pen
INTERNATIONAL

An Illustrated History

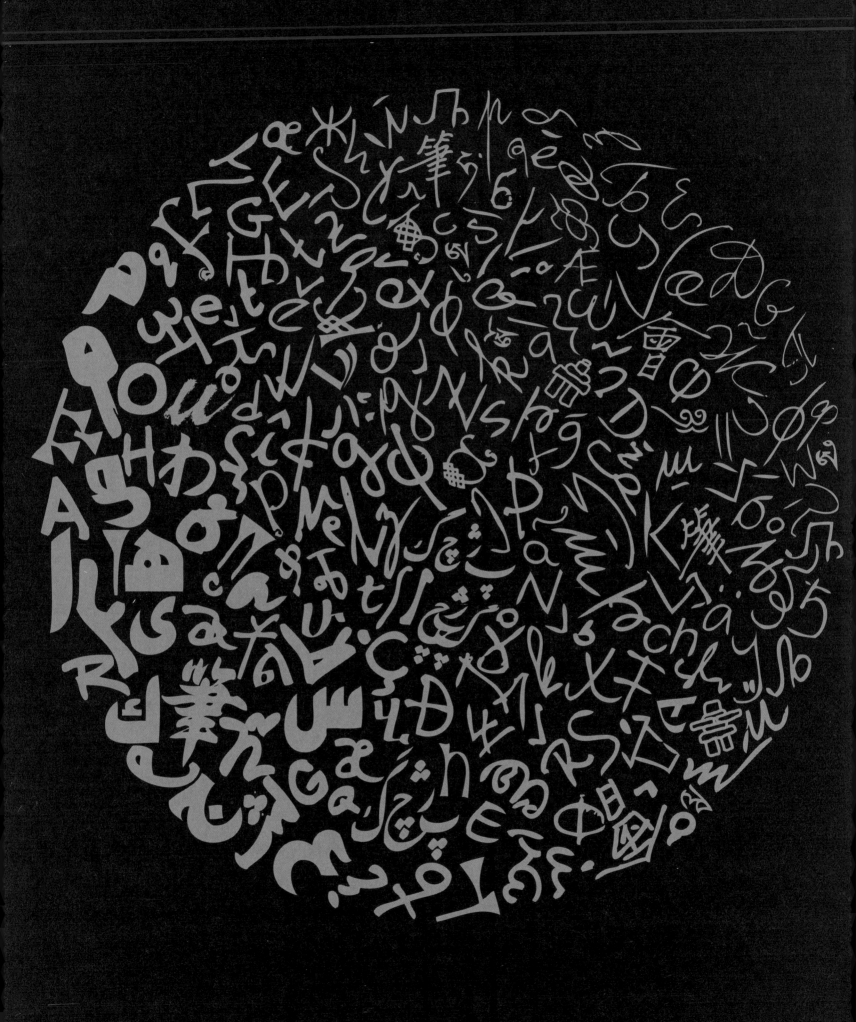

pen
INTERNATIONAL

An Illustrated History

Literature knows no frontiers

Edited by
Carles Torner & Jan Martens

Authors
Ginevra Avalle, Jennifer Clement,
Peter McDonald, Rachel Potter,
Carles Torner, Laetitia Zecchini

Interlink Books

MOTOVUN GROUP
OF INTERNATIONAL
PUBLISHERS

pen
INTERNATIONAL

Contents

PEN Key Documents 299

s no centre, where well-known writers of both sexes c
visitors from abroad can hope to find them. A dinner-
to meet socially without being under any obligation t

fications for membership are:- A book of verse publis
or American firm. A play produced by ~~a London or No~~ *any willing*
ip past or present of a well-known paper or magazine.
a wellknown London or American firm *or continental*

ion 5/- yearly, which money shall be used for statio
ial expenses. Each member shall pay his own dinner-b

—the Florence (4/-) is sugg
Tuesdays at eight o'clock at ~~an inexpensive restaur~~
ine shall telephone (7609 Hampstead) to the secretary
The first 3 ... week 4 ; then every Tuesday

ttee shall consist of six members, who shall be elec
a yearly general meeting. If for any reason a commit
esign, the committee shall elect another to take his
...eral Committee shall also be formed
hall be allowed to bring visitors; but these visitors
rights, editors, novelists, or persons of distinction
... themselves on the ...
~~will not~~ be expected to ~~wear any particular sort of~~
~~elves in the matter.~~ No formal speeches shall be mad
ers of the club shall be made as comfortable as if t
mes.

nications should be addressed :- Secretary of the /P
a Road, London, N.W.8. and shall contain a stamped,
reply.

Foreword

PEN has helped writers who have risked losing their families, homeland, livelihood, freedom and very often – too often – their lives to tell the truth. This means that, on so many levels, PEN works to protect all knowledge. This, in past times or in our times, is extraordinary.

Established to promote friendship, intellectual cooperation and exchange between writers, PEN is now the world's largest and oldest literary organisation and a champion of translation and linguistic rights. Today, as before, PEN sees literature as playing a significant role in developing mutual understanding, dialogue and peaceful debate. The opening sentence of the PEN Charter speaks to this ideal: 'Literature knows no frontiers and must remain common currency among people in spite of political or international upheavals.' While PEN originally stood for 'Poets, Playwrights, Essayists, Editors, Novelists', the membership has grown to include a broader understanding of the term 'writer' and welcomes publishers, translators, bloggers, academics and journalists. PEN works to both protect freedom of expression and honour the transformative experience of literature and telling stories.

From opposing book burning and the persecution of writers in Nazi Germany, to supporting dissident writers during the Cold War and campaigning for imprisoned writers in China today, PEN has worked to safeguard against all kinds of censorship and self-censorship. This book tells the story of PEN members all over the globe who believe in a personal responsibility to help one another, care for a stranger, challenge repressive governments and keep vigil outside of prisons.

It is impossible to know how many writers PEN has saved or helped over these 100 years, but there is no doubt that a world without PEN would be even more fragile and less hopeful. One of PEN's very first cases was that of the poet and playwright Federico García Lorca, and it is right and good to start this book on PEN's history with his words: 'The artist, and particularly the poet, is always an anarchist in the best sense of the word [... and] must heed only the call that arises within [...] from three strong voices: the voice of death, with all its foreboding, the voice of love and the voice of art.'

Jennifer Clement
President

Acknowledgements

To mark the centenary, PEN International delves into its past to tell the story of how it became what it is today. PEN visually recollects and publishes its history through letters, photographs, official documents, artwork, and personal memories for the first time.

These fragments of history draw a picture as diverse, prolific and multifaceted as PEN itself and can only be the first milestone in writing the organisation's history.

The present book is mainly based on the collective efforts of two research projects, the PEN Centenary Archive Collection and the AHRC-funded Writers and Free Expression project.

This historical research would not have been possible without the work of many people.

We wish to thank Isabel Jacobs for PEN International and Katherine Cooper, Kate Highman, and Chinmay Sharma for the Writers and Free Expression team. Their research on Yiddish PEN, English PEN, PEN International, South African PEN, and All-India PEN was as crucial as their work in obtaining copyright permission and high-resolution images. A special thanks to Sara Whyatt, who has conducted extensive research for the Centenary Archive Collection website, in particular in regards to the Writers in Prison and the Case List. Joanne Leedom-Ackerman's 'PEN Journeys' published in her blog have also been a source both of documents and inspiration.

Extended thanks go to the PEN Centres and members who shared their history, memories and materials with us. Many of the stories contained in the past 25 years of PEN would not have been possible without the support of the Swedish International Development Cooperation Agency, the Norwegian Ministry of Foreign Affairs, Fritt Ord, UNESCO and PEN's Publishers, Writers, Stage & Screen and Readers circles, as well as several other funders and donors internationally and locally, and we want to express here our gratitude to them. We are also grateful to Aline Davidoff Misrachi for her support in the creation of this book.

We appreciate the support of the Antoni Tàpies Foundation and the artists who have contributed to the book, as well as Getty Images and each of the photographers who have donated their pictures. We are all also grateful for the support of Moomin Characters OY Ltd, founded on the extraordinary legacy and vision of Tove Jansson, as we move toward the future.

We would also like to give a special mention to the Harry Ransom Centre at the University of Austin, Texas, and its archivists for their time and efforts in providing us access to PEN's archives.

Last but not least, we would like to express our deep appreciation to Jan Martens from Marot S.A. and Thierry Julliand from T'ink Studio for their constant enthusiasm, and to the Motovun Group for believing in this project and bringing it to reality.

London, August 2021

It is not chance but perfect concord that the Motovun Group is publishing PEN International's book to celebrate the organisation's 100 years protecting freedom of expression and literature. The MGIP was founded as Motovun Group Association in 1977 in the midst of the Cold War as a group committed to building bridges over the Iron Curtain between East and West. The name Motovun comes from the town in Croatia (then Yugoslavia) where the summer meetings were held in the early years. The Group was created with dedication to the principles of freedom of speech and free exchange of information and to cultural, intellectual, and spiritual values. The traditions of Motovun and a devotion to those principles and those values continue today as the essence of MGIP.

Since December 2017, we have worked together to create the concept for these pages. It has always been clear that this partnership has also been a collaboration of ideals and friendship.

Jennifer Clement
Christopher Hudson

As the humanist principle that founds the regime of freedoms and human rights on the impartiality of democratic civil power free from any religious interference, secularism obliges the state to ensure the equality, solidarity and emancipation of citizens through the dissemination of knowledge and the exercise of freethinking. The impartiality thus guaranteed to citizens, and in particular to writers, in the face of rulers, safeguards the regime of individual freedoms recognized as fundamental, universal and inseparable from human rights. These include freedom of thought, expression, conscience and religion.

However it may be called, this principle – which enables freedom of expression, the sharing of knowledge and the emancipation of peoples – must have inspired Catharine Amy Dawson Scott and John Galsworthy when they laid the foundations of the PEN Club in 1921. In doing so they wanted to contribute to world peace. Peace as imagined by Henri La Fontaine, the winner of the Nobel Prize in 1913. Peace made possible through exchange, culture and the coming together of differences perceived as a richness.

A century later, in a world where Humankind is rediscovering a common destiny, it is the duty of the Centre d'Action Laïque de Belgique to honour these pioneers of pacifism who always preferred debating to antagonism and war.

Henri Bartholomeeusen
President of the *Centre d'Action Laïque de Belgique*

" Un miracle d'amour "

Paul Valéry, 1925

" Our club, the P.E.N. Club, is materially a small organisation,
but it upholds an immense and splendid banner, the banner
of free thought and free discussion. "

HG Wells, 1936

" The belief on which the PEN is founded is threatened not from one side but
from many. [...] If we can keep alive in our country the mind which makes
Jew-baiting, concentration camps, and the suppression of
opinion all equally odious to us we are doing our duty. There is but one
way to do it. This is to insist on the excellence of just those ideas
which are hated and made a laughing stock by the Goebbelses of Europe. "

Margaret Storm Jameson, 1939

" Let every man be the exponent and the embodiment of this great ideal of
world peace, of which writers are laying the foundation. "

Mahatma Gandhi, 1945

" If you were to ask me whether PEN has a political dimension,
I would simply refer to the Charter. You find it all there. "

Heinrich Böll, 1971

" In a world where independent voices are increasingly stifled,
PEN is not a luxury, it's a necessity. "

Margaret Atwood, 1984

" In language lies the main weapon of resistance. "

Rigoberta Menchú, 1996

" With all its flounderings and failings and mistaken acts, it is still,
I think, a fellowship moved by the hope that one day the work it tries and often
manages to do will no longer be necessary. Needless to add,
we shall need extraordinarily long lives to see that noble day. Meanwhile we
have PEN, this fellowship bequeathed to us by several generations
of writers for whom their own success and fame were simply not enough. "

Arthur Miller, 2001

*" When another writer in another house is not free,
no writer is free. This, indeed, is the spirit that informs the
solidarity felt by PEN, by writers all over the world. "*
Orhan Pamuk, 2006

*" I've had a long and close relationship with PEN, both here in England and in
America, and I well remember that when I was in need of what PEN can do, that PEN
support here, in America and elsewhere, was colossally important and wonderfully
unified, and it really mattered to me a great deal. "*
Salman Rushdie, 2007

*" Freedom of expression is the foundation of human rights, the source of humanity,
and the mother of truth. To strangle freedom of speech is to trample on human rights,
stifle humanity, and suppress truth. "*
Liu Xiaobo, 2009

*" My respect for this organisation has no borders —
PEN has been fierce, so consistent and ferocious in its efforts that
it is hard to ignore their impact worldwide. "*
Toni Morrison, 2011

*" The right to mother tongue or the language of one's culture is
not a privilege to be granted or withdrawn at will, it's a human right.
PEN is one of its supporters. "*
Ngũgĩ wa Thiong'o, 2016

*" I want you to know that your letters, which have rendered
iron curtains meaningless and ineffective, have filled my two-steps'-long cell
with resistance, resolve and hope....Knowing that you are right there,
akin to keeping company to caged birds, is beyond any dream inside this cell. "*
Nedim Türfent, 2019

*" I received the PEN/Oxfam Novib award in 2013, and later on the
same year I received the Tucholsky award from Swedish PEN and the Pinter award
from English PEN. With the funds of the three awards we
founded a school in Syria that was able to shelter and educate children for
six years. Until it was bombed by the Russian forces six months ago. "*
Samar Yazbek, 2020

Origins

PEN was founded in London in October 1921 by the novelist and poet Catharine Amy Dawson Scott, who enlisted a group of fellow writers to join her in creating the first London club where writers of both sexes could meet. From the start, its founders envisaged a club with PEN Centres in every city in the world, and a PEN membership comprising all the major global writers. These expansionist efforts quickly bore fruit. By 1923, PEN had Centres in New York, Mexico City and most European cities, and its honorary members included WB Yeats, Rabindranath Tagore, Maurice Maeterlinck, Selma Lagerlöf, Maxim Gorky, Thomas Mann, Knut Hamsun, and Alfonso Reyes.

PEN organised its structures and rules quickly. Its first International Committee, with John Galsworthy in the Chair, was held in February 1922, and its first annual International Congress hosted in London in 1923. Its internationalist ambitions captured the post-war literary imagination. Galsworthy described its friendliness across frontiers as a 'great dream' in 1924, and Paul Valéry heralded it as 'un miracle d'amour' in 1925. Insisting that PEN was not political, its members also saw it as ideally placed to influence 'les grandes questions vitales', as Thomas Mann put it. At the 1924 New York Congress they agreed to commit PEN to international literary solidarity and at the Brussels Congress of 1927 approved PEN's founding principles. As PEN expanded and changed, these principles, that literature 'knows no frontiers' and 'should remain common currency' among nations, bound together the PEN literary community.

By the mid-1930s, PEN had extended its networks far beyond Europe, with Centres in Johannesburg and Cape Town in 1927, Tel Aviv and Buenos Aires in 1929, Beijing in 1930, La Paz in 1932, Baghdad and Bombay in 1933, Cairo in 1934, and Tokyo in 1936. Yiddish PEN, meanwhile, with Centres in New York, Warsaw and Vilna, was admitted into the organisation in 1930 on a 'non-territorial basis'. PEN's expansion created new aspirations and debates. In 1935, Sophia Wadia, president of the All-India Club, spoke of PEN's commitment to 'equality' among writers, not in the 'sense of identity', as she put it, but 'because they see the value of differences', an emphasis that chimed with the desire of other Centres to use PEN networks to promote the fruits of non-Western or anti-colonial literary traditions.

By the 1930s, the challenges facing the Club had also significantly changed. Harnessing its status as an organisation representing 3,000 global writers, its 1931 'Appeal to All Governments' demanded that governments respect the rights of writers imprisoned on religious or political grounds. The dire reality of German state-enforced exile and racial persecution triggered further declarations. The 1933 'Canby Resolution' announced PEN's opposition to persecution on the grounds of 'racial prejudice', while the 1934 'Raymond Resolution' committed PEN to defending the exiled author's rights to freedom of expression. After the war, PEN's 1948 Charter culled the words of previous resolutions and principles, but added a new clause on the writer's responsibilities, designed to tackle the consequences of unrestrained fascist speech and state propaganda. As the world hurtled into the heightened tensions of the Cold War, PEN would confront the political implications of defending both writers' rights and responsibilities.

← *Writer in prison* (detail), artwork created by Frederic Amat for Catalan PEN on the Day of the Imprisoned Writer 2004.

Beginnings
The 1920s

1921 The foundation of PEN

On Wednesday 5 October 1921, the PEN Club met for its inaugural dinner at the Florence Restaurant in Soho, London's lively theatre district. Long a favourite of the metropolitan literary set, the Florence had been Oscar Wilde's restaurant of choice in the early 1890s and Filippo Marinetti had declaimed his disconcerting Futurist poems there in 1913 as a guest of Wyndham Lewis. This was a more decorous affair, all black-tie formality, polite conversation, and speeches.

Over 40 writers and guests enjoyed a six-course banquet in the chandeliered splendour of the main dining room — Turbot Mornay, Médaillon de Bœuf Bordelaise, Grouse Rôtie, and more.

The unstoppable Catharine Dawson Scott, the Club's founder, had made it all happen, but it fell to the urbane John Galsworthy, the first president, to propose the toast. 'We writers are in some sort trustees for human nature', he said, 'if we are narrow and prejudiced we harm the human race. And the better we know each other [...] the greater the chance of human happiness in a world not, as yet, too happy.'

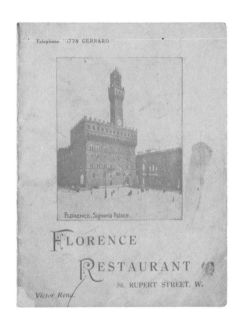

← Portrait of Catharine Amy Dawson Scott, founder of PEN, donated by her granddaughter Marjorie-Ann Watts to PEN International in 2003.

↗ → It is fitting that the inaugural meeting of the London PEN Club on 5 October 1921 took place with a lavish dinner in the Florence Restaurant on Rupert Street in London's Soho. With dishes such as 'Petite Marmite à la Française' and 'Pommes Chips Bread Sauce' the menu suggestively captured the cosmopolitan aspirations of the Club. Banquets and drinks parties were mainstays of PEN Club activities in its early years.

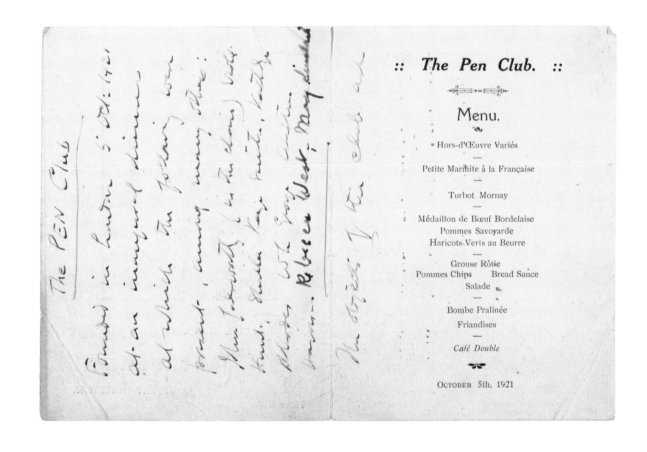

:: The Pen Club. ::

Menu.

* Hors-d'Œuvre Variés

Petite Marmite à la Française

Turbot Mornay

Médaillon de Bœuf Bordelaise
Pommes Savoyarde
Haricots-Verts au Beurre

Grouse Rôtie
Pommes Chips   Bread Sauce
Salade

Bombe Pralinée
Friandises

Café Double

OCTOBER 5th, 1921

↑   The inaugural PEN dinner. Catharine
Amy Dawson Scott is at the bottom right,
looking at the camera. John Galsworthy
is seated to her right.

> ❝ *Trustees for*
> *human nature.* ❞

Dawson Scott outlined her initial vision for the new Club in the
dinner invitation she sent out in September 1921. 'London has no
centre where well-known writers of both sexes can meet socially, no
place where distinguished visitors from abroad can hope to find
them,' she began, before adding with characteristically businesslike
aplomb: 'As a dinner-club would supply this need, it is proposed to
start one.' The annual subscription would be a modest five shillings
('for stationery, printing and secretarial expenses'), a shilling more
than the inaugural dinner itself, and the membership qualifications
uncompromisingly exclusive ('a book of verse' or 'a novel published
by a well-known Continental, London or American firm', 'a play
produced by any well-known theatre', or 'the editorship, past or present,
of a well-known paper or magazine'). The emphasis she placed on
literary prestige reflected her ambition to make the Club an eminent
and influential force for good from the start.

Catharine Amy Dawson Scott

Known as 'Sappho' to her friends, the poet, novelist, feminist, and internationalist Catharine Amy Dawson Scott created PEN as a London club where both female and male writers could meet — no such club existed at the time. With May Sinclair, Radclyffe Hall, Rebecca West, and Violet Hunt as early members, women were, and have continued to be, central to PEN's membership and functioning. The writer and Theosophist Sophia Wadia energetically headed up the Bombay PEN Centre established in 1933, while the Turkish writer, women's rights activist, and exile Halide Edib Adivar was a central figure in PEN circles throughout the 1920s and 1930s, and in discussions after the Second World War about writers' rights. Dawson Scott was vigilant in ensuring women's centrality to PEN. On discovering, at the 1928 Oslo PEN Congress, that one of the PEN Centres did not admit women she declared that this was 'contrary to the spirit of the PEN' and insisted that the principle of equality be enshrined in PEN principles. When Dawson Scott died in 1934, the organisation continued to have strong female members, including Margaret Storm Jameson, who ran the English PEN Club in the late 1930s, and, after the Second World War, many of the most prominent global women writers, including Nadine Gordimer, Toni Morrison, and Margaret Atwood. Dawson Scott's ideals also lived on in PEN's Women Writers Committee, founded in 1991, and in the *Women's Manifesto* (2017).

↗   Adolf Hoffmeister (1902–1973) was a writer, painter, journalist, caricaturist, and lawyer, who was president of the Czech PEN Club in the 1930s and had a very prominent role in the 14th PEN International Congress meeting in Prague in 1938. He caricatured Catharine Amy Dawson Scott as the mother of PEN Clubs, English PEN as the elder and wiser brother and Czech PEN, founded in 1923, as a young (and naughty) boy.

→   John Galsworthy, Catharine Amy Dawson Scott, and Hermon Ould, PEN's long-serving general secretary.

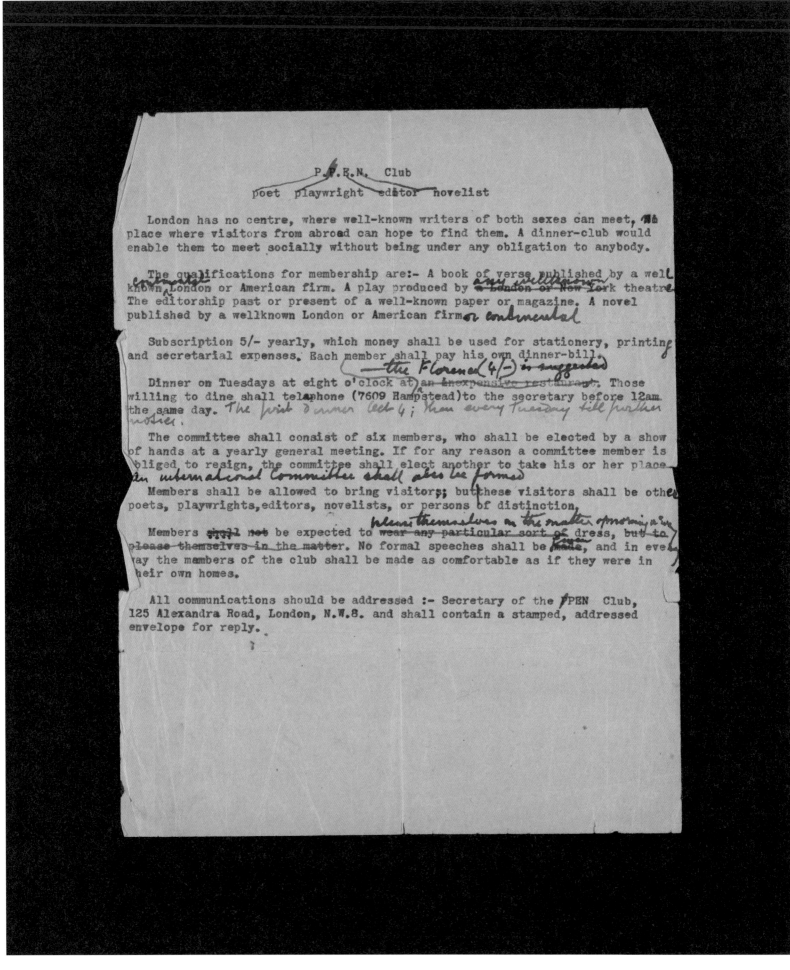

P.P.E.N. Club

poet playwright editor novelist

London has no centre, where well-known writers of both sexes can meet, no place where visitors from abroad can hope to find them. A dinner-club would enable them to meet socially without being under any obligation to anybody.

The qualifications for membership are:- A book of verse published by a well known London or American firm. A play produced by a London or New York theatre. The editorship past or present of a well-known paper or magazine. A novel published by a wellknown London or American firm *or continental*

Subscription 5/- yearly, which money shall be used for stationery, printing and secretarial expenses. Each member shall pay his own dinner-bill.

Dinner on Tuesdays at eight o'clock at an inexpensive restaurant. *the Florence (4/-) is suggested* Those willing to dine shall telephone (7609 Hampstead) to the secretary before 12am the same day. *The first dinner Oct 4; then every Tuesday till further notice.*

The committee shall consist of six members, who shall be elected by a show of hands at a yearly general meeting. If for any reason a committee member is obliged to resign, the committee shall elect another to take his or her place. *An international committee shall also be formed*

Members shall be allowed to bring visitors; but these visitors shall be other poets, playwrights, editors, novelists, or persons of distinction.

Members shall not be expected to wear any particular sort of dress, but to please themselves in the matter. No formal speeches shall be made, and in every way the members of the club shall be made as comfortable as if they were in their own homes.

All communications should be addressed :- Secretary of the PEN Club, 125 Alexandra Road, London, N.W.8. and shall contain a stamped, addressed envelope for reply.

↑   From early on, PEN established strict membership rules based on a yearly subscription and assumptions and assertions about what constituted a writer. With its multiple revisions, this early document reveals the rapidly shifting nature of these rules. While it states that members should have published a book of verse or a novel, produced a play, or edited a paper or magazine, it is also careful to insist that these publications should be with a well-known London or American firm. The word 'continental' has been added to the document's list of reputable publishing outlets to allow for PEN's expanding membership in Europe.

As the more formal draft membership rules show, Europe emerged as an afterthought in what was at first a very Anglo affair. While the document states that members should have published a book of verse or a novel, produced a play, or edited a paper or magazine, it is also careful to insist that these publications should be with a well-known London or American firm. The word 'continental' was then added, most probably in Dawson Scott's hand, to allow for PEN's expanding membership in Europe. The document also explains the name: 'P.E.N.', as it was usually written at first, was an abridged and punning acronym standing for Poets, Playwrights, Editors, Essayists, and Novelists. These exacting membership rules would haunt PEN in the century ahead. Even after it began to extend its networks beyond its Euro-American centre of gravity, it was slow to admit that publishing firms or magazines outside Europe or America were sufficient markers of literary value. Adding further complications, local PEN Centres often had their own rules, which exposed the racial or class assumptions or challenges of being a writer in different parts of the world.

" It meddles not with politics. "

To Dawson Scott's essentially social idea of a London-based, international dining club, Galsworthy, who served as president from 1921 until his death in 1933, added a particularly inflected cultural vision. 'All works of the imagination', he wrote in an article on 'International Thought' for the London *Times* on 30 October 1923, 'are the property of mankind at large' and 'any real work of art, however individual and racial in root and fibre, is impersonal and universal in its appeal'. For Galsworthy, this was not simply a matter of literary aesthetics. It concerned the writer's special calling. At a time when governments, journalists, scientists, and financiers continued to see themselves as 'trustees for competitive sections of mankind' — he had in mind the malign nationalism that led to the First World War — writers as 'trustees for human nature' had a 'plain duty' to be the heralds of a cooperative, rules-based international order and the champions of 'a new idealism'. This too entailed a certain exclusiveness. As Galsworthy's ideas of art (and lifelong aversion to English provincialism) derived largely from Matthew Arnold's *Culture and Anarchy* (1869), he had little time for modernism, or, as he put it, 'literature driven in on itself, or running riot'. Yet it was not wayward experimentalism that most concerned him. The key thing was to keep literary culture free of politics and ensure PEN's independence. 'It meddles not with politics,' he wrote in his first public statement about the new Club's aims in

THE P.E.N. CLUB.

TO THE EDITOR OF THE TIMES.

Sir.—I have been asked, as president of this international writers› club, on the eve of its first May-week international gathering, to furnish a statement of its aims and activities. Its aim is singular, if its activities are plural. A word first about its inception and growth. Its idea was that or the English novelist Mrs. Dawson Scott, and the club was founded by her in October, 1921. It has over two hundred members in this country, and it has promoted twelve sister clubs or centres in other countries – the United States, France, Belgium, Italy, Spain (two), Sweden, Norway, Denmark, Holland, Germany, and Rumania. Several centres in other countries are in process of formation.

Its aim is simply the fostering of good feeling, hospitality, and understanding among the writers of the world—poets, playwrights, editors, essayists, novelists—whence the name, P.E.N. It meddles not with politics. The meeting ground is that of «Letters».

The members of the other centres are automatically members of our London centre ; and the same principle is observed. I believe, by all the other countries. Except for this, each centre goes as it pleases, on terms of perfect equality, and each has its specially suitable method of keeping itself in existence. Our London centre adopts the method of a monthly dinner, to which each member has the right to bring a guest, preferably a writer ; and there is generally an attendance of over a hundred. To these dinners we ask foreign writers, whether members of other centres or not, who happen to be over here. The extraordinary way in which the idea is being taken up all over the world shows, we think, a real feeling towards interchange of ideas, and comradeship in the realm of literature.

In our May gathering we of the founding centre are privileged to hold the first really important social assembly of the world›s writers. We are going to try to make our distinguished guests—nearly thirty or them, we hope—feel at home and happy, to give them a little insight info the life of English writers, show them a little of our country— beautiful in spring—and exchange views on our craft. People who see politics behind everything must for once be disappointed. When we say we are not political, we mean it.

JOHN GALSWORTHY.

↑   John Galsworthy's letter to the London *Times*, dated 24 April 1923.

April 1923. 'The meeting ground is that of "Letters".' In the increasingly partisan climate of the 1920s, the decade of Julien Benda's *La Trahison des Clercs* (1927), this was not an airy statement: it was a polemical assertion of the public value of intellectual disinterestedness and of the writer's responsibility to put art before politics.

" *It would be wiser to remain quite free.* "

On this perennially vexed issue, Galsworthy had the full backing of the Club's first international council. When Boris Pilnyak, the ill-fated early critic of Bolshevism, expressed an interest in establishing a Centre in Moscow in 1923, for instance, the minutes of the council meeting for 17 June pointedly record the assurances he gave about it not being 'used politically & that it could be organised in conjunction with exiled Russian writers'. In fact, despite numerous initiatives on both sides, PEN's relations with Soviet writers remained fraught for the next 60 years — a Russian Centre was founded only in 1989. Similarly, when asked in 1925 about collaborating with the International Committee for Intellectual Cooperation (ICIC), the non-governmental precursor to UNESCO in the League of Nations, the council decided 'it would be wiser to remain quite free.' Two years later, however, after realising they had many members and interests in common — the ICIC itself was in the process of attempting to create a new globalised 'Republic of Letters' — they joined forces to promote international understanding through literary translation. And in 1928, after passing its first formal resolution against 'systematic censorship' and for 'the free international circulation of *des ouvrages de l'esprit*', PEN notified the ICIC of its decision to start monitoring the threats to free expression around the world.

The members of the founding council may have worried about political meddling, but, with Galsworthy and Dawson Scott's energetic encouragement, they quickly set about establishing the Club's activist and internationalist credentials. Drawing on their various social networks, as well as their contacts in the press, the diplomatic, and university worlds, they lost no time in spreading the word, reaching out, as the first minutes dated 22 February 1922 record, to Belgium, Italy, Spain, Norway, Sweden, Denmark, the United States, Australia, New Zealand, South Africa, Japan, and Russia.

↓   Poet and dramatist Hermon Ould served as the driving force for PEN from its foundation until his death in 1951. He served as secretary to the English Centre from its inception in 1921 and became international secretary at the Berlin Congress in 1926. During Ould's time PEN grew from a dining club for writers to an influential international organisation.

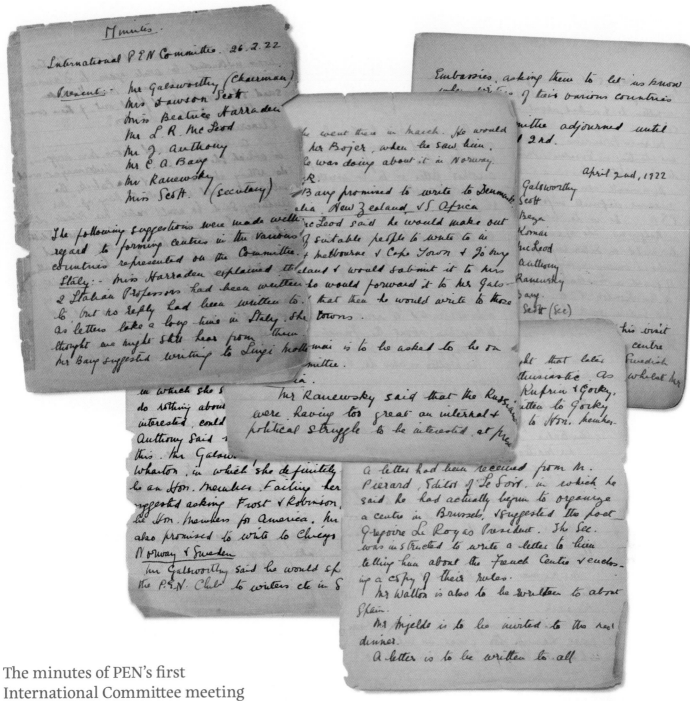

The minutes of PEN's first International Committee meeting

*Held at the founder Catharine Amy Dawson Scott's London house
(125 Alexandra Road, St John's Wood), dated 26 February 1922.*

The English novelist and founding president John Galsworthy was in the chair, and
Marjorie Scott (later Watts), Catharine's daughter, acted as secretary — so the minutes
are most likely in her hand. The other members of the committee included Beatrice
Harraden, the English novelist and suffragette, and the New Zealand-born journalist
Lewis Rose MacLeod, then literary editor of the London *Daily Mail*. As the minutes show,
PEN actively extended its membership from the start, reaching out to Italy, United
States, Norway, Sweden, Denmark, New Zealand, Australia, South Africa, Japan, Russia,
and Belgium. Galsworthy reported that he had invited the American novelist Edith
Wharton to be an honorary member, but she 'definitely refused'. A similar letter had
been sent to the Russian writers Alexander Kuprin and Maxim Gorky, but they had not
replied. The minutes also record that 'the Russians were having too great an internal &
political struggle to be interested at present in the idea [of founding a PEN Centre]', but
that 'later on they would be very enthusiastic'.

1923 London, first Congress of PEN International

1. James Louis Garvin
2. Ramón Pérez de Ayala
3. RB Cunninghame Graham
4. Miss Pérez de Ayala
5. John Drinkwater
6. Miss Rolland
7. Israel Zangwill
8. Edwin Arlington Robinson
9. John Galsworthy
10. JM Barrie
11. Countess Russell
12. Johan Bojer
13. JD Beresford
14. Romain Rolland
15. HG Wells
16. Rebecca West
17. Clemence Dane
18. Sinclair Lewis

19. Dorothy Wellesley
20. St John Greer Ervine
21. Gonnoske Komai
22. Denis Mackail
23. GR Mallock
24. MT Hogg
25. Henry Nevinson
26. AE Mann
27. Stephen Southwold
28. John Farquharson
29. Maud Churton Braby
30. Marie Stopes
31. EH Lacon Watson
32. FM Atkinson
33. Helen Williams
34. Alan Sullivan
35. ?
36. Joseph Burton Hobman

37. ?
38. Amber Reeves
39. Gerald Barry
40. Alec Waugh
41. Cynthia Stockley (?)
42. – McPeake
43. Percy Hord
44. – McGill
45. C Lewis Hind
46. Edith Shackleton Heald
47. Josep Maria Millàs-Raurell
48. Horace Shipp
49. Émile Cammaerts
50. FS Flint (?)
51. Pompeu Fabra
52. Catharine Amy Dawson Scott

Within a year, Paris, New York, Brussels, Oslo, Barcelona, and
Stockholm all had Centres, and by the end of the decade over 40 Clubs
with a total membership of around 3,000 had been created across
Africa, Asia, Europe, Oceania, and the Americas from Mexico City to
Shanghai, Warsaw to Cape Town. Argentina, Brazil, Ireland, India,
and Japan joined early in the next decade.

From the start, as Galsworthy noted in 1923, the founding London Club
served as the hub around which each newly created Centre 'goes as it
pleases on terms of perfect equality'. To make this federalist ideal a reality,
they established a tradition of annual congresses much like the League
of Nations itself — London in 1923, followed by New York, Paris, Berlin,
Brussels, and Oslo — and in March 1927 they launched *PEN News*, a
monthly bulletin in which the various Centres reported on their activities.

The table arrangements for the first International Congress, held at the Hotel Cecil on London's Strand in May 1923

This table arrangement reflected PEN's
founding ideals. Like the League of Nations,
each of the main national groupings has a
table of its own, though, as the detailed
seating plan indicates, everything was
carefully arranged to foster 'good feeling,
hospitality, and understanding among the
writers of the world' (see Galsworthy's letter

to *The Times* on page 21). The 11 tables were
accordingly arranged in alphabetical order
with hosts and guests evenly interspersed.
At the Italian table, for instance, Vita
Sackville-West, the English aristocrat and
friend and lover of Virginia Woolf, is seated
next to the Italian writer and politician
Antonio Cippico, who is next to the American

feminist Harriet Dunham, wife of the leading
Italian liberal Antonio de Viti de Marco. As
Galsworthy later put it, 'the P.E.N. does not
stand for an amalgamation of nationalities,
but for an association of nationalities.' Yet, as
the separate tables for Barcelona and Madrid
show, his idea of literary internationalism was
under pressure from the start.

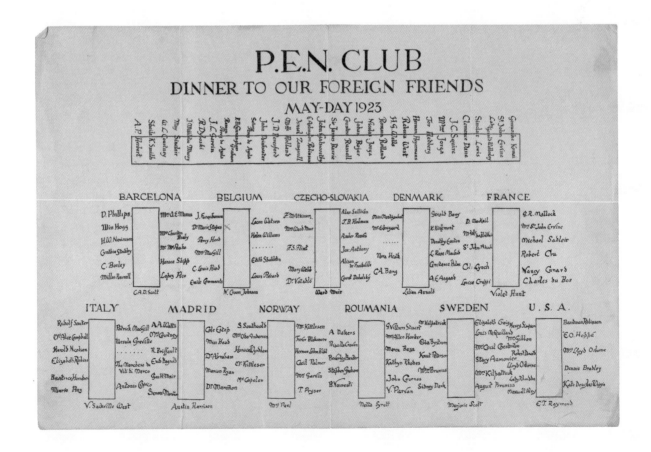

PEN spreads out

←   Anatole France,
first president of French PEN.

1922, founding of French PEN, the second PEN Club

In early 1922, French PEN was created around the figures of Paul Valéry, Jules Romains and Anatole France, who was elected its first president. The great novelist and humanist Anatole France died soon after, in 1924. In 1922, Swedish, Catalan, Romanian, Italian, Belgian, Netherlands, Norwegian, and American PEN Clubs were founded. For 75 years, English and French were the working languages of PEN, until Spanish was added as the third language in 1996.

1923, founding of Mexican PEN

PEN quickly expanded beyond Europe, particularly in Latin America. Mexican PEN was established in October 1923, with 44 members, including José Juan Tablada, Carlos Pereyra, and Alfonso Reyes. The Mexican PEN Club rules describe the group's invitation to establish itself for friendly and cooperative purposes, and reveals PEN's organisational structure of centralised and local control; Mexican PEN, it states, will accept the London PEN Club rules, in accordance with their own membership rules. Other Latin American Centres soon formed, with Pedro Prado creating Santiago PEN in 1925, and PEN clubs founded in Buenos Aires in 1929, La Paz in 1932 and Rio de Janeiro and Bogotá in 1936. These Centres created a strong Latin American literary network that was also linked closely to European cities, most notably Paris and Madrid. Reyes, for instance, who was a writer, translator, editor, and — later — politician, lived in Madrid in the early 1920s and represented Mexican PEN at the New York Congress in 1924. When the Spanish Civil War broke out in 1936, these literary networks aided fleeing exiled Spanish and Catalan writers seeking refuge in Mexico and other South American cities.

1936, founding of Japanese PEN

In March 1936, Nippon PEN was launched, with funding from the Japanese Department of Foreign Affairs and the Society for International Cultural Relations, and was accompanied with the publication of a sumptuous pamphlet detailing its membership, rules, and chief officers. With over a hundred members, and Japan's foremost novelist Tōson Shimazaki as president, and the poet Nico Horiguchi and the novelist and painter Ikuma Arishima as vice-presidents, Nippon PEN was an extremely strong and important PEN Centre in the late 1930s. Annual membership was 30 yen. Shimazaki wrote a fascinating opening notice about the Club's founding, in which he registered the Club's desire to open up Japanese literary culture to the outside world, but also registered that 'East and West are entering a stage of great transition'.

↑   The novelist Tōson Shimazaki,
first president of Japanese PEN in 1936.

1934, founding of Indian PEN

The first issue of *The Indian P.E.N.*, published on 7 March 1934, introduced the newly established Indian Centre of PEN (soon known as the All-India PEN Centre), and set out the aims of the organisation. The Club was founded by the Colombian-born Theosophist Sophia Wadia in Bombay, and its first president was Rabindranath Tagore, with famous writers Sarojini Naidu and arvepalli Radhakrishnan acting as vice-presidents. Created in order to bridge lines between Indian literatures in different languages, and between India and the rest of the world, the Centre was also premised on the need to redress a double imbalance: the invisibility of India on the world stage, and the invisibility of Indian literatures not written in English, more specifically. 'Why a Pen Club in India?' asked the first issue of *The Indian P.E.N.* The answer sounds almost defiant: 'Why not? Are Indian writers not good enough to take their place in the fellowship of the world's creative minds?' Although the Indian PEN repeatedly claimed to be non-political, it asserted India's worth and the country's capacity to 'mould' its own destiny in the context of British rule. The organisation also put extraordinary faith in translation both as a means of nation-building, to construct what it viewed as the fundamental unity underlying all Indian literatures, and as a means to reconcile 'East' and 'West'. The Club's monthly newsletter, *The Indian P.E.N.*, which was brought out until the 1990s, also served the same purpose by chronicling literary news in India and in the world. In keeping with its mission to bring together writers and literatures from different 'vernacular' languages, the organisation established a PEN All-India Advisory Linguistic Committee and organised successful All-India Writers' Conferences across India.

→
The Indian P.E.N. was the newsletter
of the All-India PEN Centre and its
first issue opened with the question
'Why a P.E.N. Club in India?'.
It was founded in 1934 by Sophia
Wadia and had Rabindranath Tagore
as its first president.

6846

THE INDIAN P. E. N.

No. 1.   7TH MARCH, 1934   PRICE 2 ANNAS.

P. E. N.

A · WORLD · ASSOCIATION · OF

Poets **E**ditors **N**ovelists
Playwrights **E**ssayists

India Office : Hill Crest, Pedder Road, Bombay.

WHY A P. E. N. CLUB IN INDIA?

Why not? Are Indian writers not good enough to take their place in the fellowship of the world's creative minds? And should not this international company derive benefit from contact with those who are precipitating a renaissance in this ancient and honourable land? The duty of Indian authors to interpret the fast-moving mind of this country to the world at large is supreme. What better method can they find than by acquainting their peers abroad with the achievements and aspirations which imperceptibly but definitely are moulding India's destiny?

This paramount duty, however, cannot be discharged adequately unless the Indian writers themselves, from Gauri Shankar to Kanya Kumari, become an organized group. Those who write in English are few and their influence on the mind of the masses is limited; they serve the Motherland less at home and more abroad. They may know each other and the world may know them; but how many among the *littérateurs* of different Vernaculars know each other? More important, what does the world know of their works? The Vernacular literary movements influence the Indian villages, but they have also something of truth and beauty to offer to the world at large. The unfoldment of native cultures is now taking place in different Provinces; each must yield its quota of members in this India-wide and world-wide organization for their own benefit as also for the sake of India and the world.

The formation of the India Centre of the P. E. N. was undertaken for this dual task.

The P. E. N. Club long since recognized India by appointing her great poet, Dr. Tagore, as one of its Honorary Members. Now it is India's turn to respond: let Indian authors share the toils and the hopes of the members of their craft the world over.

THE INDIAN P. E. N.

This is the organ of the India Centre of the P. E. N. Its programme is simple:—

(1) It will act as a link between all members in this country and will represent them in the world association of poets, playwrights, editors, essayists and novelists.

(2) It will chronicle noteworthy activities of the Indian members who may write in Sanskrit, in English, or in any of the Vernaculars. Members are requested to communicate the news of their activities and new publications to us.

(3) It will bring to its readers useful literary news from abroad; it will record Indian literary events; especially will it report developments in various linguistic areas of this vast country, as it aspires to become a channel of information about, and service of, Vernacular literatures of the past, and of their present developments. Numerous organizations are known to be working for the advance of the different Vernacular cultures. We shall be glad to hear from their workers and to receive reports of the aims, activities and achievements of such literary organizations in the Provinces and Indian States.

The INDIAN P. E. N. will be supplied free to every member in good standing.

It is not a periodical regularly to be published.

Its life and growth depend on the response made. We need members; we need financial and moral support; we need encouragement from those on whose behalf we are making sacrifices in time, money and work.

Those desiring to join the Club, or to buy the Indian P. E. N. or to acquire information are requested to address their communication to "The Hon. Secretary, P. E. N., Hill Crest, Pedder Road, Bombay."

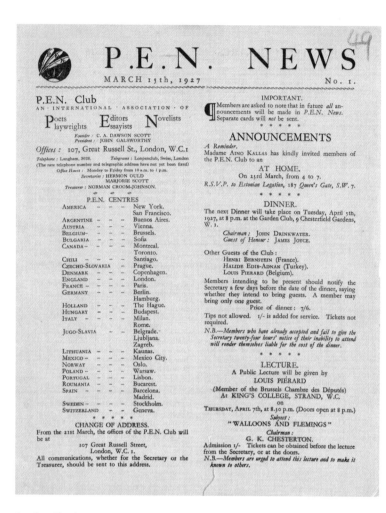

P.E.N. NEWS

MARCH 15th, 1927   No. 1.

P.E.N. Club

AN · INTERNATIONAL · ASSOCIATION · OF

Poets   **E**ditors   **N**ovelists
Playwrights   Essayists

Founder : C. A. DAWSON SCOTT
President : JOHN GALSWORTHY

Offices : 107, Great Russell St., London, W.C.1

Telephone : Langham, 3028.   *Telegrams :* Lenpenclub, Swiss, London
(The new telephone number and telegraphic address have not yet been fixed)
Office Hours : Monday to Friday from 10 a.m. to 1 p.m.
Secretaries : HERMON OULD
MARJORIE SCOTT
Treasurer : NORMAN CROOM-JOHNSON

P.E.N. CENTRES

AMERICA	– – –	New York.
		San Francisco.
ARGENTINE	– – –	Buenos Aires.
AUSTRIA	– – –	Vienna.
BELGIUM–	– –	Brussels.
BULGARIA	– – –	Sofia
CANADA –	– –	Montreal.
		Toronto.
CHILI	– – –	Santiago.
CZECHO-SLOVAKIA	–	Prague.
DENMARK	– – –	Copenhagen.
ENGLAND	– – –	London.
FRANCE –	– –	Paris.
GERMANY	– – –	Berlin.
		Hamburg.
HOLLAND	– – –	The Hague.
HUNGARY	– – –	Budapest.
ITALY	– – –	Milan.
		Rome.
JUGO-SLAVIA	– –	Belgrade.
		Ljubljana.
		Zagreb.
LITHUANIA	– – –	Kaunas.
MEXICO –	– –	Mexico City.
NORWAY –	– –	Oslo.
POLAND –	– –	Warsaw.
PORTUGAL	– – –	Lisbon.
ROUMANIA	– – –	Bucarest.
SPAIN	– – –	Barcelona.
		Madrid.
SWEDEN –	– –	Stockholm.
SWITZERLAND	– –	Geneva.

CHANGE OF ADDRESS.

From the 21st March, the offices of the P.E.N. Club will
be at

107 Great Russell Street,
London, W.C.1.

All communications, whether for the Secretary or the
Treasurer, should be sent to this address.

IMPORTANT.

Members are asked to note that in future *all announcements will be made in P.E.N. News.
Separate cards will not be sent.*

* * * * *

ANNOUNCEMENTS

A Reminder.
Madame AINO KALLAS has kindly invited members of
the P.E.N. Club to an

AT HOME.
On 23rd March, from 4 to 7.
R.S.V.P. to Estonian Legation, 187 *Queen's Gate, S.W.*7.

* * * * *

DINNER.

The next Dinner will take place on Tuesday, April 5th,
1927, at 8 p.m. at the Garden Club, 9 Chesterfield Gardens,
W. 1.

Chairman : JOHN DRINKWATER.
Guest of Honour : JAMES JOYCE.

Other Guests of the Club :
HENRI BERNSTEIN (France).
HALIDE EDIB-ADNAN (Turkey).
LOUIS PIÉRARD (Belgium).

Members intending to be present should notify the
Secretary a few days before the date of the dinner, saying
whether they intend to bring guests. A member may
bring only one guest.
Price of dinner : 7/6.

Tips not allowed. 1/- is added for service. Tickets not
required.

*N.B.—Members who have already accepted and fail to give the
Secretary twenty-four hours' notice of their inability to attend
will render themselves liable for the cost of the dinner.*

* * * * *

LECTURE.

A Public Lecture will be given by
LOUIS PIÉRARD
(Member of the Brussels Chambre des Députés)
At KING'S COLLEGE, STRAND, W.C.
on
THURSDAY, APRIL 7th, at 8.30 p.m. (Doors open at 8 p.m.)
Subject :
"WALLOONS AND FLEMINGS"
Chairman :
G. K. CHESTERTON.
Admission 1/- Tickets can be obtained before the lecture
from the Secretary, or at the doors.
*N.B.—Members are urged to attend this lecture and to make it
known to others.*

INTERNATIONAL COUNCIL; 6 October 1926

PRESENT: John Galsworthy (Chair)
          Hans Blunck from Hamburg
          Marcu Beza
          Horace Shipp
          Hermon Ould

MINUTES of the last meeting were read and confirmed.

ANNUAL MEETING RESOLUTION. Mr. Galsworthy read the
resolution which was put by him, second by Edmund
d'Auvergne and carried unanimously by the members
assembled at the Annual Meeting held after the dinner
on the 5th October. The notion reads as follows: -
    "That this Meeting be asked to empower the dele-
gates sent by the London Centre to next year's
International Congress at Brussels to vote for the
following resolution:-

    'This international gathering of the P.E.N.
    Clubs expresses the belief that the arts are
    essentially international and adopts on behalf
    of all the P.E.N. ~~Clubs~~ Centres here represented
    the principle that, even in time of war, Art,
    Music and Literature (other than propaganda)
    should remain common currency between antagon-
    istic nations; and further records its
    determination at all times to influence public
    opinion towards support of this principle.'"

The Secretary is asked to send a copy of this
Resolution to the secretaries of all centres and to
M. François Borge for publication in the Bulletin.

REPORTS FROM CENTRES.

Vienna. _ report from Fran von Urbanitsky reporting
progress was read with interest. She annouced the
forthcoming visit to London of Siegfried Trebitsch.

↑   The official PEN letterhead of the 1920s
with its pantheon of honorary members and
alphabetical list of countries from America to
Switzerland.

↗   The 'Statement of Aims' was approved
by the London Centre in October 1926, later
shared at the meeting of the International
Counsel and sent to the secretaries of all PEN
Centres as well as published in the *PEN
Bulletin*. One year later, it was revised and
developed by the Brussels Congress into the
three main guidelines of the PEN Charter.

→   Polish PEN was very active in inviting
foreign writers. This picture dated 1927 shows
Thomas Mann in a toast with Warsaw writers
following the PEN tradition of literary
dinners to welcome guests from abroad.
The news explains that the interaction was
in all directions, as Polish writer Wacław
Sieroszewski had been invited on the same
dates by the London PEN Club.

To raise the Club's public profile, they also created a prestigious list of honorary members, securing the support of over 30 major writers by the end of the decade. The list, which became part of the official PEN letterhead, included Thomas Hardy (England), JM Barrie (Scotland), Hugo von Hofmannsthal (Austria), Liang Qichao (China), Paul Valéry (France), Benedetto Croce (Italy), Maxim Gorky (Russia), Martínez Ruiz (Spain), Sholem Asch (Yiddish), and Robert Frost (United States) as well as nine Nobel Prize winners: WB Yeats (Ireland), Maurice Maeterlinck (Belgium), Henrik Pontoppidan (Denmark), Romain Rolland (France), Gerhart Hauptmann (Germany), Rabindranath Tagore (India), Knut Hamsun (Norway), Selma Lagerlöf (Sweden) and Verner von Heidenstam (also Sweden).

The list of honorary vice-presidents, many of whom are Nobel winners, continues this association today — Toni Morrison until her death in 2019, and currently Svetlana Alexievich, JM Coetzee, and Orhan Pamuk. Shortly before his own death, Galsworthy also entered the Swedish pantheon. Already too ill to receive the 1932 prize in person, he nonetheless left the £9,000 award to PEN in his will, giving it a much-needed financial boost (£250 per year) and making him its first major donor.

180

Berliner Tageblatt, 10 Apr 1927

Thomas Mann, als Gast des P. E. N. Clubs, in einem der bekanntesten Warschauer Weinrestaurants   *Keystone View phot.*

Christian Science Monitor 14 Apr 1927

HERR MANN TALKS TO WARSAW P. E. N. CLUB

WARSAW, Poland (Special Correspondence)—The idea of the P. E. N. Club, i. e., to spread friendship among authors of all nations, is being carried out as far as Poland is concerned quite in the spirit of the founders. The eminent Polish author, Waclaw Sieroszewski, has recently been the guest of the London P. E. N. Club, while Thomas Mann was invited to Warsaw, where he was entertained by the Warsaw branch of the P. E. N. Club. He was received at dinner by the literary club on March 12, after which a reception was held for representatives of the Polish intellectual and artistic world.

The following day Herr Mann delivered a public lecture, and on March 14 Polish authors received him at the famous old firm of Fukier's, where in the ancient registration books figures the signature of the German author E. T. Hoffmann, whose tales have delighted so many generations.

1927 Brussels, the foundation of the PEN Charter

John Galsworthy's other principal legacy was the PEN Charter, an idea the London Centre first proposed on 5 October 1926 as a suggested 'Statement of Aims':

> *The P.E.N. Club stands for hospitality and friendliness among writers of all countries; for the unity, integrity and welfare of letters; and concerns itself with measures which contribute to these ends. It stands apart from politics.*

The meeting also proposed a resolution affirming 'the principle that, even in time of war, Art, Music and Literature (other than propaganda) should remain common currency among antagonistic nations'. Underlining PEN's activism, it noted 'its determination at all times to influence public opinion towards support of this principle'. The following day, Galsworthy tabled this proposal at a meeting of the international council. As the minutes record, he 'wondered whether it would be possible to get the Brussels Congress in 1927 to uphold the idea that in the event of future wars the P.E.N. Club would not cease its activities during the progress of hostilities, but would, on the contrary, do all in its power to maintain the interchange of ideas through art of all kinds.'

Galsworthy was not only concerned about what PEN might do in times of conflict. He was responding to a series of questions German writers, including Bertolt Brecht, Robert Musil, Alfred Döblin, and Ernst Toller, had raised at the Berlin Congress earlier in the year. Though they were mainly troubled about their own Centre's claims to represent German literature, Toller, a German-Jewish avant-garde playwright and revolutionary social democrat, recently imprisoned for his political activities, also expressed doubts about Galsworthy's non-, perhaps even anti-political idealism. After all, he said, politics is 'everywhere and influences everything.' This was the first of many interventions Toller made in the 1920s and 1930s, all of which had a significant impact on PEN's future direction.

Following Galsworthy's proposal at the council meeting, a sub-committee duly drafted a resolution, re-working the London statement as well as some of Galsworthy's earlier public statements, which the English, Belgian, French, and German Centres then formally tabled at the Brussels Congress. This formed the basis of the Charter's three founding articles:

> 1. *Literature, national though it be in origin, knows no frontiers, and should remain common currency between nations in spite of political or international upheavals.*
>
> 2. *In all circumstances, and particularly in time of war, works of art, the patrimony of humanity at large, should be left untouched by national or political passion.*
>
> 3. *Members of PEN should at all times use what influence they have in favour of good understanding and mutual respect between nations.*

Ernst Toller

German-Jewish writer and political activist Ernst Toller (1893–1939) is known especially for his contribution to German Expressionist theatre. In his late twenties, he was serving a five-year prison sentence in the Niederschönenfeld Fortress for the part he played as founding president of the short-lived Bavarian Soviet Republic in 1919. Exiled and stripped of his citizenship in 1933, he was a leading voice in PEN throughout the interwar years and an outspoken critic of the Nazis until his suicide in New York on 22 May 1939. 'Dear Ernst', WH Auden wrote in an elegiac tribute, 'lie shadowless at last among / The other war-horses who existed till they'd done / Something that was an example to the young.'

Though the text was approved unanimously, the second article provoked some debate. The initial draft, derived from the London statement, noted that even in a time of war 'Art, Music and Literature (other than propaganda) should remain common currency between antagonistic nations', since 'the arts are essentially international'. However, Carl van Doren, president of New York PEN, felt this tied it too tightly to the spectre of the First World War, limiting the Charter's appeal as an expression of PEN's highest ideals. The less freighted final wording did not wholly solve the problem, as later revisions would show, but it epitomised the literary internationalism around which PEN's steadily expanding association of writers rallied in the 1920s. Universalist in

1928 The Oslo Congress

In June 1928, delegates travelled to Oslo for PEN's sixth annual Congress. This map shows the flight routes into Malmö, Copenhagen, Stockholm, Oslo, and Gothenburg, with delegates coming from around Europe, including Madrid, Rome, and — interestingly — Leningrad. Delegates also travelled from as far away as South Africa and Australia, while Slovenia's foremost modernist poet, Oton Župančič, made his way from Ljubljana.

Dawson Scott aptly labelled PEN a literary 'league of nations' in her opening speech. Festivities took place at the old Universal Festival Hall, and were presided over by King Haakon VII of Norway. As PEN expanded and travel became easier, PEN Congresses would increasingly attract a worldwide audience. Eight years later, at the Buenos Aires Congress, along with the usual European presence and a strong Latin American contingent, the poet

Shaul Tchernichowsky, Sophia Wadia and international studies academic Majid Khadduri traversed the seas from Palestine, Bombay, and Mosul respectively, while the modernist poet Tōson Shimazaki journeyed from Tokyo, and Johannes Anderson, poet and translator of Maori literature, made the trip from Auckland. The publisher Harriet Monroe and surrealist writer Alfonso Reyes travelled down from Chicago and Mexico City.

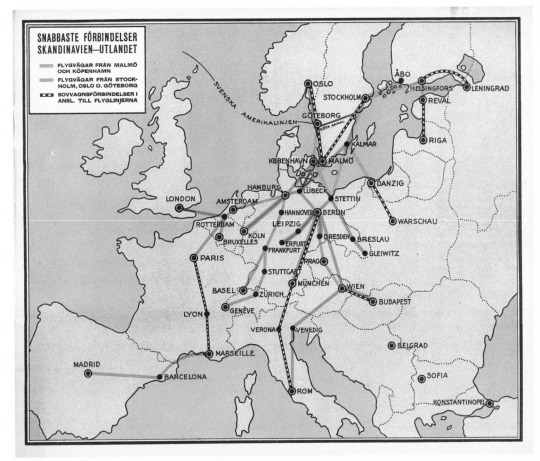

FASTEST CONNECTIONS
SCANDINAVIA–ABROAD

▨▨▨ Itineraries from Malmö and Copenhagen
▨▨▨ Itineraries from Stockholm, Oslo and Gothenburg
◼◼◼ Connections with sleeper in connection with airlines

← Map of the recommended travel routes to the Oslo Congress, 1928

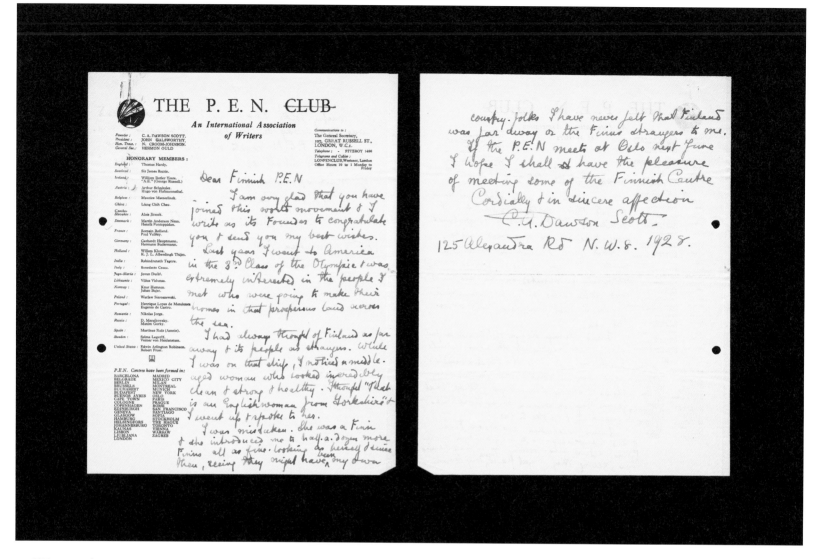

↑   PEN continued to grow with the
active participation of its founder
Catharine Amy Dawson Scott. In this
1928 letter to Finnish PEN, she looks
forward to meeting Finnish delegates
at the Oslo Congress.

↓   Official opening of the League
of Nations, Geneva, Switzerland,
15 November 1920.

aspiration and anti-nationalist in spirit — though also presupposing
the primacy of the nation at every point — it gave concrete shape to
Galsworthy's 'new idealism', while underlining his anxieties about
political meddling.

Such at least was the vision. The realities were a little different, not just
because writers like Toller thought otherwise about politics but
because some worried Galsworthy made PEN look too much like a
mirror image of the League of Nations.

In fact, since not all languages had a localised territory or the
backing of a state, alternative, culture-based Centres were created
almost immediately, beginning in 1922 with the Catalans in
Barcelona, followed a year later by the Spanish in Madrid. The
council had also discussed the question of Russian exiles, dealt with
tensions in Brussels between the Flemish and the French, and
welcomed the formation of Scottish PEN. The greatest challenge,
however, came from Yiddish writers who found themselves adrift
after the Polish Centre in Warsaw turned down their request for
co-membership. After much debate, the solution, formally accepted
in 1927, was to establish a Yiddish Centre in the contested city of

Vilna (now Vilnius, capital of Lithuania) with further branches in New York and Warsaw. Two years later, at the 1929 Congress in Vienna, it was then agreed that 'the method of dividing the PEN into sections and the right of voting at Congresses should be based on literary and cultural', rather than national grounds. Despite this, the first article of the Charter, codifying Galsworthy's vision of a literary League of Nations, remained unchanged until 2003.

> **❝ *Literature, national though it be in origin, knows no frontiers, and should remain common currency between nations in spite of political or international upheavals.* ❞**

An interlude at the 1930 Warsaw Congress: rafting on the Dunajec river

As well as the serious business of agreeing policy and making declarations, PEN Congresses also involved elaborate sightseeing tours, receptions with monarchs and politicians, visits to local cultural attractions and natural wonders, dinners, and dances. In this photograph, we see Warsaw Congress delegates being punted down the Dunajec river gorge in the Pieniny National Park. The excursion to the Pieniny and Tatras Mountains, Poland at its most 'picturesque and poetic' as Warsaw PEN put it, was a dramatic conclusion to an intricate five-day itinerary. The Congress had opened on the morning of Friday 20 June 1930 with a reception in the Great Hall of the Polish Parliamentary Assembly. Later that day, delegates enjoyed a ballet performance at the open-air Theatre of Lazienki Palace and a party at the Royal Palace, with Walery Sławek, the prime minister of Poland. On Saturday participants met representatives of Polish arts and letters at a reception hosted by August Zaleski, the minister of foreign affairs, while on Sunday they were invited to walk the streets of Warsaw and saw an exhibition at the Warsaw School of Fine Arts. On Monday, the PEN Congress decamped to Kraków, where they enjoyed a garden party in a nearby forest and visited Wawel Royal Castle. Finally, on Wednesday, they set forth to the mountains. The frenzied pace of this literary trip to

Poland, typical of PEN Congresses in the late 1920s and 1930s, suggests the extent to which they were viewed as opportunities to promote national literatures and, as the involvement of government attests, the modern nation-state. As Ferdynand Goetel predicted, in his opening address to the Congress, at the next Warsaw PEN Congress (in 1999!), there would be skyscrapers and asphalted roads.

Pamphlet produced for the Oslo Congress

This pamphlet, produced for the Oslo Congress in 1928, tells the story of PEN's first seven years, showing that it had already started to engage with the International Committee for Intellectual Co-operation, the precursor to UNESCO in the League of Nations.

It also sets out the ideals consolidated in the first Charter of 1927. By then the organisation had 41 Centres in 29 countries, the one exception being Yiddish. With no territory as such, it had Centres not just in Vilnius (then in Poland) but in Warsaw and New York. A year later, at the seventh Congress, held in Vienna in June 1929, it was decided to organise PEN into 'sections' and to base 'the right of voting at the congresses' on 'literary and cultural grounds' in order to keep the organisation 'as far as possible from national considerations'.

THE P.E.N.

An International Association of Writers

Founder :
MRS. C. A. DAWSON SCOTT.
President :
JOHN GALSWORTHY.
Honorary Member for England :
H. G. WELLS.
Representative on European Council :
GEORGE BERNARD SHAW.
General Secretary :
HERMON OULD.
Honorary Treasurer :
NORMAN CROOM-JOHNSON.

107, GREAT RUSSELL STREET, LONDON, W.C.1.
Office Hours : Monday to Friday, from 10 a.m to 1 p.m.
Telephone : Fitzroy 1486. *Telegrams :* Lonpenclub, Westcent, London.

THE P.E.N.

An International Association of

POETS	EDITORS	
PLAYWRIGHTS	ESSAYISTS	NOVELISTS

P.E.N. Centres have been founded in :

		HONORARY MEMBERS OF LONDON CENTRE
America	New York. San Francisco.	
Argentine	Buenos Aires.	Scotland Sir James Barrie.
Austria	Vienna.	Ireland Willam Butler Yeats. "A. E." (George Russell).
Belgium	Brussels.	
Bulgaria	Sofia.	Austria Arthur Schnitzler. Hugo von Hofmannsthal.
Canada	Montreal. Toronto.	Belgium Maurice Maeterlinck.
Chile	Santiago.	China Liang Chih Chao.
Czecho-Slovakia	Prague.	Czecho-Slovakia Alois Jirasek.
Denmark	Copenhagen.	Denmark Martin Anderson Nexo. Henrik Pontoppidan.
England	London.	
Estonia	Tartu.	France Romain Rolland. Paul Valéry
Finland	Helsingfors.	
France	Paris.	Germany Gerhardt Hauptmann. Hermann Sudermann.
Germany	Berlin. Cologne. Hamburg. Munich.	Holland Willem Kloos. K. J. L. Alberdingk Thijm.
Holland	The Hague.	India Rabindranath Tagore.
Hungary	Budapest.	Italy Benedetto Croce.
Italy	Milan. Rome.	Jugo-Slavia Joan Dučić.
Jugo-Slavia	Belgrade. Ljubljana Zagreb.	Lithuania Vilius Vidunas
		Norway Knut Hamsun. Johan Bojer.
Latvia	Riga.	
Lithuania	Kaunas.	Poland Waclaw Sieroszewski.
Norway	Oslo.	Portugal Henrique Lopes de Mendonca. Eugenio de Castro
Poland	Warsaw.	
Portugal	Lisbon.	
Roumania	Bucarest.	Rumania Nikolas Jorga.
Scotland	Edinburgh. Glasgow.	Russia D. Mereikowsky. Maxim Gorky.
South Africa	Cape Town. Johannesburg.	Spain Martinez Ruiz (Azorin).
Spain	Barcelona. Madrid.	Sweden Selma Lagerlöf. Verner von Heidenstam.
Sweden	Stockholm.	United States Edwin Arlington Robinson. Robert Frost.
Switzerland	Geneva.	
Yiddish	Vilna, Poland.	Yiddish Sholom Asch.

2

THE P.E.N.

⊞⊞⊞

THE P.E.N. was founded in London by Mrs. Dawson Scott in October, 1921, as an association of writers of accepted standing in the various branches of literature. The need being felt for occasional social meetings one with another, and also with the literary workers of other countries, it was held that this purpose was best served by the formation of a dining club, which, first in London and eventually in the capital cities of the world, would constitute an international association of poets, playwrights, editors, essayists and novelists, concerning itself with friendly feeling and hospitality but in no sense with politics or propaganda.

Although the fundamental idea has remained unchanged, the organisation has developed in many directions and it is no longer merely, or even primarily, a dining-club.

On the first Tuesday in every month from October to July a dinner is held in a London restaurant, at 8 o'clock. A member is permitted to bring one guest to the functions of the Club,

3

but the desire is expressed that guests shall themselves be connected with literature. The Annual General Meeting, open to Members only, is held in October. From time to time At Homes are given by members of the Centre to their fellow members.

By a principle of the association (though subject to the discretion of individual centres) membership of one centre is deemed to include membership of every centre, so that writers travelling in any country where a branch of the P.E.N. exists are enabled socially and informally to meet their fellow-writers in that country.

The members of the London centre extend a welcome to writers from abroad on the occasion of their visits here.

Each Centre elects its own Committee, its Members and Hon. Members, conducts its own business and frames its own rules. International Congresses are held every year, at which matters relating to the P.E.N. and literature generally are discussed. Every Centre has a right to send delegates to these international gatherings. The first was held in London; the second in New York; the third in Paris; the fourth in Berlin; the fifth in Brussels, and the sixth in Oslo.

4

By these means the P.E.N. has demonstrated its international character, ignoring the frontiers which in recent years have prevented the free interchange of literature and ideas. At the Paris Congress many distinguished German writers were present as guests of the French. English, French, Belgian, Jugo-Slavian and Czecho-Slovakian authors went to Berlin as honoured guests of the German Centre. The P.E.N. was privileged to remove yet another barrier when Germans were received by Burgomaster Max as the guests of Brussels.

At this Congress the following resolution, presented by the English, French, German and Belgian delegates, was passed unanimously :

1. Literature, national though it be in origin, knows no frontiers, and should remain common currency between nations in spite of political or international upheavals.

2. In all circumstances then and particularly in time of war, works of art, the patrimony of humanity at large, should be left untouched by national or political passion.

3. Members of the P.E.N. will at all times use what influence they have in favour of

5

good understanding and mutual respect between the nations.

At the Paris International Congress it was decided to give the question of translations particular attention and a scheme for collaborating with the Institut de Co-operation Intellectuelle of the League of Nations has since been developed. At present it is in its infancy, but with time should be of real service, making the best literature of the world available in all civilised languages.

Writers of recognised position desiring to become members of the P.E.N. must be proposed by two existing members for ballot by the committee. The subscription for annual membership is 26/- (twenty-six shillings) payable in advance in October.

P.E.N. News, a monthly 4 pp. circular, is sent to all members. An occasional Bulletin, circulated by the Paris Centre, is also issued free. Members pay for their dinners at the time.

6

PEN Centres
in 1930

While the mission and structures of PEN were being defined in Congresses in London, New York, Paris, Berlin, Brussels, Oslo, Vienna, and Warsaw, the first decade of the organisation saw PEN Clubs established in 45 cities across four continents.

Oslo, Norway

Helsinki, Finland

Glasgow, Scotland

Stockholm, Sweden

Tartu, Estonia

Dublin, Ireland

Edinburgh, Scotland

Riga, Latvia

Copenhagen, Denmark

Yiddish, Vilna

Kaunas, Lithuania

Hamburg, Germany

Amsterdam, The Netherlands

Berlin, Germany

Warsaw, Poland

London, England

Brussels, Belgium

Prague, Czechoslovakia

Paris, France

Freiburg, Germany

Vienna, Austria

Budapest, Hungary

Geneva, Switzerland

Ljubljana, Yugoslavia

Zagreb, Yugoslavia

Milan, Italy

Belgrade, Yugoslavia

Bucharest, Romania

Sofia, Bulgaria

Madrid, Spain

Barcelona, Spain

Rome, Italy

Lisbon, Portugal

Argentina – Buenos Aires
Austria – Vienna
Belgium – Brussels
Bulgaria – Sofia
Canada – Montreal, Toronto
Chile – Santiago
China – Shanghai
Czechoslovakia – Prague
Denmark – Copenhagen
England – London
Estonia – Tartu
Finland – Helsinki
France – Paris
Germany – Berlin, Freiburg, Hamburg
Hungary – Budapest
Iceland – Reykjavík
Ireland – Dublin
Italy – Milan, Rome

Latvia – Riga
Lithuania – Kaunas
Mexico – Mexico City
The Netherlands – Amsterdam
Norway – Oslo
Palestine – Tel Aviv
Poland – Warsaw
Portugal – Lisbon
Romania – Bucharest
Scotland – Edinburgh, Glasgow
South Africa – Cape Town, Johannesburg
Spain – Barcelona, Madrid
Sweden – Stockholm
Switzerland – Geneva
United States – New York, San Francisco
Yiddish – Vilna
Yugoslavia – Belgrade, Ljubljana, Zagreb

Towards a supra-political stand

1930 to 1948

> *“ From time to time the conscience of the world is stirred and shocked by revelations of the ill treatment, in this, that or the other country, of people imprisoned on political or religious grounds. ”*

1931 Appeal to all governments

For all the concerns about political meddling, PEN did not retreat into quietism as the already fractious climate of the 1920s gave way to the more extreme polarisations of the new decade. In 1931, following the rise of Nazism in Germany as well as fascism in Spain and Italy, the organisation issued a strongly worded public 'Appeal to All Governments' — in reality, to the 56 countries then represented in the League of Nations.

Written by Galsworthy and agreed at PEN's 1931 Amsterdam Congress, the appeal was designed to intervene in the League's World Disarmament Conference, held in Geneva in February 1932. That conference, which took place against a backdrop of German rearmament, was a turning point in the League's reputation as an effective champion of world peace. Writing on behalf of 'some 4,000 writers in 35 countries' — up from 3,000 in the manuscript — Galsworthy declared: 'From time to time the conscience of the world is stirred and shocked by revelations of the ill treatment, in this, that, or the other country, of people imprisoned on political or religious grounds.' With

APPEAL TO ALL GOVERNMENTS

We, undersigned members or honorary members of the
non-political World Association of Writers called the P.E.N.,
and representing 3,000 writers in 35 countries, respectfully
draw the attention of all Governments to the following
considerations:

From time to time the conscience of the World is stirred and
shocked by revelations of the ill treatment, in this, that or the
other country, of people imprisoned on political or religious grounds.

Without calling in question the right *or the duty of* ~~or need of~~ Governments
to maintain their laws ~~to imprison such as are in opposition to their regime~~ we submit
that, in such cases, Governments are specially bound to see that
~~the laws of~~ humanity ~~and decent conduct are~~ not violated in the
treatment of such prisoners.

We, further, urge Governments to remember that nothing so
provokes the ill will, of the world at large against a given
country, as knowledge that political or religious prisoners are
ill treated; and that such ill treatment is in these days bound,
soon or late, to become matter of common knowledge.

--oOo---

APPEL À TOUS LES GOUVERNEMENTS

Nous les soussignés, membres ou membres honoraires
de l'association non-politique et mondiale d'écrivains
dénommée le P.E.N., représentant 3,000 écrivains dans 35
pays, appelons respectueusement l'attention de tous les
Gouvernements sur les considérations suivantes:

De temps à autre, la conscience du monde est émue et
troublée par des révélations relatives à de mauvais traitements
infligés, dans tel ou tel pays, à des personnes incarcérées
pour des raisons politiques ou religieuses.

Sans vouloir mettre en question le droit des Gouvernements,
ou la nécessité pour eux, ~~d'emprisonner ceux qui font~~ *de maintenir leurs lois,*
~~opposition à leur régime~~, nous nous permettons de faire
observer que, dans de tels cas, les Gouvernements sont tout
particulièrement obligés de veiller à ce que les ~~lois de~~ *principes de*
l'humanité ~~et les convenances~~ ne soient pas violés dans le
traitement de cette catégorie de prisonniers.

Nous invitons instamment, en outre, les Gouvernements à
se rappeler que rien ne provoque autant l'hostilité du monde
en général contre un pays, que de savoir que les prisonniers
politiques ou religieux y sont maltraités; et que ces mauvais
traitements, de nos jours, ne peuvent pas manquer d'être tôt
ou tard connus de tout le monde.

---oOo---

pointed targeting and phrasing, he insisted that 'Governments are specially bound to see that [the laws of] *humanity* are not violated in the treatment of such prisoners' (italics added).

Read at the Geneva Conference, the appeal was also published in the press, signed by a roster of famous writers, including Benedetto Croce, Maurice Maeterlinck, André Maurois, Gilbert Murray, George Bernard Shaw, Rabindranath Tagore, HG Wells, and Karel Čapek. It thus combined some of the key ingredients — famous signatures, a universalist language of rights, global reach — that would feature in many of PEN's subsequent campaigns.

The high-profile 1931 Appeal to All Governments marked a new departure for PEN, but it did not represent a major shift in its thinking. That happened two years later at the first Congress under Galsworthy's successor as president, HG Wells.

↑   Book burning in Berlin, May 1933.

←   Draft typescript with manuscript additions of the 1931 Appeal to All Governments. The final version included the text in German.

1933 Dubrovnik, PEN defends freedom against the Nazis

Over three tumultuous days in late May 1933, the ancient port city of Dubrovnik, then part of the Kingdom of Yugoslavia, became the testing ground for Galsworthy's 'new idealism'. The growing persecution of writers in Germany, the book burnings, and the Nazification of German PEN — all in the months immediately following Hitler's rise to power in January 1933 — changed everything almost overnight.

Yet it was Wells's own determination to uphold what he called the 'liberty of expression' that gave a new, sharper edge to Galsworthy's dream of a non-political world 'Republic of Letters', and to PEN's early concerns about censorship. After the German Centre failed to answer questions about its recent conduct put by Hermon Ould, PEN's long-serving general secretary (1926–51), Wells insisted on giving the now exiled Ernst Toller a platform from which to speak about the realities of Nazi rule. At that point, the German delegates walked out, joined by others from Switzerland, Austria, and The Netherlands. When Toller

← The opening of HG Wells's inaugural speech as president of PEN at the Dubrovnik Congress in 1933, paying tribute to Galsworthy's 'old Liberal idea' but also committing PEN to defending the 'liberty of expression' and building 'a World Republic of Letters and Creative Effort'.

→ Klaus Mann represented the PEN Club of German writers in exile based in London. At the Barcelona Congress in 1935, he presented a resolution denouncing the incarceration of Ludwig Renn and Carl von Ossietzky and the illegal activities of the Gestapo persecuting German authors in their countries of exile.

CATALAN CONGRESS : May 1935

GERMAN PRISONERS, etc.

The P.E.N.Clubs in all countries solemnly protest against the incarceration and ill-treatment of German authors in Germany.   Authors of all countries united in the P.E.N.Club demand the release of their colleagues Ludwig Renn and Carl Ossietzky.

The authors of all countries grouped in the P.E.N. Club protest against the persecution through the agent of the Gestapo of their colleagues who have emigrated from Germany.   They demand the immediate release of the journalist Berthold Jacob who was illegally abducted from Switzerland.

Klauss Mann.

CARRIED with one dissentient (The Dutch Delegation, who explained that their objection was not to the principle of the resolution, to which they agreed, but to the stating of names.)

1933   Toller's speech

Yesterday I did not speak because I wanted to give the official German delegation a chance to answer me and deny my statements, if possible. As they had decided, in spite of the magnitude of the accusation, not to attend the session for formal reasons, I am forced to speak in their absence. They may answer elsewhere.

Many have advised me not to speak, supplying many reasons why it would be more advantageous to keep silent.

The writer is responsible to the spirit only. One who believes that life is governed by moral laws, apart from power, must not keep silent.

I can only thank my good fortune that I am standing here now. On the night when the German Reichstag was burned I was to be detained. By pure chance, I was in Switzerland. This gift of freedom is an obligation to all the comrades who are now in prison in Germany.

[Other versions of the speech include the following exchange at this point: Shouts from the floor: 'You have no right to speak because you are communist! You talk against Germany!' I do not belong to the Communist Party. I am speaking as an author not against Germany, but against all power throughout the world. During the war I fought on the German side. Only when I recognised that war was a disgrace did I rebel.]

Yesterday the German delegates passed a resolution which contained the following words: 'It is the duty of the artist to guard the spirit in its freedom so that mankind shall not be prey to ignorance, to malice, and to fear. Literature knows no frontiers and should remain common currency in spite of political or international upheavals.'

I was surprised indeed that the gentlemen from the German PEN Club supported this resolution and I wanted to ask them: Is their support compatible with reality?

A few weeks ago, ten members of the German PEN Club received a notice that they were being deprived of membership because of their Communist or similar views. I do not intend to dwell on this vague formulation. For these gentlemen, everybody who is not in their ranks is a Communist. The gentlemen of the German PEN Club opposed yesterday any discussion of political issues in the PEN Club. But if they expel writers for ideological reasons, then it is they who bring politics into PEN.

Last year in Budapest, Mr Schmidt-Pauli and Elster, members of the present official delegation, supported a decision against the persecution of poets and their works on ideological grounds. What did they do when the German writers Ludwig Renn, Ossietzky, Mühsam, Duncker, Wittfogel were imprisoned, when tens of thousands of German workers were imprisoned? [from the audience: 'They did nothing!']

On the 10th of May, books by the following German writers were burned: Thomas Mann, Heinrich Mann, Stefan Zweig, Arnold Zweig, Jakob Wassermann, Lion Feuchtwanger, Kurt Tucholsky, Emil Ludwig, Theodor Wolff, Alfred Kerr, Bertolt Brecht, von Ossietzky, Hellmut von Gerlach, Lehmann-Russbüldt, Rudolf Olden, Friedrich Wolff, Anna Seghers, Martin Buber, Jürgen Kuczinski, Erich Maria Remarque, Joseph Roth, Hans Marchwitza, Alfred Döblin, Werner Hegemann, Bruno von Salomon, Ernst Bloch, Walter Mehring, Arthur Holitscher, Prof. Gumbel, Prof. Grossmann, Siegfried Kracauer, Hermann Wendel, KA Wittfogel, Egon Erwin Kisch, FC Weiskopf, Johannes R Becher, Gustav Regler, Bruno Frei, Paul Friedländer, Heinz Pol, Otto Heller, Erich Weinert, Ludwig Renn, Hermann Duncker, Bernhard Kellermann, Leonhard Frank, Franz Werfel, Ludwig Fulda, Vicki Baum, Adrienne Thomas, Ferdinand Bruckner, Carl Sternheim, Georg Kaiser, Carl Zuckmayer, Georg Bernhard, Heinrich Simon, Arthur Eloesser, Erich Baron, HE Jacob, Ernst Toller.

What has the German PEN Club done against the burning of books? The gentlemen will say that the burning was the work of young, immature men. The burning was carried out under the auspices of Minister Goebbels and he called the burnt books, by writers who represented a nobler Germany, 'spiritual filth'.

What has the German PEN Club done against the banishment of Germany's most prominent university professors and scientists, against the banishment of Einstein, Zondek, Heller, Lederer, Bonn, Schücking, Goldstein, and others from the field of medicine, law, philosophy? They have to live abroad, exiled, separated from their work and their jobs, no longer able to serve Germany, to serve humanity.

What has the German PEN Club done about the fact that artists such as Bruno Walter, Klemperer, Weill, Busch, Eisler are prevented from working in Germany?

What has the German PEN Club done about the fact that important artists such as Käthe Kollwitz, Otto Dix, Hofer, Klee are no longer allowed to work at German academies, that the great painter Liebermann was forced to leave the Academy because he refused to work in humiliating conditions?

What has the German PEN Club done about the expulsion of great actors from German stages?

What has the German PEN Club done about the expulsion of German poets from the professional association of German writers?

What has the German PEN Club done against the blacklisting of books by those writers who are no longer published in Germany and whose works are no longer sold in German bookstores?

What has the German PEN Club done about the fact that foreign publishers who wanted to publish books by persecuted writers were threatened with boycott of their entire production in Germany?

The secretary of the German PEN Club today is one Mr von Leers. In his book *Juden sehen Dich an* (Jews are Watching You), he dared to describe the Jews as devils in human shape. Under the pictures of Einstein, Ludwig, Lessing, he wrote 'not hanged', under the picture of Erzberger who was, incidentally, not a Jew, the words 'finally liquidated'.

Will this eruption of madness and barbarity be condemned, will Mr von Leers be expelled from the German PEN Club? Will speeches and resolutions of these gentlemen be followed by deeds?

I am not talking about my personal fate, I am not talking about the personal fates of any of these people who are in exile today. It is difficult enough in itself. They are not allowed ever again to see the country in which they were born, they are persecuted, expelled, rejected. But others have suffered more.

We live in times of raging nationalism, of brutal racial hatred. The intellectuals are isolated, they are threatened and oppressed by the regime, reason is scorned, the spirit abused. [from the audience: 'Why do you speak of Germany only?'] If I speak here only about the situation in Germany, it is because it is critical and also because I know it well, but I expect you to show the same courage fighting against violence in your own countries.

I shall be accused in Germany for speaking against Germany. It is not true. I raise my voice against the methods of those who rule Germany today but have no right to identify themselves with Germany. Millions of people in Germany are not allowed to speak freely and to write freely. Speaking here, I speak also for those millions who have no voice today. The rulers evoke the spirit of great German writers. How are the spiritual claims of Goethe, Schiller, Kleist, Herder, Wieland, Lessing compatible with the persecution of millions of human beings?

Madness governs our times, barbarity rules the people. The air around us is getting thinner. Let us not delude ourselves, the voice of the spirit, the voice of humanity, is heard by the mighty only when it serves as a front for political purposes. Let us not delude ourselves, the politicians only tolerate us and persecute us when we become disagreeable. The voice of truth was never agreeable.

> " *We live in times of raging nationalism, of brutal racial hatred.* "

Throughout the centuries, whether we think of Socrates, Giordano Bruno or Spinoza, men of spirit and truth were tortured, persecuted, murdered, because they refused to bend and chose death rather than a lie, because they believed in the world of freedom, of justice, of humanity.

I doubt that there will be many opportunities for us to meet in this Europe and talk with each other. Those who resist are threatened. It depends on us. Let us overcome the fear which humiliates and insults us. We may be fighting on different sides and perhaps we shall have to confront each other; but in all of us there is an awareness of mankind that is free of barbarity, of lies, of social injustice and slavery.

Source:
Branko Matan, *Speak Now or Never: The 1933 Dubrovnik PEN Club Congress*. Zagreb-Dubrovnik: Croatian PEN Centre & Most/The Bridge, 1993.

> **❝ We don't expect you to say that this or that party or government are good, but to raise your voice against violence, killing, racism, genocide, destruction of cities. ❞**

finally spoke the next day, he denounced the Nazis' 'raging nationalism' and 'brutal racial hatred', after pointedly naming 60 major writers whose books were among the over 20,000 'un-German' volumes students had burned in Berlin two weeks earlier. At a meeting of PEN's international council in London six months later, the German Centre was formally expelled. The reason? By excluding members on political grounds, it had betrayed the Charter and Galsworthy's vision.

Did this not mean that PEN itself was now meddling in politics, as the Germans and their supporters argued? Looking back on the events 60 years later, when Dubrovnik was once again host to the PEN Congress and once again at the centre of a violent political storm, the Croatian writer and PEN activist Branko Matan confronted this central question head on:

> the defenders of freedom in Dubrovnik [in 1933] had the same problem that the Croatian defenders of freedom have now, and also Bosnian, Kosovian, Macedonian, Hungarian, and even those few Serbian ones. To all of them the same thing is being said: What you are telling us is all very nice, but what do you want us to do? To take sides in a political conflict, to support one political view against another in countries that are not ours? The answer is the same today as it was in 1933 (but not many seem to be listening): No, what we want from you is not a political, but a supra-political stand; we don't expect you to say that this or that party or government are good, but to raise your voice against violence, killing, racism, genocide, destruction of cities.

The questions and the answers may have been similar in 1933 and 1993. The context was different. At the first Dubrovnik Congress, PEN was only beginning to get a sense of what it might mean to take 'a supra-political stand', and it had not yet found a way of giving voice to Galsworthy's 'new idealism' in a language robust and global enough to confront the abuse of power wherever it occurs. It took the horrors of another world war — and the Nuremberg Trials, which established the primacy of international law, especially in relation to 'supra-political' rights — for that language to achieve canonical articulation in the Universal Declaration of Human Rights (1948).

→   Henry Seidel Canby's report on the 1933 Dubrovnik Congress, testifying to the importance of Ernst Toller's speech. Canby was then president of New York PEN.

REPORT OF THE P.E.N. CONGRESS
by
Henry Seidel Canby, American Delegate
and
Speech made at the Congress
by
Ernst Toller representing exiled authors

The Annual Congress of the International P.E.N. Clubs, meeting on May 25-28 at Dubrovnik (Ragusa) in Jugoslavia, was a lesson in what may be expected of international gatherings in the troublous year of 1933. The P.E.N. Clubs have fifty-four "centres" in forty nations of Europe, North and South America, with a beginning (unrepresented this time) in Asia. Some 400 official delegates and members were present, a polyglot group drawn from the writing professions of the world, with novelists, journalists, and poets best represented. Jules Romains was there from France, H. G. Wells, as president, from England, Ernst Toller from among the exiled Germans, and an especially strong group of poets, novelists and journalists from the Danubian countries. The Argentine was ably represented, Holland had a large and, as it proved somewhat agonized delegations; Scotland, which is to have the Conference next year, was led by Edwin Muir; Felix Salten was chairman of the Austrians.

The United States, that whirlpool into which all translatable books are finally drawn, was represented, I regret to say, only by myself; but thanks to the acumen of our New York Executive Committee, and especially Will Irwin, Robert Nathan, and Alfred Dashiell, I was able to present a Resolution which kept the Conference from being one more disaster on the rocks of Chauvinism.

These Congresses, of which I have attended several, are ordinarily harmless and most delightful social gatherings in which, especially in the smaller countries, the state opens palaces, organizes exhibitions and banquets, and in general gives the attendant moulders of public opinion a swell time. I do not speak disparagingly. A P.E.N. Conference in Poland, or Austria, or Belgium is an experience never to be forgotten, and in its course of heated oratory, informal talk, and papers and resolutions on the internationalism of art, lessons are learned of mutual tolerance and conciliation in points of view of a value second only to the personal friendships made between individuals of different races. Yet the best results of previous Congresses have been social. No issue of great importance has ever troubled the Conference or interfered with the business of exchange of views on comparative literature and contributions to the solidarity of culture.

Dubrovnik, that exquisite fortress in the Adriatic, enclosing a town built of old ivory, the half-way place for centuries between the Turk, the Byzantine, and the East, was an ideal setting for a social Congress. Its rector's palace, more beautiful I think than the Doge's palace in Venice, was the background for a Renaissance pastoral play, "Dubravka," performed on the very spot for which it was written; in one of its towers high above the ocean we dined while a chorus sang Slavic folk songs; the narrow streets were gay with Dalmatian costumes, and to swim in the sea beneath the palmy terraces was like swimming in light.

The Congress, however, was far from gay. Its agenda provided for a discussion of moral disarmament, of free speech (this is one of the most heavily censored countries in Europe), and of collectivism vs. individualism in literature. We got to none of them, and the papers prepared were unread. The sole issue was the question of Chauvinism vs. internationalism in literature forced upon the Congress by events and by the delegation representing the Berlin P.E.N. Club.

For PEN, however, the high stakes theatre of the 1933 Congress, which centred on two key resolutions, marked a significant moment in its own evolution. The first resolution, tabled by the American literary critic and editor Henry Seidel Canby, was on the formal agenda for the second session. Framed with characteristically diplomatic delicacy — it pointed no fingers but the subtext was clear — it reaffirmed the three articles of the 1927 Charter, while also condemning 'Chauvinism' and 'racial prejudice', and upholding 'the duty of the artist to guard the spirit in its freedom so that mankind shall not be prey to ignorance, to malice, and to fear'. In the course of the discussions, and without prior notice, the French-speaking Belgian poet René Lyr put forward an alternative. Faced with this breach of protocol, Wells had to find a tactful solution: while insisting they keep to the agenda, he agreed to let Lyr table his resolution later in the day, after Canby's had been fully debated — and, as it turned out, passed unanimously (i.e. with German support).

> **" *The defence of liberty of expression and that defence alone, defines a task big enough for all your efforts as a society.* "**

For all this, Lyr's resolution was not substantially different from Canby's. It said much the same thing, only with some added French flair. After noting the recent 'destruction of books' and 'attacks on the individual freedom of writers' (again Germany was not named), it set out PEN's 'general principles' as follows:

1. *the defence of the rights of the spirit [droits de l'esprit] in all circumstances.*

2. *the rapprochement of peoples by intellectual means and especially through literature.*

3. *as a consequence, the condemnation of all that threatens the rights of the spirit, or the rapprochement of peoples; in particular, racial or religious prejudice and national fanaticisms.*

Though Wells was uneasy about some of the wording — 'the rights of the spirit' probably reminded him too much of the vaguer aspects of Galsworthy's idealism — Lyr's resolution was in the end also carried, although not unanimously (10 for, 2 against, 14 abstentions). What proved most significant, however, was not the resolution itself but the fact that it brought the growing tensions at the Congress to a head. When the German delegates said they would back it only if there was no discussion, Wells was adamant: since PEN existed largely to

↓ Front cover of the 2015 re-issue of HG Wells's 1940 Penguin Special.

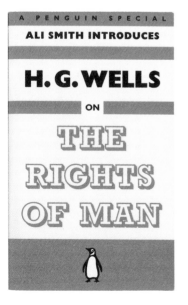

champion free expression, it had to practise what it preached. He then gave Ould the floor, precipitating the sequence of events that culminated in the German Centre's formal expulsion.

With Dubrovnik still very much on his mind, though also concerned about new British legislation suppressing anti-royalist 'Incitement to Disaffection', Wells opened the next international Congress held in Edinburgh a year later with a landmark declaration: 'The defence of liberty of expression and that defence alone, defines a task big enough for all your efforts as a society.' The prolific British novelist Ernest Raymond then took up the theme, tabling a formal resolution at Wells's dictation that captured the lessons of 1933 and clarified his evolving vision. 'The P.E.N. stands for liberty of expression throughout the world,' it began. This sounded expansive, but, as Raymond explained, he was referring primarily to 'the right of the author's existence, the right of authors to write' — recalling the 1928 resolution about 'des ouvrages de l'esprit'. This was also Wells's position as president of PEN, though in his influential Penguin Special *The Rights of Man* (1940), which began as a letter to the London *Times* on 25 October 1939, seven weeks into the war, he would go on to recast free expression as a more fundamental, universally human right.

The key resolutions passed at the Edinburgh Congress in 1934, relating to free expression, and German writers in exile and in prison.

Hermon Ould writes to the Scottish writer Compton Mackenzie outlining the 'Raymond resolution' on free expression, parts of which would eventually be incorporated into the PEN Charter.

RESOLUTIONS.

FREEDOM OF EXPRESSION.

Moved by Ernest Raymond (England).

The P.E.N. stands for liberty of expression throughout the world and view with apprehension the continual attempts to encroach upon that liberty in the name of social security and international strategy. It affirms its belief that the necessary advance of the world towards a more highly organised political and economic order renders a free criticism of administrations and institutions imperative from all points of view.

Carried. One against. Two abstentions.

GERMAN GROUP OUTSIDE GERMANY.
Moved by Hermon Ould.
The XII. P.E.N. Congress, recognising that the German members of the P.E.N. outside Germany constitute the only part of German mental expression at the present time which conforms to P.E.N. ideals, and being anxious to consolidate and preserve the unity of this mentality with a view to the final complete restoration of the German P.E.N. on German soil, proposes to recognise a common centre for this German P.E.N. de facto in London or Paris, and to accord that centre pro tem. all the respect due to any national P.E.N. Club.

Carried unanimously.

IMPRISONED GERMAN WRITERS.

Moved by Ernst Toller.

The XII. International P.E.N. congress declares:
That since the arrival to power of the National Socialist Government in German, writers have been imprisoned without trial and without having committed any offence against the laws of their land, for no other reason than that they had under former governments in former years written books the intellectual content of which was not to the taste of the present regime. This Congress demands the release of these men who have thus been deprived of liberty.

Carried unanimously.

ATTITUDE OF WRITERS IN THE EVENT OF WAR.

Emil Ludwig moved:
The Congress requests the Secretary in case of the imminence of war to call together the delegates of the International P.E.N. Association, in order to consider measures to safeguard the

10th May 1934.

Compton Mackenzie, Esc.
Tarbert,
Harris,
Inverness-shire

Dear Mackenzie,

Many thanks for your note of the 1st. I have arranged with Ernest Raymond to open the debate on Freedom of Expression. He will move the following resolution, or something like it:

"The P.E.N. stands for liberty of expression throughout the world and views with apprehension the continual attempts to encroach upon that liberty in the name of social security and international strategy.

That it emphatically records its belief that the manifest advance of the world to-day towards a more highly organised political and economic order renders all the more necessary a free criticism of administration and institutions from every point of view."

and I hope you will take part in this discussion.

Yours sincerely,

HERMON OULD

HO/GB

↑ Filippo Marinetti, PEN's arch tormentor in the 1930s.

↗ *The Indian P.E.N.* for 1 October 1936 reports on one of the more provocative moments involving Marinetti at the Buenos Aires Congress.

With a further Wellsian flourish, Raymond's resolution continued: PEN 'affirms its belief that the necessary advance of the world towards a more highly organised political and economic order renders the free criticism of administrations and institutions imperative from all points of view'. At a time when writers were 'languishing in prisons and concentration camps' and being 'driven forth into poverty and exile', he said during the discussion, it was critical for PEN to take a stand. Once again, Ernst Toller provided powerful corroborating testimony on behalf of 'tens of thousands of fugitives' who, like him, had been forced into 'poverty and exile', ensuring the resolution carried with only Italy voting against and South Africa and Romania abstaining.

Toller's rival and PEN's arch tormentor in the 1930s, the Italian Futurist, now outspoken fascist, Filippo Marinetti, was the one loudly dissenting voice. He provoked another showdown in Buenos Aires in 1936, the first Congress held outside Europe and North America. Speaking partly as a high-minded avant-gardist, Marinetti thought Raymond was being too inclusive. Only 'real writers', he insisted, not

The 1936 Congress in Buenos Aires as represented in the film
Stefan Zweig: Farewell to Europe (2016) in the moment
they are paying tribute to German Writers in exile

Stefan Zweig was one of the important guests of honour at the 1936 Buenos Aires Congress. A Jewish-Austrian humanist, and novelist, playwright, and journalist, he was one of the most famous and translated writers of the 1920s and 1930s. In the mid- to late 1930s, his writings were banned and criticised in the German-speaking world. He left Vienna in 1934 and lived in exile for the rest of his life, first in London, and then,

fearing the German advance westwards in 1940, in New York, before settling in Brazil. In 1942, he committed suicide with his wife, Lotte. On 14 September, the last day of the Buenos Aires Congress, Zweig delivered a passionate eulogy to HG Wells. Wells had recently stepped down as PEN International president, and made way for Jules Romains. Zweig spoke of his happiness at attending the Congress, and announced that,

despite the divisions, in this session writers have gathered 'under the spell of a single idea', unanimous in their desire to honour Wells, 'the great writer and indefatigable forerunner of a better humanity'. His final call to delegates that they rise and toast Wells was greeted with cheers and loud applause.

mere 'pamphleteers', merited the right to 'freedom of thought' — he said nothing of ordinary citizens in general. Echoing the Germans in Dubrovnik, however, his chief objection was that if PEN accepted Raymond's resolution it would inevitably be meddling in politics and so betraying its founding ideals.

Doubts about the very possibility of taking a supra-political stand, framed in a language of rights, would resurface on many occasions in the turbulent decades ahead, not least when Hungarian PEN was briefly suspended in the 1950s, when Afrikaans PEN excluded itself in the 1960s, and when Chilean PEN was expelled in the 1970s. And such doubts remain. In 2019, after PEN International president Jennifer Clement visited imprisoned Catalan writers, the Peruvian-Spanish Nobel laureate and former PEN president Mario Vargas Llosa publicly resigned his membership, claiming PEN had abandoned 'its long-established neutrality about internal political affairs'.

1937 PEN's campaign to free Arthur Koestler in Spain

In the course of the 1930s, PEN also began to assist exiled and imprisoned writers in more direct ways. It set up the German Writers Abroad Centre in 1934 and campaigned on behalf of individual writers in prison by various means. One method was to write directly to high-ranking government officials. On 31 January 1934, Ould sent a private letter on behalf of English PEN via the German Embassy in London to 'Your Excellency' Josef Goebbels asking him, in the politest of terms, to consider releasing Ludwig Renn from prison. Renn was one of the most important German communist writers of the interwar period. After the Reichstag fire of February 1933, Hitler seized dictatorial powers and instructions were given to arrest all members of the German Communist Party. Along with Carl von Ossietzky, Renn was one of the first German communists to be rounded up — Toller escaped because, as he explained in his PEN speech, he happened to be in Switzerland. Renn was sentenced 9 January 1934 and imprisoned for 18 months. PEN's letter to Goebbels, sent a couple of weeks later, repeated what were now familiar phrases: it was a 'non-political' organisation representing 'colleagues in the world of culture'. There

31st January, 1934

Herrn Reichsminister Dr. Josef Goebbels,
BERLIN.

Your Excellency,

        Many members of the P.E.N., an
organisation which is no doubt known to you as
a strictly non-political body of writers, have
approached me on the subject of their fellow-
author Ludwig Renn, whose works are well known
in this country and much esteemed.

        It appears from reports in the English
Press that Mr. Renn, after awaiting trial for
a year, has now been sentenced to a long term
of imprisonment. As these reports are not
very explicit, and the nature of Mr. Renn's
offense is not clear, I am sure that Your
Excellency will understand the uneasiness felt
by Renn's colleagues in the world of culture,
and that they would be glad if you would be
kind enough to throw light on the subject.

        I am, dear Reichsminister,

        Yours very truly,

                Hermon Ould,
                General Secretary

← Ould writes to
Goebbels on behalf of
Ludwig Renn in 1934.

had been some internal disagreement between Margaret Storm Jameson and HG Wells about whether such a letter would have any effect, with Wells arguing forcefully against sending it — Jameson was a prominent English novelist and future president of English PEN. Unsurprisingly, the letter failed to persuade Goebbels to release Renn. Nevertheless, this first attempt by English PEN to influence a foreign government in a case of imprisonment would certainly not be its last.

With its first successful campaign on behalf of a writer in prison, PEN adopted a different strategy. When General Franco's chief propagandist, Luis Bolín, arrested the Hungarian-born writer and journalist Arthur Koestler in Malaga in 1937, it joined a larger protest campaign, which included a cross-party group of British MPs. Unlike the correspondence with Goebbels, PEN now wrote an open letter, printed in the press and signed by a collection of famous writers. Along with PEN members, such as EM Forster, they persuaded an important non-member, Aldous Huxley, to add his name. The letter repeated the claim that PEN was a 'non-political' organisation, and stated that they wanted to defend what they called the 'immemorial rights' to free speech of a liberal journalist. The claim that Koestler was a liberal journalist at that point was premature. He had been a member of the German Communist Party for six years, and was sent to Spain on the instructions of Willi Münzenberg, chief propagandist of the Comintern in Western Europe. He became an outspoken anti-Stalinist only after his imprisonment. PEN's actions were reported widely in the British press, and they were given a welcome burst of publicity. From this point on, PEN would often publish public protest letters, signed by famous authors, to defend writers in prison.

↖ Ludwig Renn (right) with Ernest Hemingway and Dutch filmmaker Joris Ivens during the Spanish Civil War.

↓ Jules Romains, third president of PEN International.

```
Arthur Koestler,
C/o "News Chronicle",
19/22 Bouverie Street,
London, E.C.4.                    2nd June, 1937.


   Dear Sir,

      Arriving in London after more than three months of
   imprisonment in Seville I want to express my deep gratitude
   for the unstinted help your organization gave in obtaining
   my release.

      I am fully aware that it was no personal merit of my
   own, but in the deeper interests of the free expression of
   opinion which is the life-blood of democracy and humanity
   that this help was given.

      That a free public opinion should have thus proved so
   strong, is as much to me as my own personal liberty.

      May I express once more my most grateful thanks for
   everything that you have done on my behalf.

                        Yours truly,


                        Arthur Koestler,
               former "News Chronicle" Correspondent
                           in Spain.

   Herman Ould, Esq.,
   Secretary,
   The "P.E.N. Club",
   59 New Oxford Street, W.C.1.
```

↑   Arthur Koestler writes to Herman Ould, following his release on 13 May 1937 and his arrival in London, thanking PEN for its help in securing his release and for its commitment to 'the free expression of opinion which is the life-blood of democracy and humanity'. His three-month jail term would shape his writing for the next 10 years, during which time he also became a vocal anti-Stalinist. In his most famous novel, *Darkness at Noon* (1940), a depiction of the Soviet show trials, he mined his own experiences in his description of the character Rubashov's imprisonment. Koestler did not forget his debt to PEN. He became a lifelong member and used the money he made from writing to establish a PEN 'Koestler fund' to support exiled writers.

Throughout this period, PEN continued to clarify its larger aims and purposes. In 1937, the first year of the French poet Jules Romains's presidency, the international council reaffirmed its identity as 'a world association of established writers without regard to nationality, race, colour, or religion' committed to safeguarding 'the full freedom necessary for creative literature'. As early as 1926, after hearing that some Centres had been flouting the membership rules, Dawson Scott had tabled a resolution confirming that it was also open to women. The same general restatement of aims, which was endorsed at the Paris Congress in 1937, stressed that PEN 'has nothing whatever to do with State or Party politics'. Partly bred of its own hard experience, partly a response to the emergence of other more overtly politicised writers' groups, some Soviet-sponsored, others explicitly anti-fascist, this underlined the supra-political principles it was now beginning to make its own.

HG Wells in conversation with Indian writers in Bombay, December 1938

Although HG Wells stepped down from the PEN presidency in 1936, he continued to play a vital role in the organisation, and his aura was intact when he spent a few hours in Bombay on 16 December 1938. He arrived in the city in the early hours of the morning by steamer (the SS *Comorin*), boarded at Marseille and bound for Australia where he was due to attend several events as guest of honour, including a conference of the Australasian Association for the Advancement of Science. The All-India PEN Centre newsletter, *The Indian P.E.N.*, dated 1 January 1939, records Sophia Wadia greeting

Wells on board, and taking him for a drive through the city, then hosting a 'small informal gathering' at her house in his honour. There Wells met several prominent PEN members and public figures, including first chief minister of the Bombay presidency, BG Kher, home minister, KM Munshi, and Srimati Lilavati Munshi, essayist and member of the Legislative Assembly. All three were also engaged in the Freedom Struggle movement, and were imprisoned by the British. In an article in *The Indian P.E.N.*, 'HG Wells in Bombay', probably written by Sophia Wadia, it is

reported that Wells's most pressing concern was the future world order: 'what steps should people take to build a real cosmos out of the chaos?' Urging Indians to address this question for themselves, he also talked about his most recent book, the novel *The Holy Terror* (1939), which deals with democracies and dictator-ships, and evokes the 'cruel monstrosity' of the treatment of Jews in Germany.

INTERNATIONAL P.E.N. CLUB
LONDON CENTRE
————————————

APPEAL TO THE CONSCIENCE OF THE WORLD.

At this moment, when the future, not of our nation alone but that
of all nations, is being decided, we, the undersigned English writers,
ask to be heard by the writers of other countries.

Our country has been blamed in the past for actions most manifestly
taken because we hoped by them to avert war. We failed. We failed to
check the deliberate and carefully-prepared violence which has invaded
and killed in one country after another, Austria, Czechoslovakia, Poland,
Norway, Denmark, Holland, Belgium, France. Where the invading armies of
Germany have gone, unarmed men and women and children have been mercilessly
killed, and freedom of mind and spirit has been crushed out.

It is not only life which is threatened. It is freedom of
conscience, and if it is lost, as it is lost wherever the Nazi power
extends, life itself is not worth a breath. We ask all those who have
still the liberty to speak, and to think, to consider what this means.

We ask you to make it clear to people in your country that we with
our allies are not fighting only for ourselves, but for the belief we
share with every man, of any race and religion, who holds that men should
respect each other and minds should be free. We are fighting for our own
lives. We are fighting in the hope to end this war before more children,
innocent if anyone is, have been slaughtered, in their homes and as they
flee from their homes. But in as much as we are fighting for the
consciences of our children we are fighting for the people of every nation,
without exception.

We ask you to know this. We ask you, with the confidence that you
will judge us fairly, to support us as best you can in a struggle which
is not ended yet. We do not expect defeat. We expect danger and we are
able to face it. We expect your belief in us. And we pledge ourselves
on our part to remember that a lasting peace can be based only on justice.
We do not desire and we will set our faces against revenge.

We appeal to each one of you individually to pass our words on, by
every means, to the nations of the world.

> STORM JAMESON, President,
> HERMON OULD,   General Secretary,
> H. G. WELLS   )
> J.B.PRIESTLEY   ) former Presidents.
> HENRY W.NEVINSON)
>
> BONAMY DOBREE   )
> WALTER DE LA MARE)
> E.M.FORSTER   )
> GILBERT MURRAY   ) Vice Presidents.
> V.SACKVILLE-WEST)
> HUGH WALPOLE   )
> REBECCA WEST   )

Anthony Asquith, Phyllis Bentley, Vera Brittain, Gerald Bullett,
George Catlin, Guy Chapman, Richard Church, Susan Ertz, Eleanor Farjeon,
Louis Golding, G.P.Gooch, G.Rostrevor Hamilton, Nora Heald, R.C.
Hutchinson, Margaret Irwin, Henrietta Leslie, C. Day Lewis, F.L.Lucas,
Robert Lynd, Irene Rathbone, Ernest Raymond, Owen Rutter, Beatrice Kean
Seymour, Howard Spring, Olaf Stapledon, L.A.G.Strong, Frank Swinnerton,
H.M.Tomlinson, Marjorie Watts, Evelyn Wrench, Alec Waugh.

June, 1940.   G.D.H.Cole, Kingsley Martin.

1940 'Appeal to the Conscience of the World'

These principles underpinned the 1940 'Appeal to the Conscience of the World', a sequel to Galsworthy's public declaration of 1931. Signed by prominent members of English PEN, including Margaret Storm Jameson, HG Wells, JB Priestley, Walter de la Mare, EM Forster and Rebecca West, the new appeal called on writers of the world 'to make clear to the people in your country that we with our Allies are not fighting only for ourselves, but for the belief we share with every man, of any race or religion, who holds that men should respect each other and minds should be free'. It was released in June 1940, shortly after Allied Forces had been forced to retreat from Europe, leading to the mass evacuation of troops at Dunkirk. At a bleak moment in the war, the writers of English PEN wanted to reach out to like-minded liberals around the world, to spread a message of solidarity and hope. Led by the indefatigable Margaret Storm Jameson, English PEN was at that point also helping to secure grants for refugee writers and providing assistance on many other matters through the Arts and Letters Refugee Committee, which it had founded in collaboration with other organisations. By 1941, the committee was host to seven PEN Centres in exile: Yiddish, Austrian, German, Polish, Catalan, Norwegian, and Czech.

> ## " *The weakening of Liberty in one place weakens it in every corner of the world.* "

Yet, as the editorial from *The Indian P.E.N.* six months later revealed, the cause of free expression at that particular moment was fraught with tension and duplicity: if English PEN was actively for free expression in the struggle against totalitarian regimes in Europe, it was culpably silent on its suppression in the colonies beyond. 'Miltons and Shelleys — we are purposefully naming English names — always write against any attempt to limit man's Freedom of Speech,' the editorial began. It went on to protest against Nehru's imprisonment in October 1940 by the British colonial government for the part he played in Gandhi's civil disobedience campaign: 'Who can blame those who point to such unfair action as being a species of Hitlerism?' Yet the editorial was careful to insist that an anti-colonial animus was not the only motive for Indian PEN's protest. If 'the PEN (really) stands for free speech', it argued, it is the duty of all its members to uphold the principle everywhere: 'The weakening of Liberty in one place weakens it in every corner of the world.' Initially given a four-year sentence, Nehru was released from what was by then his eighth prison term in December 1941, after serving just over a year. Having been a member of Indian PEN since 1935, the year he was its delegate to the PEN International Congress in Barcelona, he became its vice-president in 1944, a position he held until his death in 1964.

←   The London Centre's 'Appeal to the Conscience of the World', June 1940.

All-India PEN, as Nehru's membership suggested, was now a significant Centre in its own right. The International Congress was scheduled to take place in Mysore in 1940, but had to be cancelled because of the war. The idea was revived with the first All-India Writers' Conference organised in Jaipur in October 1945, where writers from all over India, and foreign delegates such as Hermon Ould and EM Forster, gathered to debate 'The Development of the Indian Literatures as a Uniting Force'. Nehru, who had just been released from jail, as well as Sarojini Naidu, elected president of the organisation since Rabindranath Tagore passed away, were present. Other noted speakers included Mulk Raj Anand and S Radhakrishnan, future president of All-India PEN and president of India. Many speakers stressed that the diversity of India's linguistic cultures was PEN's great responsibility and opportunity, but also a symbol of the larger function of PEN International. Ould emphasised the importance of the event in the history of PEN because it was the first regional conference. It was also particularly significant because by promoting 'variety in unity' and fostering translation 'in India we have an example for the world'.

1946 Stockholm, PEN, and the United Nations

" *To oppose such evils of a free press as mendacious publication, deliberate falsehood and distortion of facts for political and personal ends.* "

The next major turning point in the evolution of PEN's thinking happened in the immediate aftermath of the Second World War when the American Centre put forward two resolutions at the 1946 Stockholm Congress. Both redefined the organisation's sense of purpose, linking it directly to the new international order taking shape under the auspices of the United Nations. One resolution committed PEN 'to dispel race, class and national hatreds and champion the ideal of one humanity living in peace in one world'. While these words recalled the Canby and Lyr resolutions — albeit omitting religion from the latter — they also reflected PEN's new, more broadly humanitarian outlook: they were intended, as the resolution put it, 'to rekindle the Hope in Mankind which these dark years of Terror have almost extinguished'. The other resolution reaffirmed but also radically extended PEN's commitment to free expression. Now no longer simply concerned with writers, it pledged 'our adherence to the principle of unhampered transmission of thought' and, in a handwritten addition, 'to oppose any form of *suppression of freedom of expression*' (italics added). The original wording also declared 'for a free press consistent with public order' — the last four words were cut from the final version, however, given concerns about how the wording might be manipulated in Franco's Spain. At the same time, it pledged 'to oppose such evils of a free press as mendacious publication, deliberate

→   *The Indian P.E.N.* protests at the imprisonment of Jawaharlal Nehru, December 1940, highlighting the contradictions of the period, particularly in so far as the British were concerned.

THE INDIAN P. E. N.

Editor: SOPHIA WADIA

VOL. VI. No. 12.   1ST DECEMBER, 1940   PRICE 3 ANNAS

P. E. N.

A · WORLD · ASSOCIATION · OF

Poets
Playwrights
Editors
Essayists
Novelists

All-India Office : "Aryasangha", Narayan Dabholkar Road, Malabar Hill, Bombay.

THE P. E. N. STANDS FOR FREE SPEECH

The P. E. N. is an international organization, and it is entirely non-political; men and women of all shades of political opinion are among its members. All of them are writers in good standing and it is a well-known fact that great writers are lovers of their fellow-men. It is natural, therefore, that on many occasions they combat, with their pens, tyranny and wickedness. Miltons and Shelleys—we are purposely naming English names—always write against any attempt to limit man's Freedom of Speech. The P. E. N. Club, at its various international conferences, has passed Resolutions affirming the great value and importance of Free Speech and has called upon its branches to do what they could to uphold the great ideal and to counter any attempt at curbing the free expression of ideas and opinions, especially by their own members.

This ghastly war continues to be waged to overthrow Hitlerism. One of the major characteristics which makes Hitlerism hateful is the total annihilation of Free Speech and Free Press. The enemies of Hitlerism—among whom we are—have a sacred duty not to fall prey to Hitlerian evils, by imitating Hitlerian principles. It is legitimate for any government fighting Hitlerism, as the Indian Government is doing, to safeguard its position in war time through necessary legislation, so that foul traitors shall not mar its work of prosecuting the war. But to use such special war-time legislation against sincere men and women who themselves are enemies of Hitlerism, and who are fighting their own battles of Liberty, is not fair; nay, is injurious to the cause of freedom and of democracy; and who can blame those who point to such unfair action as being a species of Hitlerism?

The All-India Centre of the International P.E.N. is not concerned with political issues, but its duty under existing circumstances in this country demands that it record its protest against the curbs which are being put on the Freedom of Speech and the Freedom of the Press. For poets and playwrights, essayists and editors, novelists and other pen-men, freedom of expression is the very breath of life, and they need it for their existence even in war time; they would fail in their sacred task of assisting the Cause of Truth and of Liberty if they were deprived of the power of free expression of views and ideas.

The trial and the sentencing to four years' rigorous imprisonment of one of our members, Pandit Jawaharlal Nehru, is a saddening event; the reasons for which the trial took place and the sentence was passed weaken the Cause of Liberty for which Britain says she is fighting. Thus Britain is playing into the hands of her own enemy. We ourselves, like Pandit Nehru, are convinced foes of that enemy. The weakening of Liberty in one place weakens it in every corner of the world. Our organization in upholding the right of Free Speech is fighting Hitlerism; and we most earnestly appeal to those who are in power to reflect calmly upon the psychological issue involved in their action. We are not writing only on behalf of those who are imprisoned, but on behalf of the Principle of Freedom itself, which, if upheld here in India, would influence the defeat of tyranny in Germany and in the territories which Hitler has annexed. How true are the words of the great Benjamin Franklin :—

They that can give up essential liberty to obtain a little temporary safety deserve neither liberty nor safety.

falsehood and distortion of facts for political and personal ends', since 'freedom implies voluntary restraint'. In a further qualifying formulation, it opposed 'arbitrary censorship in a time of peace'.

After English PEN moved to have these resolutions officially incorporated into the international rules at the Zurich Congress the following year, the council agreed to redraft the Charter. While retaining John Galsworthy's founding three articles, it added the humanitarian clause about dispelling hatreds and championing peace to the third and introduced a fourth, bringing together all the wording on free expression, along with the Wellsian sentence about the 'advance of the world' and the 'free criticism of administrations and institutions' from the 1934 Raymond resolution. After some debate about the translation of 'administrations', which does not have the same sense in French as in (American) English, the word 'governments' was added to avoid ambiguity. Inserted just before the Copenhagen Congress in May 1948, amid the gathering shadows of the Cold War, this small clarification had a powerful resonance. Though there were a number of attempts to revise and even redraft the Charter in the 1970s, the new four-article version agreed unanimously in 1948 remained unchanged for the rest of the twentieth century.

Eleanor Roosevelt holds up the Universal Declaration of Human Rights, formally agreed in 1948.

In 1945, US President Harry Truman appointed Eleanor Roosevelt as the US delegate to the newly formed United Nations General Assembly, where she would serve for seven years. She had long been a campaigner for black US civil rights and the rights of refugees, and in 1946 she became the first chair of the UN Commission on Human Rights. She helped oversee the drafting of the Universal Declaration of Human Rights (UDHR), which was finally ratified and adopted by the General Assembly in 1948. In the period immediately after the end of the Second World War, the new UN bodies were keen to work with international organisations in disseminating and promoting the UDHR. PEN International, whose members had long been defending the rights of writers in prison and in exile, were largely happy to oblige, and were particularly keen to promote the right to free expression as stated in Article 19.

1948 PEN meets UNESCO

That year also marked another key moment in PEN's evolution as an organisation. In 1948, it acquired special consultative status to UNESCO, the United Nations Education, Scientific and Educational Organization, founded in 1945, and a year later the United Nations recognised it as 'representative of the writers of the world.' For PEN, this formal association strengthened and consolidated the looser relationship it had forged in the interwar years with the International Committee on Intellectual Cooperation (ICIC), the relatively underfunded precursor to UNESCO in the League of Nations. For UNESCO, it represented a unique alliance. While all the other UN-related international associations — for the arts, theatre, and music — were creatures of UNESCO itself, PEN was and remained autonomous. In the immediate post-war years, the two organisations collaborated on a number of cultural initiatives, including conferences on the role of the writer in the post-war reconstruction, translation, international copyright, and the dissemination of the values of the Universal Declaration of Human Rights. And while a number of PEN members, such as Stephen Spender, took up active roles within UNESCO, others, particularly in the United States, eagerly worked with both the UN and UNESCO to promote the values of internationalism and free expression, some focusing on using the connection to the UN to campaign against communism.

The partnership with UNESCO, which continues today, reflected a significant shift in PEN's thinking and in the wider post-war world. When it came to its attitude to the state, PEN at its founding sided with a broadly Anglo-American tradition of civic activism and laissez-faire liberalism, setting itself against Soviet, Nazi and fascist statism. This underpinned Galsworthy's worries about politicisation, the council's anxieties about revolutionary Russia, and its initial reluctance to associate with the ICIC, even though the latter was itself determinedly non-governmental. It also informed PEN's early approach to fundraising. To boost its always modest and erratic income from membership dues and other initiatives, including public lectures and theatrical events, it sought additional support from private foundations only — the first such attempt, to the Carnegie Trust in 1926, was unsuccessful. Not all Centres shared these qualms: the Polish, French and Japanese PEN Centres, for instance, happily accepted governmental support from the start. Yet, for the early Anglo-dominated international council, being independent of the state was sacrosanct. Even Wells, who distanced himself from what he called PEN's 'good old Liberal idea' in 1933, treated this as an article of faith. During the war, he fell out with Margaret Storm Jameson, then president of English PEN, temporarily revoking his membership when she applied to the British government for funds to support refugee writers.

Though such attitudes continued to haunt PEN during the Cold War, affecting its relations with Soviet writers and its own Eastern European Centres, they also began to change. Following the emergence of a more positive social democratic vision of the state and relatively well-funded multi-state organisations like UNESCO, which had a budget well

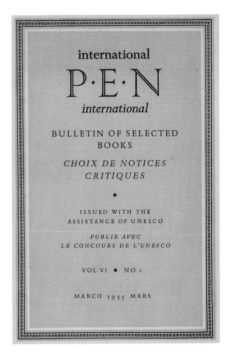

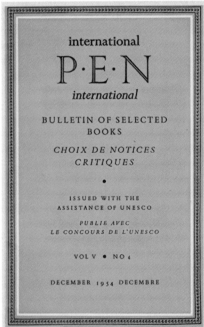

↑ The coincidence of PEN and UNESCO missions in the areas of promotion of literature, translations, and freedom of expression made UNESCO PEN's main sponsor in the 1950s. Starting in 1950, a *PEN International Bulletin of Selected Books* offered an annual review of translations and books published in 'languages of lesser currency'.

beyond the dreams of the ICIC, it began to collaborate with many public as well as private funding bodies, the most significant of which was UNESCO itself. It became PEN's chief sponsor from the early 1950s, starting with an annual subvention of around $4,500 rising to $12,500 in the 1970s. This enabled PEN to expand its operations, funding special conferences, beginning with a joint roundtable on 'The Writer and the Idea of Freedom' held in Edinburgh in 1950, and the *PEN International Bulletin of Selected Books* since 1950, an annual review of translations and books published in 'languages of lesser currency', which became the *PEN International Magazine* in 1982.

" *The true UNESCO of peoples and of individuals.* "

Yet, in all its dealings with UNESCO, PEN remained proud of its autonomy and grassroots, member-led structure. As the French writer and long-serving PEN International secretary Alexandre Blokh (also known as Jean Blot) remarked in 1986, it was always free to hold its major multi-state donor to account, reminding it (and the member states) of the clause in the preamble to its own constitution which recognises

> *That a peace based exclusively upon the political and economic arrangements of governments would not be a peace which could secure the unanimous, lasting and sincere support of the peoples of the world, and that the peace must therefore be founded, if it is not to fail, upon the intellectual and moral solidarity of mankind.*

By remaining independent of but in dialogue with its often compromised multi-state partner, PEN kept UNESCO's own founding ideals to the fore, helping to make it, as Blokh commented, 'the true UNESCO of peoples and of individuals', rather than 'of governments and civil servants.' That Blokh made these observations in a speech to UNESCO asking for more financial support says rather a lot not just about his own sustained efforts to strengthen the ties between the two organisations but about the terms of their long-standing partnership.

← Alexandre Blokh, the French writer and International PEN secretary (1981–98) who did much to strengthen PEN's ties with UNESCO. Blokh was the first secretary of PEN International who was not also secretary of English PEN. It was decided to create two separate organisations in 1981.

Letters to the Editor

WAR AIMS

THE RIGHTS OF MAN

TO THE EDITOR OF THE TIMES

Sir,—You recently did me the honour of printing a letter upon the possibility of discussing the outcome of this war while it is still going on, in which I stressed the need for free and outspoken discussion. This letter produced a considerable response, and it has been reprinted extensively in America and elsewhere. I have been favoured by the views and comments of a number of very able people. With your permission I will give certain things that have become much clearer in this discussion as it has proceeded.

The first is the extensive demand for a statement of "War Aims" on the part of young and old, who want to know more precisely what we are fighting for, and the second is the practical impossibility of making any statement in terms of boundaries, federations, and political readjustments at the present time. This demand and this difficulty are not so mutually contradictory as they seem at first. There is a way of answering the demand in a very satisfactory manner without any of the entanglements involved in map-drawing, constitution-mongering, schemes for pledges, guarantees, sanctions and the like, and it is a method which is entirely in the best traditions of the Atlantic parliamentary peoples: the method of a Declaration of Rights. At various crises in the history of our communities, beginning with Magna Carta and going through various Bills of Rights, Rights of Man, and so forth, it has been our custom to produce a specific declaration of the broad principles on which our public and social life is based, and to abide by that as our fundamental law. The present time seems peculiarly suitable for such a restatement of the spirit in which we face life in general and the present combat in particular. It would answer the first question completely; it would furnish a criterion for our subsequent treaties and behaviour.

In conjunction with a few friends I have drafted a trial statement of the Rights of Man brought up to date. I think that this statement may serve to put the War Aims discussion upon a new and more hopeful footing. It really involves nothing that is not actually observed or tacitly accepted by a great majority of reasonable men in the democratic States of to-day, it defines the spirit in which the mass of our people are more or less consciously fighting, and it is calculated to appeal very forcibly to every responsive spirit under the yoke of the obscurantist and totalitarian tyrannies with which we are in conflict.

DECLARATION OF RIGHTS

Since a man comes into this world through no fault of his own, since he is a joint inheritor of the accumulations of the past, and since those accumulations are more than sufficient to satisfy the claims that are here made on his behalf, it follows:—

(1) That every man without distinction of race or colour is entitled to nourishment, housing, covering, medical care and attention sufficient to realize his full possibilities of physical and mental development and to keep him in a state of health from his birth to death.

(2) That he is entitled to sufficient education to make him a useful and interested citizen, that he should have easy access to information upon all matters of common knowledge throughout his life and enjoy the utmost freedom of discussion.

(3) That he and his personal property lawfully acquired are entitled to police and legal protection from private violence, deprivation, compulsion and intimidation.

(4) That although he is subject to the free criticism of his fellows, he shall have adequate protection from any lying or misrepresentation that may distress or injure him. All registration and records about citizens shall be open to their personal and private inspection. There shall be no secret dossiers in any administrative department. All dossiers shall be accessible to the man concerned and subject to verification and correction at his challenge. A dossier is merely a memorandum; it cannot be used as evidence without proper confirmation.

(5) That he may engage freely in any lawful occupation, earning such pay as the need for his work and the increment it makes to the common welfare may justify. That he is entitled to demand employment and to a free choice when there is any variety of employment open to him. He may suggest employment for himself and have his claim publicly considered.

(6) That he may move freely about the world at his own expense. That his private house or apartment or reasonably limited garden enclosure is his castle, which may be entered only with his consent, but that he shall have the right to roam over any kind of country, moorland, mountain, farm, great garden or what not, where his presence will not be destructive of its special use nor dangerous to himself nor seriously inconvenient to his fellow-citizens.

(7) That he shall have the right to buy or sell without any discriminatory restrictions anything which may be lawfully bought or sold, in such quantities and with such reservations as are compatible with the common welfare.

(8) That a man unless he is duly certified as mentally deficient shall not be imprisoned for a longer period than three weeks without being charged with a definite offence against the law, nor for more than three months without a public trial. At the end of the latter period, if he has not been tried and sentenced by due process of law, he shall be released.

(9) That no man shall be subjected to any sort of mutilation or sterilization except with his own deliberate consent, freely given, nor to bodily assault, except in restraint of his own violence, nor to torture, beating or any other bodily punishment; he shall not be subjected to imprisonment with such an excess of silence, noise, light or darkness as to cause mental suffering, or to imprisonment in infected, verminous or otherwise insanitary quarters, or be put into the company of verminous or infectious people. He shall not be forcibly fed nor prevented from starving himself if he so desire. He shall not be forced to take drugs, nor shall they be administered to him without his knowledge. That the extreme punishments to which he may be subjected are rigorous imprisonment for a term of not longer than 15 years or death.

(10) That the provisions and principles embodied in this Declaration shall be more fully defined in a legal code which shall be made easily accessible to everyone. This Declaration shall not be qualified nor departed from upon any pretext whatever. It incorporates all previous Declarations of Human Right. Henceforth it is the fundamental law for mankind throughout the whole world.

Yours faithfully,

H. G. WELLS.

13, Hanover Terrace, Regent's Park, N.W.1. Oct. 23.

HG Wells's letter to the London *Times*, 23 October 1939, sketching out his vision for a Universal Declaration of Human Rights.

The first draft of HG Wells's *The Rights of Man* appeared as a letter in the London *Times* for 25 October 1939. Besides serving as the second president of PEN International from 1932 to 1935, during which time he made the freedom of expression a central concern for the organisation, Wells was a founding member of the British National Council for Civil Liberties (now called Liberty), established in 1934. EM Forster, another key figure in PEN at the time, was its first secretary. Penguin published an expanded version of *The Rights of Man* as a low-cost 'special' in 1940 and PEN's wartime council officially endorsed it two years later.

PEN Centres
in 1945

The 1945 map of PEN has radically transformed the map of the early 1930s. Many Centres had not yet existed in 1930, with new ones in Egypt, Iraq, South Africa, India, China, Australia, New Zealand and the huge expansion of PEN in both North and South America. Others remained in exile at the end of the Second World War, sheltered in London by English PEN, as totalitarian regimes consolidated in the Soviet Union or Spain, or expanded elsewhere in Eastern Europe. Yiddish PEN retained two branches of exiled writers in London and New York.

Argentina – Buenos Aires
Australia – Melbourne
Austria – in London*
Belgium – Brussels
Bolivia – La Paz
Brazil – Rio de Janeiro
Canada – Montreal, Toronto
Catalonia – in London*
Chile – Santiago
China – Address uncertain
Colombia – Bogotá
Cuba – Havana
Czechoslovakia – Prague, in London*
Denmark – Copenhagen
Egypt – Cairo
England – County Hertfordshire
France – Paris
Germany – in London*
Hungary – in London*
Iceland – Reykjavík
India – Mumbai (Bombay)
Iraq – Baghdad

Ireland – Belfast, Dublin
Italy – Rome
Mexico – Mexico City
The Netherlands – Amsterdam
New Zealand – Wellington
Norway – Oslo
Palestine – Tel Aviv
Peru – Lima
Poland – Lodz, in London*
Scotland – Glasgow
South Africa – Johannesburg
Sweden – Stockholm
Switzerland – Basel, Zurich
United States – New York, San Francisco
United States – Chicago, Los Angeles
Uruguay – Montevideo
Venezuela – Caracas
Yiddish – in London*, New York

In black: unchanged situation Centres since 1930
In red: new or changed situation Centres since 1930

* PEN Centres in exile

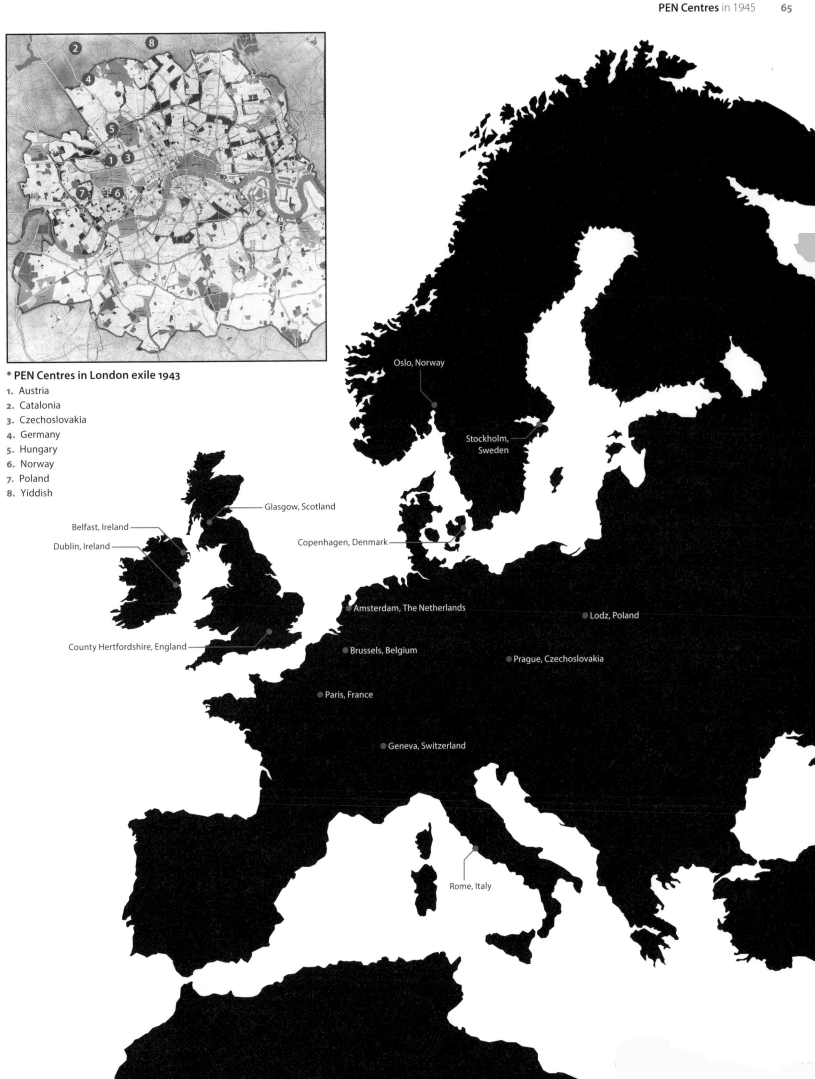

* **PEN Centres in London exile 1943**

1. Austria
2. Catalonia
3. Czechoslovakia
4. Germany
5. Hungary
6. Norway
7. Poland
8. Yiddish

Oslo, Norway

Stockholm, Sweden

Glasgow, Scotland

Belfast, Ireland

Dublin, Ireland

Copenhagen, Denmark

Amsterdam, The Netherlands

Lodz, Poland

County Hertfordshire, England

Brussels, Belgium

Prague, Czechoslovakia

Paris, France

Geneva, Switzerland

Rome, Italy

A Brief History of the PEN Charter

1927 The original PEN Charter

```
      RESOLUTION PASSED AT THE ANNUAL MEETING OF THE
        LONDON CENTRE ON 5th OCTOBER 1926
     That this meeting be asked to empower the delegates sent
 by the London Centre to next year's International Congress
 at Brussels to vote for the following resolution:-
     "This international gathering of the P.E.N. Club
     expresses the belief that the arts are essentially
     international and adopts on behalf of all the P.E.N.
     centres here represented the principle that, even in
     time of war, Art, Music and Literature (other than
     propaganda) should remain common currency between
     antagonistic nations; and further record its determina-
     tion at all times to influence public opinion towards
     support of this principle."

             ---------------------------


        SUGGESTED "STATEMENT OF AIMS."
 The P.E.N. Club stands for friendliness and hospitality
 among writers of all countries; for the unity, integrity
 and welfare of letters; and concerns itself with
 measures which contribute to these ends. It stands apart
 from politics.
             . . . . . . . .
```

The Charter of PEN International has guided, united, and inspired its members for nearly a century. Its principles were implicit at the organisation's founding in 1921 and codified for the first time in 1927. The initial formulation, not yet called the Charter, began as a proposed 'Statement of Aims' by the London Centre in October 1926:

> *The P.E.N. Club stands for hospitality and friendliness among writers of all countries; for the unity, integrity and welfare of letters; and concerns itself with measures which contribute to these ends. It stands apart from politics.*

Revised and developed during the Brussels Congress a year later, this turned into the three guiding principles of the interwar period:

1. *Literature, national though it be in origin, knows no frontiers, and should remain common currency between nations in spite of political or international upheavals.*

2. *In all circumstances, and particularly in time of war, works of art, the patrimony of humanity at large, should be left untouched by national or political passion.*

3. *Members of PEN should at all times use what influence they have in favour of good understanding and mutual respect between nations.*

Formally backed by the Belgian, French, and German Centres, with additional input from the Americans, this wording closely reflected the vision of PEN's English founder Catharine Amy Dawson Scott and the first president, John Galsworthy (1921–32), who were, like many of their contemporaries, haunted by the horrors of the First World War. Universalist in aspiration and anti-nationalist in spirit — though also presupposing the primacy of the nation at every point — it gave concrete shape to Galsworthy's 'new idealism', while underlining his anxieties about political meddling.

↑   The London Centre's first draft of the PEN Charter, 1926.

→   The final version of the PEN Charter, approved in 1927.

Brussels Congress June 1927

The federated P.E.N. Clubs declare their adhesion to the following principles:

1. Literature, national though it be in origin, knows no frontiers, and should remain common currency between nations in spite of political or international upheavals.

2. In all circumstances then and particularly in time of war, works of art, the patrimony of humanity at large, should be left untouched by national or political passion.

3. Members of the P.E.N. Clubs will at all times use what influence they have in favour of good understanding and mutual respect between the nations.

1948 The revised Charter agreed in Copenhagen

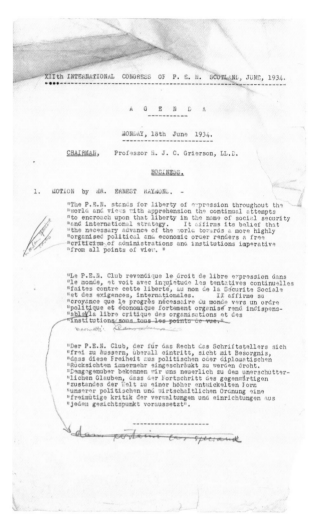

↑   The 'Raymond resolution', presented as a motion at the 1934 Edinburgh Congress, affirms PEN's commitment to the 'liberty of expression'. Key phrases from this text would be included in the fourth article added in 1948.

The three principles formed the basis for what came formally to be called the Charter at the Copenhagen Congress in 1948, an idea Leo Koenig (pseudonym of Arye-Leyb Yaffe), the president of the Yiddish Centre then based in London, first proposed in 1942 as a way of strengthening PEN's 'moral authority' and public profile. The new, expanded formulation incorporated a number of key resolutions endorsed during the interwar years, notably PEN's commitment to the freedom of expression, which Galsworthy's successor as president, HG Wells (1933–36), made a central part of the organisation's mission at the Edinburgh Congress in 1934. In Stockholm, 12 years later, American PEN presented two further resolutions. One urged PEN members 'to champion the ideals of one humanity living in peace in one world'; the other addressed the issues of free expression and censorship, taking inspiration directly from Wells and the crisis over the Nazification of German PEN that had dominated the 1933 Dubrovnik Congress. Debate over the wording and scope of these resolutions continued at the 1947 Congress in Zurich, before being agreed in Copenhagen. The original third article now included a new final clause: 'they pledge themselves to do their utmost to dispel race, class and national hatreds and to champion the ideal of one humanity living in peace in one world.' The other major addition — a wholly new fourth article — recalled the internal debates of the 1930s, though it, too, registered the specific traumas of the Second World War, much as the first statement of principles witnessed the First World War.

4. *PEN stands for the principle of unhampered transmission of thought within each nation and between all nations, and members pledge themselves to oppose any form of suppression of freedom of expression in the country and community to which they belong. PEN declares for a free press and opposes arbitrary censorship in time of peace. It believes that the necessary advance of the world towards a more highly organised political and economic order renders a free criticism of governments, administrations and institutions imperative. And since freedom implies voluntary restraint, members pledge themselves to oppose such evils of a free press as mendacious publication, deliberate falsehood and distortion of facts for political and personal ends.*

By the early 1970s, some began to feel that this wording was itself looking dated, and in 1972 Dutch and West German PEN proposed a number of changes but these were shelved. However, at the 1977 Congress in Sydney, American PEN put forward a resolution to amend the first sentence of the fourth article 'so that it would require members to oppose the suppression of freedom of expression in the world as well as in their own countries.' 'This was felt to demand too much of those who live under repressive regimes,' the *PEN Bulletin* reported, 'but, after an amendment by the Belgium, French-speaking, centre adding the words "wherever it is possible," the resolution was passed unanimously.' This amendment addressed growing concerns about the priority the Charter gave to the national and strengthened PENs' commitment to the universalist aspirations of the post-war human rights era, pledging the membership to champion free expression 'in the country and community to which they belong as well as throughout the world wherever this is possible'. For the rest, the 1948 wording stood until the new millennium. Then, on two occasions, first in 2003 and then in 2017, the organisation engaged in a more sustained process of revision, focusing initially on the first article, unchanged since 1927, and then on the addendum to the third, introduced in 1948.

↓   The final text of the revised Charter agreed in Copenhagen in 1948. The handwritten word 'governments' was added at the last minute to avoid ambiguity and the underlined word 'Unanimous' records the enthusiastic support for the text.

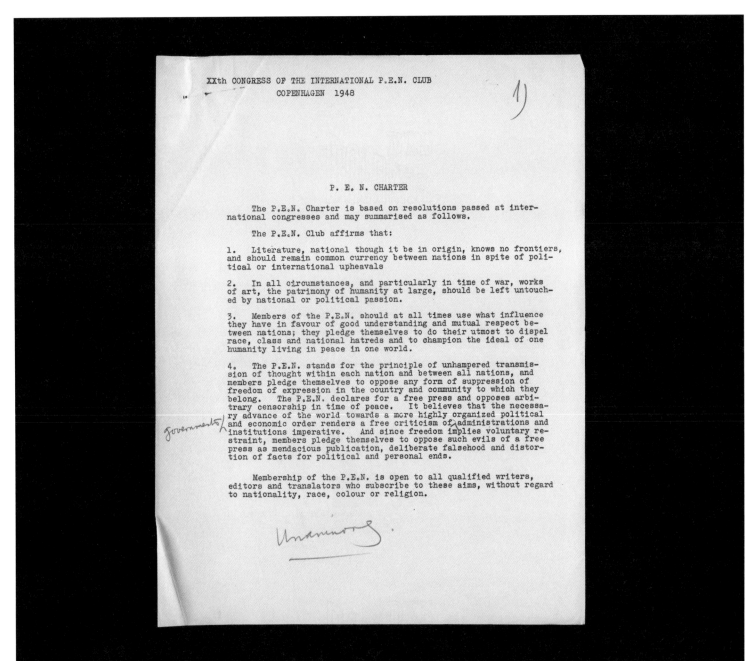

The 2003 revisions

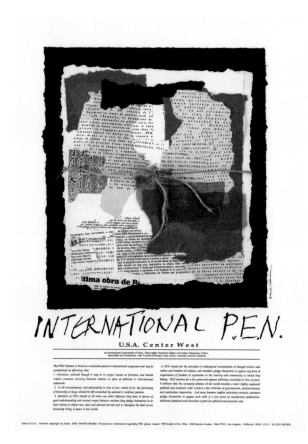

↑   Poster of the PEN Charter by artist
Sally Howell, published by PEN USA West.
In 1988, Los Angeles PEN became
independent from American PEN and was
named PEN USA West. Its presidents had
prominent roles in PEN International:
Joanne Leedom-Ackerman was chair of
the Writers in Prison Committee (1994–97)
and International secretary (2004–07),
and Eric Lax was International treasurer
(2007–13). They are both vice-presidents
of PEN International. In 2018, PEN USA
West merged again with American PEN.

John Galsworthy's version of literary internationalism as a world association, not amalgamation, of European-style national cultures tied to
relatively homogenous nation-states remained at the heart of PEN's
vision for over 70 years. Yet the first article of the three-part 1927
statement of principles raised questions from the start — for one thing,
it had no room for Yiddish writers who could not be assigned to one
nation only. At the London Congress in 2001, however, exiled writers,
led by the Iranian president of Canadian PEN, Reza Baraheni, questioned the primacy this afforded the national community as such
— that year also saw the founding of an Independent Chinese PEN
Centre — mainly in exile. Following their interventions, the
Canadian and German Centres proposed a new formulation of the
first article at the next Congress, held in the small resort town of
Ohrid, Macedonia, in 2002:

> *Literature of whatever provenance or language is a world
> cultural heritage and must be protected and upheld at
> all times as the free and common currency of all people,
> particularly in periods of political or international
> upheaval.*

This effectively removed Galsworthy's contentious subclause 'national
though it be in origin', though the sentence read like something
composed by committee via email over some months, which is, in fact,
how it emerged. Not everyone was happy. Writers from the former
Soviet Union and Eastern bloc spoke against the change, describing
what the almost talismanic PEN Charter had meant to them
throughout the dark years of the Cold War. They also worried about
the loss of the word 'national', which had acquired a new significance
for them since 1989 and for everyone in the era of globalisation. By
contrast, African writers spoke for the proposal because they liked the
word 'protected', which addressed concerns they had about marginalised languages and literatures.

For the English writer Victoria Glendinning and literary agent
Susanna Nicklin, the problems were stylistic. Feeling that the new
version was not 'in keeping with the spare, clear wording of the
Charter', they proposed an alternative, which involved subtracting
rather than rewriting. This broke with protocol (statutorily, you cannot
amend an amendment in the course of discussion). In characteristic
PEN fashion, an unfussy solution was found: the English and
Canadian delegates were sent away to redraft the amendment, a task
that took four hours. Why so long? Again characteristically, the
debates reflected everything for which PEN stands — 'communication,
tolerance, impassioned discussion, literary quotation, story-telling,
poetic digressions, tales of wrongful imprisonment, life-stories' and

more, as Glendinning and Nicklin reported. What resulted was the following small but decisive reformulation, which re-founded PEN as a truly supra-national, non-statist and intercultural association of writers, equal to the broader vision of 'language communities' articulated in the Universal Declaration of Linguistic Rights (1996), a document PEN did much to shape in the 1990s:

> Literature, ~~national though it be in origin,~~ knows no frontiers~~,~~ and ~~should~~ must remain common currency ~~between nations~~ among people in spite of political or international upheavals.

The amendment carried by the required two-thirds majority, though it was formally incorporated into the PEN Charter only after it was ratified a year later at the 69th Congress in Mexico City, a meeting otherwise dominated by reports on the growing number of attacks on writers and journalists around the world — 775 in 2003 alone.

↓   Assembly of delegates at the 80th PEN International Congress in Bishkek, Kyrgyzstan, in 2014. At PEN international Congresses, delegates sit in alphabetical order, from Afar and Afghan PEN to PEN Zambia and Zimbabwe. Procedures at the assembly of delegates are followed to vote for officers of PEN International, reports and resolutions as well as, exceptionally, amendments to the PEN Charter.

The 2017 revisions

Resolutions and amendments to the Charter are debated by the assembly of delegates at PEN Congresses.

↑↑   Assembly at the 29th PEN International Congress in Tokyo, 1957.

↑   Argentinian delegate Nina Jaramillo having the floor at the 85th Congress in Manila, 2019.

Following the 2003 change, which addressed the legacy of PEN's commitment to the 'national', the next reassessment concerned the humanitarian clause added to the third article of the 1927 principles in 1948, which the American Centre proposed in a resolution two years earlier. This pledged PEN 'to dispel race, class and national hatreds and champion the ideal of one humanity living in peace in one world'. As the Mexican-American writer Jennifer Clement noted at the Quebec Congress in 2015, something was missing: 'our Charter does not include gender in its call for a just and peaceful way of living.' 'This should change', she added, 'with millions of girls silenced all over the world, PEN must stand and say no more.' Her remarks carried weight not just because PEN had a standing committee dedicated to promoting women's rights since 1991, to say nothing of its early ties through Catharine Amy Dawson Scott to the suffrage movement. Clement was also speaking as the newly elected PEN International president — the first woman to hold the office in a long line of 31 mainly European and North American men, stretching from John Galsworthy (1921–33) to John Ralston Saul (2009–15). The exceptions in terms of nationality were Hu Shih (Chinese, who served on the collective wartime presidential committee, 1941–47), Mario Vargas Llosa (Peruvian, 1976–79), and Homero Aridjis (Mexican, 1997–2003). In the 1989 elections, the Nigerian novelist Chinua Achebe lost out to the French poet and literary editor René Tavernier.

Members of PEN should at all times uphold the human rights of all persons without regard to distinction based upon race, class, religion gender, sexual orientation, gender identity and nationality, and to champion the ideal of one humanity living in one world.

PEN Canada
suggestion
Grace Westcott

→

Canadian PEN's suggested wording for the 2017 revision, proposed by Grace Westcott.

↑   Andrew Solomon, president of PEN America (centre), at the 81st PEN International Congress meeting in Quebec City in 2015.

↓   Email correspondence between Jennifer Clement, president of PEN International, and Andrew Solomon, president of PEN America, about the changes to the Charter to be proposed at the 82nd PEN International Congress in Ourense, Spain, in 2016.

Achieving a consensus on this second change for the new millennium was not straightforward, however, as the next Congress, held in the northern Spanish town of Ourense in 2016, proved. The wording prepared in advance of the meeting in consultation with all the Centres via email proposed extending the post-war triad of 'race, class and national' to 'race, class, religious, gender, sexual orientation, gender identity, and national hatreds'. Andrew Solomon, president of American PEN, added 'gender identity' to make the list trans-inclusive. Many were in favour of the new formulation, with each term attracting its own key advocates at the meeting. South African PEN strongly supported 'gender', for instance, while Sierra Leone PEN focused on 'religious' and Galician PEN spoke for 'sexual orientation'. Yet some worried about what the new list still excluded, given the many hatreds with which they were all too familiar. After Macedonian PEN mentioned 'cultural identity' and Chilean PEN 'national minorities', Esperanto PEN wondered about all the other categories itemised in the Universal Declaration of Human Rights. 'Everyone is entitled to all the rights and freedoms set forth in this Declaration,' Article 2 states, 'without distinction of any kind, such as race, colour, sex, language, religion, political or other opinion, national or social origin, property, birth or other status.'

Others raised larger questions of practice and principle. On the one hand, some African delegates, notably those from Togo and Zimbabwe, were concerned about the implications for PEN and its activities of highlighting sexual orientation in countries that still criminalise homosexuality or prohibit positive portrayals of 'non-traditional' relationships. On the other, many European delegates, the Danish, Dutch and the three Swiss Centres in particular, took issue with the inclusion of religion, which, in their view, belonged in a different

On Sun, May 22, 2016 at 7:14 PM, Andrew Solomon <andrew.solomon@penamerica.com> wrote:

Dear J&C,

"they pledge themselves to do their utmost to dispel **race, class, religious, gender, sexual orientation, gender identity, and national hatreds**, and to champion the idea of one humanity living in peace in one world."

This makes it trans-inclusive, which gender by itself does not.

Best,

Andrew

On May 22, 2016 at 12:00 PM, Jennifer Mexico <<jennifer.clement@pen-international.com> wrote:

We propose a change in the Charter of PEN International, paragraph 3. Where it states:

Members of PEN should at all times… pledge themselves to do their utmost to dispel **race, class and national hatreds**, and to champion the idea of one humanity living in peace in one world."

To the following:

"they pledge themselves to do their utmost to dispel **race, class, religious, gender, sexual orientation and national hatreds**, and to champion the idea of one humanity living in peace in one world."

Jennifer Clement's speech
at the PEN International Congress in Ourense 2016, proposing changes to the Charter

Let us remember who we are.

Let us remember who we are. We are writers. We believe in the imagination and in being witnesses to our lives and the lives of others. In words we express our needs, desires, prejudices, hopes, suffering and also what we invent and dream.

EM Forster who was PEN President in 1946 wrote the novel *Maurice* about society's hatred toward an average white, middle-class man who was in love with a male friend. Forster showed us that to be different means to be ashamed and in danger. As the book unfolds, the author unravels stereotypes and brings the reader to the realisation that Maurice could be one of our own family members and someone we love.

PEN defends individual expression, the personal story, which as art becomes universal. We do not want literature without the heroic and ordinary stories about race, nationality, class, gender, sexual orientation, sexual identity and religion. In so many places these stories cannot be told. Freedom of expression is also freedom to read. If writers are free to write but are not allowed to be read we are not advocating for freedom of expression — especially in the case of women and girls and promoting literacy. Women and girls are excluded from literacy.

Virginia Woolf asked, 'Where are Shakespeare's sisters? Where is Judith Shakespeare?'

She was in America and is considered one of the world's greatest poets. Her name was Sor Juana Inés de la Cruz and was born in 1651. She wrote:

'I was not yet three years old when my mother determined to send one of my elder sisters to learn to read at a school for girls we call the Amigas. Affection, and mischief, caused me to follow her, and when I observed how she was being taught her lessons I was so inflamed with the desire to know how to read, that deceiving -- for so I knew it to be -- the mistress, I told her that my mother had meant for me to have lessons too. […] I learned so quickly that before my mother knew of it I could already read.'

Worldwide, more than 700 million women alive today were married before their 18th birthday. Those girls will most likely never get an education or write a book. We need to look at violence against women as censorship. Women must be allowed to be credible witnesses to their own lives.

In 74 countries it is a criminal offence to be gay and in 13 countries being gay is punishable by death. 40 countries have a 'panic clause' if provoked by a gay person and many countries have conflicting laws. In many places transgender people are still considered mentally ill and, for this group, the rates of suicide and murder are high.

We know that religious persecution and discrimination are threatening basic freedoms.

Almost 100 years ago John Galsworthy and Catharine Amy Dawson Scott drafted the first Charter and courageously named the reasons for censorship. Later, in 1946, American PEN — backed by English PEN — presented two resolutions (exactly in the same manner we are doing today). One urged PEN members 'to champion the ideals of one humanity living at peace in one world'; the other addressed the issue of censorship. The resolution became the foundation of the fourth article of the PEN Charter. Now, years later, we should be bold to name the censorship of our day.

The change in the Charter is important now because it takes us to the core of our work: writers who are excluded and despised and degraded need to tell their stories and the world needs to listen. A person who is hated is stained by that hate.

The great poet, Walt Whitman, who was gay, in his poem *Song of Myself*, wrote:

> Whoever degrades another degrades me,
> And whatever is done or said returns at last to me…

And so, yes, these additions to the charter are about freedom of expression but, as this is PEN, they are also about literature. Writers want to read — or write — those stories, which are about women's knowledge; or loving a body that looks just like one's own; or feeling lost or found by God. We want to read — or write— the poem about a boy who feels like a girl and knows he is, to quote Kafka, 'a cage in search of a bird'.

It is for all those who have no voice that we must remember who we are.

Thank you.

JC

category. Prior to the meeting, the Danish set out their objections in a detailed email. While recognising the good intentions behind the amendment, they feared that adding 'religion (or hate speech motivated on religious grounds?) to the list of ills' was 'counterproductive' because, unlike 'race, ethnicity, gender or sexual orientation', 'religion cannot be considered an inescapable identity'. Some would argue this is no less true of gender, ethnicity, sexual orientation, class, and nationality. Moreover, as an 'abstract entity', not an 'individual', a religion 'cannot suffer from defamation'. In sum, they argued, 'thoughts, beliefs, faiths and ideas', whether 'religious, political, philosophical, etc. should not be protected, only human beings should'. While acknowledging that PEN's historic commitment to defending free expression and dispelling hatreds always involved a difficult balancing act — the varied responses to the *Charlie Hebdo* killings in Paris at the Quebec Congress in 2015 confirmed this only too clearly — they believed the amended clause would make this kind of balancing harder still.

Recognising the force of these arguments, the proposal was put on hold, allowing the International Board time to review the issues and table a revised version at the next Congress a year later. In fact, over the course of the next few months, the board developed a wholly new approach, focusing not just on the PEN Charter but on PEN's broader strategies regarding women and free expression. For the latter, a group of advisors, led by Jennifer Clement and supported by the Women's Committee, produced the PEN International *Women's Manifesto* (2017). Conceived as a supplement to the revised Charter, this key document took the longstanding questions about PEN and politics in a new direction. As the manifesto's opening paragraph notes, the 'frontiers' referred to in the first article of the Charter were 'traditionally thought of as borders between countries and peoples' — that is, they were political in a broadly 'public' sense. Yet 'for many women in the world — and for almost all women until relatively recently — the first, and the last and perhaps the most powerful frontier was the door of the house she lived in: her parents' or her husband's home' — that is, political in an ostensibly 'private' sense. In the new millennium, PEN had to acknowledge, and encourage others to recognise, that this other kind of frontier constitutes a further impediment to free expression. 'For women to have free speech, the right to read, the right to write,' the manifesto continues in a formulation Virginia Woolf would have welcomed, 'they need to have the right to roam physically, socially and intellectually.' Here, too, the contemporary climate played a part. At a time when 'culture, religion and tradition are repeatedly valued above human rights and are used as arguments to encourage or defend harm against women and girls', the manifesto notes that 'violence against women', whether in the private or the public sphere, 'creates dangerous forms of censorship'. The 'act of silencing a person is to deny their existence', imposing on them 'a kind of death', it concludes, reinforcing and updating HG Wells's opening remarks at the 1934 Congress in Edinburgh.

When it came to the Charter itself, the challenge was not simply to address the concerns raised at the 2016 Congress but to make its own language as universal as possible. This particular difficulty had been

↑↑ PEN International secretary David Carver (1951–74) with his secretary Maureen Kilroe at the 29th PEN International Congress in Tokyo, 1957.

↑ International president, Mario Vargas Llosa (1977–79), and International secretary, Peter Elstob (1974–81), arriving in Sydney for the 42nd PEN International Congress in December 1977.

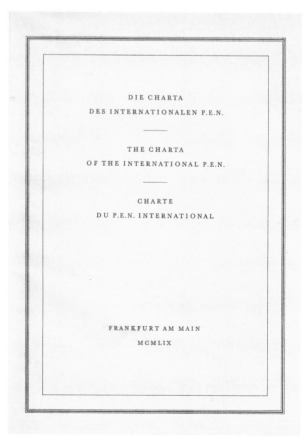

there from the start — recall Carl van Doren persuading Galsworthy to remove the word 'propaganda' in the 1920s because it tied the original statement of principles too closely to the First World War. Similar concerns had been raised about the 1948 Charter and the Second World War in the early 1970s — think only of the wording about 'race, class, and national hatreds.' The extended list proposed in 2016 brought comparable risks, albeit now in relation to twenty-first-century concerns. Balancing these competing demands, while recognising that the Charter had to remain the expression of PEN's guiding ideals, the board proposed the same elegant solution for the new Article 3 as had been adopted for the revised Article 1 in 2003: deletion combined with light but significant addition.

> *Members of PEN should at all times use what influence they have in favour of good understanding and mutual respect between nations* and people; *they pledge themselves to do their utmost to dispel* all *hatreds and to champion the ideal of one humanity living in peace* and equality *in one world. (emphasis added)*

Adding 'people' to the first clause, which was part of Galsworthy's original 1927 version, reinforced the earlier shifts away from 'nations' and the historical legacy of the 1920s. At the same time, dropping the post-war triad of specific hatreds and introducing 'equality' helped uncouple the Charter from the 1940s, making PEN's promissory note to itself and the world at once more universal and more inspirational.

The membership unanimously approved the new wording and the *Women's Manifesto* at the 2017 Congress held in the Ukrainian city of Lviv. Known as Lwów under Polish rule, Lemberg under the Habsburgs and Lvov under the Soviets, the city is now permanently associated with the two prosecutors, Hersch Lauterpacht and Raphael Lemkin, who introduced the phrase 'crimes against humanity' and the term 'genocide' into the language of human rights at the Nuremberg Trials in 1945. From the United Nations Declaration (1948) to the Geneva Convention (1949), Nuremberg had a transformative impact on international law. It also established the principles that underpin the supra-political stand PEN pioneered and continues to uphold as a leading champion of free expression, as well as of writers, readers, literatures, and linguistic communities, throughout the world.

↖   The PEN International *Women's Manifesto* passed by unanimity at the assembly of delegates of PEN International at the 83rd PEN International Congress in Lviv, Ukraine, on 21 September 2017.

←   The 30th PEN International Congress took place in 1959 in Frankfurt am Main, the city that ten years previously had regained its position of main publishing capital with the Frankfurt Book Fair. West German PEN published a book with the PEN Charter's translations in 40 languages and in different alphabets, illustrated on pages 79, 80, and 81.

ARABISCH

<hr>

٠١

لا يقر الادب اية حدود اقليمية بالرغم مب كونه قوميا ، ويقتضي عليه ايضا الاحتفاظ بصفته كـ «عملة» مشتركة يجرى تداولها بين سائر الشعوب ، حتى في ازمان الانقلابات السياسية والدولية .

٠٢

يجب ان تبقى التآليف الفنية تراث الانسانية جمعاء علو كل حال ، وجاصة اثناء الحرب ، وان تكون نعيدة عن متناول النزوات القومية والسياسية .

٠٣

يجب على اعضاء نادى «.P.E.N» بذل كل نفوذهم لاحلال التفاهم والاحترام المتبادل نين الشعوب . كما ويجب عليهم التزام مكافحة كراهية العناصر والطبقات والشعوب ، تجهيز كل قواهم للعمل علو رفعة المثل الاعلى الذى ينطوى على عيش الانسانية بسلام ، في عالم يسوده التفاهم والوثام .

٠٤

يربط نادى «.P.E.N» بعبدأ حرية تبادل الافكار ، سواء كان ذلك داخل قطر معين ام بين مختلف الاقطار . ويلتزم اعضاؤه الوقوف في وجه كل ضفط على حرية التعبير عن الراى في اقطارهم او في المحيط الجماعي الذى يعيشون فيه . يعلن نارى «.P.E.N» وقوفه بجابن حرية الصحافة وتنديده بالرقابة التعسفية قطعا ، وعلى الاخص في ازمان السلم . ويرىبانه لابر في التقدم اللازم للعالم ، المؤدى الى مرتبة اسمى من التنظيم السياسي والاقتصادى ، لابد في ذلك من امكان توجيه النقد الى الحكومات ، والادارات ، والمؤسسات بعطلق الحرية . ولما كانت الحرية تشمل التكتم الاختيارى ايضا ، فان الاعضاء يتعهدون بالوقوف في وجه مثل هذه الادران التي تعترى الحرية الصحافة ، كاصدار المنشورات المفايرة للحقائق ، ونشو الاكاذيب الحرقاء ، وتشويه الحقائق طمعا في خدمه الاهداف السياسية والشخصية .

VIETNAMESISCH

1

Văn chương dù xuất-xứ có tính cách quốc-gia nhưng không có biên-giới và cần phải được trao đổi giữa các quốc-gia mặc dầu những biến cố chính-trị quốc-gia hoặc quốc-tế.

2

Bất cứ trong hoàn-cảnh nào, đặc-biệt trong thời chiến, những công-trình văn-nghệ, tài sản chung của nhân-loại, không thể bị xâm-phạm bởi những cuồng-vọng chính-trị hoặc quốc-gia.

3

Các hội-viên của P.E.N. lúc nào cũng phải dùng hết ảnh hưởng của mình để làm tăng sự tương-tri và tương-trọng giữa các quốc-gia, phải nguyện cố gắng phá bỏ mọi hiềm-khích về chủng-tộc, giai cấp hoặc những thù oán giữa các quốc-gia, luôn luôn tranh-đấu cho một lý tưởng kiến tạo nhân-loại sống trong hòa-bình của một thế-giới duy-nhất.

4

Hội P.E.N. chủ-trương nguyên-tắc tự-do truyền bá tư tưởng trong quốc-gia và giữa các quốc-gia, và hội-viên nguyện sẽ phản đối mọi hình thức đàn áp trong xứ sở và trong đoàn thế của họ. Hội P.E.N. tuyên bố ủng hộ tự-do báo chí và phản đối sự kiểm duyệt độc đoán trong thời bình. Hội tin rằng vì thế-giới cần tiến-bộ để đạt tới trật tự hoàn mỹ hơn về chánh-trị và kinh-tế nên cần phải có sự tự-do chỉ-trích các Chánh-phủ, các Cơ-quan hành-chánh và các Tổ-chức. Vì tự-do có nghĩa là tự kiểm chế, các hội-viên tự nguyện đả phá những tệ-đoan mệnh-danh là tự-do báo chí để đăng những tin giả dối, cố ý loan tin nhảm và xuyên-tạc sự thực vì những mục-đích chính-trị hoặc tư-lợi.

INDISCH · BENGALI

যে—

১। সাহিত্য যদিও মূলতঃ জাতিগত, তথাপি সাহিত্য কোনও ভৌগোলিক সীমারেখা মানে না। কোনও রাজনৈতিক বা আন্তর্জাতিক দলীয় অভ্যুত্থান সত্ত্বেও সাহিত্য বিভিন্ন জাতির মধ্যে বরাবর সমভাবেই সচল থাকে।

২। সকল অবস্থাতেই এবং বিশেষতঃ যুদ্ধের সময় এই বিশাল মানব সমাজের পিতৃধন স্বরূপ যে শিল্প-কলা-কৃতি তাহার উপর যেন কোনো দেশের জাতীয় বা রাষ্ট্রীয় আক্রোশ হস্তক্ষেপ করিতে না পারে।

৩। পি. ই. এন সদস্যাবৃন্দের যাঁহার যতটুকু প্রভাব আছে তাহা সকল সময়েই তাঁহারা সর্বজাতির মধ্যে সদ্ভাব স্থাপনে ও পরস্পরের প্রতি শ্রদ্ধা পোষণে নিয়োজিত করিবেন। তাঁহারা এই প্রতিশ্রুতি দিতেছেন যে জাতি বর্ণ ও শ্রেণীর অন্তর্নিহিত ঘৃণা বিদ্বেষ প্রভৃতি বিরূপ মনোভাব দূর করিবার জন্য তাঁহারা যথাসাধ্য চেষ্টা করিবেন এবং একই বিশ্বে একই মানবতার অধিকারে শান্তিতে বসবাসের আদর্শ রক্ষায় ব্রতী হইবেন।

৪। পি. ই. এন পুস্তাকষ্টি জাতির মধ্যে এবং সকল জাতির পরস্পরের মধ্যে অবাধ ভাব ধারার সহজ সঞ্চরণ নীতির উপরই প্রতিষ্ঠিত। সদস্যগণ, নিজেরা নিজ দেশ ও যে সমাজের অন্তর্ভুক্ত, সেখানে, নিজ নিজ মনোভাব স্বাধীনভাবে প্রকাশের বাধা স্বরূপ সকল প্রকার দমন নীতির প্রতিরোধ করিবার প্রতিশ্রুতি দিতেছেন। পি. ই. এন, সংবাদপত্র সমূহের স্বাধীনতা ঘোষণা করিতেছেন এবং শান্তির সময় স্বৈরাচার মূলক যে কোনো নিয়ন্ত্রণ প্রথার বিরুদ্ধাচরণ করিবার সংকল্প গ্রহণ করিতেছেন। পি. ই. এন বিশ্বাস করেন যে উন্নততর ও সুগুণালীবৃদ্ধ রাষ্ট্রীয় ও অর্থনৈতিক ব্যবস্থার দিকে বিশ্বের প্রয়োজনীয় প্রগতির পক্ষে শাসনতন্ত্র ও অন্যান্য প্রতিষ্ঠানের তরফে সমালোচনা অপরিহার্যরূপে আবশ্যক। এবং, যেহেতু স্বাধীনতার ভিত্তিই হইল স্বেচ্ছাপূর্ণাদিত সংযম, সুতরাং সংবাদপত্রের স্বাধীনতার অপব্যবহারজনিত কুফল, অলীক সংবাদ প্রকাশ, ইচ্ছাকৃত মিথ্যাভাষণ এবং সত্য ঘটনাকে বিকৃত ভাবে প্রকাশ করা ইত্যাদি রাজনৈতিক অথবা আত্মস্বার্থ লাভার্থে বা অন্য যে কোনও কারণে ইহার অপব্যবহার প্রতিরোধের প্রতিশ্রুতি দিতেছেন।

GRIECHISCH

1ον)

Ἡ λογοτεχνία, ἄν καί ἐθνική στήν ῥίζα της, δέν ἀνέχεται διαχωριστικά κρατικά σύνορα καί πρέπει ἀκόμη σέ καιρούς ἐσωτερικῶν ἤ διεθνῶν ταραχῶν νά διατηρήσει τήν ἰδιότητά της, σάν κοινό νόμισμα ὅλων τῶν ἐθνῶν.

2ον)

Σέ ὅλες τίς περιστάσεις, καί εἰδικώτερα σέ περίπτωση πολέμου, πρέπει νά μένουν τά ἔργα τῆς τέχνης, κληρονομία καί περιουσία ὁλόκληρης τῆς ἀνθρωπότητας, ἀνέγγιχτα ἀπό ἐθνικά καί πολιτικά πάθη.

3ον)

Τά μέλη τοῦ P.E.N. πρέπει πάντοτε νά μεταχειρίζονται ὅλην τήν ἐπιρροή τους γιά τήν καλή συνεννόηση καί τόν ἀμοιβαῖο σεβασμό τῶν λαῶν. Ἀναλαμβάνουν τήν ὑποχρέωση νά δράσουν μέ ὅση δύναμη διαθέτουν γιά τήν καταπολέμηση τοῦ φυλετικοῦ, ταξικοῦ καί ἐθνικοῦ μίσους καί γιά τήν διαρκή προβολή τοῦ ἰδεώδους μιᾶς ἐν εἰρήνῃ ζώσης ἀνθρωπότητας σέ ἔναν κόσμο ὁμονοιασμένο.

4ον)

Τό P.E.N. πρεσβεύει τήν ἀρχή τῆς ἀπρόσκοπτης ἀνταλλαγῆς τῶν ἰδεῶν ἐντός κάθε ἔθνους καί μεταξύ ὅλων τῶν ἐθνῶν, καί τά μέλη του ἀναλαμβάνουν τήν ὑποχρέωση νά ἀντιδράσουν σέ κάθε εἶδος καταπίεση τῆς ἐλευθερίας τῆς ἐξωτερίκευσης τῆς γνώμης στόν τόπο τους ἤ στήν κοινότητα, ἐντός τῆς ὁποίας ζοῦν. Τό P.E.N. θέλει τήν ἐλευθερία τοῦ τύπου καί ἀποδοκιμάζει γενικά τήν ἀναγκαία ἀνάλιξη τοῦ κόσμου πρός μία τάξη ἀνώτερης πολιτικῆς καί οἰκονομικῆς ὀργάνωσης ἀπαιτεῖ μία ἐλεύθερη κριτική τῶν κυβερνήσεων, τῶν ἀρχῶν καί τῶν ὀργανισμῶν. Ἐφ᾽ ὅσον δέ ἡ ἐλευθερία περιέχει ἐντός αὐτῆς καί τόν ἑκούσιο περιορισμό, ἀναλαμβάνουν τά μέλη τήν ὑποχρέωση νά καταπολεμήσουν ἄρρωστα φαινόμενα τοῦ ἐλεύθερου τύπου, ὅπως μέ τήν ἀλήθεια μή συμβιβαζόμενες δημοσιεύσεις, ἠθελημένη ψευδολογία καί διαστροφή τῶν γεγονότων γιά πολιτικούς καί προσωπικούς σκοπούς.

CHINESISCH

四

筆會堅守的原則是：在各國中及各國間有不受拘束的思想交流，筆會會員保証反對其所在國家及社群中任何形式的對表達自由所加之壓制。筆會宣佈擁護出版自由，並反對平時的專橫的檢查制度。然而，自由之含義既包括自制，筆會會員保証反對出版自由之惡弊，例如虛謊之出版物，有意作偽，及為政治的與個人的目的而歪事實。

三

筆會會員應該不為國家、種族、或政治的狂熱所感染。應該不為國家、種族、階級及民族間的仇恨。

二

筆會會員應該始終盡力提高國族間的諒解和互敬，保證致力於消除種族、階級及民族間的仇恨，致力於全人類在世界大同中和平共存的理想。

一

文學的起源雖然是民族性的，却無疆界之別；它應該是各國交流的通貨，不受政治或國際動亂的影響。在任何情形下，尤其在戰爭時，作為全人類世襲財產的藝術作品，種族、階級及民族間的仇恨。

BULGARISCH

1

Литературата, макар национална по произход, не познава граници и трябва да бъде достъпна за всички без оглед на политическите и международни вълнения.

2

При всички обстоятелства, особено през време на война, произведенията на изкуството — културно наследство на цялото човечество — трябва да останат незасегнати от националните и политически страсти.

3

Членовете на ПЕН трябва винаги да използуват влиянието си за взаимното разбирателство и уважение между народите. Те обещават да направят всичко, каквото е по силите им, за да разсеят расовата, класова и национална омраза и да се борят за идеята за единно човечество, живеещо в единен свят.

4

ПЕН въздига принципа на свободното разпространение на мисълта във всяка държава и между народите; членовете на ПЕН се задължават да се противопоставят на всяко потисничество над свободата на изказ в страната и обществото, на които принадлежат. ПЕН се обявява за свободния печат и се противопоставя на произволната цензура в мирно време. Организацията смята, че необходимият напредък на света към по-съвършен политически и икономически строй изисква свободна критика на правителство, администрация и други институции. И тъй като свободата предполага доброволното ограничаване, членовете на ПЕН обещават да се противопоставят на лъжливи публикации, преднамерени фалшификации и изкривяване на истината за политически или лични цели.

HEBRÄISCH

א.

הספרות, אף על פי שמקורה לאומי, אין גבולות חוצצים בפניה, אלא היא מחלת מאומה לאומה, ושום חילוקי דעות פוליטיים ושיבושי יחסים בין אומות לא יהיו מפריעים על דרכה.

ב.

בכל הנסיבות, ובייחוד בשעות מלחמה, יהיו מעשי האומנות, שהם מחלת האומנות כולה, שמורים מפגיעתה של הקנאה הלאומית ושל הקנאה הפוליטית.

ג.

חברי פא״ן חייבים בכל עת להשתמש בכל מדה של ההשפעה שברדם, כדי להביא ללב האומה שתהיינה מבינות זו לזו ומכבדות זו את זו, ומקבלים חברי פא״ן על עצמם להשתדל בכל מדה להעביר מן העולם את השנאה שבין גזע לגזע, שבין מעמד למעמד ושבין לאום ללאום, ולהיות זורע ורומז לחזון של חיי שלום לכל באי עולם.

ד.

פא״ן מחזיק בעיקר שאין שום מעצור על דרכה של המחשבה מלפשוש בקרב כל אומה ומלפשוש מאומה לאומה, וחבריו מקבלים על עצמם להתקיים, איש איש בארצו ובעדתו, כנגד כבישת חופש הביטוי הבאה בכל צורה שהיא. פא״ן מכריז שהוא הערותיות חופשית, והוא מתנגד לכל גזירה צנזורה בימי שלום. פא״ן סבור שהתיקון הנצרך לעולם בסדרי הפוליטיקה והכלכלה, הוא התביע חירות של ביקורת על ממשלה, שלטונות ומוסדות. והואיל וגדר החירות בקבלת עול של סייגים מרצון, נוטלים חברי פא״ן על עצמם להתקיים כנגד השימוש בחומר חדש לרעה, כגון:סרסומי כזב, שקרים שבמזיד ועקימות האמת הנעשים לשם תכלית פוליטית או לתועלת הפרט.

JAPANISCH

一、文学は民族に由来するものではあるが、国境はないのであって、諸国民に共通なものである。

二、芸術作品は人類全体の遺産であるから、あらゆる場合に、特に戦時において、国家的または政治的の感情によって左右されてはならない。

三、P・E・N 会員は常に諸国家間の善意の理解ご相互の尊敬のために尽力しなければならない。P・E・N 会員は人種的、階級的、また諸国家間の憎悪を排除して、平和のうちに一つの世界に生活する人類ざい理想のために努力することをう誓う。

四、P・E・N は各国内のみならず、あらゆる国家間において、思想の交流が妨げられてはならないざいう原則を支持する。会員はその属する国、および社会において、表現の自由に対するあらゆる抑圧に反対することを誓う。P・E・N は平時における言論、報道の自由を堅持し、独断的な検閲や政治や政府や諸制度に対して自由な批判が必要であると信じる。自由は責任を伴うものであるから、会員は言論、報道の自由、即ち、政治的、個人的の目的のための虚偽や捏造や歪曲に反対することを誓う。

PERSISCH

ادبیات با وجود اینکه دراصل جنبه ملّی را دارد معهذا حدود و تغییری برای آن متصوّر نیست و باید حتّی در اوقاتی که اختلافات داخلی و بحرانهای سیاسی بین الملل وجود دارد این خاصیت راکه عبارتاز تعلق داشتن بتمام ملل جهان است از دست ندهد.

۰۲

تصنیفات هنری که تعلق موروثی بتمام عالم انسانیت دارد باید از جدالهای سیاسی و رنگهای ملی کاملا آزاد و مبرّا باشد بالاخصاص هنگام جنگ.

۰۳

اعضاء پ.۰۱.ن.باید هر موقع و زمان نفوذ و توانائی خود را برای ایجاد حسن تفاهم و مراعات احترام متقابل در بین ملل عالم بکار برند و تعهد نمایند برای مبارزه باکینه های نژادی و بغضهای طبقاتی و همچنین بر ضد نفرتها و خصومتهای ملّی سعی بلغ نموده و بمنظور زنده نگاهداشتن و اعتلاء هد ف که بمنظور آن زندگی آرام و صلح جویانه یک بشر متحد و خوشبخت میباشد با تمام قوا اقد ام کنند.

۰۴

سازمان پ.۰۱.ن. این اصل را ماخذ و مبنای رفتار خود قرارداده است که باید در بین تمام افراد یک ملت و همچنین بین کلیه ملل جهان بطور آزاد امکان تبادل نظر وجود داشته باشد و اعضاء سازمان تعهد مینمایند با هر نوع اقدامی که برای خفه کردن آزادی اظهار عقیده در کشور آنها راو در جامعه ای که در آن زند گی مینمایند بعمل می اید مخالفت ورزند . سازمان پ.۰۱.ن. اعلام مبداء که طرفدار آزادی مطبوعات است و بکار بردن هرگونه سانسوری را علی الاصول مردود میداند البته بطور اشة هنگام صلح.
پ.۰۱.ن. باین عقیده است که ترقی دنیا و پیشرفت جهان برای ایجاد یک سازمان سیاسی و اقتصادی بهتر باید پایه لزوما آزادی انتقاد و اجازه خرده گیری از دولتها و ادارات و مؤسسات عمومی را ایجاب مینماید . نظر باینکه خود داری از اظهار نظر از آزادی اظهار عقیده جزء آزادی محسوب میگردد و لذا اعضاء سازمان تعهد مینمایند در مقابل نشریات مغرضانه مطبوعات آزاد — از قبیل انتشارات مخالف حقیقت — د روغ عمدی — خلاف حقیقت نشان دادن مسائلی که برای پیشرفت منظورهای سیاسی و شخصی درج میشود مقا ومت نموده و مخالفت با آزا وجه همّت خود قراردهند .

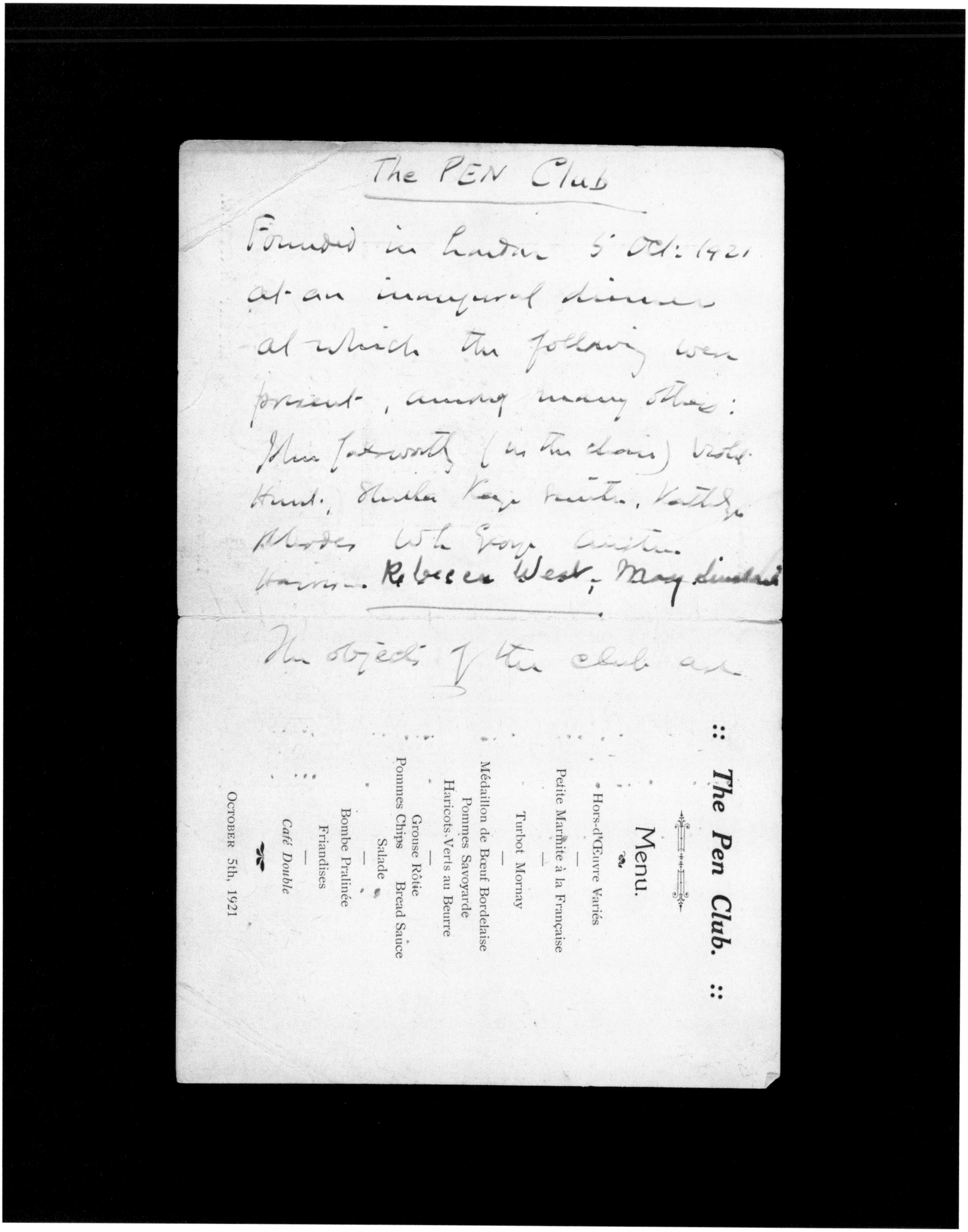

The PEN Club

Founded in London 5 Oct: 1921
at an inaugural dinner
at which the following were
present, among many others:
John Galsworthy (in the chair) Violet
Hunt, Rudolf Kaye Smith, Kathleen
Rhodes with George Austin
Harrison, Rebecca West, May Sinclair.

The objects of the club are

The Pen Club.

:: Menu. ::

* Hors-d'Œuvre Variés

Petite Marmite à la Française

Turbot Mornay

Médaillon de Bœuf Bordelaise
Pommes Savoyarde
Haricots-Verts au Beurre

Grouse Rôtie
Pommes Chips   Bread Sauce
Salade

Bombe Pralinée
Friandises

Café Double

OCTOBER 5th, 1921

↑   First draft of 'PEN identity' written on the menu of the first dinner in 1921.

The PEN Charter

1

Literature knows no frontiers and must remain common currency among
people in spite of political or international upheavals.

2

In all circumstances, and particularly in time of war, works of art,
the patrimony of humanity at large, should be left untouched by national
or political passion.

3

Members of PEN should at all times use what influence they have in favour of
good understanding and mutual respect between nations and people;
they pledge themselves to do their utmost to dispel all hatreds and to champion
the ideal of one humanity living in peace and equality in one world.

4

PEN stands for the principle of unhampered transmission of thought within
each nation and between all nations, and members pledge themselves to oppose
any form of suppression of freedom of expression in the country and community to which they belong, as well as throughout the world wherever this is
possible. PEN declares for a free press and opposes arbitrary censorship
in time of peace. It believes that the necessary advance of the world towards a
more highly organised political and economic order renders a free criticism
of governments, administrations and institutions imperative. And since
freedom implies voluntary restraint, members pledge themselves to oppose
such evils of a free press as mendacious publication, deliberate falsehood and
distortion of facts for political and personal ends.

↑   The PEN Charter in 2021.

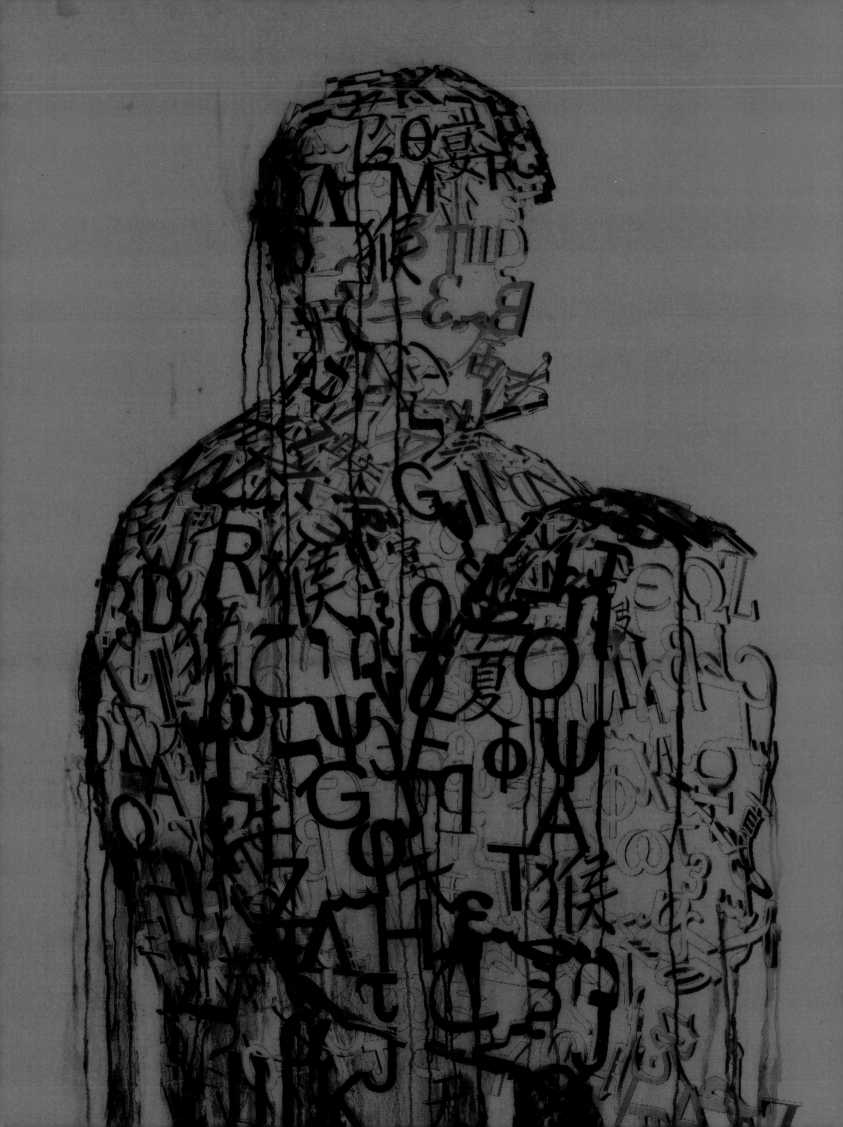

A World Republic of Letters

After the end of the Second World War and the creation of the United Nations, PEN International's mission, as defined and redefined in the PEN Charter, expanded both geographically and in response to the complexity of PEN's work. In the post-war world, exiled writers and PEN Centres in exile had become both a painful and crucial reality.

Therefore, in the following years, at PEN Congresses, members acted to create specific working committees and better develop the scope of the charter in each domain of action. A Writers in Prison Committee was created at the Rio de Janeiro Congress in 1960 with the purpose of coordinating and increasing the action of PEN Centres in solidarity with their imprisoned colleagues around the world. In the context of the Cold War, the PEN Club of Writers in Exile was instrumental in shaping a Writers in Prison Committee that, over the following 60 years, helped transform PEN into one of the leading freedom of expression organisations of the twenty-first century.

In 1978, at a Congress in Stockholm, the Translation and Linguistic Rights Committee was founded. This underscored PEN's initial mandate to support the 'translation of languages of lesser currency' and led to the establishment of a major network of every literary community without exception as well as the creation of translation programmes. In 1996, PEN drafted the ground-breaking document known as the Universal Declaration of Linguistic Rights, which not only created a vision taken on by many organisations including UNESCO, it also made PEN a home for writers in Indigenous and persecuted languages.

As PEN had been founded as a moral response of writers to the evils of the First World War, and the history of PEN having been transformed again and again by its commitment to restoring dialogue among writers in countries in conflict, it naturally followed that PEN would establish a Writers for Peace Committee. After its foundation at the 1984 Congress in Tokyo, the committee anchored itself in the lakeside village of Bled, where Slovene PEN had welcomed writers from both the Western and Eastern blocs for decades. The committee has acted on conflicts from all around the globe and the names of cities — Dubrovnik, Sarajevo, Grozny, Freetown, Kabul, Diyarbakır, Timbuktu, Simferopol, Aleppo and on and on — are inseparable from the struggle to build dialogue among writers in times of war and its ruins.

The creation of the Women Writers Committee in 1991 was a direct consequence of protests over the lack of space given to women in an organisation founded by the visionary Catharine Amy Dawson Scott. The committee — composed of both women and men — addressed freedom of expression issues directly linked to discrimination and promoted women writers by publishing anthologies and translations as well as campaigning tirelessly for women writers at risk. The election in 2015 of the first woman president of PEN International, Jennifer Clement, led to the drafting of a *Women's Manifesto*, which, through the examination of censorship on many levels, has transformed all the areas of PEN's work.

To present the expansion of the organisation, these five areas are developed in the pages ahead: 'Writers in exile', 'Writers in prison', 'Translation and linguistic rights', 'Writers for peace' and 'Women writers'. Each chapter will go back to the roots of PEN's early years and show the organisation's development and geographical expansion to 150 Centres in more than 120 countries today. Every Centre — from working with exiled writers, writers in prison, linguistic rights, women's issues or towards peace — has had a unique role in creating a worldwide body of volunteers who, at the threshold of PEN's centenary, continue to protect freedom of expression and literature throughout the globe.

← *Writer in prison*, artwork created by Jaume Plensa for Catalan PEN on the Day of the Imprisoned Writer 2008.

Writers in exile

The flood of writers, artists, and academics fleeing Germany with the rise of the Nazis gave a new shape to PEN International, as it transformed itself to support writers in exile in the 1930s. We may not have the pictures of Ernst Toller writing in London the speech that would change PEN forever at the Dubrovnik 1933 Congress, or Pablo Neruda's farewell to the Catalan and Spanish intellectuals sent from France to their exile in Chile after the Spanish Civil War, but we have their correspondence and the minutes of PEN meetings revolutionised by these hardships.

The first PEN Club in exile was German PEN, founded as early as 1934, when few civil society organisations were aware of the danger the Nazi Party meant for democracy and peace in Europe. Their fate defined the mission of PEN with regards to refugee writers: first, German PEN Club in Exile became a platform to unite the diaspora; second, it offered a platform for German writers to denounce the persecution by the Nazis of Jewish, LGBTQ, leftist, and other 'degenerate' writers and artists; and, third, it coordinated PEN's solidarity with colleagues who were at risk or in distress. Catalan PEN was the second Centre in exile, born on the very last days of the Spanish Civil War. PEN Centres in Paris and London welcomed the first waves of refugees, and later it was the turn of Chilean, Argentinian, Brazilian, and Mexican PEN.

At the end of the Second World War, the role of writers in exile within PEN did not diminish: they remained involved in the campaigning for imprisoned writers in their home countries. The Baltic PEN Clubs were initially reorganised in exile. A PEN Club of Writers in Exile, with branches in Europe and the United States, was created in 1951 and coordinated a diaspora of stateless and exiled writers during the Cold War years. The Vietnamese Writers Abroad PEN Centre was created in 1979, with members in Canada and the United States.

The occupation of Tibet by the Chinese and the subsequent repression of their language and freedoms led to the creation of PEN Tibetan Writers Abroad, based in Dharamsala together with the Dalai Lama and other Tibetan institutions in exile.

The year 1989 meant a turning point: while the fall of the Berlin Wall opened the path for PEN Centres to be refounded in Russia and Central and Eastern European countries, and for many exiled writers and intellectuals to return home, the Tiananmen Massacre led to the creation of the Independent Chinese PEN Centre, with the exiled writers of the Tiananmen generation as well as members in China, like Liu Xiaobo. In the same years, the continuous cultural repression of the Uyghur language and culture led to the creation of Uyghur PEN in Exile. In Iran, permanent repression of freedoms by the regime of the ayatollahs led to the creation of Iranian PEN in Exile in 1994. Cuban Writers in Exile PEN was founded in Miami in 1997. And, within the PEN International community, two Centres are permanent witnesses of the cruellest regimes on earth: North Korean PEN in Exile, supported by South Korean PEN, and PEN Eritrea, supported actively by Norwegian PEN.

In 2006, Norwegian PEN, Swedish PEN, Catalan PEN, and others participated in the creation of the International Cities of Refuge Network (ICORN). PEN has partnered with ICORN since then and collaborated with the more than 70 cities of the network. It's both PEN's and ICORN's mission: to welcome writers in exile and to create conditions for their writing, finding ways to reach their public either in their own countries or through translations. Mirroring the hospitality received by German writers since the 1930s, German PEN's network for exiled writers has welcomed since the beginning of the twenty-first century more than 60 writers in exile in eight German cities of refuge.

←   The list of members in 1938 of a German PEN in Exile, based in London's Oxford Street (reproduced on page 88), was used as the background image for the poster of the 1983 Bonn exhibition 'P.E.N. im Exil', commissioned by the German Exile Archive of the German National Library in Frankfurt. The poster was designed by Gunter Rambow from the studio Rambow/Lienemeyer/van de Sand.

German PEN, the first PEN Club in exile

The first PEN Centre in exile was German PEN. It was founded in 1934 and progressively incorporated the main German writers who had fled the country to escape Nazi repression and concentration camps. The impressive list of members in 1938 of a German PEN in Exile, based in London's Oxford Street, included, among others, Ernst Bloch, Alfred Döblin, Alfred Kerr, Klaus Mann, Thomas Mann, Karl Mannheim, Ludwig Renn, Anna Seghers, and Arnold Zweig.

```
                    Deutscher Pen-Club
                    ======================

          The P.E.N., a World Association of Writers, German Group

                    Adresse: c/o Pen-Club, Albion House
                            59/61, New Oxford Street
                                   London, W.C.1.

          Mitgliederliste,     18.November 1938


          Heinrich Mann, Präsident
             Vicki Baum                  + Karl Mannheim
             Joh.R.Becher                + Valeriu Marcu
          +  Georg Bernhard                Ludwig Marcuse
             Walter A.Berendsohn           Walter Mehring
             Ernst Bloch                   Peter von Mendelssohn
             Willi Bredel               + Willi Münzenberg
             Bernard von Brentano          Alfred Neumann
             Ferdinand Bruckner         2  E.E.Noth
             (Theodor Tagger)              Balder Olden
             Friedrich Burschell          Karl Otten
             Alfred Döblin                Ludwig Renn
          +  Karl Federn               +- Roda Roda
             Lion Feuchtwanger           +Walther Rode
          +  Bruno Frank                  Paul Roubiczek
             Manfred Georg             +  Anselm Ruest  Gerhard Schacher
            +Hellmuth von Gerlach      +- René Schickele
             Oskar Maria Graf             Bruno Schönlank
             E.I.Gumbel                   Leopold Schwarzschild
          +  Walter Hasenclever           Anna Seghers
             Ludwig von Hatvany         + Helene Stöcker
            +Werner Hegemann              Gerhard Schacher
          +- Max Hermann-Neisse           Willi Schlamm
             Wieland Herzfelde            Heinz Stroh
             Kurt Hiller               +  Ernst Toller
          +- Arthur Holitscher         +- Herwarth Walden
            +Ödön von Horvath             Paul Westheim
             Heinrich Eduard Jacob     +  Alfred Wolfenstein
          2  Hermann Kantorowitsch     +- Theodor Wolff
             Alfred Kerr                  Leon Zeitlin
             Kurt Kersten                 Arnold Zweig
             Hermann Kesten
             Egon Erwin Kisch
             Annette Kolb
             Fritz Landshoff
             Leo Lania
             Rudolf Leonhard
             Hubertus Prinz zu Löwenstein
             Klaus Mann
             Thomas Mann

                                      +  Rudolf Olden,
                                      +  Sekretär
```

This was the result of the 1933 Dubrovnik Congress and the expulsion of the German Centre which was aligned with the Nazi regime. German PEN had refused to sign a statement condemning the German government for the book burnings and the persecution of Jewish as well as so-called politically disagreeable artists. Ernst Toller, whose famous address to the Dubrovnik Congress initiated the process of expulsion of German PEN, returned to London afterwards and, together with Lion Feuchtwanger, Rudolf Olden, and Max Herrmann-Neisse, initiated the process of creating a German group of PEN in Exile. In December 1933, they wrote to the International Committee of PEN with the proposal of creating a German PEN in Exile.

Klaus Mann and Heinrich Mann joined soon thereafter. The group set out to contact exiled German writers and answers arrived swiftly from several other writers in exile. Heinrich Mann agreed to preside over the Club (provided it did not mean too much travelling) and pencilled in the names of other potential members.

← List of members in 1938 of a German PEN in Exile, based in London's Oxford Street, including, among others, Ernst Bloch, Alfred Döblin, Alfred Kerr, Klaus Mann, Thomas Mann, Karl Mannheim, Ludwig Renn, Anna Seghers, and Arnold Zweig.

↙ Letter from Lion Feuchtwanger, Rudolf Olden, and Max Herrmann-Neisse to the International Committee of PEN with the proposal of creating a German PEN in Exile for 'writers now living in France, Switzerland, Czechoslovakia, and elsewhere'.

↓ Letter from Heinrich Mann on 20 January 1934, written in Nice:

'Dear Sir,
I have just received your newsletter and a letter from Lion Feuchtwanger about the foundation of the German P.E.N. Club. I am happy to join this group. With best greetings I am very devoted to you, Heinrich Mann'.

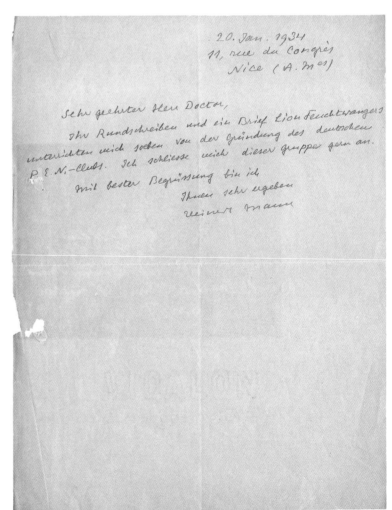

At the following PEN International Congress taking place in Glasgow in June 1934, Ernst Toller (vice-president) and Rudolf Olden (secretary of the Centre from 1934 to 1940) presented the new German PEN in Exile and were welcomed by delegates from all over the world.

German PEN Club in Exile created a network within the diaspora of German writers and represented them at Congresses, denouncing the repression of writers in Germany and gathering international solidarity. The resolution approved unanimously at the 1937 PEN International Congress in Paris denounced the German government's violence against writers as well as protesting the fact that Carl von Ossietzky had not been allowed to travel to Oslo and receive the 1935 Nobel Peace Prize.

German PEN Club in Exile became a channel of support to writers in distress. A letter by Janet Chance (who was the administrator of PEN Refugee Writers' Fund together with both Hermon Ould and Margaret Storm Jameson) to Rudolf Olden, secretary of German PEN Club in Exile, outlines the new conditions for writers to receive support. The PEN Refugee Writers' Fund offered emergency individual grants to writers in need and also supported them through translations and connections to potential publishers.

↓   Letter by Janet Chance (who was the administrator of the PEN Refugee Writers' Fund together with both Hermon Ould and Margaret Storm Jameson) to Rudolf Olden, secretary of German PEN Club in Exile, outlining the new conditions for writers to receive support. The fund offered emergency individual grants to writers in need and also supported them through translations and connections to potential publishers.

↘   Once he agreed to be their president, Heinrich Mann pencilled in the first list of the German PEN Club in Exile the names of other potential members.

→   Resolution approved unanimously at the 1937 PEN International Congress in Paris denouncing the German government's violence against writers as well as protesting the fact that Carl von Ossietzky had not been allowed to travel to Oslo and receive the 1935 Nobel Peace Prize.

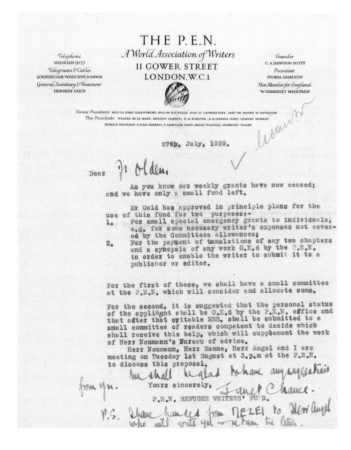

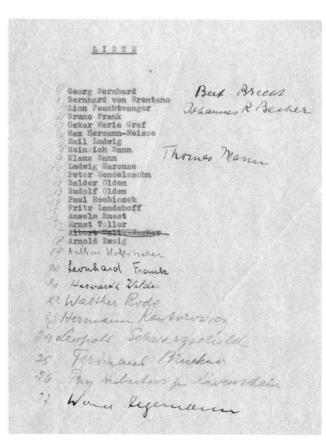

PARIS CONGRESS: June 1937.

MOTION ALLEMANDE
================

Le XV Congrès international de la Fédération P.E.N.
élève une protestation contre les violences dont de
nombreux écrivains, partisans de la liberté d'expression,
ont été victimes en Allemagne, et tout particulièrement
contre le fait que le gouvernement allemand a empêché,
par contrainte, le lauréat du Prix Nobel 1936 pour la
paix, l'écrivain Carl von Ossietzky, membre des P.E.N.
de se présenter devant le comité Nobel à Oslo et d'y
prononcer l'allocution prescrite par les statuts de la
Fondation Nobel.

Lion Feuchtwanger
(German Emigrant Group)

CARRIED UNANIMOUSLY

Stefan Zweig's exile and the Brazilian PEN Club

In May 1933, Stefan Zweig witnessed his own books being burned by the Nazis in his home city of Salzburg. He left Austria for London in early 1934, never to return.

In 1936, he attended the PEN International Congress in Buenos Aires. On his way to Argentina, he made a stopover in Rio de Janeiro, where he was welcomed by the president of the Brazilian PEN Club, Cláudio de Souza. They visited the editorial offices of the magazine *Ilustração Brasileira* and several cultural institutions.

Zweig and de Souza became friends and travelled together to Buenos Aires. At the PEN Congress, Zweig was reluctant to give public speeches. Nevertheless, towards the very end of the Congress, he finally took the floor and spoke to the assembly of delegates. His speech and praise of HG Wells, whose term as PEN International president was coming to an end, are conserved in the Congress minutes.

Zweig settled in England, from where he constantly contributed to the support of Austrian writers in exile.

In 1939, he married his secretary, Charlotte ('Lotte') Elisabeth Altmann in London, and they moved to Brazil the following year. In Rio de Janeiro, Stefan Zweig was officially welcomed by the minister of foreign affairs and he went on to develop ties to Brazilian writers linked to PEN and the Brazilian Academy of Letters. It is from Brazil that Zweig travelled in 1941 to the United States, where he completed his memoir *The World of Yesterday*. He asked the president of Brazilian PEN, Cláudio de Souza, to introduce him to American PEN and after this meeting Zweig wrote the following to De Souza: 'Dear friend, your message was read to great acclaim in front of an assembly of a thousand people. I thank your PEN centre for having been present spiritually in the meeting. Everything went fine and we received 5,600 dollars to support the survival of new writers in exile.'

On his return to Brazil, Stefan and Lotte settled in Petrópolis, where Cláudio de Souza had his summer residence. Here, on 22 February 1942 the couple, despondent from the continuous victories of the Nazi armies, took their own lives.

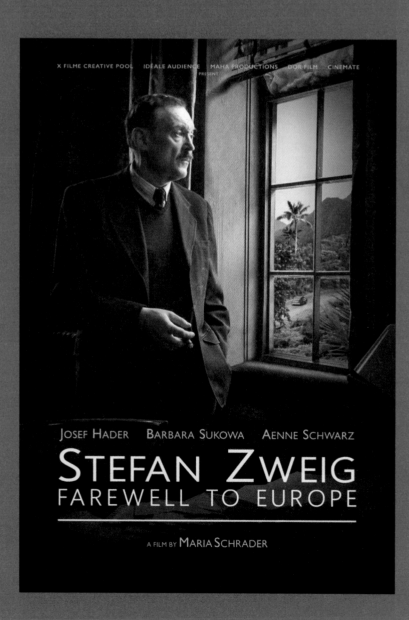

JOSEF HADER   BARBARA SUKOWA   AENNE SCHWARZ

STEFAN ZWEIG
FAREWELL TO EUROPE

A FILM BY MARIA SCHRADER

← *Stefan Zweig, Farewell to Europe* is a 2016 movie by director Maria Schrader. The first sequences of the movie take place during the 1936 PEN International Congress in Buenos Aires, where Zweig was guest of honour. The movie portrays an interview with Argentinian journalists, a session of the Congress in which a long list of persecuted German writers is read, and the tribute to Stefan Zweig, which is received by the delegates with a standing ovation.

↓ Letter from Stefan Zweig to Henrietta Leslie, supporting an appeal of the PEN Refugee Writers' Fund, dated 18 July 1938.

49, HALLAM STREET,
LONDON, W. 1.
LANGHAM 3693.

18th July 1938.

Dear Mrs. Leslie,

I enclose a cheque for five pounds for your Austrian appeal and regret that I can not send more. But I have already sent contributions to various committees on that behalf and I have not only had myself heavy continually (every day?) losses by the Austrian events but I have also to help many friends and relations of mine.

Truly yours,

Stefan Zweig

↑   Stefan Zweig and Cláudio de Souza visiting the editorial
offices of the magazine *Ilustração Brasileira* in 1936.

Catalan PEN and the bus to exile

PEN's second Centre in exile was the Catalan PEN Club. This Centre had been very active in supporting the Republic during the Spanish Civil War. The minutes taken by the International Executive Committee reflect the solidarity PEN felt for the Catalans over those years: food packages for writers in need, paper for the publication of books and magazines, and so on.

Catalan PEN had participated in a programme to bring literature to the front through a bookmobile: a library bus offering books to soldiers on the front lines. When Barcelona fell in January 1939 and during the chaos of General Franco's armies marching towards the city, one of these bookmobiles was crammed full of writers who fled to exile.

↑   Library bus used to bring books for soldiers to read at the front lines during the Spanish Civil War.

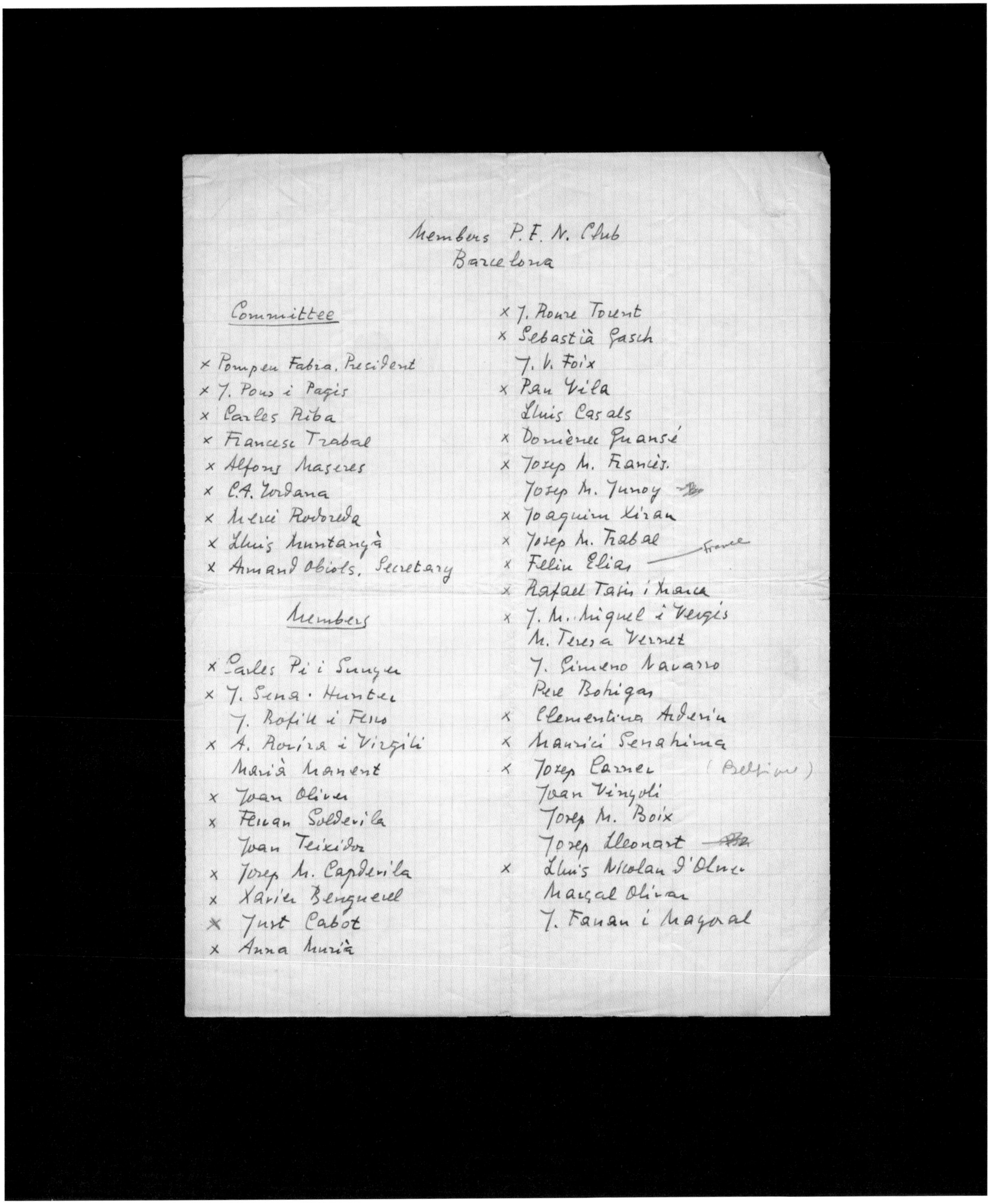

Members P. E. N. Club
Barcelona

Committee

x Pompeu Fabra, President
x J. Pous i Pagès
x Carles Riba
x Francesc Trabal
x Alfons Maseres
x C.A. Jordana
x Mercè Rodoreda
x Lluís Muntanyà
x Armand Obiols, Secretary

Members

x Carles Pi i Sunyer
x J. Serra Hunter
  J. Rofill i Ferro
x A. Rovira i Virgili
  Marià Manent
x Joan Oliver
x Ferran Soldevila
  Joan Teixidor
x Josep M. Capdevila
x Xavier Benguerel
x Just Cabot
x Anna Murià

x J. Roure Torent
x Sebastià Gasch
  J. V. Foix
x Pau Vila
  Lluís Casals
x Domènec Guansé
x Josep M. Francès
  Josep M. Junoy
x Joaquim Xirau
x Josep M. Trabal   France
x Felin Elias
x Rafael Tasis i Marca
x J. M. Miquel i Vergis
  M. Teresa Vernet
  J. Gimeno Navarro
  Pere Bohigas
x Clementina Arderiu
x Maurici Serrahima
x Josep Carner   (Bèlgica)
  Joan Vinyoli
  Josep M. Boix
  Josep Lleonart
x Lluís Nicolau D'Olwer
  Marçal Olivar
  J. Farran i Mayoral

↑   List of Catalan PEN members established in a final stop of the bookmobile
before crossing the border between Spain and France. A majority of names
appear with a cross next to them, marking those who were escaping to exile.
Among the 46 members, only 14 remained in Barcelona.

In a final stop before crossing the border between Spain and France, a list was taken: a cross next to a name marks those who were escaping to exile. Of the 46 Catalan PEN members, only 14 remained in Barcelona.

French PEN offered active support to the exiled. Very prominent writers like Mercè Rodoreda, Armand Obiols, Francesc Trabal, Carles Riba, Clementina Arderiu, Joan Oliver, and others were sheltered for several months in Roissy-en-Brie, close to Paris. Chilean poet Pablo Neruda, who was then consul in Paris, organised a ship to Valparaíso for Spanish Republican refugees, among them several Catalan writers who later joined Chilean PEN. The International Federation of PEN issued cards asking PEN Clubs to welcome Catalan refugee writers. Cards were signed by International president Jules Romains, International secretary Hermon Ould and Catalan PEN president in exile Pompeu Fabra. Xavier Benguerel used one of these cards when he was sheltered in exile by Chilean PEN.

←   Poet Joan Oliver and his wife Conxita Riera sheltered by French PEN in Roissy-en-Brie in 1939. After nine years of exile in Chile, Oliver returned to Catalonia and was the first president of the clandestine Catalan PEN re-established in 1973, with Spain still under Franco's rule.

↓   Group photograph of exiled Catalan PEN members welcomed in Roissy-en-Brie in 1939, between the end of the Spanish Civil War and the beginning of the Second World War. The novelist Mercè Rodoreda is third from left in the picture, and fourth is Francesc Trabal: both of them had been Catalan PEN delegates at the Prague Congress in 1938.

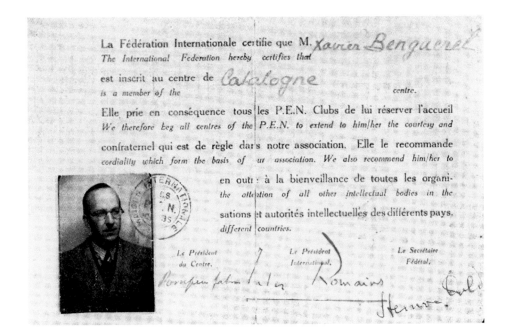

↖ Card issued by the International
Federation of PEN asking PEN Clubs to
welcome Catalan novelist Xavier Benguerel.
The card is signed by International president
Jules Romains, International secretary
Hermon Ould and Catalan PEN president in
exile Pompeu Fabra.

↑ Catalan delegates at the PEN
International Congress in New York, 1966:
Josep Maria Batista i Roca, professor at
Cambridge University, and Rafael Tasis, who
had travelled from Barcelona.

↓ Avel·lí Artís-Gener as Catalan delegate
at the PEN International Congress
in Sydney, 1977.

After the Second World War, Josep Maria Batista i Roca, a professor in
Cambridge and secretary of Catalan PEN in Exile, was able to maintain
close links with the clandestine networks in Catalonia. Writers from
those networks were leaving Spain, participating in PEN Congresses
and coming back to Catalonia, undiscovered by the regime's secret
police. Batista i Roca and Rafael Tasis were the Catalan delegates at the
1966 PEN International Congress in New York.

In 1973, two years before the death of General Franco, a large group of
writers from Catalonia, the Balearic Islands, and Valencia decided to
re-establish Catalan PEN, with the agreement of the International
secretary Peter Elstob. The novelist Avel·lí Artís-Gener rented a bus
and organised a tour, with a complicit driver who would not alert the
police, to the abbey of Poblet, which is more than a two-hour drive
from Barcelona. Forty-four writers, each carrying proxy votes, filled
the bus and went on the excursion. On the road, they approved the
constitution of the re-established Catalan PEN and elected the
members of the new board, with Joan Oliver (who had returned from
his exile in Chile) as president. Catalan PEN is a Centre that was
reborn in clandestinity. After the death of the dictator in 1975, Catalan
PEN was able to openly participate in PEN activities. In 1977, at the
Sydney PEN Congress, Avel·lí Artís-Gener was the Catalan delegate.

PEN Club of Writers in Exile

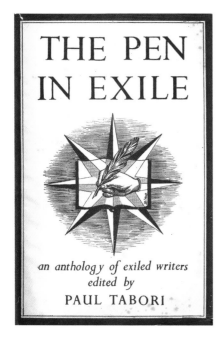

The Hungarian-Jewish author and journalist Paul Tabori chaired the PEN Club of Writers in Exile. The Centre was welcomed by the PEN community at the Lausanne Congress in 1951 and, the following year, a delegation from the Centre participated in PEN's International Congress in Nice. Paul Tabori produced an anthology of exiled writers in 14 languages. The anthology was supported by the Intellectual Freedom Fund, created by Arthur Koestler.

The letter sent by Paul Tabori to the novelist Maria Kuncewiczowa, who became president of the PEN Centre of Writers in Exile, was written on 26 May 1952 and gives the scope of their work. The PEN Club of Writers in Exile had been created with the knowledge that the totalitarian governments in Eastern Europe, the Soviet Union and Spain were well established and, therefore, many of their writers would be working from exile. In the table of contents, Tabori outlines the different literatures in exile present in the anthology: 'Bulgaria, Esthonia, Romania, Latvia, Lithuania, Russia, Hungary, Poland, Czechoslovakia, Slovakia (as a separate linguistic territory), the Ukraine (again as a different linguistic unit), Catalonia, Spain, Yougoslavia.'

↓   Letter sent by Paul Tabori to the novelist Maria Kuncewiczowa, written on 26 May 1952.

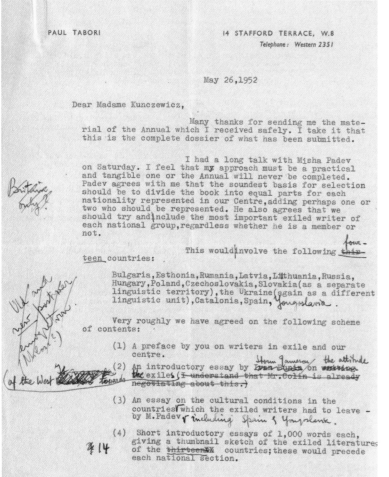

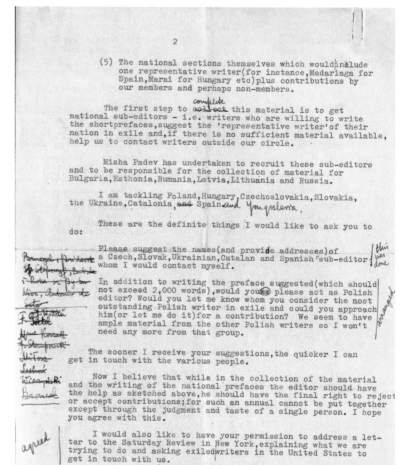

Estonian PEN and other Baltic Centres asked to be considered PEN Centres in Exile after the Second World War and the annexation of their countries by the USSR. The petition was addressed to the International Executive Committee meeting on 2 June 1946 and accepted at the meeting on 24 January 1947. Later on, when some of those Centres dissolved, their members joined the PEN Club of Writers in Exile, as can be read in the minutes of the executive committee of PEN on 9 April 1959: '(iv) Latvian Centre-New York Branch. Mr. Carver [International secretary] reported that this Branch was now dissolved, its members having transferred to the Branch of the Writers in Exile Centre in New York.'

↓   Estonian, Latvian, and Lithuanian PEN asked to be considered PEN Centres in exile after the Second World War and the annexation of their countries by the USSR. The petition was accepted by the International Executive Committee meeting on 24 January 1947, and the decision minuted with the coda 'No other statement seemed to be called for or desirable'.

> 3.
>
> BALTIC STATES: The Secretary made a state-
> ment concerning the present position of the
> Estonian, Latvian and Lithuanian Centres.
> Ants Oras presented the case for recognising
> a Group of Estonian writers outside Estonia
> as the accredited Estonian P.E.N.Centre.
> The same circumstances were operative in
> connection with Latvian writers.   After
> considerable discussion it was agreed that
> the existence of the Estonian and Latvian
> Centres should be confirmed although their
> headquarters were outside their national
> territories.   No other statement on the
> subject seemed to be called for or
> desirable.

↓   PEN Club of Writers in Exile: Czesław Miłosz, the Nobel Prize in Literature laureate of 1980, was during his exile years in San Francisco the first vice-chairman of PEN Writers in Exile. He was very warmly received by Polish PEN when he came back to Poland after the fall of the communist regime. Together with Wisława Szymborska, he read his poetry at the opening ceremony of the 66th PEN International Congress in Warsaw in 1999.

Cuban Writers in Exile

↑   The birth of the Cuban PEN Club took place on 4 October 1945 at the Restaurante Paris in Havana, with Francisco Ichaso Macías and Jorge Mañach chairing the table.

↓   The first person on the front row is Ángel Cuadra, Cuban delegate at the 77th PEN International Congress in Belgrade, 2011. Ángel Cuadra was imprisoned for 15 years in Cuban prisons and, after his release and exile to Miami, was the founder and first president of Cuban PEN in Exile. Cuadra died on 13 February 2021, being President Emeritus of the Centre.

A Cuban delegate, Jorge Mañach, was a participant at the New York World Congress of Writers in May 1939, but it was not until after the Second World War that Cuban writers united to create a PEN Centre. The birth of the Cuban PEN Club took place on 4 October 1945 at the Restaurante Paris in Havana, with Francisco Ichaso Macías and Jorge Mañach chairing the table. The Centre ceased to exist during the Cuban Revolution and under Fidel Castro's regime. Worldwide, PEN Centres actively campaigned for their Cuban colleagues in prison.

The poet Ángel Cuadra, imprisoned in Cuba from 1972 to 1987, had been an honorary member of Swedish PEN, which campaigned tirelessly for his freedom. When Cuadra left Cuba for exile in Miami, he was able to gather together a group of writers in exile. Cuban PEN in Exile was founded in 1997 and has since then promoted Cuban literature abroad with an emphasis on works by imprisoned writers.

In March 2000, Cuban PEN in Exile organised a meeting of Latin American PEN Centres in Miami. The meeting was chaired by the president of PEN International, Homero Aridjis, and Jennifer Clement, a future president of PEN International, was among the delegates.

The final statement created at this meeting affirmed:

> *Literature can only be developed in full when there's the freedom to create, and thus literature and freedom are inseparable concepts. We deplore that writers may defend, praise or support governments and political systems that curtail or suppress freedom of expression.*

Since 2017, a new Cuban PEN based in Havana has joined the PEN network. The founder of the new PEN Centre, Antón Arrufat, addressed delegates at the Quebec PEN International Congress in 2015. Two years later, it was the Cuban novelist and playwright Reinaldo Montero who attended the Lviv 2017 PEN International Congress, where the new Centre was formally welcomed by the assembly of delegates.

↓   In March 2000, Cuban PEN in Exile organised a meeting of Latin American PEN Centres in Miami. The meeting was chaired by the president of PEN International, Homero Aridjis, and Jennifer Clement, a future president of PEN International, was among the delegates. The final statement created at this meeting affirmed: 'Literature can only be developed in full when there's the freedom to create, and thus literature and freedom are inseparable concepts. We deplore that writers may defend, praise or support governments and political systems that curtail or suppress freedom of expression.'

PRIMER ENCUENTRO DE CENTROS PEN DE HISPANOAMERICA
Convocado por:
PEN CLUB DE ESCRITORES CUBANOS EN EL EXILIO
FILIAL DEL PEN INTERNACIONAL

(Declaración final de los Delegados asistentes)

-----Los Centros de PEN de Hispanoamérica, reunidos en su Primer Encuentro, en Miami, bajo el lema LITERATURA Y LIBERTAD, ratificamos nuestra adhesión a los principios generales recogidos en los Estatutos del PEN Internacional en defensa de la libertad de expresión y de creación.

-----Entendemos que en Hispanoamérica la lucha por la libertad ha sido una motivación constante en la historia de nuestros pueblos, cuyos hijos han sufrido la opresión frecuente de gobiernos dictatoriales, y la consecuente supresión o condicionamiento de la libertad de expresión.

-----Los representantes de los PEN de Hispanoamérica aquí reunidos, manifestamos nuestro rechazo a todo gobierno que, en nombre de cualquier ideología política totalitaria, restrinja o suprima la libertad de expresión y de creación, y manifestamos, además, nuestro respaldo a todo escritor o periodista que en su país sea acosado, agredido o encarcelado, en violacion de sus derechos a la libre expresión del pensamiento.

-----Afirmamos que la literatura alcanza sólo su plenitud cuando se crea en libertad, por lo que literatura y libertad son conceptos inseparables.. Lamentamos que existan escritores que defiendan, halaguen y apoyen gobiernos y sistemas políticos que restringen o suprimen la libertad expresión. Alentamos y admiramos a aquellos escritores, periodistas e intelectuales que, como exponen en su Apartado 4) los Estatutos del PEN Internacional, se oponen "a toda forma de su-

(Cont.)

presión de la libertad de expresión en el país y dentro de la comunidad a la cual pertenecen, así como en el ámbito mundial dondequiera que ello sea posible".

En Miami, a los 19 días del mes de marzo del año 2000.

Homero Aridjis
(Presidente PEN Internacional)

Gloria Guardia
(Miembro del Comité Ejecutivo del PEN Internacional)

Lucina Kathmann
(chair del Comité de Estoras, PEN Internacional)

Gaby Vallejo
(Presidenta PEN de Bolivia)

Cecilia Balcazar
(Presidenta PEN de Colombia)

Luis Mario Cerda
(PEN de Guadalajara)

Nedda G. de Anhalt
(PEN de México)

Víctor Manuel Mendiola
(Presidente PEN de México)

Martha Cerda
(Presidenta PEN Guadalajara)

Rosa María Britton
(Presidenta PEN de Panamá)

Jennifer Clement
(PEN ... México)

Angel Cuadra
(Presidente PEN de Escritores Cubanos en el Exilio)

PEN Vietnam **in Exile**

In September 1976, the former president of PEN Vietnam Vũ Hoàng Chương died only days after being released from prison by the government of the Socialist Republic of Vietnam.

The Vietnamese Writers Abroad PEN Centre was created in 1978 and welcomed by the PEN community at the PEN International Paris Congress in 1979. The poet and reporter Minh Đức Hoài became the first president of the Centre in exile and Trần Tam Tiệp its secretary general. The Centre started its activities connecting the diaspora of Vietnamese writers though meetings and publications. Trần Thanh Hiệp, who was president of the Vietnamese Abroad PEN Centre from 1984 to 1988, worked tirelessly to expand the Centre to North America after a meeting of the 1989 executive board in Montreal. The Vienamese Writers Abroad PEN rooted itself in Canada and gained year after year new members and social recognition — Ontario's premier, Kathleen Wynne, said in her 2017 greetings: 'The stories of our Vietnamese Canadian community are an integral part of their history and heritage. Ontario is proud to be home to a large and vibrant Vietnamese community whose rich literary traditions have contributed to the diverse body of work we enjoy in our multicultural society. I thank the board and members of the Vietnamese Abroad PEN Centre for their commitment to nurturing the extraordinary voices and stories of our Vietnamese community.'

Living in a foreign land has been the condition for Vietnamese Abroad PEN members, many of whom reached exile as refugees. The president of the Centre in 2020 is a good witness of this life journey: Dương Thành Lợi (Lloyd Duong) was a child refugee and one of the boat people, and now celebrates freedom, solidarity, and literature with his colleagues at literary galas attended by more than 500 people.

Other Vietnamese refugee writers have joined the PEN Centres of their countries of exile. Nguyên Hoàng Bao Viêt, imprisoned for years in a concentration camp because he had published a poem in honour of Federico García Lorca, joined the Swiss Romand PEN Centre and has been a PEN International advocate at the sessions of the United Nations Human Rights Council since the 1990s. At the 42nd session of the Human Rights Council in 2019, Nguyên Hoàng Bao Viêt reported on freedom of expression violations by the Socialist Republic of Vietnam and about 'forced labour concentration camps, where prisoners are punished by isolation, malnourished and deprived of medical care'.

↖ In September 1976, the former president of PEN Vietnam, Vũ Hoàng Chương, died only days after being released from prison by the government of the Socialist Republic of Vietnam, having refused to write poems to serve political objectives.

↗ The Vietnamese Writers Abroad PEN Centre was created in 1978. The poet and reporter Minh Đức Hoài became its first president.

↑ Trần Thành Hiệp, president of Vietnamese Abroad PEN Centre from 1984 to 1988, worked tirelessly to expand the centre to North America.

← Dương Thành Lợi (Lloyd Duong), president of Vietnamese Abroad PEN Centre since 2018, was among the boat people, refugees who fled Vietnam in the wake of the end of the Vietnam War.

Iranian PEN in Exile and Faraj Sarkohi

Iranian PEN was born after a meeting of the Iranian Writers' Association in the Netherlands in 1994. Initiated by 20 Iranian writers in exile, the new Centre travelled in the following autumn to the PEN International Congress in Prague. The Congress was attended by Arthur Miller, president of PEN International 1966–69, who met the Iranian delegation, and supported the new PEN Centre and the call 'We are the author' — a call against censorship in Iran, also known as 'Text of the 134' as it was signed by 134 Iranian writers, artists and intellectuals. Iranian PEN in Exile was welcomed to the PEN community at the Prague 1994 Congress.

Faraj Sarkohi, founder of the cultural magazine *Adineh*, considered to be the spokesperson of the 'Text of the 134', was detained in 1996 and sentenced to death one year later. A PEN International campaign as well as other international protests resulted in the verdict being overturned. Members of Iranian PEN in Exile conducted demonstrations together with Moris Farhi, chair of the PEN International Writers in Prison Committee. Faraj Sarkohi was awarded the Kurt Tucholsky Prize by Swedish PEN in 1997. He went into exile in Germany, where he was honorary member of German PEN. He was a host of the German PEN network for exiled writers from 2000 to 2006 and lives in Frankfurt am Main.

↖   Faraj Sarkohi, founder of the cultural magazine *Adineh*, considered to be the spokesperson of the 'Text of the 134', was detained in 1996 and sentenced to death one year later. A PEN International campaign as well as other international protests resulted in the verdict being overturned. He was welcomed in exile by German PEN.

←←   Iranian PEN was born after a meeting of the Iranian Writers Association in the Netherlands in 1994 and welcomed as a new PEN Centre by the delegates of the 61st PEN International Congress in Prague.

←   Moris Farhi, chair of PEN International Writers in Prison Committee from 1997 to 2002, is holding the banner in a demonstration for the liberation of Faraj Sarkohi, together with members of Iranian PEN in Exile, outside the Iranian Embassy in London.

Uyghur PEN **connecting the diaspora of Uyghur writers**

↑   Members of Uyghur PEN welcomed
delegates of Turkish, Estonian,
Hungarian, South Korean, and Central
Asian PEN at their network conference in
Mongolia in 2011.

Uyghur PEN was founded in Stockholm in 2006 by the Uyghur
musician and writer Kurash Kosen and other Uyghur writers in exile.
The new Centre was formally accepted as a member of PEN
International during the 74th PEN International Congress in 2008 in
Bogotá. Meetings of Uyghur PEN take place in different countries, the
majority of members being from Kazakhstan and other Central Asian
countries, with others based in Europe and North America. Members
work in fields ranging across academia, media and film production,
translation, and literature. The Centre network meetings invite other
PEN Centres supporting Uyghurs in exile, as at the conference celebrated in Mongolia in 2011, which saw the participation of delegates
from Turkish, Estonian, Hungarian, South Korean, and Central Asian
PEN. The Centre publishes *Uyghur PEN Magazine*, in both Uyghur
and Russian, connecting in this way to the diaspora of Uyghur writers.

Tibetan Writers **Abroad**

↑   On 5 May 2017 the Dalai Lama received Jennifer Clement and Carles Torner, president and executive director of PEN International, and thanked them for PEN International's support of Tibetan writers.

↘   The poet and singer Lhoudup Palsang, here wearing dark glasses, is the current president of PEN Tibetan Writers Abroad. On his left is Nyima Tso, sociologist and general secretary of the Centre. First on the right is Lokdun, vice-president and school director, and on his left, Buddha Kyab, fulltime children's book writer for the network of Tibetan schools in exile. They all crossed the Himalayas, escaping from Tibet as teenagers.

'I came from Tibet crossing the chilly snowy mountains and the strong running rivers for forty-two days and nights by walking on bare foot. Many times we had to pass very closely through Chinese military camps and there was so much fear […] We had often lost our paths in the night. Fortunately, we all escaped from the bullets of Chinese army.' The leadership of PEN Tibetan Writers Abroad is made up of young writers, all of whom escaped through the Himalayas when they were teenagers. They joined the Tibetan community in exile in Dharamsala, in the Indian state of Himachal Pradesh. In 2017, the board of PEN Tibetan Writers Abroad included Lhoudup Palsang, Lokdun, Nyima Tso, Buddha Kyab, and others.

PEN Tibetan Writers Abroad organises readings and meetings of Tibetan writers. From its offices, it publishes Tibetan literature, smuggling manuscripts out of Tibet, printing them in India, circulating them widely and sending copies back to Tibet through clandestine networks. PEN Tibetan Writers Abroad has published several reports on freedom of expression and writers in prison in Tibet, as well as newsletters and journals of Tibetan literature like the monthly magazine *Chitsok Melong*. Its report on human rights in Tibet was banned in China, as well as the one on censorship in Tibet.

By integrating the PEN International community, PEN Tibetan Writers Abroad has become a platform for the international presence of Tibetan writers. Tibetan delegates participate at each PEN International Congress and PEN Tibetan Writers Abroad is one of the driving forces of the Translation and Linguistic Rights Committee of PEN International. Tibetan writers participated actively in the drafting of the Universal Declaration of Linguistic Rights and used it to analyse the systematic replacement of Tibetan by Mandarin Chinese in the schools of Tibet.

ཕྱི་ཚོགས་མེ་ལོང་།

Chitsok Melong

ཚོས་དེ་ཡང་ཤེས་དགོས་ལ།   ཤྱིད་དེ་ཡང་ཤེས་དགོས།

བཅར་འདྲི་ཕོད་མིའི་རང་དབང་དམངས་གཙོ།

↑   PEN Tibetan Writers Abroad publishes reports,
newsletters, and journals of Tibetan literature, like
the monthly magazine *Chitsok Melong*, that connect
the diaspora of Tibetan writers.

PEN and the International Cities of Refuge Network (ICORN)

The year 2006 saw the creation of the International Cities of Refuge Network (ICORN), encompassing representatives of 15 cities and several PEN Centres, with the ICORN Secretariat established with support from the Norwegian city of Stavanger. PEN International and ICORN signed an official cooperation agreement, as ICORN shares the main challenge PEN has faced since the 1930s, when PEN Centres mobilised themselves for refugee writers fleeing Germany, Spain, Austria, and Czechoslovakia: supporting colleagues in exile and offering them the possibility to continue their commitment as writers. Chenjerai Hove, a leading figure of postcolonial Zimbabwean literature, who was forced into exile in 2001 by the regime of Robert Mugabe, became the first guest writer in the city of Stavanger and later in Miami City of Refuge.

The map of ICORN cities has grown non-stop. Since 2006, more than 70 cities around the globe have joined the network, and no fewer than 250 writers and artists have found shelter in an ICORN member city. The commitment by these cities is both very concrete and deeply symbolic: the writer or artist escapes from imminent threat and persecution; the host city offers sanctuary; and the values of hospitality, solidarity, and freedom of expression become further enshrined in the ethos of that city. PEN members in the city offer guest writers and

↑↑   Cities join ICORN in public ceremonies. Gdańsk became a member of the International Cities of Refuge Network in 2017. The agreement is being signed, from right to left, by ICORN director Helge Lunde, the director of the Gdańsk City Gallery, Piotr Stasiowski, and the mayor of Gdańsk, Paweł Adamowicz, a symbol of the struggle for democracy and freedom in Poland, who was assassinated in 2019.

↑   The mayor of Paris, Anne Hidalgo, participating in the general assembly of ICORN celebrating the tenth anniversary of the network in Paris in 2016.

→   The poet and translator Basim Mardan had to flee Iraq in 2006 and became the first ICORN guest writer in Norway. In 2016, he joined the PEN International Protection of Writers at Risk team at the London Secretariat and has been central to PEN–ICORN collaboration. Here he is shown on the panel, speaking about 'The Role of the Writer in Countering Xenophobia' at the conference of ICORN and PEN's Writers in Prison Committee in Rotterdam, May 2019. Left to right: Karin Karlekar, PEN America; Basim Mardan; Naeimeh Doostdar, an Iranian journalist and ICORN guest writer in Malmö; Gautam Bhatia, PEN Delhi; Dr Ma Thida, president of PEN Myanmar; Salil Tripathi, chair of the Writers in Prison Committee. The empty chair is dedicated to Oleg Sentsov, Ukrainian filmmaker, writer and activist from Crimea, who was serving a twenty-year prison sentence in Russia. He would be released as part of a prisoner exchange in 2019.

artists a community of fellow colleagues, translation of their work into the local language, and participation in solidarity campaigns. ICORN and PEN enable them to continue to express themselves freely in a place where they are safe but not silent. Through digital media, they can reach audiences to whom they were denied access before leaving.

The ICORN Secretariat works closely with PEN International and its Writers in Prison Committee, and every two years a major ICORN/PEN conference analyses common challenges, develops strategies to face them, and celebrates writers in exile and their literature. PEN International's Protection of Writers at Risk team evaluates the authenticity of authorship and artistic production as well as declared danger of the candidates to be welcomed in the cities of the network, and thus the two international secretariats work in daily collaboration.

↖ From 15 cities when it was founded in 2006, ICORN has grown to become a well-connected solidarity network of 74 cities in 2020 working in collaboration with local PEN Centres and PEN International. The ICORN world map extends from the United States to Brazil and from the Mediterranean to Northern Europe.

Eaten Fish, alias for Ali Dorani

Ali Dorani, an Iranian refugee, chose the alias 'Eaten Fish' after the boat carrying him to Australia sank and he had to be rescued from the ocean. He was locked up in the immigration detention centre at Manus Island, in Papua New Guinea, as part of Australia's 'deterrence' policy. In the detention centre he suffered persecution and lived under very harsh conditions that included beatings and unsanitary conditions. In some cases, it meant death for the inmates, as was the case for Ali Dorani's friend Faysal Ishak Ahmed. Eaten Fish worked tirelessly to describe in detail the unbearable conditions endured by the detainees.

PEN International and ICORN, after a long period of campaigning on his behalf, were able to relocate Ali Dorani to Stavanger, Norway, in 2018. One of PEN and ICORN's priorities is to make sure that refugees maintain their identity as writers and artists and help to have their work published and translated. Eaten Fish's international career as a cartoonist has thrived since he reached Stavanger, and his work has been exhibited in Norway and abroad.

A major exhibition of his work took place in Germany in 2019, when Norway was the guest of honour at the Frankfurt Book Fair.

← Christopher Downes, together with many cartoonists from Australia and from all over the world, participated in the campaign for the liberation of Ali Dorani, with the support of Cartoonist Rights Network International, PEN International, and other freedom of expression organisations. Two years of intense campaigning and the support of ICORN succeeded in relocating Eaten Fish to Norway.

↓ The picture shows the close collaboration between PEN International and ICORN. From left to right, after a meeting at PEN International London offices: Cathy McCann, manager of the Protection of Writers at Risk team at PEN International, supporting refugee writers worldwide and connecting them with ICORN; Ali Dorani (PEN name Eaten Fish), Iranian cartoonist detained in Manus Island until he was welcomed by ICORN in 2018; Lotte Løkeland Hovda, coordinator of Friby Stavanger, the city's programme for refugee writers. Stavanger is among the funders of ICORN and Ali Dorani is the 11th refugee writer welcomed in the city.

↑   A major exhibition of Eaten Fish's work took place in
Germany in 2019, on the occasion of the Frankfurt Book Fair.
The lead image of the exhibition was this tropical version
of Edvard Munch's *The Scream*.

The Independent Chinese PEN Centre

↑   Liu Xiaobo, a professor at Beijing
Normal University, addressing
demonstrators in Tiananmen Square
in May 1989, during the student-led
protests that led to the massacre of
4 June.

The short-lived democracy movement in China began on 15 May 1989
with student demonstrations and ended on 4 June with the Tiananmen
Square Massacre. Liu Xiaobo, then a professor at Beijing Normal
University, was among the speakers who addressed the demonstrators.
The crackdown meant death for many, exile for many more, or long
years of repression for those inside of China.

In 2001, the Independent Chinese PEN Centre was established, its
membership drawn from writers based in China and Hong Kong as
well as those living in exile. Among the members were Liu Xiaobo
and Liu Xia in Beijing. The list of founding members of the Centre
was sent to Jane Spender, secretary at PEN International, by Bei Ling,
who later became president of the Independent Chinese PEN Centre.

↗   Liu Xia, widow of Liu Xiaobo, on 10 July 2018,
on her way to Berlin where she was welcomed by members
of Independent Chinese PEN and German PEN.

→   The president of Independent Chinese PEN Centre, Tienchi Martin, in
conversation with Marian Botsford Fraser, chair of the Writers in Prison
Committee 2009-15, at the Lviv PEN International Congress, in early October
2017. The conversation was a tribute to Liu Xiaobo, who had died two
months earlier. The empty chair was for Liu Xia, widow of Liu Xiaobo, who
was unofficially detained at home, outside of any legal process.

The drafting of the Charter of the Independent Chinese PEN Centre
was a participatory process. An initial document was sent to all
members taking part in a forum, and the final Charter, approved by
the members in October 2003, was translated into English and shared
with all PEN Centres.

The Independent Chinese PEN Centre was registered in New York,
with Liu Xiaobo as one of its directors, even though he was based in
Beijing. Years later, Liu Xiaobo was one of the writers who drafted
Charter 08, signed by 303 Chinese dissident intellectuals and human
rights activists. Among other things, Charter 08 called for the Chinese
government to amend the constitution and create a separation of
powers, legislative democracy, an independent judiciary, public control
of public servants and a guarantee of human rights and freedom of
expression. Liu Xiaobo was detained and in 2009 was sentenced to
11 years in prison. PEN campaigned worldwide for his release.

Liu Xiaobo received the 2010 Nobel Peace Prize. He was only
released from prison with a terminal illness a few weeks before his
death in 2017.

PEN Eritrea, the youngest PEN Centre in exile

↑   Participants at the third Congress of PEN Eritrea in Exile, meeting in Rotterdam in 2019. They had travelled from their cities of exile in Norway, Sweden, Germany, Switzerland, and the Netherlands.

↓   PEN Eritrea's 'Breaking the Silence' project is a civil society programme of PEN International, with the support of SIDA, consisting of creative writing workshops for Eritrean refugee writers in Egypt and Uganda. This group photograph is from the Cairo workshop in 2019.

The establishment of PEN Eritrea was proposed by Norwegian PEN in 2014 at the 80th PEN International Congress in Bishkek, Kyrgyzstan, and was welcomed unanimously by the PEN community. Dessale Abraham Berekhet, who had been guest writer in Bø City of Refuge from 2012 to 2014, gave an impassioned speech before the entire assembly of delegates, describing his and his colleagues' repression within Eritrea as well as the painful journey into exile that many have endured. As he began to speak in Tigrinya, the conference hall came to complete silence. Switching to English, Dessale began to show photographs of his colleagues and friends, including Dawit Isaak — in prison for 13 years, with no contact with family or the outside world.

Since its foundation in 2014, PEN Eritrea in Exile has celebrated three Congresses. The second one met in Rotterdam in 2019, with participants travelling from Norway, Sweden, Germany, Switzerland, and the Netherlands. The third conference was conducted via Zoom in July 2020.

The Centre promotes the work of diaspora writers. The PEN Eritrea website publishes literature and journalism in Tigre and Tigrinya as well as in English. At the First Vienna International Strategic Conference on Human Rights in Eritrea in 2017, PEN Eritrea presented the anthology *Uncensored Voices* with the support of PEN Austria. The second conference, uniting PEN Centres active in the support of Eritrean writers, took place in 2019.

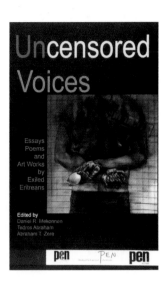

↗   At the First Vienna International Strategic Conference on Human Rights in Eritrea in 2017, PEN Eritrea presented the anthology *Uncensored Voices* with the support of PEN Austria.

↓   Action by PEN Eritrea in defence of the 17 plus journalists detained since 2001, who have subsequently remained incommunicado. Although Eritrea's foreign minister claimed in a 2016 interview that all of the journalists and politicians arrested in 2001 were still alive, no proof has yet been provided.

Yirgalem Fisseha Mebrahtu

At the PEN International Bishkek Congress in 2014, when Dessale Abraham Berekhet made his impassioned call for the urgent need to create a PEN Eritrea in Exile, he presented to the delegates photograph after photograph of writers who had been detained for several years in Eritrea's appalling prisons. Among them, was Yirgalem Fisseha Mebrahtu, who at the time had been imprisoned for five years.

Arguably one of Eritrea's finest women poets, a radio presenter, and short-story writer, Yirgalem Fisseha suffered six years of arbitrary arrest in the country's most notorious military prison. In February 2009, the educational station Radio Bana, where Yirgalem had worked, was raided by the military who took more than 30 staff members and journalists associated with the radio station into custody. The majority were only released after four years, but Yirgalem and five others were released after six years and without ever facing trial. While in custody, she became

an iconic and symbolic figure of unlawful detention by the Eritrean regime and her images were widely shared on social media as were posters calling for her release, some of them created by PEN International.

Yirgalem left Eritrea in March 2018 and went to live in Uganda. While in Uganda, she published her poems and her first-hand account of her experience in prison (the latter on the PEN Eritrea website). Yirgalem received a scholarship from the Writers-in-Exile Programme of PEN Germany and arrived in Munich in December 2018.

Since 2018, Yirgalem has been travelling around Europe to read her poetry at festivals and PEN gatherings.

In June 2019, Yirgalem received the first PEN Eritrea's Freedom of Expression Award in front of more than 200 delegates from PEN Centres and ICORN cities at the 'At Home Everywhere' conference in Rotterdam.

↙ Dessale Abraham Berekhet calls for the creation of a PEN Eritrea in Exile by showing delegates faces of writers who had been detained for several years in Eritrea's prisons.

↓ Yirgalem Fisseha Mebrahtu receives PEN Eritrea's Freedom of Expression Award from Carles Torner, executive director of PEN, at the PEN Writers in Prison/ICORN Conference in Rotterdam, 2019.

↑   A portrait of Yirgalem Fisseha
Mebrahtu created by artist Caroline
Glover for a PEN campaign on the
occasion of International Women's
Day in 2019.

German PEN's Writers-in-Exile Programme

← Writers welcomed by
German PEN's Writers-in-Exile
Programme in 2018, from left to
right: Enoh Meyomesse
(Cameroon), Fatuma Yimam
(Ethiopia), Sajjad Jahan Fard
(Kurdish from Iran), Arpita
Roychoudhury (Bangladesh),
Aleksei Bobrovnikov (Ukraine),
Şehbal Şenyurt Arınlı (Turkey), and
Zobaen Sondhi (Bangladesh).

German PEN has been very active in welcoming writers in exile.
Founded at the end of the twentieth century, German PEN's Writers-
in-Exile Programme has sheltered more than 60 authors. With
sponsorship from the Federal Commissioner for Cultural and Media
Affairs, German PEN provides foreign scholars with a furnished
apartment, a monthly stipend, and health insurance for one or two but
no longer than three years. During this time, German PEN protects
and advises refugee colleagues. It gives them a short breather to
recover from some of the trauma they have been through in their
countries, and it encourages them to continue their work as writers.

German PEN has also promoted actively their writing. *Zuflucht in
Deutschland* (Refuge in Germany) is an anthology of 20 writers in
exile in Germany, from Chechnya, Iran, China, Syria, and several
other countries, all of them welcomed by German PEN's network of
writers in exile. One of the priorities of the network is to translate the
work of their foreign colleagues and welcome them to Germany's
literary landscape.

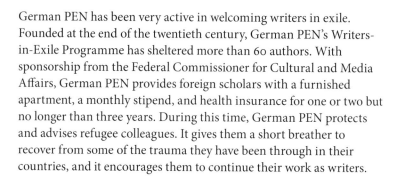

← The former president of German PEN Joseph Haslinger (2013–17)
campaigning against Turkish anti-terror legislation and in solidarity
with Ayşe Berktay in 2013, when she was in Bakırköy Women's Prison
in Istanbul. German PEN has actively campaigned for writers
imprisoned in Turkey, and over the years has welcomed in Germany
the following Turkish writers, journalists, and filmmakers: Fethiye
Çetin, Mehmet Selim Çürükkaya, Ahmet Kahraman, Pınar Selek,
Can Dündar, Şehbal Şenyurt Arınlı, and Aslı Erdoğan.

Das Writers-in-Exile-Programm des PEN

Zuflucht in Deutschland

Texte verfolgter Autoren

Herausgegeben von
Josef Haslinger und Franziska Sperr

← The book cover of the anthology *Zuflucht in Deutschland. Texte verfolgter Autoren (Refuge in Germany. Texts by persecuted authors)*, published in 2017 by the German PEN's Writers-in-Exile Programme.

↓ Official reception on the occasion of 20 years of the Writers-in-Exile Programme on 8 October 2019 at the Bundeskanzleramt, Berlin.
Front row (left to right): Najet Adouani, Franziska Sperr, Regula Venske (president of German PEN since 2017), Monika Grütters (Federal Commissioner for Culture and the Media), Khalil Rostamkhani.
Second row: Leander Sukov, Christa Schuenke, Sanath Balasooriya, Liu Dejun, Fatuma Yimam.
Third row: Zaza Burchuladze, Kerstin Martini, Şehbal Şenyurt Arınlı, Can Dündar, Sajjad Jahan Fard, Yassin al-Haj Saleh, Yirgalem Fisseha Mebrahtu.
Back row: Umar Abdul Nasser, Aleksei Bobrovnikov, Yamen Hussein, Sandra Weires-Guia.

Can Dündar: #WeAreArrested

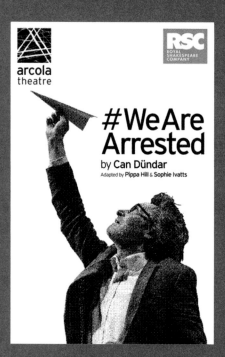

On 29 May 2015, Can Dündar, a member of PEN Turkey and editor-in-chief of the oldest Turkish newspaper, Cumhuriyet, published the news that Erdoğan's regime was illegally supplying weapons to radical groups fighting the war in Syria. Dündar was immediately threatened on live TV by President Erdoğan_ who said: 'He will pay a heavy price for this, I won't let him be.' Dündar was later detained together with the editor of Cumhuriyet, Erdem Gül. At the moment the judge handed down his sentence, Can Dündar sent a tweet with the now famous hashtag #WeAreArrested.

Local and international solidarity was immediate. There were large demonstrations in front of Cumhuriyet, and a vigil of solidarity began in front of Silivri Prison. The vigil lasted several months, and delegates of Turkish, Kurdish, Norwegian, Swedish, Flemish, Welsh, Swiss Italian, English, and German PEN Centres travelled to Istanbul to participate in the vigil.

On 25 February 2016, the constitutional court of Turkey ruled 12 votes against three that the imprisonment of journalists Can Dündar and Erdem Gül amounted to a violation of their rights. The two were let out of jail while the trial continued. On 6 May, in a break during court proceedings, Can Dündar narrowly missed an attack on his life when a gunman fired at him outside the Istanbul courthouse. The assassin only missed his target because Dündar's wife, Dilek, and a Member of Parliament managed heroically to jump the assassin. The same day, Can Dündar and Erdem Gül were sentenced to five years in prison and they immediately appealed. Dündar was allowed to go home and, surprisingly, the court did not issue a travel ban.

After these events, Can Dündar travelled to Barcelona to complete his book in safety. In July 2016, he was forced to opt for exile in Berlin after the attempted coup in Turkey, which immediately resulted in a crackdown on free expression, with the number of arrested journalists rising from 23 to over 170. Dündar was welcomed in Berlin by German PEN and Reporters Without Borders. A few weeks later he participated at the 82nd PEN International Congress meeting in Ourense, Galicia, Spain. Dündar was the keynote speaker at the Congress: 'Dear Friends, […] Those who hide dirty secrets, profit from war, and stand by as innocent people suffer, don't like our pens. They understand that the way to hide secrets, prolong wars and exploit the innocent is to break our pens and prosecute writers. That's why those who hold a pen can't escape persecution. My relationship with the pen grew like this. It became my closest friend from the day I picked it up. It taught me to express myself. It listened to my troubles and wrote them down, it was a companion in my misfortune; penning my secrets and concealing them. I won my first girlfriend's heart thanks to it. I bought my first books with its money. I was tried, jailed and shot at because of it. But never once did I give it up… Or betray it.' From Berlin, Can Dündar has joined PEN in campaigns defending writers in prison and in exile.

When travelling to be reunited with her husband in exile, Dilek Dündar's passport was seized by the Turkish police although there were no legal charges against her. They kept her in Turkey on the grounds of guilt by association. The family was separated for three years, until she was able to escape from Turkey.

↑   The prison diary of Can Dündar, titled #WeAreArrested, was translated into over 20 languages. The Royal Shakespeare Company in the UK has staged a version of #WeAreArrested to much acclaim.

→   Can Dündar visited the imprisoned Catalan writer and social leader Jordi Cuixart and also spoke out on his case in interviews on Spanish TV. The photograph shows Dündar with Txell Bonet, Jordi Cuixart's wife, in front of the gate of Lledoners Prison, Barcelona, in December 2018. During the prison visit, Dündar told Cuixart: 'Your wife, who travels the world seeking solidarity for your cause, reminds me of Dilek's trips abroad when I was imprisoned.'

↑   On 6 May 2016, in a break during court proceedings,
Can Dündar narrowly missed an attack on his life when a
gunman fired at him outside the Istanbul courthouse.
The assassin only missed his target because Dündar's wife,
Dilek, and a Member of Parliament managed heroically
to jump the assassin.

Eo autem libêtius hoc quicquid
est laboris suscepi, quòd nimium sibi placere nonnullos
ob annotatas d se nescio quot Graecas cum Ciceronis in-
terpretatione uoculas animaduerterem : quasi uerò
pro pauculis illis, non essent omnibus in promptu propè
innumerabiles: omnibus dico, quos(ut loquitur cultus et
tersus poeta) nõ inertia tardat. Sed et alia me ad hûc
suscipiendum impulsum fuisse causa, nequaquam dissi-
mulabo. Nimirum ut sinistrorum quorundam Ciceronis imitatorum(quos etiã iure optimo seruum pecus ap-
pellare quis possit)fastum ἀδόχετον mehercle, οὐχ ὅπ ex-
χ τòν, siqua ratione possem, reprimerem: et illis pudorem

Writers in prison

For one century, imprisoned writers have shaped PEN International from behind bars. A turning point was the 1933 Dubrovnik Congress, followed by PEN International's break from German PEN after the burning of books in Nazi Germany and the founding of a German PEN Club in Exile with its formal address on Oxford Street in London. The subsequent International Congress was held in 1935 in Barcelona. Here delegates were given information on the imprisoned Haitian poet Jacques Roumain along with translations of his poetry. For the first time, PEN International wrote a letter to a government asking for the release of an imprisoned writer. At the same Congress, delegates demanded the release of Ludwig Renn and Carl von Ossietzky and protested against the abduction of Berthold Jacob from Switzerland. A historic letter had already been drafted in 1934 to Joseph Goebbels asking for the release of Ludwig Renn. The 1936 Buenos Aires Congress paid tribute to exiled German and Austrian writers like Stefan Zweig as well as to Federico García Lorca, the poet killed by fascist squads during the first weeks of the Spanish Civil War.

In the 1950s, in the context of the Cold War, the creation of the PEN Club of Writers in Exile was instrumental in the work to gather names of writers imprisoned by totalitarian regimes in communist countries as well as those in Spain and Portugal. The first lists of PEN cases, consisting of writers in prison for whom the organisation campaigned, were compiled by exiled writers from Albania, Romania, Hungary, and Czechoslovakia.

In 1960, at the Rio de Janeiro International Congress, a committee to denounce the imprisonment of writers was created and named the Writers in Prison Committee (WiPC). Year by year the committee grew in importance as more and more PEN Centres became involved in the defence of their imprisoned colleagues. As an added consequence, this work became the central part of debates at PEN Congresses. In the 1990s, specialised staff at the London Secretariat coordinated a PEN Case List, which often had over a thousand cases.

Not a year went past in the 1990s without a PEN Centre sending a mission to a country to meet with writers in prison and their families or to observe trials, an indication of the growing capacity of the Centres. In 1991, a joint Canadian PEN/PEN USA West mission went to Mexico to raise concerns about the high rates of attacks on journalists. Japan PEN visited South Korea in 1993 to petition for Hwang Sok-yong, a leading writer in prison who had been detained for several years, and Swedish PEN followed in 1995. Japan PEN also visited Myanmar and met with Aung San Suu Kyi under house arrest, and, in 1995, visited Indonesia to petition for Pramoedya Ananta Toer who was another long-term prisoner. Norway's Eugene Schoulgin's visit in 1997 to Yemen eventually led to the release and successful asylum of the poet Mansur Rajih who had been sentenced to death and who had already served fifteen years in prison. Missions became a constant tool for PEN to campaign for imprisoned colleagues and raise international awareness, with some crucial successes like the change in the laws for crimes against journalists in Mexico in 2012.

Each PEN Centre created its own WiPC and, by the turn of the century, campaigning for writers at risk, in prison, or in exile had become central in all PEN gatherings. Conferences for the coordination of campaigns, mission planning, and training of leaders of the local WiPCs were organised on a biannual basis. The first one took place in 1998, hosted by Danish PEN in Helsingør, followed by conferences in Chichester, Kathmandu, San Miguel de Allende, Barcelona, Istanbul, Glasgow, Kraków…

Over the years, campaigning for imprisoned writers has changed the face of PEN Centres worldwide. The fall of the Berlin Wall meant that dissident and exiled writers joined the newly created PEN Centres in Eastern Europe and Russia. PEN South Africa became a driving force in PEN after the fall of the apartheid regime. This was a reflection of how imprisoned and persecuted writers became the core work of PEN Centres globally. Ma Thida, who had been PEN's main case in Myanmar in the 1990s, became president of the new PEN Myanmar in 2013 and was later elected a member of the PEN International Board. Dina Meza, a Honduran journalist at risk who was at the core of PEN reporting to the United Nations and the Inter-American Commission on Human Rights about crimes against journalists in her country, became first president of PEN Honduras in 2014. And Svetlana Alexievich, who was welcomed by PEN and ICORN during her exile in Germany and Sweden and received the Nobel Prize in Literature in 2015, became the president of Belarus PEN when she returned to her homeland.

← Page by Henri Estienne from a 1557 edition redacted by censorship in Geneva. *Deletrix* (a Latin word denoting 'destruction') is the title chosen by photographer Joan Fontcuberta for his exhibition on censorship, through a series of examples of censored texts from various periods accumulated through visits to libraries and archives throughout Europe and North America. The project was developed in collaboration with art critic Manel Guerrero and Catalan PEN.

Roumain, Renn, Lorca, Koestler:

the first four writers in prison for whom PEN campaigned

Since its early days, PEN International embodied the mission to defend writers who were imprisoned for their use of the freedom of the word. PEN had taken sides against the persecution by the Nazis of Jewish, pacifist, religious, liberal, anarchist, socialist, communist, 'decadent', and other authors at the Dubrovnik 1933 Congress. After this, support to individual writers took shape. A first step was the motions presented by the PEN's 'German Group Outside Germany' at the Edinburgh Congress in 1934: about 'German members of P.E.N. outside Germany constituting the only part of German mental expression at the present time which conforms to P.E.N. ideals', about 'Imprisoned German Writers' and about the 'attitude of writers in the event of war'. But no individual names of writers were yet mentioned in PEN resolutions.

This happened at the next Congress in Barcelona, 1935. The first writer in prison for whom PEN campaigned was the Haitian Jacques Roumain. At the Catalan Congress, the American delegate, professor, critic, and editor Henry Seidel Canby, made an impassioned request to the delegates meeting in Barcelona: according to the minutes, 'Dr. Canby called attention to the case of imprisonment of the Haitian author, Jacques Roumain.

From information received it would appear that an error of justice had been committed, and without in any way pre-judging the circumstances thought than an enquiry should be made. He therefore moved that the Government of Haiti be asked to re-consider the case.' Roumain was founder of the Haitian Communist Party and arrested several times for his opposition to the US occupation of Haiti. Two of his poems were translated and circulated at the Congress. It was the first case for which PEN was raising its voice, and the motion, supported by the writer and pacifist Henrietta Leslie from English PEN, was carried unanimously. The same period saw the letter to Joseph Goebbels signed by PEN International secretary Hermon Ould, asking for the liberation of Ludwig Renn.

In the first weeks of the Spanish Civil War, the poet Federico García Lorca was executed in Granada by a fascist squad. He was a great and popular poet, as well as a socialist and homosexual. It happened so fast that the PEN community was in shock. At the following Congress in Paris, a unanimous resolution recorded that 'Poet García Lorca was not involved in political struggles and his works, connected to popular poetry and the eternal literary traditions of Spain as expressed in the

Romancero, Cervantes and Lope de Vega. PEN pays tribute, with pain, to the memory of the poet.'

After the shock of Lorca's assassination and the incapacity of PEN to intervene, the campaign for the liberation of Arthur Koestler can be considered the first important success of the organisation in this field. An open letter signed by many, including EM Forster and Aldous Huxley, succeeded in the Spanish fascist authorities liberating Koestler from prison after more than three months of detention in Seville. Koestler wrote to Hermon Ould, PEN International secretary, saying 'I am fully aware that it was no personal merit of my own, but in the deeper interests of the free expression of opinion which is the life-blood of democracy and humanity that this help was given'. Koestler continued to support refugees through PEN International.

← Jacques Roumain, Ludwig Renn, Federico García Lorca.

→ Arthur Koestler.

The creation of PEN's Writers in Prison Committee

← The Hungarian poet and writer Tibor Déry became a spokesman for the Revolutionary government that tried to end the Soviet occupation in October 1956. When the Hungarian Uprising was suppressed, he was condemned to nine years in prison.

↓ Minutes of the PEN International Congress in Rio de Janeiro, 1960. The Austrian manifesto, seconded by PEN Argentina, acknowledges the creation of a 'Permanent P.E.N. Committee for Writers in Prison to re-establish the Freedom of Writing wherever it is suppressed.'

'The 31st International PEN Congress protests against the persecution of writers still suffering for their writings and opinions […] The congress therefore calls upon PEN Centres to do their utmost in the spirit of the Charter to support the work of the Permanent PEN Committee for Writers in Prison to re-establish the freedom of writing wherever it is suppressed.' The Rio de Janeiro Congress in 1960 marked a major step forward for PEN in the defence of imprisoned colleagues. PEN Centres worldwide started to welcome foreign writers in prison as honorary members, and pledged to support them until their release. This work created a network of contacts for families of detainees and their lawyers while PEN Centres were giving publicity to the situation of their honorary members among the literary community and the media. The Congress issued appeals for Manolis Glezos, sentenced to five years in Greece, the Catalan poet Luis Goytisolo (both of them accused of pro-communist activities), and the censored Portuguese writer Aquilino Ribeiro.

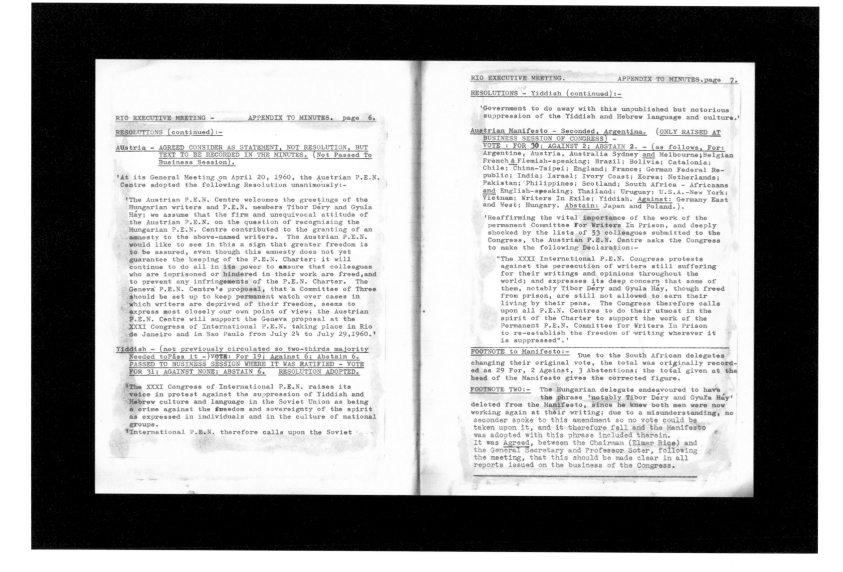

← Paul Tabori, president of PEN
Club of Writers in Exile.

↖ Margaret Storm Jameson,
president of English PEN.

↑ Victor E van Vriesland, president
of Dutch PEN and president
of PEN International (1962–65).

In post-war Europe, the persistence of fascist regimes in Spain and Portugal and the expansion of communist regimes in Central and Eastern Europe multiplied reports of imprisonment, censorship and travel bans. The creation of the WiPC was directly related to the division of Europe into two blocs and the continuity of the network of writers in exile within PEN. The Hungarian Uprising of 1956 had seen writers and intellectuals front stage, later being among the first victims of repression. The Hungarian playwright Paul Tabori, president of Writers in Exile PEN Club, had obtained the suspension of the Hungarian PEN Centre's membership because it did not help obtain information about writers in Hungarian prisons. The Centre was readmitted at the Rio Congress after two of the most prominent imprisoned Hungarian writers, Julius Hay and Tibor Déry, were released. Just a few months before the Berlin Wall was built in 1961 and the tension between West and East German PEN Centres became irreconcilable, PEN decided to create the WiPC.

The proposal had come as a resolution proposed by both the Swiss Romand and Swiss Italian PEN Centres, where it was said that 'In view of the increasing dangers threatening the principles of the Charter of PEN' a 'permanent Committee of three members' should be created, being 'charged with the carrying out of any action they judge to be necessary and proper to aid those writers during the intervals between the meetings of the International Executive Committee' and able to coordinate information and actions of the centres. The three members of the committee appointed by the Rio delegates were Paul Tabori himself, together with the president of English PEN Margaret Storm Jameson, who, since the years of the Second World War, had been very active in supporting writers in exile, as well as Victor E van Vriesland, president of Dutch PEN, who, in 1962, was elected president of PEN International.

Arthur Miller, president of PEN International (1966–69), writes in his autobiography about the poet Alexey Alexandrovich Surkov, a high-profile nomenklatura figure in the USSR.

*At last Surkov said flatly,
'Soviet writers want to join PEN'…
'I couldn't be happier', I said.
'We would welcome you in PEN.'
'We have one problem', Surkov said,
'but it can be resolved easily.'
'What is the problem?'
'The PEN Constitution…'*

Musine Kokalari

Musine Kokalari's first collection of poems *As My Old Mother Tells Me* is said to be the first collection to be published by an Albanian woman writer in Albania. She had two collections of short stories published in the early 1940s: *How Life Swayed* and *Around the Hearth*.

In 1943–44 she became one of the founding members of the Social Democratic Party and was closely associated with the party newspaper *Voice of Freedom*. Born into a wealthy and politically active family, her two brothers were owners of a printing company and both were executed by communist leaders in 1944.

In 1946 Kokalari was arrested and sentenced to 20 years in prison for being an 'enemy of the people'. Prior to her arrest she had sent a letter to the Allied Forces based in the Albanian capital of Tirana, calling for free elections and freedom of expression. At her trial, Kokalari made a statement, which has since become emblematic of the struggle for freedom in Albania:

'I don't need to be a communist to love my country. I love my country even though I am not a communist. I love its progress. You boast that you have won the war, and now you are the winner and want to extinguish those who you call political opponents. I think differently from you but I love my country. You are punishing me for my ideals!'

Kokalari was released in 1964, after being imprisoned for 18 years, and transferred to a labour camp where she worked as a labourer on construction sites. When Kokalari became ill, she was allowed to go to Tirana for treatment at a hospital. Subsequently, she was transferred to the Community Cleaning Department where she served for the rest of her days. Kokalari was never allowed to resume her writing.

Kokalari was among over 30 writers from Albania, France, Hungary, and Czechoslovakia to be considered to be PEN cases by the first meeting of the 'Committee of Three' in 1960. When PEN presented a letter calling for Kokalari's release, along with other prisoners, Albanian president Enver Hoxha is said to have retorted 'Is that bitch still alive?'

In 1993, Kokalari was posthumously declared a 'Martyr for Democracy' by the president of Albania.

← Musine Kokalari dressed in traditional Gjirokastran costume, date unknown.

↓ In 2017, the Albanian Post Office issued a postage stamp commemorating the centenary of Musine Kokalari's birth.

↑   In 1946, the poet Musine Kokalari was arrested in Albania and sentenced to 20 years in prison for being an 'enemy of the people'. She was among the first cases for whom the new WiPC campaigned in 1960. Her name appears in the first Case List, included in an appendix to the minutes of the 1960 PEN Congress in Rio de Janeiro.

Evolution of the Case List

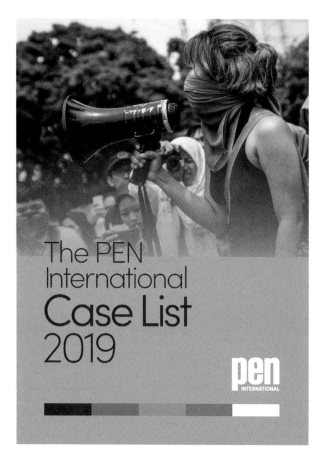

The PEN
International
Case List
2019

pen
INTERNATIONAL

↑   Cover of *Case List 2019*. To date the Case List is a key
document for research, a source for national and international
advocacy, and also a profound and painful reflection on the
continuing need for PEN's work in the world.

PEN's first four cases from the 1930s revealed the organisation's
unique position on freedom of expression. Since the beginning,
priority has always been given to the victim of repression: the writer.
This position underscores individuality and resists any attempt to
justify repression in the name of ideologies. The priority of PEN's
action is the person under detention. Over the years, PEN referred to
these writers as 'PEN cases', which also became the 'Case Lists'.

This understanding of international solidarity meant that writers in
prison and the PEN members campaigning for their release were
colleagues. Attention was given by PEN to both writers in prison and
their body of work, and, therefore, often to the translation of such
work. PEN's focus on the respect for an author's work means that
there is, and continues to be, a long list of translations of books
written by jailed writers such as Ángel Cuadra, Ken Saro-Wiwa, Yaşar
Kemal, Anna Politkovskaya, Mahvash Sabet, Liu Xiaobo, and Samar
Yazbek as an integral part of PEN action. PEN Centres around the
globe have also held countless readings, meetings with ambassadors,
street demonstrations, prison visits, trial observations, advocacy
missions, and other forms of campaigning that PEN developed.

Paul Tabori, Margaret Storm Jameson, and Victor E van Vriesland,
the 'Committee of Three', presented the first Case Lists to the Rio de
Janeiro PEN International Congress in 1960. Those very first lists
appeared as an appendix to the minutes of the Congress and had been
compiled by exiled writers. The minutes are testimony to this: the
seven names of imprisoned writers in Albania had been compiled by
'Arshi Pipa, imprisoned in '56, later escaped to West'. The 25 writers in
Czechoslovakian prisons were compiled by Ivan Jelínek, who was
living in exile in England. The 13 writers in Hungarian prisons were
listed by Paul Tabori, the nine imprisoned in Romania by 'Silviu
Craciunas, writer who left Romania recently'. The two writers in
prison in France were the exception, as they were proposed by French
PEN, who before the Rio Congress had already acted on behalf of
Henri Alleg and Mustafa Lasheraf, writers — the former French, the
latter Algerian — detained and tortured in 1957 for calling for Algerian
independence. French PEN had met with the French minister of
justice, and had published letters in *Le Monde* and other newspapers.

Until the mid-1980s, the Case Lists were published as an addendum to
the minutes of the Congresses, alongside resolutions and statements.
By the mid-1980s, they began to be printed as separate documents.
This change occurred because the lists became so long PEN needed a
more manageable document, as these were key internal documents the
PEN membership used in their global campaigns. At this time, Case
Lists were issued four times a year and later on this was changed to
twice a year. By the 1990s, the numbers of writers listed on the case list
had grown, often to over a thousand. The rise in numbers reflected
PEN's greater capacity, the fact that PEN was sharing information with
a greater number of NGOs who were covering freedom of expression,
as well as the growth in the number of PEN Centres contributing to
information and support. The internet also made research easier and
more extensive, and PEN was able to share the *PEN Case List* on its
website. The last print version was issued in 2015. Online versions
continue to be produced every year.

RIO EXECUTIVE MEETING.   APPENDIX TO MINUTES.p.8.

Names of Prisoners - Lists Circulated At The Congress Gave

Fuller Details About Many Of These

· Imprisoned Writers (still available
from Glebe House):

ALBANIAN WRITERS IN PRISON:

Peter Gjini (15 year sentence in 1946)
Etehem Haxhiademi (life imprisonment,1946)
Musine Kokalari (woman writer;20 year sentence,1946)
Kudret Kokoshi (life imprisonment,1944)
Donat Kurti (Franciscan monk; 20 year sentence,1945)
Mark Ndoja (10 year sentence,1955) (List compiled by Arshi
Kocho Tasi (life imprisonment,1945) Pipa,imprisoned to '56,
                                      later escaped to West.)
CZECHOSLOVAK WRITERS IN PRISON:

Dr.Oldrich Albert (20 year sentence announced Rude Pravo,1952)
Dr.Stanislav Gerounsky (20 years, announced Rude Pravo,1952)
Dr.Silvester Braito (15 years,announced Rude Pravo,1950)
Jan Dokulil (12 year sentence,1959)
Dr.Bedrich Fucik (14 years,announced Rude Pravo,1952)
Ladislav Jehlicka(14 years,announced Rude Pravo,1952)
Dr.Zdenek Kalista(15 years,announced Rude Pravo,1952)
Ladislav Karhan (18 years,announced Rude Pravo,1952)
Dr.V.Klima   (life sentence,announced Rude Pravo,1952)
Josef Kostohryz (life sentence,announced Rude Pravo,1952)
Frantisek Krelina(12 years,announced Rude Pravo,1952)
Josef Palivec (20 years,announced first in Rude Pravo in
               1959,but apparently sentenced in 1949)
Vaclav Prokupek (22 years,announced Rude Pravo,1952)
Vaclav Renc   (25 years,announced Rude Pravo,1952)
Dr.F.Silhan   (25 years,announced Rude Pravo,1950)
Vit Bohumil Tajovsky (20 years,announced Rude Pravo,1950)
Jan Josef Urban (14 years,announced Rude Pravo,1950)
Jan Zahradnicek (13 years,announced Rude Pravo,1952)
Dr.Stanislaw Jarolimek (20 years,announced Rude Pravo,1950)
Dr. Adolf Kajpr (12 years,announced Rude Pravo,1950)
Josef Marsalek   (15 years,announced Tribuna Ludu,(Poland)1952
Jan Anastaz Opasek(Benedictine Abbot; life imprisonment,
                      announced Rude Pravo,1950)
Dr.Miloslav Skacel (17 years,announced Rude Pravo,1952)

                                        · · · · · · · · · · · ·

↑   The first Case List of PEN International was included
as an appendix to the minutes of the 31st PEN International
Congress in Rio de Janeiro, 1960.

Wole Soyinka

In 1965, Wole Soyinka was arrested after he manned a radio station at gunpoint and broadcast a message denouncing electoral fraud in western Nigeria. By then, he had produced no fewer than 11 plays, several essays, and had published his novel *The Interpreters*. His detention was followed by international protests. Some of the poems Soyinka wrote in prison were smuggled out and published. Soyinka was finally freed on a judicial technicality.

When Nigeria was thrown into a civil war in 1966 after Colonel Odumegwu Ojukwu declared south-east Nigeria to be the independent Republic of Biafra — and after two military coups — Soyinka attempted to negotiate between the federal government and the Biafra separatists. He was arrested and accused of being on the side of the rebels. PEN International, under the presidency of Arthur Miller, and along with Amnesty International, observed the trial in Nigeria. Three years later, the civil war ended and Soyinka was released under an amnesty. His experiences as a prisoner were chronicled in his book *The Man Died: Prison Notes*. After his release, he left Nigeria for six years before returning — and then in 1983 went into exile again. In exile, he learned that *The Man Died: Prison Notes* had been banned in Nigeria.

↓   Wole Soyinka's experiences as a prisoner were chronicled in his book *The Man Died: Prison Notes*, published in 1972.

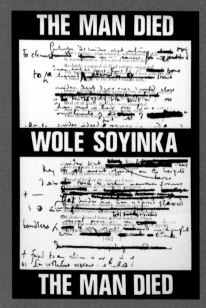

In 1986, Soyinka was the first African writer to be awarded the Nobel Prize in Literature. He returned to Nigeria once again and continued to write plays and essays; however, in 1994, he was yet again forced to flee Nigeria and go into exile. In 1997, he was charged *in absentia* with treason by General Sani Abacha's regime. These charges were lifted following Abacha's death in 1998.

Soyinka has continued to be active in PEN. Among many PEN events, he participated in a tribute to Anna Politkovskaya in Barcelona a few weeks after her assassination, he gave the Arthur Miller Lecture at the closing ceremony of the World Voices Festival in New York in 2011, and he was the keynote speaker at the 2012 PEN International Congress in Gyeongju, South Korea.

'Marilyn Monroe had nothing to do with it'

One of the stories that have been told by generations of PEN activists relates to the letter written by Arthur Miller, president of PEN International, to General Yakubu Gowon, who was heading the military government of Nigeria. The letter asked for the release of Wole Soyinka, who was facing execution. According to one of the many versions of the tale, in a meeting of the military junta, General Yakubu Gowon asked: 'Who is this Arthur Miller who dares to write to me asking for the liberation of Soyinka?' Someone answered that Miller was a famous playwright, a writer of international prestige, and the president of PEN. No doubt the junta would have shared their amazement that a writer dared to write to a president in this way. At this point, someone else chimed in, 'And this Miller is also the husband of Marilyn Monroe'. Soyinka was liberated immediately. The story is too good to be true, but it has been told and even published several times. When PEN America invited Wole Soyinka to give the Arthur Miller Lecture at the closing of the 2011 PEN World Voices Festival in New York, Soyinka himself addressed the rumour:

'I am, as many of you are aware, a compulsive mythologist. And nothing would have been more fulfilling than to stand here today and affirm a frankly delightful piece of mythology. It concerns the ancestor in whose name we are all gathered here today — that ancestor being of course Arthur Miller. It has not been easy to bring myself to debunk that mythology, especially as it links me also to one of the greatest works of pulchritude that the cinema has ever celebrated, Marilyn Monroe, whom I've never met in real life. Like any former prisoner I remain deeply appreciative of the efforts of the literary world, human rights organisations just as Amnesty International, etc., to obtain my liberty from the Nigerian military government during the Biafran war of secession

1966–69. Those who doubt that these efforts are of immense value to the physical and moral welfare of the prisoner, even if they do not immediately lead to his or her release, should take this testament of the prisoners themselves and of their immediate colleagues and relations a little more seriously. I could not receive any indication of these efforts through normal channels, while incarcerated, but as with most prisons news has a way of percolating even the stoutest walls. I was aware that the world of letters had not forgotten my existence and it mattered. Arthur Miller was at the forefront of agitators on my behalf and I was able to thank him in person, when we eventually met. However, and here comes the moment of deflation, I am afraid my release had nothing to do with him being then married to Marilyn Monroe. Since this anecdote kept cropping up, and still does, I became curious and checked the truth of it from impeccable sources, including from the man who signed both my detention and release orders. I'm afraid Marilyn Monroe had nothing to do with it. Now, if instead of signing petitions and writing letters Arthur Miller had dispatched Marilyn Monroe as his personal ambassador, I'm convinced that I would have been released much earlier. Since the PEN is mightier than the sword, and beauty is mightier than the PEN… Beauty would have shattered the generals' swords in no time. I wish that were also true. […] We shall shift temporarily away from the mythological realm to the factual, but we shall be back. Factual does not, of course, equate indisputable, so let who will dispute the following claim for which this platform, PEN International, is singularly appropriate — and deserving.'

↑   After spending close to two years in prison,
Wole Soyinka sits between two statues of gods
outside his house in Ibadan, Nigeria, in 1969.
At the time, Soyinka was working as a lecturer in
drama at Ibadan University and also writing plays.
While he was in prison, his plays were produced
to great acclaim in Accra, London, and New York.

WRITERS IN PRISON!

(ARGENTINA) Francisco Urondo. (BENGLADESH) S.G.M. Badruddin, Maswami, Salahuddin Mohammed. (BRAZIL) Renato Ferreira Nunes, Paulo da Costa Ramos, Enio Silveria. (CUBA) Andreas Cao Mendiguren, Emilio Adolpho Rivero Caro, Angel Cuadra Landrove, Ernesto De La Fe Perez. (CZECHOSLOVAKIA) Rudolph Battek, Jozef Belda, Milan Knizak, Hejdanek, Milan Huebl, Ladislav Kalina, Karel Kosik,[1] Karel Kyncl, Jiri Lederer, Jaroslav Meznik, Vladimir Nepras,[2] Milan Otanal, Ludek Pachman, Arnost Prazak, Jaroslav Sabata, Jaroslav Sedivy, Vladimir Skutina, Jan Tesar, Vlastimil Vavra(?), Premysl Vondra. (EGYPT) Sayyid Loufti, (GREECE) Basil Filias, Kostas Filinis, Yannis Kapsis, Dionysios Karageorgas, Kostas Koulofakos, Constantine Kyriazis,[3] Achilles Kytiazie,[3] Negrepontis, Stephen Nestor, Constantine Nikolopoulos,[3] G. Notatas, Alexios Papalexiou, V. Papajissis,[3] Harris Papamargaris, Stylianos Porrakis, Spyros Plaskovitis,[4] Jannis Ritsos, Jean Starakis, Tassos Vournas, P. Zannos, Alexandros Zografos. (HUNGARY) Rev. Sandor Somogyi. (INDONESIA) Abdual Mana Adinda, Tom Anwar, Rivai Apin, Arispranowo, Dahono, Go Bing Kwan, S. Hadi, Bandaharo Harahap, Juliarso, A. Jusuf, A. Karim, D.P., Naibaho, Nio Ham Djoe, Oei Hay Djoen(Samandjaja), Njoman S. Pendit, Pramoedya Anatatoer, Hasjim Rachman, Mrs. Rusijati, Bujung Saleh, Satyagraha, Mrs. Sugartis Siswadi, Djoni Hendra Sitompul, Sitor Situmorang, Djoko Sugito, Mrs. Lies Sukatno, Sjarief Sulaiman, Supijo, Suroto, Marion Tampubolon, Benni Tjung, Pramoedya Anata Tur, Wahjudi, Walujo. (MAURITIUS) Harve Masson. (MEXICO) José Revueltas. (PAKISTAN) Husain Naqi, Altaf Hussain Qureshi, Mjibur Rehman Shami. (PARAGUAY) Dr. Antonio Maidana. (PHILIPPINES) Hernando Abaya, Renato Constantino, Petronlio B. Davoy, Amando Dornila, Rolando Fadul, Dolores Stephens Feria, Rosalinda Galang, Teodosio Lansang, Luis Teodoro Jr, Teodoro Locsin. (RHODESIA) William Dzamanda Musarurwa. (SINGAPORE) Shamsuddin Tung Tao Chang, Ly Sing Ko, Lee Mau Seng, Mohammed Said bin Zahari. (SOUTH AFRICA) Rev. Cosmas Desmond, Peter Magubane. (SOUTH KOREA) Kim Chi-hah. (SOUTH VIETNAM) Chan Tin. (SPAIN) Gonzalo Arias Bonet,[5] José Maria Moreno Galvan, Luciano Rincon Vega, Carlos Rivera Urrutia. (SUDAN) Abdullahi Ali Ibrahim. (TAIWAN) Chang Tung, Chen Yu-hsi Chien Kuo-shu, Chou Chung-ping, T.M. Hsieh, Huang Yi-hsing, Li Ao, Li Chung-sun, Meng Hsiang-ko, Po Yang (Kuo Yi-tung), Shen Chien-chou, Yao Yun-lai, Young Kun-ning, Yu Chi, Albert Yuan, Rizal Yuyitung. (TURKEY) Ismail Besikci, Kemal Burkay, Turhan Dilligil, Mete Dural, Suleyman Ege, Abdullah Emre, Vahap Erdogdu, Cetin Altan, Selahattin Eyuboglu,[6] Nasih Nuri Ileri, Alpay Kabacali, Ilhan Selcuk, Abdullah Nefres, Altan Oeymen, Dogan Ozdugen, Osman Saffet, Zeynep Sagnak, Ilhami Soysal, Mumtaz Soysal, Mrs. Sergi Soysal, Ahmet Tumul, Erol Turegun, Yasar Ucar, Sabri Yilmaz.

(U.S.A.) Martin Sostre. (U.S.S.R.) Andrei Amalrik, Nikolai Braun, Vladimir Bukovsky, Vasilii Chernyshov, Vyacheslav Chornovil, Ivan Dzyuba, Aleksandr Ginzburg, Natalya Gorbanevskaya,[7] Bohdan Horyn, Svyatoslav Karavansky,[7] Annasoltan Kekilova, Mykhaylo Masyutko, Vladimir Maximov, Taras Migal, Valentin Moroz, Aleksandr Petrov, Oleksa Riznykiv, Anatolii Shevchuk, Stefania Shabatura, Ivan Sokulsky, Iryni Stasiv-Kalynets,[7] Vasil Stus, Yerhen Sverstyuk, Ivan Svitlychny, Anatolii Yakobson, Piort Yakir. (YUGOSLAVIA) Ante Bruno Busic, Adem Demaci (Albanian), Ante Glibota, Vlado Gotovac, Jozo Ivicevic-Bakulic, Zvonimir Komarica, Mihajlo Mihajlov, Vlatko Pavletic, Dr. Hrvoje Sosic, Dr. Franjo Tudjman.

[1] Released but undergoing interrogation. [2] Provisionally released. [3] Publisher. [4] Sentence suspended one year. [5] In exile. [6] Deceased. [7] In Psychiatric hospital.

THE CHARTER OF INTERNATIONAL P.E.N. ~ A WORLD ASSOCIATION OF WRITERS ~ AFFIRMS THAT "MEMBERS PLEDGE THEMSELVES TO OPPOSE ANY FORM OF SUPPRESSION OF FREEDOM OF EXPRESSION IN THE COUNTRY AND COMMUNITY TO WHICH THEY BELONG." THE ABOVE LIST HAS BEEN COMPILED BY AMERICAN P.E.N. FROM VARIOUS SOURCES. IT DOES NOT CLAIM IN ANY WAY TO BE DEFINITIVE. ANY SUGGESTIONS FOR UPDATING THIS LIST AND ANY SUPPORT FOR P.E.N. IN ITS WORK TO HELP WRITERS IN PRISON AND THEIR FAMILIES WILL BE GRATEFULLY RECEIVED BY

P.E.N. AMERICAN CENTER *
156 FIFTH AVENUE
NEW YORK CITY 10010

*A TAX EXEMPT ORGANIZATION

The Writers in Prison Committee during the Cold War

Paul Tabori, the leading force behind the 'Committee of Three' in charge of supporting writers in prison worldwide, died in 1974. After various attempts to appoint his successor, the English-American writer Michael Scammell, who had been the founder of the magazine *Index on Censorship*, was approached to take Tabori's place. Scammell has vivid memories of that moment:

> I was invited to a meeting of the Writers in Prison Committee at the London Congress that year and the only two people present were the International Secretary, Peter Elstob, and the Swedish writer Per Wästberg, who was the International PEN president. I looked around at the empty room and they said, 'We've invited you here because we want you to try to re-start the Writers in Prison Committee'. So I set to work to build the committee from scratch into a real, worldwide committee representing many centres. One result was that I became the absolute bête noire of the East European centres. [...] It was only after Perestroika that the Russians began sending a delegation to PEN Congresses. But there were a bunch of East European centres, which had survived from the pre-Cold War days when they had not been part of the Communist Bloc. Bulgaria had one, Romania had one, Hungary had one, East Germany had one — as a result there were both East and West German centres. There was also a Polish Centre and a Czech Centre. They all defended the Soviet Union and they usually spoke and acted as a bloc, so Russia was always a ghostly presence in the wings.

Scammell's reports to the assemblies of delegates at PEN Congresses created the context for PEN's growing commitment to writers in prison. According to Scammell: 'when South American military regimes came to power, in Brazil, Argentina, Chile in particular, and Peru to a certain extent, I certainly was as critical about their censorship and treatment of writers as I was on the Eastern Bloc regimes, and then we had the curious position where I was on the same side as the Hungarians, Bulgarians, and East Germans, because we all agreed that these dictatorships were responsible for hundreds of deaths and for putting writers in jail.'

← Poster by American PEN in the early 1970s listing names of imprisoned writers who were PEN cases in several countries and citing the PEN Charter as a reference irrespective of political ideologies: 'Members pledge themselves to oppose any form of suppression of freedom of expression in the country and community to which they belong'.

↓ Michael Scammell, founder of the magazine *Index on Censorship* and chair of the WiPC of PEN International from 1974 to 1986.

↑   Fall 1990. Left to right: Elizabeth
Paterson, administrative secretary
at PEN International (1968–97);
Joanne Leedom-Ackerman, president
of USA West PEN; Per Wästberg,
PEN International president (1979–86)
and interim president (1989–90);
Siobhan Dowd, director of the WiPC;
Bill Barazetti, International treasurer.

↓   The Swedish publisher Thomas
von Vegesack was chair of the WiPC of
PEN International from 1986 to 1994.

These actions coincided with PEN Centres giving persecuted writers
honorary membership of their Centres, a practice that also became a
central tool for advocacy that continues to this day. It is also a good way
to measure the loss of freedom of expression from year to year.

Scammell not only led to the creation of a more active, more incisive,
more professional WiPC, after 10 years he also established a network
of PEN Centres devoted to campaigning for their imprisoned
colleagues.

In 1986, over 600 writers from around the world participated to the
New York City 48th PEN International Congress, where Francis King
was elected as president of PEN and Michael Scammell's success in
transforming the WiPC was celebrated. There were elections in New
York, and Scammell was followed as chair of the WiPC by the
Swedish publisher Thomas von Vegesack. The WiPC's finances grew
stronger as PEN Centres made voluntary contributions to its work,
along with funders such as the Swedish International Development
Cooperation Agency. Progressively, more Centres became engaged in
advocacy. To be considered a member of the WiPC, a Centre first of
all had to form a committee in its own country, with a national chair
who would be the contact person for PEN International. Secondly, it
had to pay the additional membership fee, and thirdly it had to elect
at least two writers in prison as honorary members. This meant that
they were committed to lobbying for those cases, contacting their
families, lawyers, and supporters, and, where possible, drafting letters
to the writers in prison.

The PEN Emergency Fund

The idea of creating a special 'writers-in-need fund' emerged in the context of the WiPC. It began with the Dutch writer A den Doolaard. In 1971, he set up the PEN Emergency Fund, an international fund for writers in dire straits, based in the Netherlands. Also in 1971, Heinrich Böll was elected president of West German PEN and, the year after, he was elected president of PEN International. Böll received the Nobel Prize in Literature while being president of PEN and gave half of the award to the PEN Emergency Fund, and other donors followed. Since then, the fund has provided assistance to seriously persecuted writers and writers in exile in an emergency.

In the beginning, the financial transfers were akin to something out of a crime novel. In one example of this, Den Doolaard mailed one half of a playing card, which had been cut in two pieces, to a Czech author who was in trouble. The other half was then given to a courier who, in this case, was very popular in Czechoslovakia as a writer. When visiting Prague to see an editor, the courier also visited the colleague in need. When the two writers met and the two halves of the card fitted, each knew that this was the right person and the money could be safely handed over. Nowadays, the transfers take place by bank accounts.

The chair of the PEN Emergency Fund always gives a report on the fund at the yearly PEN Congress, and for many years it was the task of Henk Bernlef. For half a century, many writers throughout the world have received this aid. The reports are always secretive so the writer who was helped cannot be recognised. As Job Degenaar, chair of the fund since 2016, puts it: 'The concept of the fund is clear, effective and cheap. We don't have expensive buildings, we can decide very quickly and all the money we receive is used for the writers in need.'

↑ Heinrich Böll, president of PEN International 1971–72, received the Nobel Prize in Literature during his presidency. He remained committed to refugee writers. He is seen here welcoming Alexandr Solzhenitsyn to his exile in West Germany in 1974.

He escaped from extremists in Bangladesh

'I would like to express sincere thanks and gratitude to Margaret Atwood. Margaret has made me a partner today in her own accomplishment. I am delighted and humbled. This encouragement and inspiration will undoubtedly fortify me for the difficult journey ahead', said Tutul when receiving the 2016 PEN Pinter International Writer of Courage award. Margaret Atwood had chosen him to share the award, given by English PEN in a ceremony at the British Library. Since 2013, secular and freethinking writers and publishers had been the target of intimidation and violence in Bangladesh, eight of them had been murdered, and several more had suffered grave injuries.

Ahmedur Rashid Chowdhury (aka Tutul) was born in Sunamganj, Bangladesh, in 1973. In 2004, he established the publishing house Shuddhashar, which became famous for publishing young and free-thinking writers and to date has published more than a thousand books. On 31 October 2015, Tutul was attacked in his offices by Islamic fundamentalists and left critically injured. Since the attack, he has been living in Norway as one of the International Cities of Refuge Network's guest writers.

In his escape from Bangladesh, Tutul was supported by the PEN Emergency Fund.

Writing letters

'Kindness will save the world

'I am sending my heartfelt greetings, love and thanks to all dear friends who came together in Frankfurt Book Fair, and show solidarity with us. In my view, the best ways to keep hope and courage alive, grow the struggle and thereby solidarity with the resistance of oppressed communities and societies is art and literature. Accordingly, I extend a special thanks to everyone who put their efforts and hearts on the table for this end. Surely kindness will save the world. With my sincere regards,

Selahattin Demirtaş,
Edirne Prison'

↓   Letter writing at Zehra Doğan's exhibition at Tate Modern in May 2019.

In Cameroon, a prisoner is summoned after the sun goes down and is brought to the office of the prison director. He is asked to answer this question: 'Why do you organise an international campaign against me? I am only the director of this prison, why do you ask so many people to write letters to me?' The prisoner's answer is simple: 'It would be difficult for me to organise anything against you or ask anyone to write letters to you because we have never been introduced, I do not even know your name.' And then the director, annoyed, sent him back to the cell, but before the prisoner leaves, he gives him a basket full of letters: more than 200 letters. He reads a postcard: 'Cher Enoh, tenez bon!' (Dear Enoh, have courage!). And it's from Australia. Letters and postcards from Canada, from Belgium, Switzerland, Norway, Scotland, Mexico… The prisoner's name is Enoh Meyomesse. After his release, he wrote to PEN members with very warm words of thanks.

Since the creation of a PEN International committee in charge of supporting writers in prison in 1960, letters have been the main tool for PEN members to take care of their persecuted colleagues — letters to prisoners, their families, and lawyers. Advocacy letters are also sent to presidents, ambassadors, and the directors of prisons. For over 60 years, PEN Centres have organised gatherings where writers or students meet to write letters, which are later posted to prisons in Iran, China, Chile, Russia, Cameroon, and so on.

Since the very beginning, letter writing has worked both ways: letters enter and leave the prison. The letters from prisoners are often smuggled out by family members, lawyers, or PEN members after a visit. Very often, the letters from the prisoners are addressed to their fellow writers who are campaigning for their freedom. A good example of this is the letter from the Kurdish writer and leader Selahattin Demirtaş, which was read aloud to the participants at an event held at the Frankfurt Book Fair in 2019.

A letter from a Very Important Prisoner

Letter sent to the delegates meeting at the 81st PEN International Congress in Quebec, 2015.

Dear Delegates,
Dear Colleagues,

I won't keep you long, because what I have to say to you is short.

I would simply like to offer you my infinite gratitude for what you did for me, while I was in prison in Yaoundé, Cameroon.

I received hundreds of letters and postcards from you, which continued to rain down on me in prison, and even more now that I am no longer there.

The Prison Director found this greatly offensive, but, at the same time, his opinion of me immediately changed, as well as that of all the guards and all the other prisoners. Suddenly, I stopped being a criminal inmate who deserved his punishment, and instead became a V.I.P., not a 'Very Important Person', but in fact a '*Very Important Prisoner*', whose release was called for throughout the whole world.

What to say of the letters addressed to the Prime Minister of Cameroon and to the Minister of Justice, of which my lawyer brought me copies?

You're probably not aware, but, let me tell you that, thanks to them, the Cameroonian Government arranged for my release to avoid being unpopular internationally, because national opinion, they do not care about, but international opinion, on the other hand, scares them greatly.

Dear Delegates,
Dear Colleagues,

In securing my release, you have at the same time demonstrated to the Cameroonians that a writer was not the useless being they thought, but indeed rather a personality whose existence and above all, well-being, is cared about throughout the world.

Thank you again, and best wishes to all.

Enoh Meyomesse

I managed to avoid all of this, especially when PEN started to write letters.

The prison administration started to realise that this "old man", as they called me, was an intellectual

and he has support abroad. Everything changed.

↑   After his release from prison, Enoh Meyomesse was welcomed by the Writers-in-Exile Programme of German PEN.

Yannis Ritsos

Yannis Ritsos was born in May 1909 in Monemvasia, Greece. In 1934, his first collection of poems entitled *Tractor* was published, which was the same year he joined the Communist Party of Greece. Two years later, in 1936, his second collection of poems, *O Epitaphios*, was published followed by *The Song of My Sister* (1937) and *Symphony of Spring* (1938). His early writing has been described as 'militant'. Copies of *O Epitaphios* were symbolically burned in front of the Acropolis under the fascist Metaxas government. Ritsos joined the anti-fascist resistance during the Greek Civil War and spent four years in detention camps during which time he continued to write poetry including the collections *Romiosyni*, published in 1947, and *The Moonlight-Sonata*, published in 1956.

Under the military junta, which ruled Greece from 1967 to 1974, he was successively interned on the Greek islands of Yaros and Leros, before being moved to house arrest in Samos. Despite being banned from publishing his work until 1972, he continued to write and paint. He died in Athens on 11 November 1990. Over his lifetime, Ritsos published 117 collections of poetry, novels and plays. He is said to be Greece's most widely translated poet. He was nominated for the Nobel Prize in Literature nine times in his career and in 1977 was awarded the Lenin Prize for Peace.

To mark the celebration of the 75th anniversary of PEN International in 1996, an anthology of texts by imprisoned writers was published with the title *This Prison Where I Live*. The work was compiled by the Irish writer Siobhan Dowd, who had been a researcher for the WiPC in London and later director of the Freedom to Write programme of PEN America in New York. The book describes the sequence of events in a prison: arrival, crossing the threshold, entrance into the cell, closing of the cell door, conditions of imprisonment, relationships with fellow inmates, torture, and, after months or years, the experience of leaving the prison behind. Texts included, among others: 'The Cell Door Closes' by Arthur Koestler; 'First Cell, First Love' by Alexandr Solzhenitsyn; 'The Eye' by Jacobo Timerman; 'You Left Me My Lips' by Osip Mandelstam; 'Writing on Toilet Paper' by Ngũgĩ wa Thiong'o; 'The Day Your Letter Comes' by Ángel Cuadra; and 'Ruth vs. the Torturer' by Alicia Partnoy. PEN Centres around the world translated the book into many languages such as English, French, German, Spanish, and Catalan, to name a few. 'Broadening' was the fragment chosen for Yannis Ritsos:

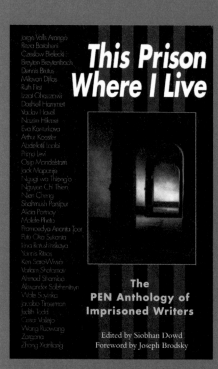

We were to stay here, who knows how long.
Little by little we lost track of time, of distinctions — months, weeks,
days, hours. It was fine that way. Below, way down,
there were oleanders; higher up, the cypress trees; above that, stones.
Flocks of birds went by; their shadows darkened the earth.
That's the way it happened in my day too, the old man said. The iron bars
were there in the windows before they were installed, even
if they weren't visible. Now
from seeing them so much, I think they're not there — I don't see them.
Do you see them? Then they called them guards. They opened the door,
pushed in two handcarts full of watermelons. The Old man spoke again:
Hell, no matter how much your eyes clear up, you don't see a thing.
You see the big nothing, as they say: whitewash, sun, wind, salt.
You go inside the house: no stool, no bed; you sit on the ground.
Small ants amble through your hair, your clothes, into your mouth.

↑   The poetry of Yannis Ritsos is in deep communion
with the earth and the sea of Greece, as we can see in this
photograph of the poet. It has been written that Ritsos
saw nature through a painter's eye. He painted stones
with figures taken from his own poetry as well as from the
Trojan War and other Greek myths.

Day of the Imprisoned Writer

↑↑   Jordi Sarsanedas, president of Catalan PEN, in a cage in the Rambla of Barcelona on the Day of the Imprisoned Writer in 2000.

↑   Day of the Imprisoned Writer in Dharamsala, where the Tibetan institutions in exile are based, in the Indian state of Himachal Pradesh. Here Tibetan PEN members, as well as speaking out for writers from Sri Lanka, Egypt, Turkey, Mexico, and Uganda, call for the freedom of five Tibetan writers: Yeshi Choedon, arrested in Lhasa 2008; Lobsang Jamyang, arrested in 2015; Kunchok Tsephel, in 2008; Pema Gyatso, and Tashi Wangchuk, in 2018. Close to 300 people attended the event. Nyima Tso, general secretary of Tibetan Writers Abroad, is addressing them.

In the 1970s, we begin to see the first references to what was to become the annual Day of the Imprisoned Writer, a key yearly campaign date for all PEN members. Initially, it was an idea proposed in the late 1960s by the then PEN president, Arthur Miller, who had suggested an 'Annual Day of World-Wide Demonstration for Freedom of Writers' but he had not been able to get the proposal through the Congress despite several attempts, as the initiative required a majority vote of two-thirds for it to be implemented. It is likely that those PEN members who blocked or abstained from the vote were from authoritarian states and feared the repercussions from being associated with such an event. Nevertheless, by the end of the 1970s, Centres were starting to organise their own annual days in October, marking the day PEN was founded. The present date is the 15 November and is linked to the founding of the PEN Emergency Fund.

The celebration of the Day of the Imprisoned Writer grew year by year and became in the twenty-first century a worldwide network of simultaneous events. In 2019, it was celebrated with an exceptional series of events worldwide. Among many others, American PEN in New York and Washington, DC, expressed support for the Ukrainian journalist Stanislav Aseyev with readings and rallies. PEN Bangladesh held a panel event during the Dhaka Literature Festival where panellists discussed hate speech and also raised their voices in solidarity for the five PEN main cases for the day, Lydia Cacho (Mexico), Stella Nyanzi (Uganda), Shakthika Sathkumara (Sri Lanka), Nedim Türfent (Turkey), and Galal El-Behairy (Egypt). Bosnian PEN organised a literary event during which their members read poetry in solidarity with imprisoned writers. Catalan PEN inaugurated an exhibition of 15 years of artworks related to the Day of the Imprisoned Writer and awarded the Moroccan journalist Ali Lmrabet the 'Free Voice' award. PEN Guinea put out a short statement on the worrying situation for freedom of expression in the country and held a press conference, receiving lots of media attention as a result. German PEN's Hermann Kesten Award was granted to Philippe Lançon, a journalist working for *Charlie Hebdo*, who was wounded in the terrorist attack perpetrated against the satirical publication in 2015. Hong Kong PEN had planned to do a film screening of *Call Me Kuchu* together with post-screening discussion; however, due to the repression in Hong Kong they had to cancel. PEN Netherlands organised a 'Night of the Imprisoned Writer' with interventions by the Syrian poet and journalist Faraj Bayrakdar about his time in and out of prison while Hamide Dogan, the Dutch translator of Ahmet Altan, read parts of the latter's memoir *I Will Never See the World Again*. PEN Nigeria put together a press statement and very successful social media campaign condemning the persecution and intimidation of Nigerian writers, including the publisher Omoyele Sowore, the blogger Dadiyata and the journalists Jones Abiri, Mary Ekere, Agba Jalingo, Stephen Kefas, and Kofi Bartels who were arrested in the course of carrying out their work. Romania PEN hosted a debate about the novelist Aslı Erdoğan from Turkey, recently translated into Romanian. San Miguel Allende PEN took action on behalf of Stella Nyanzi. Swiss

German PEN and Swiss Romand PEN invited the Chinese writer and dissident Liao Yiwu to take part in events in Basel, Zurich, Bern, and Geneva. Sydney PEN hosted a popular event with broadcaster Quentin Dempster and Jennifer Robinson, legal counsel for Julian Assange and WikiLeaks. PEN Tibetan Writers Abroad held a literary and freedom of expression event with an audience of more than 280 academics, teachers, college students, writers, journalists, and PEN members. Ukrainian PEN focused its campaign on the case of Stanislav Aseyev with an event highlighting all Ukrainian journalists imprisoned in Crimea and in occupied Donetsk such as Mykola Semena, Oleh Halaziuk, Nariman Memedeminov, Remzi Bekirov, Osman Arifmemetov, Rustem

→

Poster by PEN South Africa announcing a reading of imprisoned artists in solidarity with Dawit Isaak (Eritrea), Miroslava Breach Velducea (Mexico), Wael Abbas (Egypt), Oleg Sentsov (Ukraine), and Shahidul Alam (Bangladesh) on the 2018 Day of the Imprisoned Writer.

15 NOVEMBER 2018 • 17:30 • HIDDINGH HALL, UCT

PEN SOUTH AFRICA & THE INSTITUTE FOR CREATIVE ARTS PRESENT

DAY OF THE IMPRISONED WRITER

READINGS FOR JAILED ARTISTS AROUND THE WORLD

MASTER OF CEREMONIES
Khanya Mncwabe, PEN SA

ADDRESS & UPDATES ON 2017 CASES
Nadia Davids, PRESIDENT OF PEN SA
on Mother Mushroom, VIETNAM, Dareen Tatour, ISRAEL &
Ramon Esono Ebale, EQUATORIAL GUINEA

PRESENTATIONS
Rustum Kozain on Dawit Isaak, ERITREA
Desiree Lewis on Wael Abbas, EGYPT
Yewande Omotoso on Miroslava Breach Velducea, MEXICO
Wamuwi Mbao on Oleg Sentsov, UKRAINE
Nick Mulgrew on Shahidul Alam, BANGLADESH

PEN
SOUTH AFRICA

FREE
WRITING

institute for
creative arts

15. studeni 2011.
MEĐUNARODNI DAN PISACA U ZATVORIMA

TRIBINA HRVATSKOG P.E.N. CENTRA,
UTORAK, 15. STUDENOG 2011., 20.00 SATI,
U PROSTORIJAMA KNJIŽNICE I ČITAONICE
BOGDANA OGRIZOVIĆA, PRERADOVIĆEVA 5.
SUDJELUJU: TOMICA BAJSIĆ, BORIS BECK, ŽARKO PUHOVSKI.

"Najpodmukliji od strahova je onaj koji se maskira u zdravi razum ili mudrost, pa osuđuje kao glupa, brzopleta, nevažna i bezvrijedna, čak i najmanja, svakodnevna djela hrabrosti koja pomažu očuvati samopoštovanje i dostojanstvo čovjeka." AUNG SAN SUU KYI, BURMA.

劉曉波

LIU XIAOBO
Miš u zatvoru

Mali se miš provukao kroz rešetke
i nervozno hoda uz rub prozorskog okna.
Ogoljeli zidovi ostaju iza njega,
a tako i komarci otežali od krvi.
Uspio je privući srebrno svjetlo neba
i činilo se kao da leti.
Takva je vrsta ljepote rijetka.
Noćas, miš je pristao gospodin.
Ne jede, ne pije, niti brblja u prazno.
Širom je otvorio oči poput izdajnika
kada odlazi tragom mjesečine.

Liu Xiaobo, dobitnik NobeLove nagrade za mir 2010, zbog
"svoje neiscrpne i nenasilne borbe za osnovna ljudska prava
u Kini," jedan je od 40 kineskih pjesnika i pisaca još
uvijek u zatvoru, osuđen zbog "anti-državne subverzije."

PEN INTERNATIONAL
Day of the Imprisoned Writer
2011.

hrvatski p.e.n. centar
croatian p.e.n. centre
founded 1927

1960: MUSINE KOKALARI
1961: HENRI ALLEG
1962: MOCHTAR LUBIS
1963: JOSEF BRODSKY
1964: WOLFGANG HARICH
1965: WOLE SOYINKA
1966: ANDREI SINYAVSKY
       YULI DANIEL
1967: ANGEL CUADRA
1968: RAJAT NEOGY
1969: YANNIS RITSOS
1970: JOSE REVUELTAS
1971: NGUYEN CHI THIEN
1972: XOSE LUIS MENDEZ
1973: NIEN CHENG
1974: SHAHRNUSH PARSIPUR
1975: BREYTEN BREYTENBACH
1976: KIM CHI-HA
1977: ALICIA PARTNOY
1978: GEORGI MARKOV
1979: VACLAV HAVEL
1980: ALAÍDE FOPPA
1981: NAWAL EL SAADAWI
1982: NGUGI WA THIONG'O
1983: MANSUR RAJIH
1984: MARTHA KUMSA
1985: IRINA RATUSHINSKAYA
1986: ADAM MICHNIK
1987: JACK MAPANJE
1988: FARAJ BAYRAKDAR
1989: SALMAN RUSHDIE
1990: AUNG SAN SUU KYI
1991: RAGIP ZARAKOLU
1992: PRAMOEDYA ANANTA TOER
1993: TAHAR DJAOUT
1994: MARÍA ELENA CRUZ VARELA
1995: KEN SARO-WIWA
1996: TASLIMA NASRIN
1997: FARAJ SARKOOHI
1998: PIUS NJAWE
1999: MAMADALI MAKHMUDOV
2000: YEHUDE SIMON MUNARO
2001: SIHEM BENSEDRINE
2002: DAWIT ISAAK
2003: THÍCH HUYEN QUANG
2004: ALI LMRABET
2005: LYDIA CACHO
2006: ANNA POLITKOVSKAYA
2007: HRANT DINK
2008: SAYED PARVEZ KAMBAKHSH
2009: LIU XIAOBO

Sheikhaliev, and Ruslan Suleimanov. Turkish PEN held a very well-attended conference in Istanbul in association with the Turkish Writers' Union, the Journalists' Association of Turkey, and the Turkish Publishers' Association and issued a statement calling for the freeing of Nedim Türfent along with the more than 120 other writers and journalists languishing in prison in Turkey. Vietnamese PEN in Exile organised a successful programme honouring the poet Vũ Hoàng Chương, president of PEN Vietnam, who died in 1976 only five days after being released from prison, having refused to write poems to serve political objectives.

Also on 15 November 2019, Czech PEN continued to commemorate the International Day of the Imprisoned Writer by annually publishing a book written by an author unable to publish freely — that year a book of short stories written by the Afghani prose writer Muhammad Ásef Soltanzáde. PEN International and English PEN hosted a panel discussion at the Frontline Club in London, with Oleg Sentsov, two months after his liberation from Russian prison, in conversation with Natalia Kaliada, from Belarus Free Theatre. The sold-out event included Oleg Sentsov signing copies of his latest book for every member of the audience.

← Celebration of the 50th anniversary of the WiPC: poster made by Croatian PEN for the Day of the Imprisoned Writer, with the names of 50 writers in prison. It honoured one writer for each year since the committee's founding in 1960. The main case in 2009 was that of the Chinese dissident Liu Xiaobo.

↓ Ukrainian PEN campaigned on the Day of the Imprisoned Writer in 2019 for the liberation of Stanislav Aseyev. Left is Oleksandra Matviychuk, chairwoman of the Centre for Civil Liberties of Ukraine, and right is Tetiana Teren, Executive Director of PEN Ukraine.

Day of the Imprisoned Writer artworks

PEN International produced the report *Antiterrorism, Writers and Freedom of Expression* in the wake of the 'War on Terror' after 9/11 and the use of anti-terror laws to repress journalists such as Anna Politkovskaya in Russia and Fikret Başkaya in Turkey, and the suppression of newspapers and journals such as the closing of the Basque newspaper *Egunkaria* in Spain. The Catalan artist Antoni Tàpies produced the painting *Llibertat* for the cover of the report as well as the posters for the Day of the Imprisoned Writer 2003. Since then, Catalan artists have been producing specific works for the Day of the Imprisoned Writer.

← Antoni Tàpies, *Llibertat*, Day of the Imprisoned Writer 2003.

→ Narcís Comadira, Day of the Imprisoned Writer 2010.

← Frederic Amat,
Day of the Imprisoned Writer 2004.
Poster designed by cla se.

↙ Joan Fontcuberta, *Deletrix*,
Day of the Imprisoned Writer 2011.
Poster designed by cla se.

↓ Eulàlia Valldosera,
Day of the Imprisoned Writer 2009.
Poster designed by cla se.

→ Jaume Plensa,
Day of the Imprisoned Writer 2008.
Poster designed by cla se.

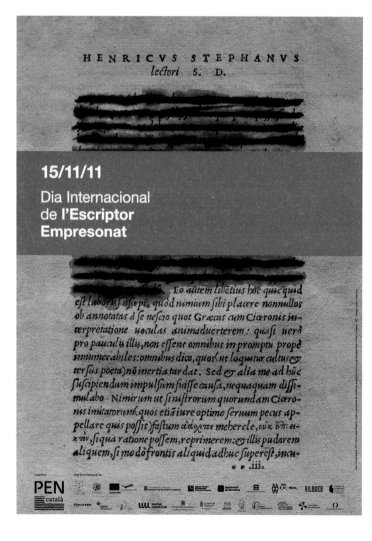

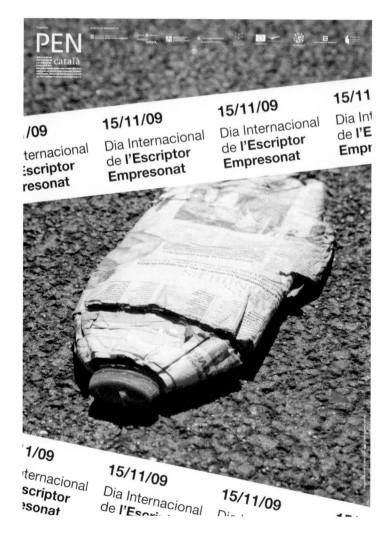

15.11.18
Dia Internacional
de
l'Escriptor Perseguit

Obra: Francesc Torres

Organitza: Amb la col·laboració de:

PEN
català

 Generalitat de Catalunya Diputació Barcelona Ajuntament de Barcelona Ajuntament de Lleida Consorci de Catalunya Institució de les Lletres Catalanes pen

  Ajuntament d'Alaró   Institut d'Estudis Baleàrics LiteRariA GENERALITAT VALENCIANA   CCCC Centre del Carme Cultura Contemporània FULL ASIL.CAT

←   Francesc Torres,
Day of the Imprisoned Writer 2018.
Poster designed by cla se.

↑   Francesc Abad,
Day of the Imprisoned Writer 2015.
Poster designed by cla se.

↗   Mar Arza,
Day of the Imprisoned Writer 2017.
Poster designed by cla se.

→   Mireia Sallarès,
Day of the Imprisoned Writer 2019.
Poster designed by cla se.

PEN missions to Turkey

↑   The photograph appears to show a group of writers and publishers standing in a field of snow. However, it is what we cannot see in the photograph that makes it significant — armed police and soldiers with their weapons ready. At the very moment the group stood together to give their PEN statement in front of Silivri Prison, they were suddenly surrounded by armed police and soldiers. Only after a tense negotiation was the group allowed to take a photograph, although they were not allowed to use the prison as a backdrop. In January 2017, PEN organised the largest mission ever to Turkey. There were participants from Lebanon, Estonia, Serbia, Sweden, Norway, Germany, USA, Canada, Mexico, Basque Country, and Catalonia as well as Kurdish and Turkish colleagues.

In 1980, the number of cases included in the *PEN Case List* consisted of 70 writers. Within four years, it had risen to over 470. A large number of these were writers who had been victims of the mass disappearances in the Americas: over 150 writers were listed as disappeared in Argentina, for example. Other countries represented heavily in the *PEN List* were Iran, China, Libya, and Syria. Even at that time, Turkey was cited as the country holding more writers in prison than any other, and this continues to be the case in 2021.

In 1985, PEN International conducted its first fact-finding trip to Turkey followed by a mission in 1986 led by Harold Pinter who, after conversations with witnesses on life in Turkish prisons, had started to write his play about torture, *One for the Road*. Pinter agreed to go on the mission with Arthur Miller, who had been president of PEN

International in the late 1960s, as both of them had continued to be very active in PEN. It was Orhan Pamuk, a member of PEN Turkey, who welcomed them at Istanbul airport and acted as their guide and translator.

PEN's commitment to writers imprisoned in Turkey has continued throughout the years, in collaboration with Turkish and international freedom of expression organisations. PEN members have attended trials in Turkey and actively supported their Turkish colleagues. A mission to Turkey led by Joanne Leedom-Ackerman, chair of the WiPC from 1994 to 1997, as part of a larger delegation, found her thrust into the limelight speaking in support of writers on trial through a megaphone on a Turkish university campus.

As the situation in Turkey deteriorated under a still more repressive government, PEN's campaigns increased. These included reports, from 2014 and 2016, on the aftermath of the 2013 Gezi demonstrations. Also, a high-level mission in 2013, led by the president of PEN International John Ralston Saul and members of the PEN International Board, PEN Centres, and PEN Turkey, met with the then president Abdullah Gül and other officials. PEN members constantly maintained a presence at the many trials against writers as well as participating in joint actions with PEN Centres and fellow freedom of expression organisations in Turkey and internationally.

The reaction of President Recep Tayyip Erdoğan's government to the attempted coup in July 2016 led to greater deterioration in both human and civil rights in Turkey. At the Frankfurt Book Fair 2016, Turkish writers and publishers, who were feeling the weight of isolation and deep concern about impunity in their country, asked PEN to organise a visit to Turkey. Three months later, in January 2017, the largest PEN

↑   Joanne Leedom-Ackerman, chair of PEN International's Writers in Prison Committee, participating at the inaugural 'Gathering in Istanbul' in 1997. Behind her, among other PEN delegates, is Aleksandr 'Sasha' Tkachenko, general secretary of PEN Russia. This was a mission of 21 writers from around the world and more than one thousand Turkish writers.

↓   The first PEN mission to Turkey took place in 1985. Here Arthur Miller from American PEN and Harold Pinter from English PEN are welcomed at the airport by a young writer and member of PEN Turkey named Orhan Pamuk who would act as their translator during the mission.

↑   When she was elected International Secretary at the 70th PEN International Congress in Tromsø in 2004, Joanne Leedom-Ackerman continued PEN's commitment for freedoms in Turkey, including the linguistic rights of the Kurds. Pictured here are participants in the 2005 PEN International seminar on cultural diversity in Amed/Diyarbakır (see page 216). First and second from right, Jane Spender, programme director at PEN 1997–2009 and editor of *PEN International* magazine, and Joanne Leedom-Ackerman. First and second from left: Tove Skutnabb-Kangas, member of the Scientific Council of the Universal Declaration of Linguistic Rights; Zerdeşt Haco, president of Kurdish PEN.

↘   Per Wästberg, president of PEN International 1979–86 and chair of the Nobel Prize in Literature, at the closing ceremony of the mission to Istanbul, January 2017.

International high-level mission in its history visited Ankara and Istanbul. The mission was led by PEN International president Jennifer Clement, president emeritus and chairman of the Nobel Prize in Literature committee Per Wästberg, president emeritus John Ralston Saul, and vice-president Eugene Schoulgin. Other participants included the Turkish writers Burhan Sönmez and Zülfü Livaneli, the German writer Peter Schneider, the publishers Eva Bonnier and Ronald Blunden, the PEN executive director Carles Torner, and the PEN Centre presidents Iman Humaydan (Lebanon), William Nygaard (Norway), Vida Ognjenović (Serbia), and Urtzi Urrutikoetxea (Basque PEN). In their week-long visit, the mission met with writers, journalists, human rights defenders, civils society actors, as well as the minister of culture Nabi Avcı, the leader of the Republican People's Party Kemal Kılıçdaroğlu, the full leadership of the pro-minority People's Democratic Party (HDP), and political figures from across Turkey's political landscape. The delegation also visited the offices of Turkish newspapers that had faced the most severe clampdowns: *Cumhuriyet*, *BirGün Gazetesi*, *Agos*, *Evrensel*, and *Özgürlükçü Demokrasi*.

❝ *I am elated to be here among you who have witnessed a frightening erosion of human rights in Turkey. […] Imagination, the ability to find out how others live or how they would want to live, is the basis of literature. Thus literature is a unique means of crossing frontiers of time and space, of getting us to realise that the tears and laughter of other peoples far away are just as real as our own. Literature should not be judged as a mirror or a protocol of what is happening in society. Literature is no branch of sociology. The immediate usefulness of creative writers is uncertain. Art does not abolish tyrannies. Still García Lorca's work remains while Franco is gone. Solzhenitsyn's works stand as a beacon for the 20th century; Gulag is closed, his witness remains.* ❞

Arthur Miller

Dear Yasar;

Your current crisis reminds me of the pleasurable hours in your home when with Harold Pinter I learned so much about Turkey from your sharp yet tolerant observations. And earlier in our meetings in Khirgizia, when with my wife Ingeborg Morath, along with writers from so many places on the earth we experienced the incredible hour when Gorbachev first seemed to be opening up Russia to the world. Do you recall our cautious hopefulness that perhaps the road ahead might be climbing toward a new vista of freedom, not only for Russians but the world? At last the end of the waste of human energy and talent and creativity that was the cold war!

Now, as I understand it, you have a judicial sentence hanging over your head should you ever utter another word in defense of your own people. Knowing your love of Turkey and the Turkish people as well as the Kurds, you must be stunned by this action.

In this age, when we send our thoughts anywhere at the touch of a button, you are forbidden, on pain of imprisonment, of letting certain thoughts past your lips. What a painful absurdity! And what power is coiled in this evil seed of suppression that it can be destroyed, so it would seem, in one country only to rise on the wind to sprout again in another! If it were not so serious it would be a theme for a comedy, a farce, in fact. But of course farce is not at all what this is for you and for human freedom.

Yasar, dear friend, there are people everywhere in the world who know you through your books and their life-affirming humanity, people who are with you in spirit now. I am sure they look upon this repression with incredulity if not anger and disgust, and salute you with the greatest respect.

Your friend,
Arthur Miller

↑   When she participated in the 1997 mission to Turkey, Joanne Leedom-Ackerman
carried a letter from Arthur Miller to the Kurdish writer Yaşar Kemal, whom he had met
12 years before in his own mission to Turkey together with Harold Pinter.

The Salman Rushdie affair

↑ Extreme conservative Muslims burning copies of Salman Rushdie's novel *The Satanic Verses* in front of Bradford City Hall on 14 January 1989.

← Ayatollah Khomeini, first supreme leader of Iran, who issued the fatwa of death against Rushdie on 14 February 1989.

The year 1989 was a crucial one for PEN International. To begin with, the fall of the Berlin Wall opened the path to the refounding of PEN Centres in Russia and all Eastern European countries. The massacre in Tiananmen Square ended all hope of economic and human rights reform in China and this, after a few years, led to the creation of the Independent Chinese PEN Centre. But before these events, on 14 February, the Ayatollah Khomeini issued a fatwa ordering Muslims to execute Salman Rushdie. The first supreme leader of Iran condemned not only the author of *The Satanic Verses* but also anyone else involved in the book.

Published in 1988, the novel had led to outcry among extreme conservative Muslims and within months had been banned in many countries around the globe including India, Bangladesh, Sudan, and South Africa. In January 1989, members of the British Muslim community staged a public burning of the book, and the fatwa of death came one month later. Rushdie went into hiding where he was to remain until the fatwa was lifted in 1998. The international response against the death threat was instantaneous. Within days, a worldwide statement against the fatwa was published with over a thousand writers' signatures. PEN International and English PEN joined other free expression organisations to form the International Committee for the Defence of Salman Rushdie and his Publishers, a high-level campaign that engaged both public advocacy and behind-the-scenes diplomacy to fight for the lifting of the threat.

Religious defamation and blasphemy became recurring themes for PEN from then on as extremists from all religions took action against writers who challenged their beliefs. Hitoshi Igarashi, the Japanese translator of *The Satanic Verses*, was killed on 11 July 1991 and mourned by the whole PEN community.

Canadian PEN had a major role in breaking Salman Rushdie's isolation in the UK by inviting him to appear, without any prior announcement, at a benefit of Canadian PEN in Toronto in 1992. This is a deeply memorable moment in PEN history. The following year, Rushdie was welcomed by Ronald Harwood, who had just been elected president of PEN International, to the PEN International Congress in Santiago de Compostela. At the unexpected appearance, Rushdie told the PEN delegates: 'Both people who attack me and who defend me are often mistaken: they see my words as something exceptional, and they are not. There are many other writers suffering the same kind of persecution and, every time, it is an unequal fight where you have on one side bullets and words on the other side.'

In October 1993, less than a month after Rushdie's appearance at the Congress, William Nygaard, the Norwegian publisher of *The Satanic Verses*, was shot outside his home in Oslo and left for dead. Nygaard survived and became a symbol of PEN's unwavering commitment to the freedom to publish. Nygaard was elected president of Norwegian PEN and, from 2014 to 2019, he played an essential role in PEN International campaigns and missions (most notably to Turkey) as well as advocating for PEN Centres in Afghanistan and Ethiopia, and supporting Eritrean PEN in Exile.

Rushdie came out of hiding in 1998 and settled in New York, where he remained a committed member of PEN. He became president of American PEN in 2004 and was the keynote speaker that year at the WiPC Conference in Barcelona. Rushdie was the founder, together with Esther Allen and Mike Roberts, of PEN World Voices Festival in New York.

↑   Appearance of Salman Rushdie at the 60th PEN International Congress in Santiago de Compostela in September 1993. From left to right: György Konrád, outgoing president of PEN International; Salman Rushdie; Ronald Harwood, incoming president of PEN International.

↓   William Nygaard, president of Norwegian PEN, who was shot for publishing the Norwegian translation of *The Satanic Verses*, at the PEN International Congress in Quebec in 2015. Here he stands with the leaders of PEN Ethiopia who were being persecuted back home.

Code Name *Sally*

Code Name Sally is a short documentary by Ari and Sturla Gunnarsson that celebrates the 25th anniversary of Canadian PEN's finest hour. In the autumn of 1992, Salman Rushdie was in deep hiding somewhere in England, condemned to death, when in Toronto a small group of Canadian PEN leaders launched an audacious secret mission to help him regain his freedom. There were so many things to consider: Was this the best way to break Rusdhie's complete isolation in England? Would the English police allow Rushdie to travel? What about security? How would the Canadian authorities react? What could be done if Air Canada refused to carry him? *Code Name Sally* details each move made by Louise Dennys, then president of Canadian PEN, and other PEN members including Marian Botsford Fraser, Ric Young, John Ralston Saul, and Adrienne Clarkson, to bring Rushdie out of the shadows in complete secrecy.

In the documentary, Rushdie recalls how he emerged from hiding to attend a Canadian PEN benefit in Toronto and how there, on stage, Ontario's premier, Bob Rae, became the first head of government to welcome Rushdie in a public forum anywhere in the world — and he did so with what is now a famous kiss! Rushdie also recounts how he was brought to the Houses of Parliament in Ottawa and met Canada's foreign affairs minister Barbara McDougall. Rushdie says: 'In the beginning of the meeting it was made clear to me that this meeting "didn't happen". By the end of the meeting it was clear that she was willing to go on the record.' McDougall took Rushdie by the arm and

↑   The premier of Ontario, Bob Rae, was the first head of government to welcome Rushdie at a public forum.

walked down the corridor, knowing full well that she was thus forcing the Canadian government to commit to publicly supporting Salman Rushdie, and, in this way, the silence was broken. Rushdie, on camera, says: 'People, including politicians, discovered their ethical sense.'

Code Name Sally is a documentary based on the memories of one of its directors, Sturla Gunnarsson, who participated in the 1992 event. Gunnarsson recalls:

> *I was at the PEN benefit twenty-five years ago and still remember what an electric, communal moment it was when Rushdie emerged from deep hiding to appear, unexpectedly, on the Winter Garden stage. There was this powerful sense of community and of moral clarity, a feeling I've associated with Canadian PEN ever since. What I didn't know at the time was what a compelling behind-the-scenes drama bringing Rushdie to Canada had been. Nor did I realise, until much later, that this was the seminal moment in his journey from fatwa to freedom. [...] To me this is a profoundly Canadian story about what a small group of people animated by a righteous ideal are capable of achieving. A modest little film with a big theme.*

↑   The autumn of 1992, at a Canadian PEN benefit, saw the first public appearance of Salman Rushdie after the fatwa of death was pronounced in February 1989. He was welcomed on stage by Margaret Atwood.

Louise Dennys   — *Salman had said to me, early early on: I don't want to be there just for me, I don't want to be on stage alone.*

Salman Rushdie   — *It was putting myself back in the environment I felt I belonged to. To be able to speak as a writer amongst writers. I thought it was the right thing to do.*

Marian Botsford Fraser   — *That's when we had the idea of really not making him be alone on stage, and we developed the plan to fill the stage with writers, filmmakers and musicians. We filled the stage with people before we asked him to step on that stage.*

Salman Rushdie   — *This was going to be a theatrical moment. I was kind of looking forward to it.*

Marian Botsford Fraser   — *And then Margaret Atwood came up to the podium, and I remember looking over at her and… She was Margaret Atwood, she had her handbag on her arm and…*

John Ralston Saul   — *… and then she turned and said: Salman Rushdie! And invited him on stage…*

↓   Salman Rushdie
Louise Dennys - John Ralston Saul - Marian Botsford Fraser.

Ma Thida

Ma Thida took part in the 1988 democracy movement in Myanmar, working for the information section of the National League for Democracy (NLD). She says: 'I was lucky enough to be safe in July 1989 while our leader Aung San Suu Kyi was put under house arrest after the military regime raided her compound. However, I couldn't stop my political activities against the National Convention which moved toward drafting the new constitution instead of transferring the rule to the NLD, the winning party of the 1990 general election. Then, on October 10, 1993, I was sentenced to twenty years in prison.' She entered Insein prison on charges of 'endangering public peace, having contact with illegal organisations, and distributing unlawful literature.'

Thida studied medicine in the early 1980s, becoming a trained physician and later volunteering as a general practitioner at a charity clinic. She gained a reputation as a progressive writer at a young age, and her books deal with the political and social situation in Myanmar. Her involvement in the 1990 general election campaign led to her first book, *The Sunflower*, which was banned in Myanmar in the early 1990s, after the military refused to accept the result of the elections and crushed the democracy movement.

In prison, Thida was denied medical care for various health ailments over the six years of her prison sentence, which she served in inhumane conditions. During her time in prison, she turned to the Buddhist meditation technique of Vipassana. This, she explains, contributed to her wish not to hold a grudge against the regime for her time in prison.

PEN Centres around the world campaigned for Thida's freedom, and she was one of the focus cases for the Day of the Imprisoned Writer in 1994. In 1996, Thida was the recipient of that year's PEN/Barbara Goldsmith Freedom to Write Award given by American PEN. She was released in 1999 on humanitarian grounds due in part to her declining health and international pressure.

When Myanmar PEN was founded in 2013, as the country took its first steps away from the military dictatorship, Thida became its first president. She placed freedom of expression, literary translation, and the establishment of literature as part of the country's educational curriculum as well as bringing together writers from all languages of a diverse and fragmented country into the core of PEN Myanmar's values. The Centre plays a central role in national advocacy to bring about human rights policy changes to the country. In 2016, Thida was elected a member of the board of PEN International and was succeeded by Myo Myint Nyein as president of Myanmar PEN.

↑   Dr Thida after being elected to her second term as PEN International Board member, with PEN Myanmar delegates at the 85th PEN International Congress in Manila, 2019.

←   Ma Thida was a focus case for PEN Centres campaigning on the Day of the Imprisoned Writer in 1994.

DAY OF THE IMPRISONED WRITER -15 NOVEMBER 1994

November 15 1994 marks International PEN's 14th annual Day of the Imprisoned Writer. On this day, writers from around the world will be commemorating their colleagues who have been imprisoned, tortured and even killed for practising their professions.

The most recent WiPC caselist documents over 900 cases of writers and journalists who have been persecuted for the practice of their profession since the beginning of 1994. Among these are 28 cases of killings, over 50 unsolved disappearances and the detention of over 350 others. Also recorded are numerous death threats, beatings and other forms of harassment aimed at intimidating writers and journalists into silence. PEN works to highlight these cases so that they are not forgotten.

This year, PEN is focusing on five writers: **Ma Thida** (pictured above right), a short-story writer from Burma who was sentenced to 20 years in prison for her writings; **Ali-Akbar Saidi Sirjani**, an eminent Iranian writer and author of several banned novels who is held on a variety of charges, all of which carry the death penalty; **Koigi wa Wamwere**, a Kenyan human rights activist and writer who is on trial for reasons widely believed to be in connection with his opposition activities; **Gunay Aslan**, a writer serving a two-year sentence in Turkey for his writings on Kurdish issues; and **Gustavo Garzon**, an Ecuadorean writer who was last seen in November 1990 and whose disappearance is thought to be linked to his previous political imprisonment.

Last year, seven cases were highlighted, including one of a killing in Turkey of poet **Metin al-Tiok** and another of the death threats against Bangladeshi writer **Taslima Nasrin**. The other cases were detained writers **Hwang Suk-young** of South Korea, **Ken Saro-Wiwa** of Nigeria, **Yndamiro Restano** of Cuba, **Mansur Rajih** of Yemen and **Bozor Sobir** of Tajikistan. Of these, only Sobir is now free, although living in exile in Russia. Although Nasrin was able to leave Bangladesh, she is still required to return to face trial at an as yet unfixed date and calls for her death continue. However, the focus on these cases by PEN has resulted in increased publicity about their plight and will ensure that the governments concerned are not allowed to feel that they can restrict the rights of writers with impunity.

For further details about the Day of the Imprisoned Writer, contact the WiPC.

↑   Ma Thida (sitting third from
the left in the back row) participated in
the democracy movement, with Aung
San Suu Kyi, as part of the information
services of the National League for
Democracy.

1990s and 2000s: towards a worldwide Writers in Prison Committee

↑ Václav Havel had been PEN's main case when he was imprisoned in 1979 as an author, together with Jan Patočka and others, for supporting Charter 77, which called for human rights in Czechoslovakia. When Czech PEN welcomed delegates from around the globe to the 1994 Prague International Congress of PEN, Havel gave the keynote speech as president of the Czech Republic and received delegates at Prague Castle. Here he is sitting next to Arthur Miller and PEN International's then president, Ronald Harwood.

In the 1990s, PEN's WiPC took on a more strategic approach to its work. In late 1990, after six years as its programme director, Siobhan Dowd left the WiPC to head PEN America's Freedom to Write programme in New York. She was followed by Sara Whyatt who set up the Rapid Action Network to respond to writers under imminent risk, coordinating appeals to governments and raising publicity.

At this time, PEN International began sending observers to the United Nations Human Rights Commission (now Council) in Geneva, along with the active support of Swiss Romand PEN. Delegates were increasingly making interventions from the floor and sending cases to the various UN Working Groups and Rapporteurs. At that time, it was also a venue where face-to-face meetings with government officials were possible, and frequently tense discussions were held with delegations from Cuba, China, and Iran, among other countries, where writers were detained. With Czech writer and dissident, Jiří Gruša, just having been elected president of PEN International in 2003, one of the most surreal meetings was at the North Korean Embassy where Joanne Leedom-Ackerman and Sara Whyatt, as chair and director of the WiPC, together with Fawzia Assaad of Swiss Romand PEN, raised the cases of long-term prisoners in North Korea over dinner.

The WiPC also saw a growth and stabilisation of income, with grants from the Dutch development agency, NOVIB, the Norwegian Ministry of Foreign Affairs, and Fritt Ord adding to the existing long-term support of the Swedish International Development Cooperation Agency, among others. This enabled the recruitment of more staff, and a greater capacity to work with the PEN membership through both the Writers in Prison Conferences and reports.

At the 73rd PEN International Congress in Dakar in 2007, Karin Clark was elected chair of the WiPC. It was her decision that all PEN Centres have been welcome to participate in the WiPC Conferences and sessions held at PEN Congresses. In the past, some Centres may have seen the WiPC as the political wing of the organisation; today, however, it is a core feature in all of PEN's global work.

↑　Orhan Pamuk at the conference with Sara Whyatt, programme director of the Writers in Prison Committee.

At the Istanbul conference of the WiPC in 2006, religious defamation was a key issue, coming just a few months after the Danish Cartoons Crisis, where cartoonists in Denmark had been threatened with death for their depictions of the Prophet Muhammad. States were called upon to remove laws criminalising religious offence and to protect those attacked for their commentary on religion.

❝ *When a home is suddenly gone, family scattered, livelihood and career and ambitions all uprooted, one is forced to consider what endures, and what one can take with him. Home moves from a physical place to a place in consciousness. The ability to speak with others and to tell the story is especially important and makes the idea of language as homeland compelling, also imagination as homeland, literature and art as homeland, and particularly relevant to PEN, a community of fellowship as homeland.* ❞

↑　Intervention by Joanne Leedom-Ackerman, International secretary of PEN, at the 71st PEN International Congress 2005, Bled, Slovenia.

←　PEN delegates at the Kathmandu Writers in Prison Conference, welcomed by Nepal PEN in 2000. Holding the Buddhist prayer wheel is Moris Farhi, chair of the WiPC (1997–2000). Behind him, on his left, is Joanne Leedom-Ackerman, chair of the WiPC (1993–97) and Sara Whyatt, director of the WiPC (1990–2010), and behind Sara, on her right, is Eugene Schoulgin, WiPC chair (2000–04). On the second row, second from right, is Terry Carlbom, PEN International secretary (1998–2004).

Mission to Peru

↑↑   Miguel Castro Castro high-security
prison in Lima, 1999.

↑   In the prison library: from left to right,
Eugene Schoulgin (Swedish PEN), Marian
Botsford Fraser (Canadian PEN), Yehude
Simon Munaro, Jens Lohmann (Danish PEN),
and Carles Torner (Catalan PEN).

'At noon on Friday, we report to Miguel Castro Castro prison for what becomes a five-hour visit with Yehude Simon. The prison is layer upon layer of iron gates, thick concrete walls, narrow, high corridors, an outer perimeter wall studded with watchtowers; beyond, the bleak sandy mountain glints with observation stations. On the roof, guards practising silently the manoeuvres of attack: run, crouch, pivot, aim; boys playing at war, or a dress rehearsal for a movie.

'It is not a movie inside. The design of the prison is claustrophobic, a tight circle of six hulking pavilions, thick concrete walls broken by grids of iron. No windows, of course. Men still sleep three to a cell (rotating on two concrete berths), and all cells are open to the weather. The only shade is a narrow band next to the walls, where guards stand and dogs sleep. Food wagons with iron wheels screech over the hard ground. All sounds are magnified: clanging doors, shouts that echo, heavy footsteps, dripping water.

'Yehude Simon's conditions have improved. The current prison governor is a compassionate man, and Yehude is a leader among prisoners in one of two pavilions now set up as minimum security. He has started a library in a small room where we meet with him privately, eat the lunch we've brought, take photos. His health is uncertain, his despair is palpable; he has been told several times that his release was a sure thing; on December 24th he was even told to pack his things, he would be leaving the next day; not true.

'He is soft-spoken, kindly. He freely admits his former radicalism, but says "spilling one drop of blood cannot be justified." (We're told he was convicted not for what he said, but for what he did *not* say; he did not explicitly denounce terrorism, because he thought dialogue would work.) He asks for books for the library, literature he says, he wants to teach literature to the prisoners.'

In February 1999, Swedish PEN, Canadian PEN, Danish PEN, and Catalan PEN went to Lima on a mission to advocate for Yehude Simon Munaro. The quote above is from Marian Botsford Fraser's narration of the mission. Yehude Simon was '51, a veterinary surgeon, a congressman from 1985 to 1992, when he was on congressional Human Rights and Justice Committees. In those days, an outspoken, radical leftist, leader of the small Patria Libre party, editor of *Cambio* magazine. A man who believed he could negotiate with Shining Path and MRTA [Túpac Amaru Revolutionary Movement] leaders. Some accuse him only of idealism and naivety; others of being a leader in the MRTA and party to violent acts. In June 1992, right after President Alberto Fujimori's "self-coup", Yehude Simon was arrested, charged with collaboration with terrorists on a motley body of evidence, and sentenced by a faceless judge for 20 years, the minimum sentence for terrorism.'

The mission interviewed Father Lannsiers, head of the commission in charge of presidential pardon to prisoners, as well as MPs, ministers, and human rights organisations and was even received by President Alberto Fujimori himself. In the following months, Yehude's wife, Nancy Valcárcel, travelled to Europe and spoke at PEN assemblies in Barcelona, Stockholm, and Oslo. When Fujimori escaped to Japan one year later and democracy returned to Peru, Yehude Simon Munaro, after spending eight years behind bars, was the first political prisoner to be liberated. In 2001, Swedish and Catalan PEN returned to Lima and obtained the liberation of Juan Jara Berrospi, the last journalist still in prison from the Dirty War years during Fujimori's regime when trials were conducted by faceless judges. In 2008, Yehude Simon Munaro was appointed as President of the Council of Ministers in Peru.

↑ The mission members preparing the interviews to be held with ministers and President Fujimori together with Susana Villarán, president of Peru's federation of human rights organisations.

↙ Thank you letter from Yehude Simon Munaro, who had just received the Freedom of Expression Prize from the Norwegian Authors Union:

'Prison, June 1999

'Dear Carles and Eugene,

'I drank your words until the last one. The feeling in my own spirit in front of such a strong solidarity I've received is an amazing one, it's difficult to express. There's so much love for a brother unjustly imprisoned! My oceanic gratitude to you, also from my dear Nancita and all my children. […] Receiving the prize is a joy because it is not because of me but because of you. Ahhh,… my dear Eugene, it's only yours. And as you are so generous that you offer it to me, my answer is that it does not belong to me but to all the people who struggle for freedom and to each person suffering unjust imprisonment.'

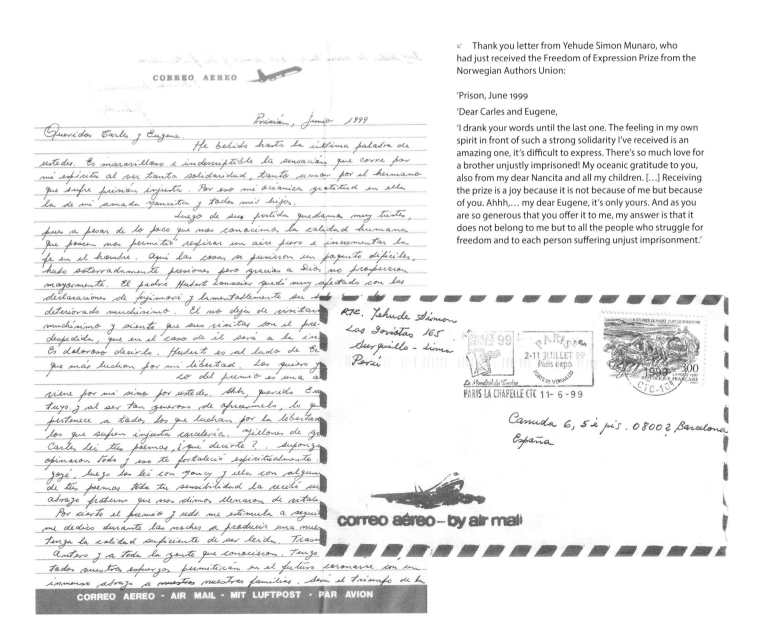

Ken Saro-Wiwa

Joanne Leedom-Ackerman was chair of the WiPC when PEN campaigned for Ken Saro-Wiwa. She narrates the struggle in her blog:

'One of the most noted of PEN's cases in the mid-1990s was Nigerian writer and activist Ken Saro-Wiwa who was hanged 10 November 1995. Ken understood they would hang him, but PEN members did not accept this. Ken was an award-winning playwright, and environmental activist who took on the government of Nigerian president Sani Abacha and Shell Oil on behalf of the Ogoni people whose land was rich in oil and also in pollution and whose people received little of the profits.

'I was living in London when Ken Saro-Wiwa, who had been arrested before for his writing and activism, visited PEN and other organisations in support of the Ogoni cause. He met at length with PEN's researcher Mandy Garner, providing her books and documentation of how he was being harassed in case he was arrested again. When he returned to Nigeria, he was arrested again and imprisoned in May 1994, along with eight others, and charged with masterminding the murder of Ogoni chiefs who were killed in a crowd at a pro-government meeting. The charge carried the death penalty.

'PEN mobilised quickly and stayed in close contact with his family. Ken Saro-Wiwa was an honorary member of PEN Centres in the USA, England, Canada, Kenya, South Africa, the Netherlands, and Sweden so these Centres were contacting their diplomats and government officials. At PEN International we met with members of the Nigeria High Commission. "I remember sitting opposite all these guys in sunglasses wearing Rolex watches, spouting the government line," Mandy recalls. We also talked with ambassadors, including from England, the US and Norway. We met with Shell Oil officials to ask that they intervene to save Ken Saro-Wiwa's life. English PEN mounted candlelight vigils outside the Nigerian High Commission with writers including Wole Soyinka, Ben Okri, Harold Pinter, Margaret Drabble, and PEN International president Ronald Harwood attending.

'The activity in London mirrored activity at PEN's more than 100 Centres around the globe, from New Zealand to Norway, from Malawi to Mexico. From every continent signed petitions were faxed to the Nigerian government of General Sani Abacha and to the writers' own governments, the United Nations, and to the press calling for clemency for Ken Saro-Wiwa. Through the International Freedom of Expression Exchange (IFEX) of which PEN International was a founding member, the word spread to freedom of expression organisations worldwide.

'Ken managed to get word out that he was tortured and held in leg irons for long periods of time. He wrote to Mandy, "A year is gone since I was rudely roused from my bed and clamped into detention. Sixty-five days in chains, many weeks of starvation, months of mental torture and, recently, the rides in a steaming, airless Black Maria to appear before a kangaroo court, dubbed a Special Military Tribunal, where the proceedings leave no doubt at all that the judgement has been written in advance. And a sentence of death against which there is no appeal is a certainty."

'When the death sentence was handed down at the end of October, PEN International launched a petition signed by hundreds of writers from around the globe seeking Saro-Wiwa's and others' release. A few days later, I was standing outside the Nigerian Embassy in a vigil, along with representatives from Amnesty and other organisations, when word was sent out to us that Ken Saro-Wiwa had been hanged that morning in Port Harcourt.'

→   PEN Centres contributed to an anthology of 100 poems for Ken Saro-Wiwa published one year after his execution. The title, *Dance the Guns to Silence*, was taken from one of Saro-Wiwa's own poems, 'Dance'. The foreword was written by Ken Wiwa, Ken Saro-Wiwa's son, and editorial advice was given by the renowned Malawian exiled poet Jack Mapanje. It included poems from Australia, New Zealand, Scotland, Catalonia, Mexico, South Africa, Uganda, Zimbabwe, Malawi, Bangladesh, and Canada.

↓   A 1996 WiPC newsletter explaining the intense campaigning for Ken Saro-Wiwa the year before.

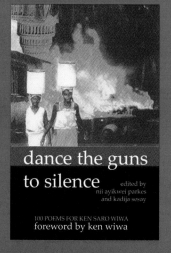

dance the guns to silence

edited by nii ayikwei parkes and kadija sesay

100 POEMS FOR KEN SARO WIWA
foreword by ken wiwa

Nigeria Campaign

PEN centres around the world took part in the campaign to free Nigerian writer Ken Saro-Wiwa imprisoned in May 1994 and hung in November 1995. He was charged with inciting the murder of four leading Ogoni figures in May 1994 and brought before a Special Tribunal which fell short of international standards for fairness. It is widely believed that the real reason for his arrest was his campaigning on minority rights issues and against environmental pollution in the Ogoni region of southern Nigeria.

Articles were published in newspapers from Canada and Mexico to Zimbabwe and Australia. Despite the shocking execution of Saro-Wiwa, International PEN centres will continue to campaign for justice for him and his family and for other writers and journalists who fall foul of the repressive military régime in Nigeria. Centres are currently working for:

Christine Anyanwu, editor-in-chief of TSM magazine, arrested on 4 June 1995 and originally sentenced by a military tribunal to life in prison for an article she published in connection with the alleged coup attempt in early 1995. The sentence has been reduced to 15 years in prison after international protests.

Drawing by Maxine Young

Diary of the Ken Saro-Wiwa campaign

• May 1993: Ken Saro-Wiwa, a founder member of Nigerian PEN, visits the International PEN office and talks about his minority rights campaign. He says he has been detained three times in recent months and fears plans are being laid for his long-term arrest. International PEN sends an appeal to the Nigerian authorities concerning the harassment of Saro-Wiwa.

• June 1993: International PEN sends a Rapid Action alert (RAN) for Saro-Wiwa after learning of his arrest on 21 June. Centres around the world also send appeals. Articles are written by centres and PEN. Saro-Wiwa is elected an honorary member of Dutch PEN.

↗   In 1995, PEN campaigned and advocated tirelessly for Ken Saro-Wiwa, a writer and member of the Ogoni people in Nigeria. Saro-Wiwa became president of the Movement for the Survival of the Ogoni People and led a non-violent campaign against environmental degradation of the land and waters of Ogoniland in the Niger Delta by the operations of the multinational petroleum industry, especially Royal Dutch Shell. An outspoken critic of the Nigerian government, he was detained, tortured, and condemned to death.

The empty chair

→   This sculpture by Antony Gormley is on permanent display at the British Library, London, and is titled *Witness*. It was commissioned by English PEN to mark its 90th anniversary. Cast in iron, the work depicts the empty chair, which English PEN has used as a symbol in its events for 30 years. The picture was taken in October 2015, on the day the publisher Ahmedur Rashid Chowdhury (aka Tutul) won the PEN Pinter International Writer of Courage Award after having to escape from Bangladesh because he was attacked by an Islamic fundamentalist extremist group and left critically injured.

↓   The empty chair devoted to Azimzhan Askarov was presented by his wife at the beginning of the 2014 PEN International Congress in Bishkek, Kyrgyzstan. Paintings of the writer in prison were on display and sold to collect funds for his legal defence.

↓↓   The Swedish Academy used the symbol of the empty chair when the writer and PEN leader Liu Xiaobo received the Nobel Peace Prize while being imprisoned in Beijing.

At the very beginning of any PEN meeting, an empty chair is placed front stage and the participants at the event are introduced to the imprisoned writer. In this way, the absent, imprisoned writer symbolically chairs the PEN meeting. The ceremony of the empty chair was started by English PEN and Canadian PEN and soon thereafter became a tradition after Salman Rushdie, as the keynote speaker in Barcelona at the 2004 Writers in Prison Conference, presented the empty chair. Today, hundreds of PEN meetings across the globe are chaired by imprisoned writers. The Swedish Academy used the ceremony of the empty chair when the writer Liu Xiaobo, leader of the Independent Chinese PEN Centre, was awarded the Nobel Peace Prize.

In 2019, in a speech to the Motovun Group in Greece, Jennifer Clement, president of PEN International, addressed the symbolism of the empty chair, 'In PEN, we talk about "our prisoner". What we mean, of course, is that this is a person we are advocating for and is in the PEN *Case List*. But this ownership is so profound to me. It is like saying, "This prisoner does not belong to the state, the government, a powerful leader, a jail, a corrupt judge, a prosecutor, a religious cleric, or a jail guard, but belongs to us and this belonging is also a kind of freedom because who we belong to matters."'

↑   *The Chair*, by Aline Martineau, is on display at the Quebec City House of
Literature, main partner of the 81st PEN International Congress in 2015. The sculpture
is a tribute to all imprisoned writers and is dedicated to Djibril Ly, president of
Mauritanian PEN, who died during the Quebec Congress. Ly, a writer in Fula, was
committed to the survival of all Mauritanian languages and had been imprisoned
for five years in Oualata Prison after distributing his *Manifesto of the Oppressed
Negro-Mauritanian*. He had also written plays such as *The Tree at the Criminal Court*.

Portraits of imprisoned writers for the empty chairs

Since the 2004 Writers in Prison Conference in Barcelona, all PEN Congresses, committee meetings, and PEN assemblies at national or regional level start with the ceremony of the empty chair. The authors are presented in detail and sometimes one of their texts is read, while their portrait sits in the empty chair. The artist Maxine Young has collaborated with PEN brilliantly for over 15 years by drawing the portraits of imprisoned writers, thus giving support to the imagination of PEN members when they make present their absent colleagues. At PEN meetings, participants are invited to sign the portraits that are later sent to families of those who suffer injustice, or hung in the walls of PEN offices as a remembrance of international solidarity.

Chimengül Awut
(چچ مهنگۇل ئاۋۇت):
#EmptyChair #ImprisonedWriter

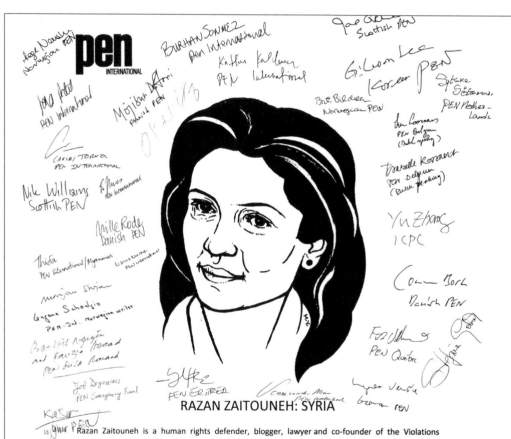

RAZAN ZAITOUNEH: SYRIA

Razan Zaitouneh is a human rights defender, blogger, lawyer and co-founder of the Violations Documentation Centre in Syria (VDC). She is the winner of the 2011 Sakharov Prize for Freedom of Thought, the 2011 RAW in WAR Anna Politkovskaya Award and the 2012 Ibn Rushd Award for Freedom of Thought. On December 9, 2013, Zaitouneh, along with her colleagues Samira Khalil, Nazem Hamadi and Wa'el Hamada (her husband) were abducted during a raid by a group of armed men on the offices of the VDC in Douma, near Damascus. They had been documenting human rights violations after fleeing Syrian government controlled area. There has been no news of their whereabouts since, but they are presumed to be held by an Islamic armed group in control of Douma.

PEN International is calling on the armed groups in control of the area and the governments who support them to do everything in their power to facilitate the immediate release of Zaitouneh, Hamada, Al-Khalil and Hamadi.

PAVEL SHEREMET: UKRAINE

Pavel Sheremet was a Belarusian-born Russian journalist and free speech advocate, who died in a car bomb explosion in Kiev on 20 July 2016. Sheremet, among other things, wrote for the independent news website *Ukrainski Pravda* and hosted a morning radio show on the independent broadcaster *Radio Vesti*. In his writing, Sheremet commented on political developments in Ukraine, Russia and Belarus, for which he frequently faced threats and retributions. He also won numerous awards for his work, including the Belarus PEN Center's Adamovich Prize (1995), the Committee to Protect Journalists' International Press Freedom Award (1998), and the Organization for Security and Cooperation in Europe's Prize for Journalism and Democracy (2002). Shortly before he was assassinated, he had written about corruption among law enforcement officials in Belarus, alleged corruption among government officials and police in Ukraine, and the work of government propagandists in Russia. His murder remains unresolved. The May 2017 documentary 'Killing Pavel', produced jointly by the Organized Crime and Corruption Reporting Project and Slidstvo.info, revealed many shortcomings in the investigation.

NEDIM TÜRFENT: TURQUÍA

El jefe de redacción, periodista y poeta Nedim Türfent se encuentra cumpliendo una condena de prisión de ocho años y nueve meses por cargos de terrorismo inventados tras un juicio injusto. Durante dicho juicio, decenas de testigos dijeron que habían sido torturados para que declararan en su contra. A Türfent se le negó repetidamente el derecho a comparecer físicamente ante el tribunal y experimentó graves problemas de interpretación. Cuando presentó su testimonio en idioma Kurdo Kurmanji a través de un enlace de video, el intérprete, que no pudo escucharlo correctamente debido a problemas técnicos, repitió frases recurrentes y cometió graves errores en la traducción. La cultura y el idioma kurdos siguen siendo duramente reprimidos en Turquía. PEN International pide la liberación inmediata e incondicional de Türfent.

PARAGUAY: NELSON AGUILERA

Writer, professor and member of PEN Paraguay, Nelson Aguilera was sentenced to 30 months in prison for alleged plagiarism on 4 November 2013. His conviction is subject to an appeal before the Supreme Court. Aguilera stands accused of plagiarizing Maria Eugenia Garay's novel *El túnel del tiempo* (*The Time* Tunnel) in his 2010 children's novel *Karumbita: La patriota* (*Karumbita: The Patriot*). Independent experts and writers have found that the similarities in the two works cannot be described as plagiarism. PEN believes Aguilera's sentence to be unjust and calls on the Paraguayan authorities to quash his conviction without further delay.

TAL AL-MALLOUHI: SYRIA

Tal al-Mallouhi is a Syrian blogger and poet who was taken from her home by Syrian forces when she was 19 years old and remains detained almost nine years later. After her arrest on 27 December 2009, Tal was charged with 'spying for a foreign country' without any evidence, by the now abolished Supreme State Security Court, and sentenced to five years in prison. It is widely believed that Tal's sentence and detention are related to the content of her blog in which she criticised government's policies and promoted human rights and peace in the Middle East.

Tal was first questioned in 2006 by the Syrian security service after she published an open letter to the Syrian President, Bashar al-Assad in which she called on him to accelerate the democratic change in the country. She was repeatedly questioned by the same service in 2007 and asked to stop writing. Tal's arrest and sentence have sparked controversy and public outcry across Syria, as she was the youngest known convicted prisoner of conscience in the country.

On 19 October 2013, Tal's name was included in a prisoner exchange agreement between the government and armed opposition groups, and it was reported that she had been released after the State Security Court's decision ordered her release. However, she was taken from Douma prison to the State Security Department in Damascus, where she is still believed to be held incommunicado. PEN International calls for her immediate and unconditional release.

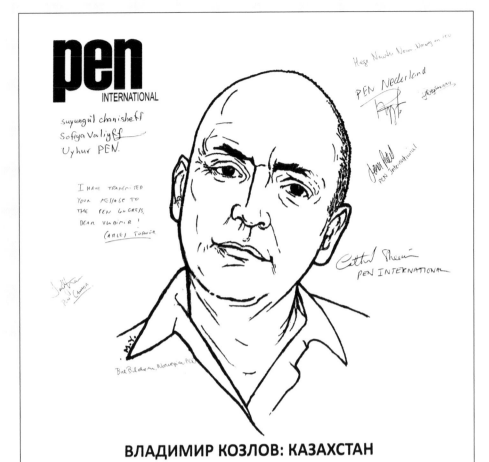

suyungül chanisheff
Sofiya Valiyff
Uyhur PEN.

I HAVE TRANSMITED
YOUR MESSAGE TO
THE PEN CONGRESS,
DEAR VLADIMIR !
(CARLES TORNER)

PEN Nederland

PEN International

PEN INTERNATIONAL

ВЛАДИМИР КОЗЛОВ: КАЗАХСТАН

Владимир Козлов – журналист, правозащитник и основатель "Алга!"(Вперед!), оппозиционной политической партии. В дополнение к его деятельности в печатных СМИ, он также работал в качестве редактора на AKTiVi ТВ и стал соучредителем одной из первых частных телеканалов Казахстана "Актау-Лада". В октябре 2012 года он был признан виновным в "разжигании социальной розни" и попытке свержения конституционного строя государства. Он был приговорен к семи с половиной годам лишения свободы, которые он в настоящее время отбывает в колонии общего режима в поселке Заречное, Алматинской области. Его арест и судебное разбирательство последовали после его сообщения в Европейский Парламент об убийстве полицией около 15 бастующих нефтяников в Жанаозене и о пытках в полиции после случившегося. Козлов публично призвал к проведению международного расследования этих событий.Независимые наблюдатели уверены, что суд над журналистом был несправедливым. Международный ПЕН-клуб и другие правозащитные организации считают его приговор политически мотивированным и призывают к его немедленному и безоговорочному освобождению.

Sedigeh Vasmaghi
#EmptyChair #ImprisonedWriter

GAURI LANKESH: INDIA

Gauri Lankesh, a senior journalist and editor of the weekly Kannada-language tabloid *Gauri Lankesh Patrike*, was shot dead at her home in Bengaluru, Karnataka state, on 5 September 2017. Lankesh was a tireless campaigner for freedom, justice, human rights, and liberal values, and stood firm in support of the marginalised and the vulnerable.

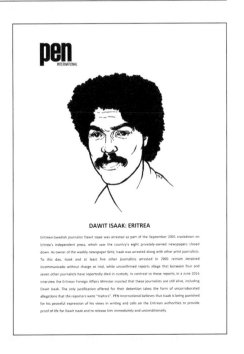

DAWIT ISAAK: ERITREA

Eritrean-Swedish journalist Dawit Isaak was arrested as part of the September 2001 crackdown on Eritrea's independent press, which saw the country's eight privately-owned newspapers closed down. As owner of the weekly newspaper *Setit*, Isaak was arrested along with other print journalists. To this day, Isaak and at least five other journalists arrested in 2001 remain detained incommunicado without charge or trial, while unconfirmed reports allege that between four and seven other journalists have reportedly died in custody. In contrast to these reports, in a June 2016 interview the Eritrean Foreign Affairs Minister insisted that these journalists are still alive, including Dawit Isaak. The only justification offered for their detention takes the form of uncorroborated allegations that the reporters were "traitors". PEN International believes that Isaak is being punished for his peaceful expression of his views in writing and calls on the Eritrean authorities to provide proof of life for Dawit Isaak and to release him immediately and unconditionally.

Anna Politkovskaya

PEN welcomed in the twenty-first century in Russia. In 2000, the 67th PEN International Congress took place in Moscow and, over those days, issued very strong resolutions against Vladimir Putin's government and its involvement in the Second Chechen War and the killing of journalists in Chechnya. Both Russian PEN and PEN International, faithful to their mission, were a bastion for persecuted writers in Russia.

One year later, Anna Politkovskaya stormed the 68th PEN International Congress in London. The journalist from *Novaya Gazeta* had been in trouble a few months earlier when, during one of her investigations, she was detained in a military camp by the FSB, the Russian security service. The world's attention having been alerted by *Novaya Gazeta*, an immediate international campaign succeeded in having her liberated, but not without a clear warning. During her detention Politkovskaya was taken to a courtyard between two military barracks where she was subjected to a simulated execution – she was shot at with a machine gun that was not

loaded. Due to this, Politkovskaya had a nervous breakdown and went into exile in Vienna. When she stormed the 68th PEN International Congress in London she had already resolved to go back to work as a jounalist in Russia and to investigate the crimes in Chechnya, specifically the crimes of the army against civilians:

'I have published only one book,', said Politkovskaya to the delegates, 'but I'm a special writer because quite all the characters in my book are already dead. It makes my life atypical, because I've decided to be faithful to them and do my best for the international community to stop this war. […] When people are executed in a given territory and because of their nationality, we can call it "genocide". Destruction involves children, women, even pregnant women, anyone. I have seen with these eyes mass graves with all corpses having clear signs of torture and many even have been scalped. Hands and feet were tied with wire. These were medieval tortures, amputated bodies. I can even understand that all men are seen by the

Russian army as suspicious of being fighters, but when you see the corpses of women and children in the graves, then you know it's a genocide.'

The following year, Anna Politkovskaya took part in the 69th PEN International Congress in Ohrid, Macedonia, and several PEN Centres agreed on a campaign to try to protect Politkovskaya by inviting her, promoting, and translating her writing, and thus make the Russian authorities aware that she was a journalist with international prestige. PEN organised events in Los Angeles, Toronto, Oslo, Stockholm, and Barcelona, among others. In January 2004, she received the Oxfam Novib/PEN Freedom of Expression Award in The Hague. Only six months later, she was poisoned on a flight while going to mediate between the Russian army and the Chechen fighters who had taken a school in Beslan hostage.

On 7 October 2006, Anna Politkovskaya was shot dead in the lift of her apartment building in central Moscow. In May 2014, after a lengthy farcical retrial, five men were convicted of having been involved in Politkovskaya's murder. The masterminds of her assassination remain free. Every 7th of October PEN pays tribute to her memory.

← Anna Politkovskaya revising her notes after her speech at the PEN International Congress in London 2001.

↓ Tribute to Anna Politkovskaya at the Frankfurt Book Fair on 8 October 2006, the morning after her assassination. In the front row are Politkovskaya's French publishers, Moris Farhi, chair of PEN International's WiPC, and Kjell Olaf Jensen, president of PEN Norway.

↑   Anna Politkovskaya addressing a crowd of
students at Pompeu Fabra University in Barcelona
on 15 November 2002, just three weeks after she had
tried to obtain from a Chechen commander the
liberation of hundreds of hostages at the Dubrovka
theatre in Moscow.

2010s: beyond the 50th anniversary of the Writers in Prison Committee

↑   In January 2015, the horrific murder of 12 people, mostly staff, at the offices of the French satirical magazine, *Charlie Hebdo*, by gunmen claiming to be offended by the publication's depiction of the Prophet Muhammad led to writers and PEN members protesting at the deaths and demanding that governments recognise the dangers posed by fanatics using violence aimed at shutting down criticism of religion.

In 2010, PEN International celebrated the 50th anniversary of the WiPC. A booklet was published featuring 50 cases of writers for whom PEN had sent appeals and staged campaigns over the half-century, each one emblematic of the year in which they were imprisoned. The first, representing 1960, was Musine Kokalari, imprisoned in Albania in 1960 and whose name was among those in the first *Case Lists* presented at the inaugural meeting of the WiPC. The final, representing 2009, was that of Liu Xiaobo serving an 11-year sentence in China and who went on to win the 2010 Nobel Peace Prize.

The murders at the offices of *Charlie Hebdo* on 7 January 2015 were an earthquake for PEN. Two days after the killing, PEN International president John Ralston Saul, International treasurer Jarkko Tontti, and executive director Carles Torner paid tribute to the victims at the memorial outside *Charlie Hebdo*'s offices. They were accompanied by the president of French PEN, Emmanuel Pierrat, who was the lawyer of two of the victims.

During these years, as the situation in Turkey deteriorated, PEN's campaigns increased including reports on the aftermath of the 2013 Gezi demonstrations published in 2014 and 2016. A high-level mission led by members of PEN International's board, PEN Centres and PEN Turkey met with the then President Abdullah Gül and other officials. Throughout the decade, PEN members maintained a constant

presence at the many trial hearings against writers, and took part in joint actions with PEN Centres and fellow freedom of expression organisations in Turkey and internationally. Other countries of focus included India, with three reports issued in 2015, 2016 and 2018, in collaboration with Canadian PEN and the University of Toronto, that covered the wide range of abuses from censorship of the internet and movies, threats by Hindu nationalists, blasphemy laws and sedition, and the murders of journalists.

Alongside the increased reporting on countries and themes, PEN's work at the United Nations also grew, with statements and reports, written and oral, submitted to most of the sessions on countries including Vietnam, Cambodia, Eritrea, Ethiopia, Kazakhstan, Myanmar, Honduras, Hungary, Bangladesh, Mexico, Spain, and Turkey. PEN also brought to the UN writers who had been subjected to repression to testify to their experiences within the Palais des Nations itself, and worked alongside the UN Special Rapporteur on Freedom of Expression and other rapporteurs covering abuses including torture, extra judicial executions and cultural rights. Marian Botsford Fraser acted as chair of the WiPC from 2009 to 2015, when Indian writer and journalist Salil Tripathi took on the role. After 23 years heading PEN's freedom of expression programme, Sara Whyatt left in 2013 to be succeeded by Ann Harrison.

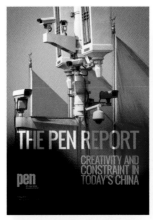
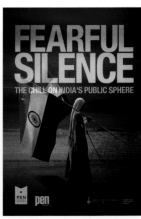

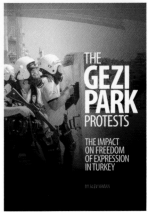

↑ PEN International reports on freedom of expression in India, China, and Turkey.

↓ In a square in rue Saint-Jean in Quebec City, a sculpture of the empty chair was raised during the 81st PEN International Congress in 2015, and each morning delegates assembled there to bear witness to imprisoned colleagues. Ensaf Haidar, wife of the imprisoned Saudi writer Raif Badawi, presented the empty chair for him together with their three children. Next to the empty chair stands Marian Botsford Fraser, chair of the WiPC (2009–15), and Émile Martel, president of Quebec PEN.

The assassination of Hrant Dink

← Hrant Dink with Hilde Keteleer, chair of the WiPC of Flanders PEN, at the 2006 Writers in Prison Committee Conference in Istanbul.

'The saddest day in my life. We had dinner together in my flat in Istanbul the night before Hrant Dink was murdered in 2007', Eugene Schoulgin, who had been chair of the WiPC from 2000 to 2004, remembers. 'We had a lively conversation with enthusiasm and complicity, he was a long-time supporter of PEN, we were good friends… He was a victim of the structural hate against Armenians in Turkey.'

Hrant Dink helped found the weekly news-paper *Agos* in 1996 and became its editor. *Agos* featured articles in Turkish and Armenian (as well as an online English-language edition) and focused its coverage on human rights abuses, minority rights, and Turkish–Armenian relations. From its inception, the magazine and its staff suffered death threats from extremist nationalist groups.

Dink was charged under Article 301 of the Penal Code. He was accused of 'insulting Turkishness' for his writings that challenged the Turkish government's refusal to acknowledge that there had been an Armenian genocide in 1915, and called for reconciliation. Dink was one of the few to be convicted. In October 2005, he was given a six-month suspended sentence for a 2004 article entitled 'The Armenian Identity'. In

2006, he was again charged under the same laws after referring to the 1915 massacre of Armenians by Ottoman Turks as 'genocide' in an interview with Reuters. One of the most high-profile cases was that of writer Orhan Pamuk, subsequently awarded the Nobel Prize in Literature, who also was charged for his comments on Armenia to international outcry. His case was dropped in early 2006.

Despite receiving numerous death threats — threats that the Turkish police reportedly refused to take seriously — Dink continued to live a public life. He was awarded the Oxfam Novib/PEN Freedom of Expression Award, and he attended the award ceremony in The Hague on 18 November 2006, where he was welcomed with warmth by Dutch PEN and the audience of the Writers Unlimited Festival.

Two months later, on 19 January 2007, he was shot dead while walking to the offices of *Agos*. His murder provoked massive protest marches, with over 100,000 protestors carrying banners saying 'We are all Armenians', 'We are all Hrant Dink' and '301 Murderer'. Dink's murder has sparked debate on the revision or repeal of Article 301, which many believe marked Dink out as a target for ultra-nationalists.

← Police officers photographed posing with Hrant Dink's murderer, Ogün Samast, who stands behind a Turkish flag immediately after his arrest. In 2011, Samast was sentenced to 23 years in prison.

↑   The killing of Hrant Dink in 2007
was an earthquake in Istanbul's society.
Against the background of the
Armenian Genocide and its forbidden
memories, the will to mourn and reject
the hate that destroyed the life of
Hrant Dink brought a crowd of citizens
to the streets of Istanbul.

The Oxfam Novib/PEN Award

Since 2005, every year begins for PEN in The Hague: the Oxfam Novib/PEN Award for Freedom of Expression is a literary award made in collaboration between PEN International, the PEN Emergency Fund, and Oxfam Novib (the Dutch affiliate of the international Oxfam organisation). The award has been given yearly at the opening ceremony of the Writers Unlimited Festival with the active participation of Netherlands PEN. It recognises writers who have been persecuted for their work and continue working despite the consequences.

↑   In 2020, the Oxfam Novib/PEN Award was given to the Ugandan poet and academic Stella Nyanzi, who was at the time kept in Ward Two at Luzira Prison. She had been arrested in November 2018 after she posted a poem on her Facebook page that implied Uganda would be better off if the president had died at birth. She was absent from the ceremony on 18 January 2020. One month later, Stella Nyanzi won her appeal against the charges and was released. PEN Uganda organised a reception at the library of the Uganda Museum in Kampala where she could finally receive the award.

↖   In 2016, the Russian novelist Mikhail Shishkin gave the keynote speech. The prestigious investigative journalist Malini Subramaniam received the award. Subramaniam, who was based in Bastar, Chhattisgarh, where she sought to shine a light on the plight of those living in a region rocked by insecurity and Maoist insurgency, reporting on the alleged torture of journalists, human trafficking, and allegations of sexual violence committed by the security forces in Bijapur, was forced to flee her home after local authorities failed to defend her in front of a vigilante group protesting outside her home and calling for her. With both of them are Jennifer Clement, president of PEN International, and Oxfam Novib/PEN director Farah Karimi.

←   The 2018 Award was given to Venezuelan writer and journalist Milagros Socorro. Three months later, she welcomed a PEN International mission to Venezuela in the most difficult circumstances. The report of the mission was published and distributed to all delegates participating in the 2018 PEN International Congress in Pune, India. From right to left: Pauline Krikke, mayor of The Hague; Milagros Socorro; Ton van de Langkruis, director of the Writers Unlimited Festival; Jennifer Clement, president of PEN International, and Farah Karimi, director of Oxfam Novib.

→ 'It is a great honour for me to write this award speech, although I am writing while seated on the floor of Ward Two at Luzira Women Prison. It is 02:16am here. The mosquitos fly and sing with such liberty. The lice and bed bugs bite deeply. Most of my prison-wardmates are deep asleep in their prison uniforms. Some are nude. Some snore. Some fart. [...] Tonight, there are seventy-two women prisoners in this overly congested prison-ward. We have only five beds in the entire ward. Three ward-leaders, one foreigner and one long-termer occupy the beds. The rest of us squeeze our bodies on the floor.'

Stella Nyanzi wrote a very moving letter of acceptance that was smuggled out of prison and read at the award ceremony in The Hague, bringing the audience of the Writers Unlimited Festival to tears. The award and the flowers for her were left in the empty chair.

Honorees of the Oxfam Novib/PEN Award

2005
- **Sihem Bensedrine** (Tunisia), journalist and human rights activist
- **Neziha Rejiba** (Tunisia), journalist and editor
- **Sarah Mkhonza** (Swaziland), novelist and columnist
- **Claudia Anthony** (Sierra Leone), journalist
- **Duong Thu Huong** (Vietnam), novelist

2006
- **Simon Mol** (Poland), journalist
- **Andrei Dyńko** (Belarus), journalist
- **Roya Toloui** (Iran/Kurdistan), journalist and human rights activist
- **Faraj Bayrakdar** (Syria), poet
- **Hrant Dink** (Turkey), journalist

2007
- **Fatou Jaw-Manneh** (Gambia), journalist
- **Svetlana Alexievich** (Belarus), writer
- **Lydia Cacho Ribeiro** (Mexico), writer
- **Ekbal Baraka** (Egypt), novelist, screenwriter and journalist

2008
- **Dejan Anastasijević** (Serbia), journalist
- **Pierre Roger Lambo Sanjo** (Cameroon), writer
- **Christopher Mlalazi** and **Raisedon Baya** (Zimbabwe), playwrights
- **Maung Thura** and **Saw Wei** (Myanmar), poets

2009
- **Chi Dang** (Vietnam), writer
- **Maziar Bahari** (Iran/Canada), journalist

- **Irakli Kakabadze** (Georgia), writer
- **Sonali Samarasinghe Wickrematunge** (Sri Lanka), journalist
- **Daniel Coronell** (Colombia), columnist

2011
- **Andrei Nekrasov** (Russia), filmmaker and journalist
- **Sakit Zahidov** (Azerbaijan), journalist and poet
- **Nedim Şener** (Turkey), journalist
- **Jayaprakash Sittampalam Tissainayagam** (Sri Lanka), journalist

2012
- **Asieh Amini** (Iran), journalist, blogger, and activist
- **Jesús Lemus Barajas** (Mexico), journalist and writer
- **Mikhail Bekhetof** (Russia), journalist
- **Rachid Nini** (Morocco), newspaper editor
- **Alhaj Warrag** and **Abdul Moniem Suleman** (Sudan), newspaper founder, editor and columnist (respectively)

2013
- **Samar Yazbek** (Syria), writer and journalist
- **Enoh Meyomesse** (Cameroon), writer and activist
- **Narges Mohammadi** (Iran), journalist and activist
- **Déo Namujimbo** (Congo), journalist
- **Büşra Ersanlı** (Turkey), writer and academic

2014
- **Abdiaziz Abdinur Ibrahim** (Somalia), freelance journalist
- **Oksana Chelysheva** (Russia), journalist, activist
- **Dina Meza** (Honduras), journalist, activist

2015
- **Bahman Ahmadi-Amouee** and **Jila Bani Yaghoub** (Iran), journalists
- **Razan Naiem Almoghrabi** (Libya), writer, journalist, and advocate of women's rights
- **Abdelmoneim Rahama** (Sudan), poet, writer and journalist

2016
- **Amanuel Asrat** (Eritrea), poet, writer and editor-in-chief
- **Can Dündar** (Turkey), writer and journalist
- **Omar Hazek** (Egypt), poet and writer

2017
- **Ashraf Fayadh** (Palestine), poet
- **Malini Subramaniam** (India), journalist

2018
- **Eskinder Nega** (Ethiopia), journalist
- **Milagros Socorro** (Venezuela), journalist

2019
- **Dareen Tatour** (Palestine), poet
- **Gioconda Belli** (Nicaragua), author
- **Roberto Saviano** (Italy), journalist

2020
- **Stella Nyanzi** (Uganda), academic, writer, and feminist activist

Missions to Mexico

↑   Participants at the PEN Pregunta event in February 2015, asking the Mexican government why it was failing to protect journalists from assassination. Clockwise from top left: Mexican poet and writer Homero Aridjis, president of PEN International (1997–2003); poet and novelist Gioconda Belli, president of Nicaraguan PEN; novelist and short-story writer Luisa Valenzuela, president of Argentinian PEN; Aline Davidoff Misrachi, president of Mexican PEN, and John Ralston Saul, president of PEN International, giving a Courage Award to journalist Pablo Ferri; Mexican novelist Elena Poniatowska, who received on that day the Mexican PEN Award.

In 2010, the first mission on Mexico, 'State of Emergency: Censorship by Bullet', consisted of an evening of solidarity in New York City with Mexican journalists, which was organised by Mexican PEN, American PEN, the Committee to Protect Journalists, and the John S and James L Knight Foundation. Luis Miguel Aguilar, Paul Auster, Jon Lee Anderson, Jennifer Clement, Don DeLillo, Laura Esquivel, Alberto Ibargüen, José Luis Martínez, Victor Manuel Mendiola, Carmen Aristegui (CNN en Español), Adela Navarro Bello (Tijuana-based *Zeta*), Rocio Gallegos (*Diario de Juárez*), and Julia Preston (*New York Times*) participated. This event occurred in the aftermath of the *Diario de Juárez*'s front-page headline on 19 September 2010 asking directly: 'Qué Quieren de Nosotros?' (What Do You Want from Us?) after the local cartel had killed two of their young photographers. This headline made news all over the world.

On 29 January 2012, in Mexico City, PEN International, Mexican PEN and other PEN Centres as well as prominent writers and journalists gathered at the 'PEN Protesta!' event to protest against the killing and disappearance of journalists in Mexico. They stated that the impunity and the government's lack of action against these crimes were intolerable, making the country the most dangerous for journalists in the world. The PEN event was the first international gathering organised in Mexico to protest against these crimes.

A statement of solidarity was signed by prominent writers from around the globe expressing solidarity with Mexico's writers and journalists and was published in the Mexican newspaper *El Universal*. In the aftermath of the mission, legislation making crimes against journalists a federal crime was passed by the Mexican Senate.

The second mission to Mexico, 'PEN Pregunta', led by PEN International president John Ralston Saul and Mexican PEN president Aline Davidoff, occurred in 2015 in Mexico City. More than 50 writers attended the event and each was given one minute to ask a question of the Mexican authorities.

↑ After the international delegation had participated in the PEN Protesta! public event in 2012, the president of the Mexican Senate José González Morfín and PEN International president John Ralston Saul met at the Senate of the Republic.

Censorship by Bullet in Mexico

Speech by Jennifer Clement, president of Mexican PEN, at the Censorship by Bullet in Mexico: An Evening in Solidarity with Mexican Journalists event in New York with PEN America.

The storyteller is the story

For Mexicans today it is hard to interpret the words around us. In these sad and crazy times we read newspapers where messages from the drug traffickers have been published, right beside the real news or in the classified section where narco messages appear in the broken thumb language of text messaging. We read the writing on walls and on the enormous white cotton sheets covered with messages that have appeared hanging from bridges and buildings. In news coverage we read letters that were pinned to dead bodies. We also try to decipher words actually carved into the skin of victims as if it were paper — across a belly, down an arm, we read a skin graffiti.

Weeks ago, after the assassination of photojournalist Luis Carlos Santiago, some narco graffiti appeared on a wall in Juárez signed by the La Linea Cartel that stated: *Nosotros no matamos periodistas*: we do not kill journalists. It was a highly unusual declaration. I logged on to the Blogdelnarco to see the response to this new graffiti. Blogdelnarco is an internet site that appeared about six months ago and is covering stories that the mainstream media are feeling threatened to stay away from. It is a place where all sides seem to communicate — drug

traffickers, law enforcement, and ordinary citizens. This controversial site contains everything from violent videos of torture and decapitations to a section on Mexican narco corridos and even narco jokes.

Regarding the graffiti that claimed *Nosotros no matamos periodistas* written on a white wall in red spray paint to look like blood, I found 392 posts. They were not about the message itself or the violence against journalists but were 392 vitriolic and sarcastic comments about the abominable spelling and poor syntax of this graffiti (it should read Nosotros no matamos a periodistas). One blogger said he was ashamed by the narcos' lack of education and, he continued, even our narcos are Third World. Another stated that it is not the alphabet that kills: bullets kill. One person wrote emphatically that she preferred to read the messages and graffiti from the rival cartel because at least they knew how to spell. After I read over more than one hundred outraged comments, a sheepish and mortified 'spelling apology' was posted, which might have been placed there by the cartel. To this expression of regret one blogger answered: You criminals are so good at killing you've even killed the Spanish language.

Yes, these are sad, and crazy, times for Mexico.

So, to stand here in your company is deeply moving for us who are living this madness. At this moment it is so important for Mexicans to feel that the rest of the world cares about this land that is a victim of corruption, poverty, US drug consumption and immoral gun selling and a land where the storyteller has become the story.

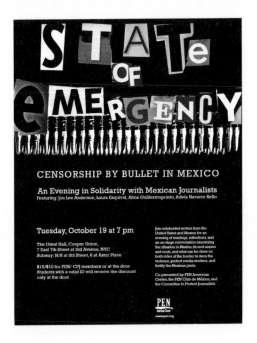

Day of the Dead

↑   *Vivan los periodistas! Long life to journalists!*
In this PEN Day of the Dead altar, an ironic yet celebratory banner unfurls over a montage of journalists' skeletons, sitting down companionably together with their typewriters and writings.

↑↑   Brendan de Caires, director of Canadian PEN, at the altar of the Day of Dead, 2012.

↑   Jens Lohmann, chair of Danish PEN's WiPC, speaking at a tribute to journalists killed around the world on the Day of the Dead in Copenhagen in 2014.

↓   Elena Poniatowska is one of the 66 Latin American writers whose texts and poems where published in the 2012 PEN anthology *Escribe contra la impunidad/ Write against Impunity*.

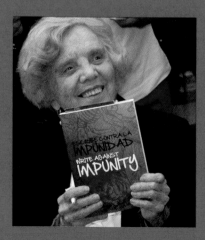

Themed campaigns became an essential for PEN throughout the 2010s. PEN International and its Centres in Latin America and the Caribbean started to mark the Day of the Dead, and soon, to events in Mexico, Chile, Argentina, Paraguay, Guatemala, Haiti, or Nicaragua, were added events in London, Zagreb, Paris, or Barcelona. All events were calling on Latin American governments to break the cycle of impunity, and protect their journalists from persecution, as well as commemorating the lives of those who have been killed for exercising their right to freedom of expression and whose cases have gone unsolved. At a global level, Latin America, together with the Caribbean, was in the second decade of the twenty-first century the second most lethal region in which to work as a journalist.

In 2012, the anthology *Escribe contra la impunidad/Write against Impunity* gathered together 66 texts from writers in 13 Latin

American countries in support of their colleagues who had been killed. The 2012 campaign created a tradition by including PEN Centres from across the world creating altars in honour of the murdered writers. This campaign underscored the fact that the killing of writers and journalists is inseparable from the total impunity for these crimes. It has become a regular feature of the PEN campaign calendar. In 2019 all Latin American PEN Centres participated in the campaign as well as many other PEN Centres from around the globe.

'In Mexico, telling the truth means risking your life. Every reporter, every young man or woman who takes up the frontline for a newspaper should be asked: "Are you ready to die?" In the northern cities of the Republic, journalists are preyed on like rabbits, and until now nobody has ever protected them,' said Elena Poniatowska from Mexican PEN at the PEN Protesta! event in January 2012.

↑   A tribute to journalists killed around the world on the
Day of the Dead in Denmark. The Day of the Dead
campaign underscores the fact that the killing of writers
and journalists is inseparable from the total impunity for
these crimes. It has become a regular feature of the PEN
campaign calendar. In 2019, all Latin American PEN
Centres participated in the campaign as well as many
other PEN Centres from around the globe.

Repealing criminal defamation laws in Africa

↑   PEN delegation to the United Nations Human Rights
Council in June 2018. From right to left: Daniel Sikazwe
(Zambian PEN), Andrew Caruana Galizia, Dina Meza
(Honduran PEN), Laurens Hueting (African PEN coordinator),
Allieu Kamara (Sierra Leonean PEN), barrister Jonathan Price,
Gautam Bhatia (Delhi PEN), Sarah Clarke (PEN advocacy
manager), Carles Torner (PEN executive director), Danson
Kahyana (Ugandan PEN).

In recent years, in many countries in Africa, governments continue to
stifle freedom of expression, open debate, political criticism, and
media reporting using laws that make it a crime to say, write, or
publish anything that they consider defamatory or insulting. These
laws are usually vague and sweepingly broad, opening them to such
wide interpretation that they act as an ever-present constraint,
particularly on investigative journalism and other aspects of the
media's capacity to perform its public watchdog role. In 2018, PEN
International produced, with the support of the United Nations
Democracy Fund, the report *Stifling Dissent, Impeding Accountability:
Criminal Defamation Laws in Africa*. The report was based on a
survey undertaken with writers across the continent on the impact of
criminal defamation, libel, and insult laws and on an analysis of four
focus countries: Uganda, Zambia, Sierra Leone, and South Africa. It

also looked at the example of Ghana, which, in 2001, became the first country in Africa to decriminalise defamation. The report was presented at a parallel event to the 38th Regular Session of the UN Human Rights Council, with the participation of the UN Special Rapporteur on the promotion and protection of the right to freedom of opinion and expression, David Kaye.

The debate, with representatives of Ugandan PEN, Zambian PEN, Delhi PEN, and Honduran PEN, reported that important developments relating to the decriminalisation of defamation, notably the landmark 2014 *Konaté vs. Burkina Faso* judgment of the African Court on Human and Peoples' Rights, have concluded that criminal defamation laws should not include custodial sentences. In the wake of this decision, numerous African countries have moved to decriminalise defamation. However, major challenges persist globally both in terms of criminal defamation and broad civil defamation laws which carry crippling fines.

Reflecting on his experiences, Lohé Issa Konaté told PEN International that, despite the African Court's ruling in his case, his conviction and imprisonment by a Burkina Faso court in 2012 had been disastrous for him and his newspaper, *L'Ouragan*. The newspaper's suspension meant that its staff lost their jobs, while he served 12 months in prison and was then barred from returning to his work as a journalist for an additional six months. After that, it took half a year more before *L'Ouragan* could again become a weekly publication, and during that period it incurred serious financial losses. The repercussions Konaté and his newspaper suffered underscore the deterrent effect of criminal defamation laws and the risks faced by journalists and editors prepared to report on issues that governments consider sensitive or damaging. Konaté stated for the PEN report: 'In Burkina Faso, we accepted to sacrifice ourselves for freedom of expression and press freedom. Some have lost their lives, like Norbert Zongo; 70 others have been through the torments of imprisonment, like us. It is without a doubt due to a part of our sacrifices that today laws have been changed so a journalist will not be jailed on defamation charges anymore.'

One emerging area of concern today is the increased use of defamation claims in Strategic Lawsuits Against Public Participation (SLAPPs), which are routinely taken against investigative journalists to prevent them from reporting on corruption and human rights abuses — as happened with the many SLAPPs against the Maltese journalist Daphne Caruana Galizia. At the Geneva panel, the empty chair was Daphne Caruana Galizia, and her son Andrew introduced her brave work as investigative journalist, and recalled her struggles with SLAPPs. Before she was killed in 2017, Caruana Galizia was attacked with dozens of libel cases that were filed by companies, government officials and individuals.

↑ Danson Kahyana, president of Ugandan PEN, presenting the report *Stifling Dissent, Impeding Accountability*. Daniel Sikazwe, president of Zambian PEN, chaired the event. On his right is David Kaye, United Nations Special Rapporteur on the promotion and protection of the right to freedom of opinion and expression, who valued PEN's campaign and the urgent need to repeal criminal defamation laws in Africa.

↓ The president of Gambian PEN, Musa Sheriff, presenting the petition led by African PEN Centres and signed by over 150 writers and NGOs across the African continent, to the chair of the African Commission on Human and Peoples' Rights, Madame Soyata Maiga, calling on African states to abolish criminal defamation and 'insult' laws.

Dina Meza and PEN Honduras

↑   PEN International addresses the Inter-American Commission on Human Rights in March 2014. For many years, Dina Meza has been under the protection of Peace Brigades International due to the threats against her and her family. She has reported being followed, watched, and threatened and that the authorities have intercepted her communications. Cars regularly follow her during her daily activities, and armed men frequently come to her house. Constant intimidation resulted in her having to spend five months in exile in 2013.

Dina Meza, an award-winning journalist, human rights defender and author, was the victim of harassment and threats over many years. Her case featured in PEN International's 2013 Day of the Imprisoned Writer as the threats against her escalated. In 2014, she was awarded the Oxfam Novib/PEN International Freedom of Expression Award in acknowledgement of her defence of freedom of expression despite grave threats to her personal safety.

PEN International submitted a joint shadow report to the United Nations on the situation of freedom of expression in Honduras, with a focus on impunity for crimes against journalists. The report was written in collaboration with Canadian PEN and the International Human Rights Program at the University of Toronto Faculty of Law (IHRP) as well as in cooperation with several writers and journalists. In the aftermath of the publication of the report, a new Honduran PEN Centre was launched with Dina Meza as its president. The Honduran PEN Centre was officially established at the 80th PEN International Congress in Bishkek, Kyrgyzstan, on 1 October 2014.

PEN International had been working closely with Honduran PEN both on the report to the United Nations and on a campaign for journalist and founding member Julio Ernesto Alvarado. Alvarado, who had faced a 16-month work ban imposed in December 2013 due to his coverage of alleged corruption by a university dean, saw his sentence lifted by the Inter-American Commission on Human Rights (IACHR).

When Honduran PEN was created in 2014, the country had one of the highest murder rates in the world — six times the global average — and journalists and human rights defenders were particular targets. State institutions, marred by corruption and abuse, rarely bring those responsible for crimes against writers and journalists to justice. Meza continued to live under threat, while remaining one of the most visible human rights defenders in the country. Her voice was instrumental in calling for justice for protestors beaten by police, and for the environmental activist Berta Cáceres, who was murdered in 2016.

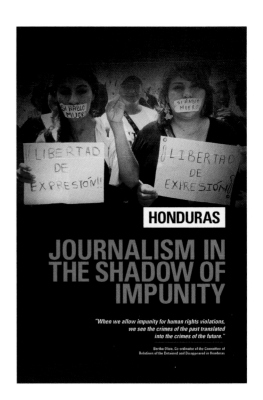

↑   PEN International, Canadian PEN, and the International Human Rights Program at the University of Toronto published a joint report about crimes against journalists in Honduras in 2014.

→
On 1 October 2014, the newly founded Honduran PEN was welcomed at the 80th PEN International Congress in Bishkek, Kyrgyzstan. Three months later, it was visited by a PEN International and Canadian PEN high-level delegation to support the Centre, and meet authorities, writers and journalists. Next to Dina Meza, on her left, is the journalist Julio Ernesto Alvarado, for whose freedom to work as a journalist PEN advocated for at the IACHR. Behind Dina is John Ralston Saul, president of PEN International, and on his left are Tamsin Mitchell, Latin America coordinator at PEN International, and Honduran PEN board members Cesario Padilla Figueroa and Kenia Oliva Cardona.

PEN stands with all LGBTQI freedom of expression activists

↑   Panel on LGBTQI writers and freedom of expression at the Bishkek Congress in 2014. From left to right: Syinat Sultanalieva, an activist with the Labrys organisation in Kyrgyzstan; the Russian journalist Masha Gessen, who in 2013 left Russia in fear of reprisals and moved to New York; Marian Botsford Fraser, chair of the WiPC. Juliet Jacques, a transgender writer from the UK, also took part in the panel.

In 2014, at the 80th PEN International Congress in Bishkek, a resolution on 'Anti-LGBTQI legislation which restricts the right to freedom of expression' was approved. Marian Botsford Fraser, who was the chair of the Writers in Prison Committee (WiPC) at this time, said: 'Between Congresses, freedom of expression issues emerge, or simmer, or sometimes actually blow up. Over several months, new pieces of legislation are proposed, in Russia, Kyrgyzstan, Uganda, threatening the LGBTQI community. It is not enough to address these issues in reactive news releases, or by signing online petitions or generating social media activity. It is essential that, as a leading freedom-of-expression organisation, PEN create a comprehensive statement that we can use in international meetings, and that individual Centres can use in their own campaigns. The resolution approved in Bishkek related to anti-LGBTQI legislation which threatens freedom of expression in one of them.' As a follow-up to the resolution, PEN International launched PEN Outwrite, an online portal to reflect the experiences of LGBTQI writers and denounce curtailments to their freedom of expression worldwide.

Resolution on anti-LGBTQI legislation which restricts the right to freedom of expression

In recent months and years, several countries, and cities and provinces within countries, have introduced legal prohibitions on 'homosexual propaganda'. These repressive pieces of legislation join an array of laws elsewhere which are used to repress the freedom to express positive views about members of the Lesbian, Gay, Bisexual, Transgender, Queer and Intersex (LGBTQI) community or even impose a ban on same-sex practices and gender variance. In the name of protecting 'public morals' or 'traditional values', such laws attempt to silence LGBTQI individuals and their supporters, effectively denying their right to freely express their sexual orientation and gender identity, and stifling their right to give and receive information about issues of sexual orientation and gender identity. Prominent among such laws are the following:

- In June 2013, the State Duma of the Russian Federation, defying international criticism, passed the so-called 'gay propaganda' law, prohibiting and criminalising the 'propaganda of non-traditional sexual relationships among minors'. […]

- A 'gay propaganda' law, similar to the Russian law but broader in scope, is at the time of writing before the Kyrgyzstan Parliament. If passed it would impose criminal sanctions for the dissemination of information on non-traditional sexual relationships, in particular activities directed at the formation of a positive attitude towards such relations. It would restrict freedom of expression and freedom of assembly within the LGBTQI community by restricting 'the organisation of and participation in peaceful gatherings that aim to make available to society any information regarding positions on any form of non-traditional sexual relations'. […]

- Nigeria has also targeted the LGBTQI community with its Same Sex Marriage (Prohibition) Act. […]

- In Iran, not only is consensual same-sex sexual activity illegal and can even lead to the death penalty, but those who are regarded as behaving or dressing in ways that do not conform to officially sanctioned gender stereotypes can face arbitrary arrest and imprisonment as well as torture and other ill-treatment including the cruel punishment of flogging. Even those who write about the existence of the LGBTQI community in Iran face reprisals: Siamak Ghaderi was released in July 2014 after serving a four-year sentence imposed in connection with blog entries he posted, including a piece in which he interviewed several gay Iranians. […]

Being queer in Tehran

Bosnian and Herzegovinian PEN, with the support of PEN International, developed a programme of dialogues among LGBTQI writers to analyse the several forms of censorship they faced. Three Iranian writers and LGBTQI activists, Elham Malekpour, Maryam Sheikh, and Babak Salimzadeh, were guests of Bosnian and Herzegovinian PEN and participated in

workshops and public events in Sarajevo and Tuzla in 2015. These young civil activists spoke about the problems facing the contemporary LGBTQI community of Iran, about the arrests, pressure, and threats from the authorities which forced them to leave their country. Babak Salimzadeh said: 'I wrote poetry highlighting the problems in society, I did artistic, committed

performances and that commitment of mine was always followed by various kinds of pressure — from my superiors interrogating me in my workplace through to "information meetings" at the Iranian security services, constant telephone calls and threats. I edited some publications that dealt with literary theory and criticism and represented views that were not in favour with the authorities, and this was an additional reason for me to be exposed to pressure. Our web portals were also under constant surveillance and often blocked, hacked… Just recently several of my friend writers were arrested due to texts that they had published. All of this lasted several years and ultimately culminated in me no longer being able to stay in Iran. It wasn't just the major psychological pressure, but my physical well-being was also being threatened.'

←   From left to right: Maryam Sheikh, Elham Malekpour, and Babak Salimzadeh at the 2015 Bosnian and Herzegovinian PEN event in Sarajevo about the forms of censorship faced by LGBTQI writers in Iran.

Gui Minhai

↑   PEN International and the International Publishers Association campaign
together for imprisoned publishers. In January 2018, the president of PEN, Jennifer
Clement, was the speaker at the 32nd International Publishers Congress in New
Delhi where the Prix Voltaire was awarded to Gui Minhai. Angela Gui, Gui Minhai's
daughter, thanked the audience for the award in a videoconference from Sweden.

In October 2015, Gui Minhai was kidnapped while on holiday in Thailand. Minhai was one of five individuals associated with publisher Mighty Current and its retail arm, Causeway Bay Book Store, to have disappeared, only to reappear in the custody of the Chinese authorities three months later. Minhai was held incommunicado before appearing on a televised 'confession' widely believed to have been coerced. On the 2016 Day of the Imprisoned Writer, PEN Centres campaigned for him across the globe.

A Chinese-born Swedish citizen, Gui Minhai is a member of the Independent Chinese PEN Centre (ICPC) and a co-founder of Mighty Current, a publishing house based in Hong Kong which prints books often critical of the Chinese Communist Party (CCP). Gui Minhai moved to Sweden as a student, and subsequently obtained citizenship there.

Two years after his disappearance, in October 2017, Gui Minhai was released on condition that he did not leave China and was required to report regularly to the police. However, he was rearrested on 20 January 2018 while travelling by train to Beijing in the company of two Swedish diplomats on his way to an urgent medical assessment at the Swedish Embassy. In February 2018, Gui Minhai appeared in a video in which he confessed to 'wrongdoing' and accused Sweden of manipulating him. The statement is thought to have been made under duress.

On 15 November 2019, Swedish PEN bestowed its Tucholsky Award — given to a writer or publisher who faces persecution or has been forced into exile — upon Gui Minhai in recognition of his work as a publisher in Hong Kong and the persecution that he has faced as a result. The decision was met with condemnation from the Chinese authorities and veiled threats from the Chinese Embassy to Sweden. In a highly unusual move, the Chinese ambassador requested that no Swedish authority should attend the Swedish PEN award ceremony. Nevertheless, the Swedish culture minister, Amanda Lind,

delivered the award and, in addition, the leader of the Swedish parliamentary opposition also attended the event.

In February 2020, Gui Minhai was convicted and sentenced to 10 years in prison on charges of 'providing intelligence'. PEN International has led protests against the sentence, noting that it had been imposed in retaliation for his work as a publisher and calling for his freedom.

DAGENS NYHETER. Nyheter   Ekonomi   **Kultur**   Sthlm   Gbg   Sport   Ledare   DN Debatt   Insändare   ≡ Mer

| Kultur

Amanda Lind: "Svensk yttrandefrihet gäller"

UPPDATERAD 2019-11-19   PUBLICERAD 2019-11-15

Kulturminister Amanda Lind delar ut priset till Gui Minhai vid Svenska PEN:s sammankomst. Foto: Magnus Hallgren

Sverige vägrar att backa efter Kinas hot om "konsekvenser".

Kulturminister Amanda Lind (MP) delade på fredagskvällen ut Svenska PENS Tucholskypris till regeringskritiske förläggaren Gui Minhai - trots att hon varnats för att bli portad från Kina.

- Vi har från regeringens sida varit tydliga med att svensk yttrandefrihet gäller, säger hon.
"Det allvarliga misstaget från den svenska sidan skapar oundvikligen allvarliga svårigheter att upprätthålla vänskapliga utbyten och samarbeten mellan Kina och Sverige", skriver Kinas ambassad i ett uttalande på sin hemsida sent på fredagskvällen.

↑   Even though the Chinese ambassador to Sweden had condemned the 2019 Tucholsky Award to Gui Minhai, and even requested that no Swedish authority should attend the Swedish PEN award ceremony, the minister of culture, Amanda Lind, stood up to give the award to an absent Gui Minhai in front of the cameras of Swedish and international media.

Sts'ibuel ta bats'il
k'opetik te sk'oplalul
pajel cha'we

Translation and linguistic rights

In 1996, PEN International proclaimed, with the support of UNESCO and together with a network of 61 other international organisations, a Universal Declaration of Linguistic Rights (UDLR). The document shaped PEN's vision of linguistic communities as empowered to develop their languages in all spheres of social life. The UDLR got the immediate support of President Nelson Mandela, Archbishop Desmond Tutu, His Holiness the Dalai Lama, Rigoberta Menchú, and other Nobel Peace Prize winners such as José Ramos-Horta, Adolfo Pérez Esquivel, Yasser Arafat, and Shimon Peres. Writers who had been recipients of the Nobel Prize in Literature also joined including Octavio Paz, Wisława Szymborska, and Seamus Heaney. For the next decade, the document shaped PEN's relationship with UNESCO and its Linguapax programme.

This vision to encompass all languages was an idea already expounded by PEN's founders. The 1928 Oslo and 1929 Vienna Congresses had decided 'that the method of dividing the International P.E.N. in sections, and the right of voting at congresses, should be based upon literary and cultural ground.' From the creation of Yiddish PEN in 1928 to Tibetan and Uyghur PEN in the twenty-first century, PEN's understanding of internationality welcomed literary communities without exclusion.

In 1978, at the Stockholm Congress, PEN International's Committee for Translation and Linguistic Rights was founded with the mission of promoting both translation from 'literatures of lesser currency' and the equal rights of all language communities. The powerful translation programmes of English PEN and American PEN have actively supported the increase in the translations of world literatures into English. The World Voices Festival in New York City, which has been organised by American PEN since 2005, is one of the world's most active venues for bringing the world's literatures together.

In 2007, at the Frankfurt Book Fair, the Committee for Translation and Linguistic Rights presented the report *To Be Translated or Not to Be*, which explored the international network of policies on translation and defined strategies for the increase of translation into the English language.

In PEN, the translation and the promotion of local languages work hand in hand. At the turn of the century, PEN Centres in Africa developed projects for the promotion of creative writing in schools in African languages with tens of thousands of participants in countries like Sierra Leone, Guinea, Ghana, Malawi, South Africa, and Zambia. PEN also participated in the research and promotion of best publishing practices for African national literatures, understanding the translation of African languages as 'Culture's Oxygen', which was the title of a 2016 PEN report.

The founding of a South India PEN, gathering writers in Tamil, Malayalam, Telugu, Konkani, Kannada, and Marathi, was welcomed at the 2018 PEN Congress in Pune, which celebrated all the world's 6,000 languages. The following year, in Chiapas, Mexico, together with UNESCO and the very active network of Mayan writers, PEN gathered authors from Indigenous languages of the Americas, India, Europe, Philippines, and Australia and announced a vision of seeing themselves as 'Writing the Future in Indigenous Languages'.

The Universal Declaration of Linguistic Rights greatly influenced other documents created by PEN. The 'Girona Manifesto of Linguistic Rights' and the 'Quebec Declaration on Literary Translation and Translators' have been the tools used by PEN Centres to promote its vision on the equality of languages and translation as a key part of cultural exchange. These two were followed by the 'Donostia Protocol to Ensure Language Rights' in 2017, which PEN, along with more than 200 institutions and organisations from Europe's civil society, signed on to.

As a spokesperson for the Universal Declaration of Linguistic Rights, Rigoberta Menchú said, 'In language lies the main weapon of resistance'. PEN members have been using this weapon daily, tirelessly and against all odds.

← The poster for the Chiapas meeting of PEN's Translation and Linguistic Rights Committee was designed by artist Sergi Rucabado Rebés, recreating a classical Maya motif with the sign of a pen and in the form of a star in the blue sky of Chiapas. The title of the meeting in Tseltal language reads 'Writing the Future in Indigenous Languages'. The Zoque and Spanish versions of the poster can be seen on pages 230 and 231. It was produced in five other Mayan languages as well as English.

Oslo 1928 and Vienna 1929
PEN Centres based upon 'literary and cultural ground'

JUNE, 1928   P.E.N. NEWS   3

NEW HONORARY MEMBERS
H. G. WELLS
We have much pleasure in announcing that Mr. H. G. Wells has consented to be Honorary Member of the London Centre in the place of Thomas Hardy.

SHOLOM ASCH
We also extend a hearty welcome to the distinguished novelist and dramatist, Mr. Sholom Asch, who joins the ranks of Honorary Members as a representative of our newly established Yiddish Centre in Poland. The following biographical note from "Who's Who in American Jewry" may be of interest:
Born November 1st, 1880, in Poland. Began literary career writing in Hebrew and Yiddish 1900. Author: The Village (translated into many languages), 1903; The God of Vengeance (played in various languages throughout the world), 1905; Mary (first novel translated into Russian, German, Polish), 1908; Came to America 1910. Member staff Jewish Daily Forward 1910. Wrote "America," an impression of the United States; returned to Europe, settled in the United States 1914. Author: Motke the Vagabond, 1914; Uncle Moses, 1916; Kidush Hashem (first historical novel, translated into English, Russian, German), 1918; The Witch of Castilia, 1920; The Mother (novel of American immigrant life), 1924; The Electric Chair, 1925. All works translated into European languages. Member: J.D.C.; Drama and Music Society, Leningrad. Clubs: Jewish Writers, Warsaw; Poetry Writers, New York City. Residence: 5 rue Emile, Bellevue (S. et O.), France. Office: 175 East Broadway, New York City.

* * *

Mr. Martin Andersen Nexo, Honorary member for Denmark, has sent us in German a most inspiring message which we are eager to publish:
Sehr geehrte Herren!
Von einer weiten Reise zurück finde ich Ihren werten Brief vom 24 Januar vor und danke Ihnen recht herzlich für die Mitteilungen.
Mir der grössten Freude erfahre ich aus Ihrem Briefe, dass der P.E.N. CLUB fortwährend Eroberungen macht und bald die ganze Erdrunde umspannt. Mögen Ihre schöne Ziele immer mehr in Erfüllung gehen und Ihr grossartiger Club sich eines Tages als Mutter einer geistigen, weltumspannenden Kameradschaft sehen!
Mit hochachtungsvoller Bewunderung!
Ihr ganz ergebener
Martin Andersen Nexo.

* * *

MEMBERS GOING ABROAD
If members visiting other countries will write to the Secretary, enclosing a stamped envelope, they will receive a card introducing them to Secretaries of other centres. A few notes on their literary work should be given. This card will constitute an introduction to all centres in other countries and should be signed and retained by the holder.

NOTE ON JUNE DINNER
This dinner—when we had the pleasure of entertaining Sir Thomas Beecham, with Mr. Drinkwater in the chair—attracted an unusually large number of representative men and women. Not only was there a good muster of our own members but among the guests were Madame Vajkai, the leading authority on Child Welfare in Hungary, who has invented a system of autonomous training which is practised in the Save the Children Fund's work-schools in Budapest; Sir Edmund Phipps, of the Board of Education; Mr. Robert Loraine, the actor; Lady Heath, the well-known airwoman; Dr. Curt Otto, Director of the famous publishing firm Tauchnitz; Dr. Percy Buck, Music Master at Harrow; Miss Daisy Kennedy, the violinist; Mr. Pool Knudsen, Danish dramatist and translator of Vedekind and Maeterlinck; Madame Aino Malmberg, author of many books on English celebrities. We were also happy to have with us the Founder of the South African Centre, Mrs. Sarah Gertrude Millin, who will attend the Oslo Congress as delegate.

ENJOYABLE AFTER-DINNER PARTY
We wish to record our appreciation and to thank Miss Henrietta Leslie for the very enjoyable party she arranged for London members on May 26th. A surprise delight of the evening was the madrigal-singing by vocalists from the London College of Choristers.

C. E. MONTAGUE
Since our last issue we have lost by death one of our most distinguished members. Through being domiciled in Manchester, Mr. Montague was, unfortunately for us, seldom able to take part in our functions, but in many other ways he proved himself to be a good friend to the P.E.N.

OUTSTANDING SUBSCRIPTIONS
Still a few members have not taken it sufficiently to heart that subscriptions are due each year on the 1st October in autumn. An appeal is made to those who have not paid to help the P.E.N. by doing so without delay, and thereby save an expenditure of time and money on personal letters. Kindly make the cheque for 26/- payable to Mr. Norman Croom-Johnson, 107, Great Russell Street, W.C.1.

WHEN YOU CHANGE YOUR ADDRESS
Members changing their addresses are particularly asked to note that we do not alter our Address Book unless specially instructed to do so. This is made necessary because many members frequently write from temporary addresses.

* * *

N.B.   With the July dinner the P.E.N. Season comes to an end and P.E.N. NEWS will not be issued again until October.

↑   *PEN News* from June 1928, announcing that both HG Wells and Sholem Asch, as representative of the newly established Yiddish PEN, had been welcomed as honorary members by English PEN.

↓   Helen Cruickshank was founder of Scottish PEN together with Hugh MacDiarmid, Herbert Grierson, and Neil Gunn.

↘   Press cards of Louis Piérard, founder of Belgian PEN in 1922.

→   Fernand Victor Toussaint van Boelaere, president of Flemish PEN, commemorated on a postage stamp in 1976.

From the very start, PEN International welcomed two Clubs in Spain, one in Barcelona for Catalan literature and one in Madrid for writers in the Spanish language, and both were present at the 1923 PEN Congress in London. Slovenian PEN based in Ljubljana and Serbian PEN in Belgrade followed in 1926, and Croatian PEN based in Zagreb in January 1927. But as the organisation grew, a reflection about how to structure PEN Centres was developed. Between the 6th PEN International Oslo Congress in 1928 and the 7th Congress in Vienna in 1929, several debates took place until the decision was taken that literatures and not countries would be the basis for establishing PEN Centres. A celebrated resolution by Henry Seidel Canby from American PEN, carried unanimously at the Vienna Congress, laid down the principle 'that the method of dividing the International P.E.N. in sections, and the right of voting at congresses, should be based upon literary and cultural ground'.

At the Oslo PEN Congress, Scottish PEN fought off claims that it did not represent a separate culture. The Centre had been founded by Hugh MacDiarmid, Helen Cruickshank, Neil Gunn, and others. The journalist William Power made Scottish PEN's case at the Oslo Congress. The decision on Scottish PEN was received as a radical cultural act in Scotland. This coincided with the decision to welcome another PEN Centre solely based on a language: Yiddish PEN, with a main office in Vilna and branches in Warsaw and New York.

In Belgium, where Louis Piérard had founded Belgian PEN in 1922, a separate Flemish PEN was founded in 1930, and Fernand Victor Toussaint van Boelaere became its first chair. All PEN Centres were actively welcoming foreign writers in Glasgow, London, Brussels, Stockholm, Madrid, Warsaw, Barcelona… Dinners, or teas, became the PEN way of celebrating the kinship between literatures.

→   The Canby resolution establishing that PEN Centres should be based upon 'literary and cultural ground' at the 1929 Vienna Congress.

VIENNA CONGRESS: June 1929

RIGHT OF REPRESENTATION AT CONGRESSES

The P.E.N. lays it down as a principle that the method of dividing the International P.E.N. in sections, and the right of voting at congresses, should be based upon literary and cultural ground.   The International Executive Committee will study the question and will propose a resolution at the next Congress for carrying out this principle.

                              Dr.Henry Seidel Canby (America)

CARRIED UNANIMOUSLY

The Yiddish PEN Club

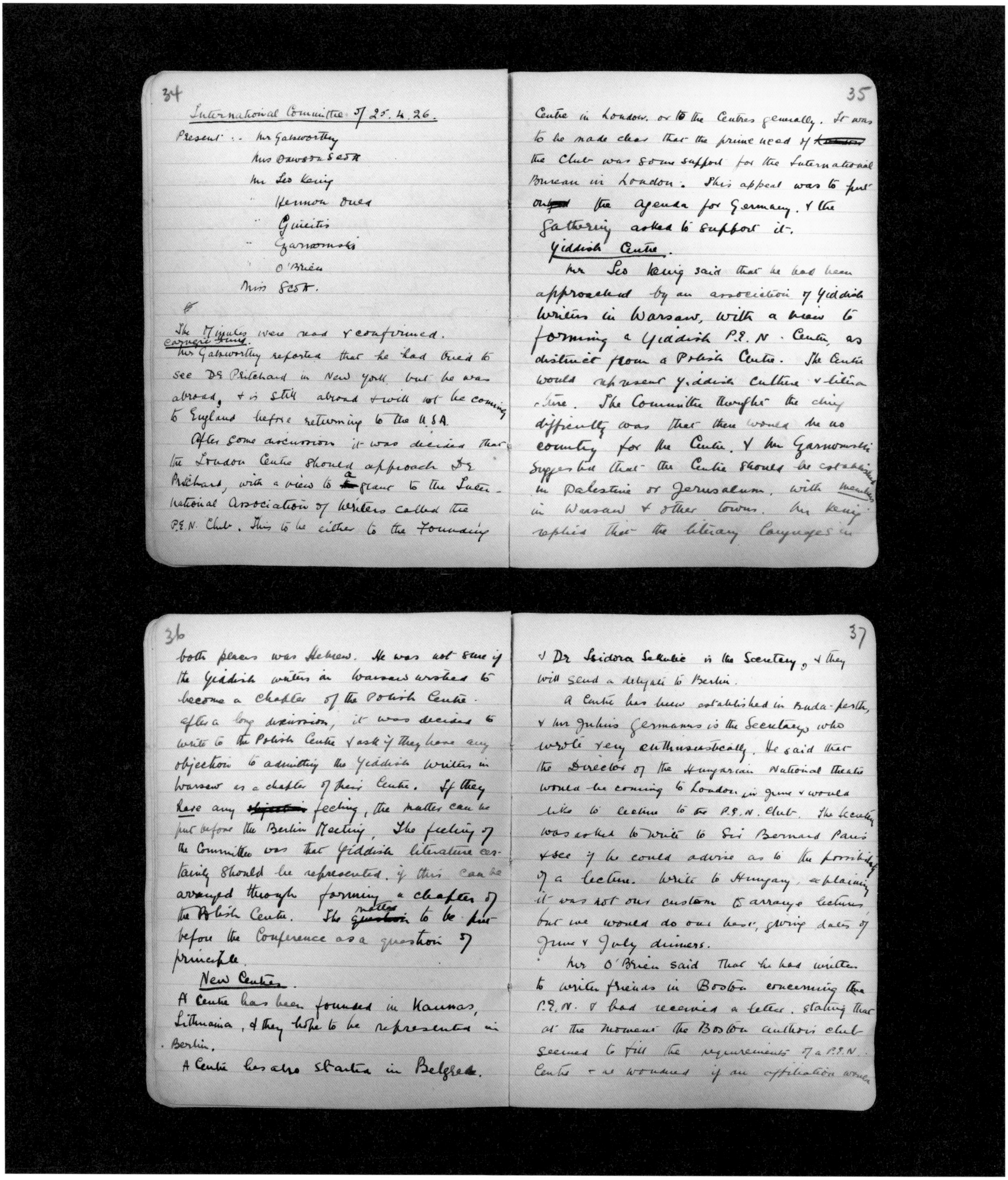

[handwritten notebook pages]

34

International Committee of 25.4.26.

Present:- Mr Galsworthy
          Mrs Dawson Scott
          Mr Leo Kenig
          " Hermon Ould
          " Guieitis
          " Garnomski
          " O'Brien
          Miss Scott.

The Minutes were read & confirmed.
Carnegie Fund
Mr Galsworthy reported that he had tried to see Dr Pritchard in New York but he was abroad, & is still abroad & will not be coming to England before returning to the U.S.A.

After some discussion it was decided that the London Centre should approach Dr Pritchard, with a view to a grant to the International Association of Writers called the P.E.N. Club. This to be either to the Founding

35

Centre in London. or to the Centres generally. It was to be made clear that the prime need of the Club was some support for the International Bureau in London. This appeal was to be put only on the agenda for Germany, & the Gathering asked to support it.

Yiddish Centre.

Mr Leo Kenig said that he had been approached by an association of Yiddish Writers in Warsaw, with a view to forming a Yiddish P.E.N. Centre, as distinct from a Polish Centre. The Centre would represent Yiddish culture & literature. The Committee thought the chief difficulty was that there would be no country for the Centre. & Mr Garnomski suggested that the Centre should be established in Palestine or Jerusalem, with members in Warsaw & other towns. Mr Kenig replied that the literary languages in

36

both places was Hebrew. He was not sure if the Yiddish writers in Warsaw wished to become a chapter of the Polish Centre.
After a long discussion, it was decided to write to the Polish Centre & ask if they have any objection to admitting the Yiddish Writers in Warsaw as a chapter of their Centre. If they have any feeling, the matter can be put before the Berlin Meeting. The feeling of the Committee was that Yiddish literature certainly should be represented. if this can be arranged through forming a chapter of the Polish Centre. The matter to be put before the Conference as a question of principle.

New Centres.

A Centre has been founded in Kaunas, Lithuania, & they wish to be represented in Berlin.
A Centre has also started in Belgrade.

37

& Dr Isidora Sekulic is the Secretary, & they will send a delegate to Berlin.
A Centre has been established in Buda-Pesth, & Mr Julius Germanus is the Secretary who wrote very enthusiastically. He said that the Director of the Hungarian National theatre would be coming to London in June & would like to lecture to the P.E.N. Club. The Secretary was asked to write to Sir Bernard Paris & see if he could advise as to the possibility of a lecture. Write to Hungary, explaining it was not our custom to arrange lectures, but we would do our best, giving dates of June & July dinners.
Mr O'Brien said that he had written to writer friends in Boston concerning the P.E.N. & had received a letter stating that at the moment the Boston authors club seemed to fill the requirements of a P.E.N. Centre & he wondered if an affiliation would

Yiddish writers from Warsaw approached PEN's International Committee to propose the creation of a Yiddish PEN. In 1927, after long debates in which Warsaw was turned down as their PEN location, PEN International formally recognised Yiddish PEN Club in Vilna (now Vilnius), with branches in Warsaw and New York. Outstanding Yiddish writers like Sholem Asch, who was the honorary president of the Club, and Isaac Bashevis Singer were closely tied to Yiddish PEN. In 1935, Yiddish PEN published Singer's debut novel, *Der śotn in Goray* (*Satan in Goray*), for the first time in book form.

Yiddish PEN Club was decimated in Warsaw by the Nazis and suspended in Vilnius after the Soviet occupation of Lithuania. There was a debate about a manifesto provided by the Yiddish PEN Centre at the 31st PEN International Congress in Rio de Janeiro in 1960, the same Congress that created the Writers in Prison Committee (WiPC). Many writers advocated to adopt a resolution that expressed solidarity and also protested against the suppression of Yiddish and Hebrew literatures in the Soviet Union. With its 'Yiddish resolution' from 1960, PEN International paid a posthumous tribute to Yiddish writers murdered in the Soviet Union.

The branch of Yiddish PEN in New York existed until the end of the twentieth century.

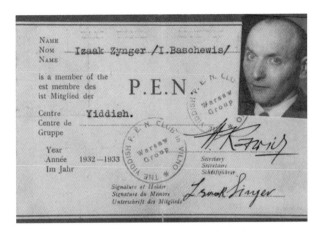

↑ In 1935, Yiddish PEN published the first novel by Isaac Bashevis Singer. In 1978, Singer was awarded the Nobel Prize in Literature.

↙ Sholem Asch (Szalom Asz) became honorary president of Yiddish PEN Club after establishing himself in the USA in 1939. The picture shows Sholem Asch (second from left) attending the PEN Congress in Warsaw in 1930, together with the art historian Stefania Zahorska, welcomed in exile in London in 1939 by English PEN and Polish PEN in Exile, and Michał Weinzieher, art critic and director of the Historical Museum of Lviv, who died in 1944 at the hands of the Gestapo.

↓ The Yiddish resolution at the 31st PEN International Congress in Rio de Janeiro in 1960.

← Minutes of the PEN International Committee meeting of 25 April 1926, attended by the Yiddish critic and journalist Arye-Leyb Yaffe (known as Leo Koenig), who had been living in London since 1914: 'Mr Leo Koenig said that he had been approached by an association of Yiddish Writers in Warsaw, with a view to forming a Yiddish PEN Centre, as distinct from the Polish Centre. The Centre would represent Yiddish culture and literature. The committee thought the main difficulty was that there would be no country for the Centre. And Mr Galsworthy suggested that the Centre should be established in Palestine or Jerusalem, with members in Warsaw and other towns. Mr Koenig replied that the literary languages in both places was Hebrew. He was not sure if the Yiddish writers in Warsaw wished to become a chapter of the Polish Centre. After a long discussion, it was decided to write to the Polish Centre and ask if they have any objection to admitting the Yiddish writers in Warsaw as a chapter of their Centre. If they have any objection, the matter can be put before the Berlin Meeting. The feeling of the committee was that Yiddish literature certainly should be represented if this can be arranged through forming a chapter of the Polish Centre. The matter to be put before the Conference is a question of principle.'

P.E.N., INTERNATIONAL EXECUTIVE.RIO.JULY 24/60.   Page 11.

Afternoon Session.

In the absence of the International President, Mr. Elmer Rice, International Vice-President, assumed the Chair.

Resolutions (continued):-

(vii) Austria The Chairman (Elmer Rice) said in his view this was a statement of opinion rather than a Resolution; he asked if the Austrian delegation would be satisfied to have it thus recorded in the Minutes, without further debate; the Austrian delegates agreed.

YIDDISH CENTRE'S MANIFESTO Mr.Rice suggested that this statement should also be recorded only, but Jacob Bolosansky urged that it be considered as a Resolution although at present in the form of a Declaration; he felt its adoption would be a posthumous tribute to Yiddish writers murdered in the Soviet Union, as well as evidence that P.E.N. would not silently tolerate such matters. Mr.Sowden asked if the original hope that Russians might be present as individual observers had prompted this Resolution; Mr.Rice said as they were not present, and no application to form a Soviet P.E.N. Centre had yet been received, so perhaps this Resolution was premature. Mr.Bolosansky said the possibility that Russian observers might have been present was immaterial to the importance of his Resolution, which urged that P.E.N. should formally protest against the suppression of Yiddish and Hebrew literature and languages in the USSR. Paul Tabori suggested that if the last paragraph only were used, with the opening phrase 'At the same time' omitted, it would be a workable Resolution. The Chairman agreed (as did the Yiddish delegate) but reminded delegates as this had not been circulated by P.E.N. rules it would require to receive a two-thirds majority vote in its favour to pass to the Business Session. Alexander Janta (Exile Centre,New York) and Lewis Sowden(South Africa) jointly seconded this Resolution. Yves Gandon said while not wishing to appear to doubt the accuracy of the Yiddish delegation, he doubted if this Resolution should be recorded unless the claims it made were known to be true. Mr. Rice said undoubtedly it must be recorded in the Minutes, as would any Resolution presented by a Centre; delegates would be able to vote for or against it in the normal way. Roger Caillois said it was a fact that the matter contained in this Resolution was perfectly true; it was known to most readers of

Pompeu Fabra, a language in exile

↑↑   Pompeu Fabra at the first PEN
International Congress in London in 1923.
Front row second from right is Josep
Millàs-Raurell, the other Catalan delegate.

↑   Pompeu Fabra with PEN International
president HG Wells chairing the 1935
PEN International Congress in Barcelona.

Pompeu Fabra was an engineer and a grammarian. From his position as chair of the Philological Section of the Institut d'Estudis Catalans (the Catalan Academy), he presided over the completion of the Catalan grammar and dictionary. He was called 'the architect of modern Catalan' and became a figure of enormous cultural prestige. Fabra was chosen as president by the group of young writers who founded the Catalan PEN Club in April 1922. Together with Josep Millàs-Raurell, he attended the first PEN International Congress in London in 1923, and they were welcomed at the gala dinner by members of the English PEN Club.

Pompeu Fabra co-chaired the 1935 PEN International Congress held in Barcelona together with PEN International president HG Wells. The card with both International and Catalan PEN boards was included in the delegates' documents for that Congress, and news in *La Vanguardia* on the Congress reproduced selections from the inaugural speeches of both presidents.

In 1939 the whole board of Catalan PEN went into exile. Pompeu Fabra remained in the commune of Prades (*Prada de Conflent* in Catalan) in France, by the Spanish border in

the so-called 'Northern Catalonia'. As the father of the Catalan dictionary, he embodied the exile of a language persecuted at home. Pau Casals, the internationally acclaimed cellist and composer, also spent his years of exile in Prades, and there are several pictures of both Fabra and Casals at the time. In 1948, Casals organised a concert to celebrate Fabra's birthday, only a few weeks before his passing.

Before his death, Fabra had met a notary in Andorra, the tiny state in the Pyrenees, which was the only place in the world where he could draft his will in Catalan, a language forbidden in Spain for decades.

↑   Pau Casals, the internationally acclaimed cellist and composer, also spent his years of exile in Prades, and there are several pictures of both Fabra and Casals at the time. In 1948, Casals organised and played at a concert to celebrate Pompeu Fabra's eightieth birthday, only a few weeks before his passing.

1978 Stockholm: Committee for Translation and Linguistic Rights

The PEN International Translation and Linguistic Rights Committee was established at the 43rd PEN International Congress in Stockholm in 1978. Since its foundation, PEN had been developing programmes to support translation. As early as 1928, PEN signed an agreement with the International Institute of Intellectual Co-operation, a committee of the League of Nations. A meeting taking place in Geneva in July 1928, with the participation of, among others, John Galsworthy, Salvador de Madariaga, Vittorio Rossi, and Elena Văcărescu, approved a resolution taking note of the agreement between PEN and the Institute: 'It has accordingly been arranged that each P.E.N. Club centre shall furnish for its own country a list of not more than twenty works which it would recommend for translation (works published in the original language before 1900). The Institute would then communicate these lists to publishers and the Press in various countries. The Sub-Committee notes the undertaking given by the P.E.N. Clubs to furnish translators, including translators of texts set to music, with such information as they may think desirable.'

In 1978, with Mario Vargas Llosa as president of PEN International, Swedish PEN welcomed delegates from the whole world at the 43rd PEN International Congress in Stockholm. Per Wästberg, president of Swedish PEN, insisted that the agenda include the importance of translators and gathered together a network of PEN Centres willing to work together in this area. Originally called the Programme and Translation Committee, it aimed to encourage and promote translation from all literatures without exception. The committee began by producing anthologies of literatures that were rarely translated to widely spoken languages. Supported by PEN Centres, anthologies between Portuguese and Catalan poets or Macedonian and French poets were published. From the very beginning, the intention was to facilitate contacts and support literatures with little international visibility.

The committee rejected a hierarchy among languages and moved away from conversations on 'small' languages to calling these 'minoritised' in the publishing market, meaning languages turned into minorities because of their limited access to translation. Under the presidency of the poet Ana Hatherly from Portugal PEN in the late 1980s and early 1990s, and with the strong support of the PEN Centre of Hungarian Writers in Romania and Romanian, Finnish, Norwegian, Swedish, Kurdish, Scottish, Welsh, Quebec, Basque, Galician, Catalan, Macedonian, Croatian, Slovenian, Kenya and Guinean PEN Centres, the committee affirmed that translation was inseparable to the defence of the rights of cultural communities and, therefore, changed its name to 'Committee for Translation and Linguistic Rights.'

↑↑   Per Wästberg, president of Swedish PEN, welcoming delegates from PEN Centres across the globe to the 43rd PEN International Congress in Stockholm. Here he is in conversation with Wole Soyinka.

↑   Nadine Gordimer, left, with another delegate from South African PEN at the PEN International Congress in Stockholm in 1978.

6   P.E.N. NEWS   NOVEMBER, 1928

TRANSLATION SCHEME

The International Institute of Intellectual Co-operation Sub-Committee on Arts and Letters met in Geneva from 16th to 19th July. The Literary Section of the Sub-Committee was presided over by M. Paul Valèry, of the French Academy.

The following were present : Mm. Destrée, Deputy, former Belgian Minister of Sciences and Arts ; De Reynold, professor at the University of Berne ; John Galsworthy; Jelinek, Counsellor to the Ministry of Foreign Affairs at Prague ; Kippenberg, Director of the "Insel Verlag," Leipzig ; Salvador de Madariaga, professor of Spanish Literature at Oxford ; Vittorio Rossi, professor of Italian Literature at the University of Rome ; Mlle. Hélène Vacaresco, Roumanian delegate to the League of Nations.

Having heard the report of the International Institute of Intellectual Co-operation on the question of Translation, the following resolution was adopted :

It notes the agreement reached between the Institute and the Federation of P.E.N. Clubs, as explained in the statements made in the Sub-Committee by the Chief of the Literary Relations Section of the Institute and by Mr. Galsworthy, President of the P.E.N. Club Foundation Centre.

It has accordingly been arranged that each P.E.N. Club centre shall furnish for its own country a list of not more than twenty works which it would recommend for translation (works published in the original language before 1900).

The Institute would then communicate these lists to publishers and the Press in the various countries.

The Sub-Committee notes the undertaking given by the P.E.N. Clubs to furnish translators, including translators of texts set to music, with such information as they may think desirable.

The Sub-Committee requests the Institute to compile a handbook of such information, to be placed at the disposal of authors, publishers and any others who may be interested.

The Institute will be asked to ascertain what steps should be taken to arrange with publishers that translations shall always bear the original title of the work and the names of the author and the translator.

On the basis of catalogues already published, the Institute, with the help of the P.E.N. Club Centres if necessary, will compile a bibliography of translations published during the preceding year.

The Institute may also communicate with literary societies in various countries in order to obtain from them any information that may be of value in connection with this question.

The Sub-Committee, being of opinion that the question of translations cannot be settled without the co-operation of publishers, requests the Institute to arrange for the resumption of the series of International Publishers' Congresses held prior to 1914.

The Sub-Committee approves the steps taken with a view to the publication of a series of translations in various languages of works by Latin-American writers.

PUBLICATIONS RECEIVED

We acknowledge with thanks the receipt of :

Times Literary Supplement.

London Mercury.

New Zealand News

La Bulgarie

International Institute of Intellectual Co-operation Bulletin, August.

Knjizevni Zivot, Zagreb.

Die Bottcherstrasse, Bremen.

Pax, Paris.

↑   The November 1928 issue of *P.E.N. News* reports on the recent agreement between 'The Federation of P.E.N. Clubs' and the League of Nations' Institute of Intellectual Co-operation to promote a translation scheme.

Ngũgĩ wa Thiong'o

↖   Ngũgĩ wa Thiong'o with Amanda Hopkinson, chair of the Translation Committee of English PEN (1993–96), in conversation in London on International Translation Day 2013.

↑   In *Decolonising the Mind: The Politics of Language in African Literature*, Ngũgĩ wa Thiong'o explains the process by which he reached the decision to write in Gikuyu, his mother tongue, and makes a call to African writers to go back to writing in African languages.

Ngũgĩ wa Thiong'o was already a writer of international prestige in 1977 when he wrote a controversial play in the Gikuyu language, *Ngaahika Ndeenda* (*I Will Marry When I Want*). The play was performed in Limuru, Kenya, in an open-air theatre, and the actors were workers and peasants from the town and surrounding area. Sharply critical of the inequalities and injustices of Kenyan society, the play communicated with the audience in the language of their daily lives. Ngũgĩ wa Thiong'o was arrested and imprisoned without charge at Kamiti Maximum Security Prison on the last day of 1977. His memoir *Detained: A Writer's Prison Diary* (1982) describes his decision to abandon English and write in Gikuyu, his mother tongue. He elaborated this position in *Decolonising the Mind* (1986). However, in prison, he had already written, on toilet paper, his novel *Caitaani Mũtharabainĩ* (1981), which was translated into English as *Devil on the Cross* (1982).

Ngũgĩ wa Thiong'o was a PEN International's main case. Together with Amnesty International, PEN campaigned and secured his release in December 1978. However, the Moi dictatorship barred him from jobs at colleges and universities in the country.

He resumed his writing and his activities in the theatre, and thus continued to be an uncomfortable public voice. While in Britain for the launch and promotion of *Devil on the Cross*, Ngũgĩ wa Thiong'o learned about a plot to assassinate him on his return. The regime's coded language for this plot was to say the country must give Ngũgĩ wa Thiong'o a 'red carpet' welcome upon his return to Kenya and so he was forced into exile. When Ngũgĩ wa Thiong'o's next Gikuyu novel, *Matigari ma Njiruungi*, was published, thinking that the novel's main character was a real living person, President Daniel Moi issued an arrest warrant but, on learning that the character was fictional, had the novel 'arrested' instead. Undercover police removed the book from bookshops across the country.

When PEN International launched the process towards the Universal Declaration of Linguistic Rights in 1994, Ngũgĩ wa Thiong'o contributed to the drafting and became one of its main supporters: 'The Declaration may be a good starting point for the liberation of all languages. It is an important complement to the Universal Declaration of Human Rights. Even before being incorporated by the world's highest institutions, it must already be considered as a first-class document for its contents and because it has obtained the support of significant non-government organisations from all over the world.' In 2017, Ngũgĩ wa Thiong'o was the keynote speaker at the Norway Writers in Prison/ICORN Conference in Lillehammer, launching the 'Make Space' campaign in support of writers in exile. At the 84th PEN International Congress in Pune, India, in 2018, his unflinching promotion of African national literatures was recognised when he was elected vice-president of PEN International.

↑   When PEN International launched the process
towards the Universal Declaration of Linguistic
Rights in 1994, Ngũgĩ wa Thiong'o contributed to
the drafting and became one of its main supporters:
'The Declaration may be a good starting point for
the liberation of all languages.'

World Conference on Linguistic Rights

↑   Delegates from 61 NGOs, 41 PEN Centres, and 40
experts in linguistic rights from all over the world
met in Barcelona for the World Conference on
Linguistic Rights. Here they are listening to a
reading of the UDLR in the Great Hall of Barcelona
University.

On 6–8 of June 1996, 61 NGOs, 41 PEN Centres and 40 experts in
linguistic rights from all over the world met in Barcelona. The World
Conference on Linguistic Rights (WCLR) was an initiative of PEN
International's Translations and Linguistic Rights Committee and
Barcelona's Centre Internacional Escarré per a les Minories Ètniques
i les Nacions (CIEMEN) research centre, along with the moral and
technical support of UNESCO.

Ronald Harwood, president of PEN International (1993–97), welcomed
the participants: 'It is because we are writers that our commitment
for linguistic rights exists. And it is because we are writers that we know
full well we cannot influence in isolation, cannot live in a vacuum,
or reside in a *tour d'ivoire*. We cannot flourish as some self-regarding

elite, separate and above the rest of society. Which is why we are here this evening. Because we have understood the need for and worked hard for cooperation and collaboration with all the Non-Governmental Organisations you represent, to come together to write and support the Universal Declaration of Linguistic Rights.'

Isidor Marí was the chair of the Scientific Council, a group of 28 linguists, sociolinguists, and jurists from the five continents. He said, 'All predictions indicate that during the twenty-first century, 80 per cent of the languages from all over the world may disappear. Therefore, the Declaration is a text that becomes necessary to correct linguistic imbalances with a view to ensuring the respect and full development of all languages and establishing the principles for a just and equitable linguistic peace throughout the world as a key factor in the maintenance of harmonious social relations.'

The Assembly of Participants at the WCLR approved the UDLR in a ceremony held on 6 June at the Great Hall of the University of Barcelona. There were delegates from the World Council of Indigenous Peoples, Finnish PEN, the Academy of Mayan Languages, Belorussian PEN, and the Assembly of the Guarani People, Israeli PEN, and Palestinian PEN, the Rromani Unia, the Kurdish Institute in Paris, the PEN Centre of Hungarian Writers in Romania, South African PEN, the Institute for Occitan Studies, and the Maori Language Commission... The delegates from NGOs, PEN Centres, and experts signed the document during the ceremony and presented the document with all the signatures to the official representative of UNESCO. A month later, Federico Mayor Zaragoza, director general of UNESCO, received the organisers of the conference, welcomed the initiative by PEN and the other NGOs, and defined the process for UNESCO to initiate its own deliberation about the UDLR.

Literature and Peace Nobel Prizes in favour of the Universal Declaration of Linguistic Rights

← Adolfo Pérez Esquivel, the Argentinian artist and human rights activist whose grandmother was a Guarani speaker, was the fourth Nobel Peace Prize laureate to support PEN and the UDLR: 'I am writing to express my support […]. What is more, I hope that unlimited respect for linguistic rights becomes a reality for it is a basis for coexistence and pacific cultural exchange between countries. Peace and goodwill.'

↓ The UDLR was very actively supported in the UNESCO debates by the South African ambassador.

Nelson Mandela (left) was among the first supporters.

Anthony Fleischer (centre), president of South African PEN and actively involved in the drafting of the declaration, brought a personal message from President Mandela, which read: 'The ideal of formulating linguistic human rights is indeed a magnificent undertaking and also long overdue. However, in view of the fact that the Declaration is still under discussion, I am at this stage only prepared to endorse the general spirit of the undertaking. I wish you well with this project.'

Archbishop Desmond Tutu (right) was also enthusiastic: 'I am pleased to endorse the Universal Declaration of Linguistic Rights. I believe it is the right of every person to be able to express themselves in the language of their choice. This right has been enshrined in the new South African Constitution and my sincere hope is that may be accepted at the next UNESCO General Meeting. In recognising the value of individual languages we acknowledge the dignity and worth of our fellow human beings. I appreciate your effort to promote this basic right. God bless you.'

In language lies the main weapon of resistance

Rigoberta Menchú, a leader of the international Indigenous movement, received the Nobel Peace Prize in 1992. She appears in the photograph above, after a coordination meeting for the promotion of the UDLR with Carles Torner from PEN, Aureli Argemí and Oriol Ramon from CIEMEN, and Kendal Nezan, president of the Kurdish Institute in Paris. In her presentation on the UDLR, Menchú told the United Nations: 'I am convinced that language is the vehicle that permits thought to be in accordance with the knowledge and the world vision of a given culture, of a given people, who have inherited this from their ancestors and which, at the same time, makes it possible to pass it on to the new generations. In language lies the main weapon of resistance of those cultures which for centuries have suffered the imposition of alien cultural values, as is the case of the native peoples of Latin America.'

↑   A few months after the UDLR was proclaimed, the East Timorese foreign minister in exile José Ramos-Horta won the Nobel Peace Prize together with Carlos Filipe Ximenes Bello, bishop of Dili, East Timor. When asked to support the Declaration, Ramos-Horta sent a quote from his Nobel lecture: 'More than half a century after the Jewish holocaust and centuries after the genocide of the Indigenous peoples of Australia and the Americas, the same attitude that has allowed these crimes to take place persists today. Opinion-makers and leaders, academics, writers and journalists who pretend to be objective and neutral in the face of racism and discrimination, the rape of a small nation by a larger power, the persecution of a weaker people by a ruthless army, must share the guilt. […] Indigenous peoples continue to see their ancestral land taken over by developers, their culture and beliefs, and their very existence reduced to a tourist commodity.'

↓   When the declaration was proclaimed, three Literature Nobel laureates supported it immediately: Wisława Szymborksa of Polish PEN (left), Octavio Paz of Mexican PEN (centre), and Seamus Heaney of Irish PEN (right). Both Szymborska and Heaney offered poems for the promotion of the declaration: Szymborska's poem was 'Into the Ark' and Heaney's 'Alphabets'.

The Dalai Lama and PEN's defence of the Tibetan language

↑   The Dalai Lama welcomes Jennifer Clement, president of PEN International, to his headquarters in Dharamsala, India, which is also the site of the Tibetan Parliament in Exile, PEN Tibetan Writers Abroad, and several other institutions of the exiled Tibetan community.

In 1996, four delegates from the group of exiled writers who were then creating PEN Tibetan Writers Abroad participated in the World Conference on Linguistic Rights. On their return to Dharamsala, they gave the Dalai Lama the UDLR. His Holiness responded with the following statement: 'I am honoured to receive a copy of the Universal Declaration of Linguistic Rights and would like to extend my full support for it. I believe that all language communities have the right to preserve their linguistic and cultural heritage. The encouragement and promotion of these will go a long way in enriching the linguistic and cultural diversity of our common world.' Twenty years later, when he received the president and the director of PEN International in his headquarters in Dharamsala, he expressed his gratitude once again: 'Thanks for your support to Tibetan writers. Thanks for your support of our literature in exile', and then he added: 'Practise having a peaceful mind to get a compassionate world.'

In 2017, the Tibetan Centre for Human Rights & Democracy published a report entitled *Bilingual Education Policy in Tibet: the Systematic Replacement of Tibetan Language with Mandarin Chinese.* The report reveals the replacement of one language by another, and Tsering Tsomo, director of the Centre, told PEN: 'We are very grateful to PEN International for its Universal Declaration of Linguistic Rights. It has given us the language to describe our situation and to claim the universality of our linguistic rights. Inasmuch as all linguistic communities have the same rights, Tibetan too!'

The cover of the report, reproduced on this page, is telling. It explains the way the Chinese government works against the language: by delegitimising Tibetan as a language of knowledge to its speakers, teaching the Tibetan alphabet through Chinese ideograms, and showing how Tibetan works through Chinese to children whose mother tongue is Tibetan. This may seem absurd, but in the minds of children it has the effect of denigrating the value of their own language and replacing it with the foreign one. The idea is to destroy the language and thereby destroy the culture and faith that resists Chinese occupation.

PEN Tibetan Writers Abroad also works to create a network of writers and journalists of the Tibetan diaspora. PEN continuously reports on attacks on freedom of expression and linguistic rights, and campaigns for imprisoned Tibetan writers. Faced with so many forms of destruction and repression by the Chinese government, PEN also responds in a complex way: 'To these many faces of repression, PEN responds with many faces of resistance.'

↑ Cover of the 2017 report from the Tibetan Centre for Human Rights & Democracy on the replacement of the Tibetan language by Mandarin Chinese.

↙ The journalist and poet Tsering Kyi reported on the persecution of the Tibetan language at the Translation and Linguistic Rights Committee meeting in Chiapas in May 2019.

Kunchok Tsephel Gopey Tsang

→
Members of the PEN
Tibetan Writers Abroad
Centre on the Day of the
Imprisoned Writer 2014.
The first demonstrator
from the right holds a
picture of Enoh Meyomesse,
from Cameroon, while
the fifth holds a portrait
of Kunchok Tsephel
Gopey Tsang.

↑   Kunchok Tsephel
Gopey Tsang.

Kunchok Tsephel Gopey Tsang is a Tibetan writer who, along with the leading poet Kyab-chen, created the Tibetan language website *Chomei* (*The Lamp*): www.tibetcm. com. Launched in 2005, this first ever Tibetan literary website features both classical and contemporary Tibetan writing, and provides a platform for contemporary Tibetan-language writers to have news on their own and international literature and translations as well as voicing their experiences and concerns. It is closely monitored by the Chinese authorities and was shut down several times during 2007 and 2008.

In March 2008, the Chinese authorities launched a crackdown on the Tibet Autonomous Region following the staging of anti-government protests in Lhasa and other areas. In the wake of this, Tibetan writers and artists were increasingly at risk for writing critical articles, poems, and books and composing songs. Gopey Tsang was arrested by Chinese security officials at his home in the town of Nyul-ra, Gannan Tibetan Autonomous Prefecture, Gansu Province, on 26 February 2009. At the time of his arrest, Gopey Tsang was working as an environmental officer for the Chinese government.

According to his family, he was deeply concerned about the issue of environmental protection and worked tirelessly in his spare time to document environmental degradation in the Tibetan grasslands.

On 12 November 2009, Tsang was convicted of 'disclosing state secrets' and is currently serving a 15-year prison sentence. On the basis of the available evidence, PEN International believes that he is imprisoned solely for peacefully exercising his right to freedom of expression, and PEN has called tirelessly for his immediate and unconditional release.

Gopey Tsang has been the empty chair writer at many PEN International Congresses and gatherings around the globe. As Chinese government policies continue to seek to devastate Tibetan language, culture, and religious expressions, PEN's Translation and Linguistic Rights Committee is deeply committed to this case.

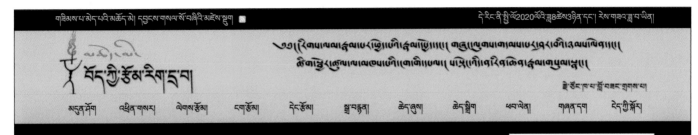
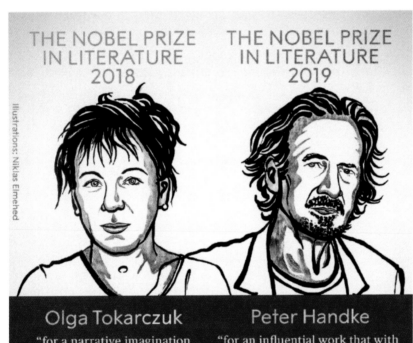

↑　*Chomei* (*The Lamp*): www.tibetcm.com is a Tibetan literary website publishing poems and articles and giving news about international literature.

World Voices Festival: *To Be Translated or Not to Be*

→
Esther Allen, chair of the
American PEN Translation
Committee (2003–06), co-founder
of the World Voices Festival
and editor of the report
To Be Translated or Not to Be.

→ →
Michael Henry Heim (1943–2012),
a professor of Slavic Languages at
UCLA and translator of Bohumil
Hrabal and Milan Kundera.
He established the PEN/Heim
Translation Fund Grants.

↑   The Hungarian writer, playwright,
and essayist Péter Nádas opens the PEN
World Voices Festival in 2013.

Everywhere writers long to be translated into English, and the
English language suffers because of a lack of translations. It is a kind
of paradox: the language that perceives itself as the primary international means of communication, with authors from all continents
from Canada to New Zealand and from India to South Africa, is in
fact one of the more isolated literary communities. American PEN
has had a prominent role in helping to shape PEN International's
translation guidelines. In 2004, Esther Allen, Salman Rushdie, and
Michael Roberts founded the World Voices Festival in New York, a
celebration of international literature with a clear focus on translation.
Allen was the chair of the Translation Committee of American
PEN, Rushdie was American PEN president, and Roberts was the
director of the Centre.

In 2007, PEN International's Translation and Linguistic Rights
Committee published the report *To Be Translated or Not to Be. On the
International Situation of Literary Translation*, edited by Esther Allen.
The document included case studies from six countries, a catalogue of
good practices for policies on translation, and an international survey
of more than 30 PEN Centres headed by Simona Škrabec. In her
introduction, Allen wrote: 'The world's richest language, in economic
terms — English — is also one of its most impoverished when it
comes to taking in the literary wealth that exists beyond it. Rather
than acting as a true lingua franca to facilitate communication among
different languages, English all too often simply ignores whatever is
not English, mistaking the global reach and diversity of the world's

dominant language for the world itself.' Esther Allen presented the report, which was co-produced by the Ramon Llull Institute, at the 73rd PEN International Congress in Dakar and the Frankfurt Book Fair in 2007.

The American PEN Translation Committee, recipient of an extra-ordinary donation from Michael Henry Heim, a professor of Slavic Languages at UCLA, established the PEN/Heim Translation Fund Grants to support translations from all languages into English. Heim, a renowned translator of Czech writers such as Bohumil Hrabal and Milan Kundera, wanted to change the 'dismayingly low number of literary translations currently appearing in English'. Managed by the Translation Committee of American PEN, the PEN/Heim Translation Fund Grants have promoted the translation and publication of world literature into English by giving yearly awards to a select number of literary translators, based on quality of the translation as well as the importance of the original work. Since 2003, the fund has promoted translation from 33 languages into English.

↑   Jessica Lange reading *The Time of the Doves* by Mercè Rodoreda at the PEN World Voices Festival 2009.

TO BE TRANS-LATED OR NOT TO BE

PEN / IRL REPORT ON THE INTERNATIONAL SITUATION OF LITERARY TRANSLATION

Esther Allen (ed.)

institut ramon llull
Catalan Language and Culture

To Be Translated or Not to Be

Produced by PEN International and the Ramon Llull Institute, *To Be Translated or Not to Be. On the International Situation of Literary Translation* was edited by Esther Allen, with case studies in the Netherlands, Argentina, Catalonia, Germany, China, and France, and a catalogue of good practices in policies on translation. Headed by Simona Škrabec, the report included an international survey with the participation of more than 30 PEN Centres.

Preface to the report *To Be Translated or Not to Be* by Paul Auster

Dostoevsky, Heraclitus, Dante, Virgil, Homer, Cervantes, Kafka, Kierkegaard, Tolstoy, Hölderlin, and scores of other poets and writers who have marked me forever — I, an American, whose only foreign language is French — have all been revealed to me, read by me, digested by me, in translation. Translators are the shadow heroes of literature, the often forgotten instruments that make it possible for different cultures to talk to one another, who have enabled us to understand that we all, from every part of the world, live in one world.

I would like to offer a salute and a declaration of thanks to all these men and women, these translators, who toil so selflessly to keep literature alive for everyone.

Egunkaria and Martxelo Otamendi

At the time of his arrest in February 2003, Martxelo Otamendi was a reporter and director of the Basque-language newspaper *Egunkaria*, the only daily newspaper published entirely in the Basque language. The Spanish authorities claimed that *Egunkaria* was financed by the Basque separatist group Euskadi Ta Askatasuna (ETA), and subsequently closed down the newspaper. According to the Spanish authorities, *Egunkaria*'s anti-ETA stance was a ploy that disguised its true links to a terrorist organisation.

While in prison, PEN campaigned for Martxelo Otamendi and, after his liberation, Otamendi was one of the keynote speakers at PEN's 2004 WiPC Conference in Barcelona along with Salman Rushdie. Joan Smith, the chair of English PEN's Writers in Prison Committee, introduced Otamendi and explained that the closure of *Egunkaria* was one of a number of trends seen around the globe on new anti-terrorism legislation since the terrorist attacks in the USA on 11 September 2001. Under the new Spanish anti-terrorist legislation, prisoners could now be held in custody for up to five days without charges. Otamendi spoke of his arrest and torture in prison.

In 2010, the final and unanimous verdict by the Criminal Court of the Spanish 'Audiencia Nacional' stated that there were no grounds to have the newspaper closed. The court confirmed 'the narrow and erroneous view according to which everything that has to do with the Basque language and with culture in that language is promoted and/or controlled by ETA leads to an incorrect assessment of facts and figures, and to the inconsistency of the accusation.' It goes on to note that the closure was an 'interference with press freedom' and declares: 'the allegations have not proven that the defendants have the slightest relation with ETA, and this determines in itself the acquittal with all pronouncements favourable to the defendants.'

In 2012, the European Court of Human Rights issued a judgment saying that the Spanish authorities should have carried out a genuine investigation into allegations of police brutality during the time that Martxelo Otamendi was held in solitary confinement while in police custody. The court considered that there had been a violation of Article 3 (prohibition of inhuman or degrading treatment) of the European Convention on Human Rights.

The arbitrary closing down of the only newspaper in the Basque language created a strong response from Basque civil and literary society. In 2004, at the 70th PEN International Congress in Tromsø, Norway, PEN delegates from the whole world welcomed a new Basque PEN Centre and its president, Laura Mintegi.

↙   The press conference held during the 2004 Writers in Prison Conference in Barcelona. Salman Rushdie, president of American PEN, expressed his support for Martxelo Otamendi and demanded to know why the allegations of torture had not been investigated. Both men were keynote speakers at the conference.

↓   Demonstration in front of the offices of *Egunkaria* newspaper on 20 February 2003, the day it was closed down by the Spanish authorities.

↑   Demonstration in Donostia
(San Sebastian) on 22 February 2003,
against the closing of *Egunkaria*,
the only newspaper in the Basque language.

PEN and the linguistic rights of the Kurds

In March 2005, PEN's first international meeting on linguistic rights took place in the city of Diyarbakır — or Amed as it is called by the local Kurdish population — in collaboration with UNESCO and the city's municipality. The sessions had simultaneous Kurdish/Turkish/English translation. The PEN delegates from abroad were told it was the first time in the city's history that a session was held where the Kurdish language was included in international dialogue. It was also the first time that a session organised by the Committee for Translation and Linguistic Rights had the rare privilege of being interrupted by the sonic boom of low-flying military combat planes. It was a warning.

The writers Mehmed Uzun and Murathan Mungan were special guests at the meeting where the UDLR and its relevance in Turkey were at the centre of debate. Kata Kulavkova, chair of PEN's Translation and Linguistic Rights Committee, affirmed publicly that Turkey is made up of different linguistic communities, and the only path to peace for the country is by respecting cultural diversity and linguistic rights. The final document stated the need for the full and free use of the Kurdish language in the fields of literature and literary translation, as well as in culture, education, and communication. PEN also affirmed that the Turkish government needed to respect the use of the original Kurdish names of people and places. Delegates debated at length on the introduction of bilingual education in schools. This gathering was organised by both Kurdish and Turkish PEN, and it also included a celebration of the Newroz festivities, the Persian New Year celebrated by many Kurds.

Since the founding of the Republic of Turkey in 1923, which enshrined a monocultural national identity, the country's large Kurdish minority has often been banned from expressing its culture or from speaking the Kurdish language. But 2005 was a time of new openness in Turkish society, and the participants in the Diyarbakır seminar were able to explore a future in which the Kurdish and Turkish languages would have equal status. The UDLR affirms that 'All language communities have the right to use place names in the language proper to the territory, both orally and in writing, in the private, public and official spheres.' At the end of the 2000s, President Recep Tayyip Erdoğan loosened some of the restrictions against Kurdish culture, but, in July 2015, the repression of the Kurdish population came back in full force with the total breakdown of the peace process between the Turkish authorities and the Kurdistan Workers' Party (PKK). Subsequently, the Kurdish language was banned from schools and more than 11,000 Kurdish teachers lost their jobs. When, in October 2016, the mayors of Diyarbakır were detained and imprisoned (like so many other elected officials from the pro-minority HDP party), the Kurdish words on the City Hall's facade were torn down.

↑↑   Workers tearing down the Kurdish words from the Diyarbakır/Amed City Hall in October 2016.

↑   Chairing the presentation of the UDLR to the Dyarbakir audience were, among others, Zerdeşt Haco, president of Kurdish PEN; Kata Kulavkova, chair of PEN's Translation and Linguistic Rights Committee; and Joanne Leedom-Ackerman, the PEN International secretary.

←   Participants in the 2005 PEN International seminar on cultural diversity in Amed/Diyarbakır travelled to the Tigris to express their solidarity with organisations struggling for the preservation of Heskîf/Hasankeyf. They argued that the loss of this potential World Heritage Site due to the building of an artificial lake, part of the *Ilısu* hydroelectric dam project, would be a tragedy. Continuously inhabited for more than 10 millennia by the Byzantines, Romans, Mongols, Ottomans, and, for centuries, the Kurds, these civilisations' artefacts and architecture were all layered upon each other — ancient cave dwellings, amphitheatres, aqueducts, mosques, minarets. Heskîf/Hasankeyf would have been a UNESCO World Heritage Site (and the flood avoided) if Turkey had applied for it. Fifteen years later, and despite the struggle to save it, the whole view captured in this picture was under water. The visit was a way for PEN delegates to witness the many faces of Turkey's policies of cultural destruction against Kurdish heritage, culture, language, and community.

Kurdish PEN and the unity of all
Kurdish literary communities

Founded in 1988 by Huseyîn Erdem, Emîne Erdem, Yayla Mönch-Bucak, Haydar Işik, Evdirehman Neqşîbendî, Huseyîn Kartal, Mostoo Xêro and Riza Topal, Kurdish PEN celebrates meetings and campaigns for freedom of expression as well as the cultural and linguistic rights of the Kurds in Turkey, Syria, Iran, and Iraq. Congresses and network meetings take place in the Kurdish lands and also around the communities of Kurdish exiles in Germany in Dresden, Oldenburg, and Berlin.

↑   Seminar in Slemani, Iraq, 2013.

↗   Berivan Dosky, Osman Ozçelîk, Netîce Altûn, and other Kurdish PEN board members celebrating their election at the 2016 Congress in Diyarbakır/Amed, Turkey.

→   Participants at the Kurdish PEN Congress in Dresden, Germany, 2018.

↘   Kurdish PEN event in Rojava, Syria, in 2015.

←   Zara Mohammadi is a Kurdish teacher and director of the Nojin Cultural Association, whose activities include teaching the Kurdish language and literature, with classes for children and adults at all levels. She was apprehended by Iranian security forces at her home in Sanandaj, detained for six months and sentenced to 10 years' imprisonment just for teaching Kurdish literature. While she was waiting for the result of her appeal, she intervened in a digital event of Kurdish PEN on the Day of the Imprisoned Writer 2020.

← Participants in the Writers for Peace meeting in Amed/Diyarbakır in April 2016 presenting their conclusions to the delegates of the 82nd PEN International Congress in Ourense, 2016. From left to right: Berivan Dosky, president of Kurdish PEN; Jennifer Clement, president of PEN International; Can Dündar; Eugene Schoulgin, vice-president of PEN International; Zeynep Oral, president of PEN Turkey.

'Even saying the word "peace" is dangerous'
The assault by Turkish armed forces on Kurdish PEN's office in Diyarbakır/Amed

In December 2015 and January 2016, Turkish armed forces launched a massive attack against young Kurdish militants, and for two months much of Sur — the ancient heart of Diyarbakır/Amed, a UNESCO World Heritage Site — was under 24-hour curfew and the site of battles, with hundreds of killings and more than 30,000 people fleeing the city. In January, five more districts were also given curfews and attacked. The devastation of the Millennial City of Sur by Turkish army tanks, assault vehicles, and thousands of troops destroyed almost all traces of its Kurdish, Jewish, Muslim, Christian, Persian, Arab, Armenian, and Turkish peoples — who all had left their mark on the city. The destruction of entire neighbourhoods, including archaeological sites, clearly revealed the Turkish government's agenda.

PEN International united in the defence of more than 1,000 academics in Turkey who signed the manifesto *We Won't Be Party to this Crime*. The document claimed that, as a result of the curfews and bombings, 'the right to life, liberty, and security, and in particular the prohibition of torture and ill-treatment protected by the constitution and international conventions have been violated. […] These actions are in serious violation of international law. We demand the Turkish state to abandon its deliberate massacre and deportation of Kurdish and other peoples in the region.'

On 4 February, the offices of Kurdish PEN in Sur Amed were attacked, sculptures and paintings were destroyed, documents were stolen, and the premises were set on fire. The global PEN community protested in unity and demanded that those responsible be brought to justice and that all Kurdish peoples and PEN members be protected from harm.

Just a few weeks after the end of the curfew, Kurdish PEN, Turkish PEN, and PEN International organised a meeting in Amed/Diyarbakır. Tone Peršak, chair of the Writers for Peace Committee, and Eugene Schoulgin, PEN vice-president, joined with Kurdish PEN and Turkish PEN to proclaim: 'At present, even uttering the word "peace" is dangerous, open to accusation, punishment and attacks. In spite and because of this situation, we have united for an invitation to peace. We have decided that our demand for peace be heard. We have got together in harmony with the dear memories of our losses including Hrant Dink and Tahir Elçi, who were also working for the same goals. We underscore once again our individual responsibility to leave our children a better world and to help them to realise their dreams.'

Zehra Doğan

In March 2017, the journalist, painter, and poet Zehra Doğan was convicted of 'propagandising for a terrorist organisation' in her work. She spent 500 days in prison. The criminal charges against her related to a painting in which she recreated a photograph by the Turkish military taken during the three-month curfew imposed on the town Nusaybin, which showed Turkish flags on top of destroyed buildings. Doğan was also convicted for her social media activity and for her newspaper reporting on the fighting between the Turkish army and the PKK in Nusaybin.

During her imprisonment, PEN campaigned nonstop for her freedom. When Doğan was released, she wrote PEN a letter: 'I couldn't believe that so many people from all over the world were writing to me. There were many (PEN members) from Belgium, the USA, people from the UK sent many, people from India and the Philippines… I've received letters from Belgium almost every other day. I truly felt my voice was heard far beyond the parameters of my jail sentence and this global solidarity gave me strength to endure and almost transcend my conditions. We read the letters together, often excitedly in a crowded jail cell and before it was banned, they sent me all sorts of pictures, scents and card posts. I wrote back to almost all of them, and still keep the ones the prison hasn't taken from me. I'm very grateful to PEN members for their support.'

↑↑   Zehra Doğan's painting *Nusaybin* (2016) showing Turkish flags on buildings destroyed by government forces led her to be charged with propagandising for terrorism and imprisoned.

↑   The UK street artist Banksy painted a mural in solidarity with Doğan on a wall in Houston Street, Manhattan. The mural was a collaboration with the graffiti artist Borf, who has spent time in jail for his work.

→   Zehra Doğan leaving Tarsus prison on 25 February 2019.

↑ After her liberation, Doğan was invited by English PEN to be a writer in residence in London. With the support of Ege Dündar from PEN International, she produced the exhibition *E Li Dû Man* (*Left Behind*) at Tate Modern. As a journalist covering the clashes in Kurdish cities in Turkey from 2015 to 2016, Doğan took the small objects she found in the debris as testimony of a war no one was talking about. This installation told the stories of those who fled through what they left behind. It also invited visitors to participate in the crafting and performance of stories about place and displacement.

PEN International in defence of translators at risk

In 2010, the Committee for Translation and Linguistic Rights met in the town of Girona in Spain to discuss methods to help PEN Centres promote linguistic rights at a grassroots level. The complexity of the UDLR was important for lobbying at the level of the United Nations and state parliaments, but PEN felt there was a need to have a streamlined document for defending linguistic diversity around the world. The *Girona Manifesto* was created at this meeting and was presented and approved by the assembly of delegates at the 76th PEN International Congress in Belgrade. To date, it has been translated into 42 languages.

In 2014, Simona Škrabec, from Catalan PEN and a translator of Slovenian origin, was elected chair of the Translation and Linguistic Rights Committee. Working on the initiative of Émile Martel, the president of PEN Quebec, the committee drafted the Declaration on Literary Translation and Translators, which was approved in 2015 in Quebec City during the 81st PEN International Congress. The document states: 'All cultures are not equal when it comes to translation. Some cultures translate by choice, others by obligation. Translation is a key to the protection of languages and cultures.' The committee also asserted that the translator was also an author: 'Respectful of authors and original texts, translators are nevertheless creators in their own right. They seek not only to reproduce a literary

The moral duty of the USA to Iraqi translators

Basim Mardan, a journalist and translator from Mosul, Iraq, had to escape his home country and was welcomed by Norwegian PEN as the first ICORN guest writer in the country in 2006. Since 2016, he has been part of the Protection Team for Writers at Risk at PEN International. His testimony can be read in full on ICORN's website: 'Al-Qaida was actually killing everyone, as long as you are an easy target, you do not carry a weapon or have bodyguards, then you are exposed to be kidnapped, tortured, and they might as well let you dig your own grave before they end your life. However, for me, every element of my social and intellectual life was leading to that morbid scenario. I belong to a politically active family, I am the child of a mixed marriage (father is Shia and mother is Sunni, living in a Sunni-dominant city), the stigma of publishing a book of poetry that got too much unfriendly attention when I was still a university student, my work in an NGO that

promoted democracy and human rights, my work as a translator/ interpreter with the local government, and finally my name in Al-Qaida hit list and their threatening messages and phone calls were actually the reasons why I felt like I should abandon the ship and seek help somewhere else.'

American PEN, whose Freedom to Write programme was directed by Larry Siems, built pressure in the USA to recognise and fulfil a moral duty to those who had been translators and interpreters for US forces, NGOs, and media, and whose lives were in danger because of their work. Three op-eds pages were filled with Basim Mardan's and other translators' experience in the *New York Times* in November 2006. There were meetings with the State Department to press Congress to set aside refugee slots for Iraqi translators and interpreters and speed their resettlement to the USA. Siems went to Damascus with a crew from the television news

show *60 Minutes* to help them prepare a story about translators and interpreters who had fled to Syria and were stuck and in grave danger there. Over the next couple of years, many translators were able to resettle in the USA, and

American PEN contributed to the pressure that made that happen, alongside veteran groups and other organisations.

↓   Basim Mardan.

↓   Larry Siems.

work but to move the work forward, to expand its presence in the world. Translators are not simply messengers: though they speak for others, their voices are also their own. In particular, they act in favour of cultural diversity by remaining loyal to marginalised authors, literary styles and social groups.'

Since the beginning of the twenty-first century, with the proliferation of online hate speech and attacks on freedom of expression by extremist groups and especially in post-war zones, PEN has witnessed a growing number of translators at risk. The Quebec Declaration clearly states that 'the rights of translators must be protected' and the 'physical safety and freedom of expression of translators must be guaranteed at all times.' Through the collaboration of Larry Siems, from American PEN, and Kjell Olaf Jensen, president of Norwegian PEN, Basim Mardan, a translator from Mosul, escaped from death and became the first ICORN guest writer in Norway in 2006. In 2019, PEN participated in an *#ProtectLinguists* event at the United Nations headquarters in New York in order to raise awareness of the need for greater legal protection of local civilian translators and interpreters in conflict and post-conflict zones.

↖   *The Girona Manifesto on Linguistic Rights* in Zulu. The manifesto has been translated into 42 languages, including Armenian, Occitan, Berber, Mayan, Japanese, Creole, Sesetho, Somali, Tshivenda, and Xhosa.

↓   A panel at the 79th PEN International Congress in Reykjavik in 2013, from left to right: Vigdís Finnbogadóttir, president of Iceland (1980–96) and UNESCO's Goodwill Ambassador for languages; Josep Maria Terricabras, chair of the TLRC and a sponsor of the *Girona Manifesto*; Émile Martel, president of PEN Quebec, and the writer who led in the creation of the Quebec Declaration on Literary Translation and Translators.

↓↓   Members of the Translation and Linguistic Rights Committee with PEN International president John Ralston Saul in Girona in 2011 to draft the *Girona Manifesto on Linguistic Rights*. Present at the meeting were the Basque, Amazigh, Xhosa, Uyghur, Occitan, Quebec, Swiss Italian, Japanese, Catalan, Croatian, and Slovenian linguistic communities.

pen
INTERNATIONAL

Eminyakeni eyishumi nanhlanu eyedlule, isibophezelo samalungelo okusetshenziswa kwezilimi nesaziwa ngokuthi yi-Universal Declaration of Linguistic Rights sethulwa okokuqala emphakathini edolobheni laseBarcelona sethulwa Yikomidi Lezokuhumusha kanye Namalungelo Okusetshenziswa Kwezilimi ngaphansi kwe-PEN International.

Namhlanje-ke futhi, lelo Komidi elifanayo, liye lahlangana eGirona nalapho lifike khona lavumelana ngazwi linye ekwethuleni Izethulo zemigomo eyishumi enqala Yokuzibophezela Kukawonkewonke emhlabeni.

1. Ukwehlukana ngokwezilimi yinto eyigugu emhlabeni wonke futhi kumele ithokozelwe futhi ithakaselwe.

2. Inhlonipho ebhekiswe kuzona zonke izilimi kanye namasiko kuyingqalasizinda yokwakha kanye nokugcina inkulumompikiswano ikhona futhi iphilile.

3. Bonke abantu bafunda ukukhuluma emongweni womphakathi obanika impilo, ulimi, isiko kanye nokuzazi kanye nokuzazisa.

4. Izilimi ezahlukene kanye nezindlela ezahlukene zokukhuluma akusizona nje izindlela zokuxhumana kuphela ezikhona, kodwa futhi lokhu kungamanyathelo abantu abakhula ngawo kwakhiwe namasiko ngawo.

5. Noma yimuphi umphakathi okhuluma ulimi oluthile unelungelo lokusebenzisa njengolimi olusemthethweni lolo lulimi endaweni yawo oyakhele.

6. Indlela okufundwa ngayo esikoleni kufanele ibambe iqhaza elibonakalayo ekukhuliseni ulimi olukhunywa umphakathi okuleyo ndawo.

7. Kuhle futhi kuyancomeka ukuthi abantu bakwazi ukukhuluma izilimi ezahlukene ngoba lokho kusho ukuzwelana kanye nokuvuleka komqondo, kanti kwenza nokuthi umuntu alwazisise nolimi lwakhe lwebele.

8. Ukuhunyushwa kwemibhalo, ikakhulu imisebenzi emikhulu ekhuluma ngamasiko, kusho into ebaluleke kakhulu ohlelweni lokuqonda kanye nenhlonipho ekhona phakathi kwabantu bodwana.

9. Abamaphepha, abemisakazo kanye nabamathelevishini bayizizinda ezikhuluma kuzwakale uma kubhekwa izindaba zezilimi futhi yibona kanye abangenza ukuthi izilimi zibekwe esicongweni esizifanele.

10. Ilungelo lokuthi umuntu azisebenzisele ulimi lwakhe lwebele kufanele lihlonishwe yiNhlangano Yezizwe njengelinye lamalungelo ayisisekelo.

YiKomidi Lokuhumusha kanye Namalungelo Okusetshenziswa Kwezilimi Ngaphansi Kwe-PEN International

PEN in Africa: language exchange through translation is Culture's Oxygen

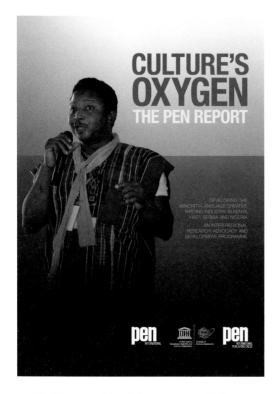

↑   The PEN report *Culture's Oxygen*, was provided by Ngũgĩ wa Thiong'o, vice-president of PEN International, who wrote the preface: 'One of my favourite quotes is from Aimé Césaire's *Discourse on Colonialism* [...] Languages are central to all cultures, big and small. So, [...] language exchange, through translations, is the oxygen of culture, but this assumes their equality.'

↘   Johannesburg, March 2016. Delegates from African PEN Centres and members of the Translation and Linguistic Rights Committee with its chair, Simona Škrabec (in a yellow dress).

A large gathering of the Translation and Linguistic Rights Committee took place in Johannesburg in March 2016 in order to debate issues of linguistic rights with all African PEN Centres. Welcomed to their country by South African PEN and Afrikaans PEN, there were delegates from PEN Centres in Egypt, Ghana, Guinea, Malawi, Mali, Mauritania, Nigeria, Senegal, Sierra Leone, Uganda, Zambia, and Zimbabwe, as well as Eritrean PEN in Exile and invited writers from Angola and Sudan. The meeting was dedicated to discussing the publication and circulation of African literature in African languages. Projects relating to mother-tongue education were presented, and the promotion of creative writing, critical thinking, and African stories was discussed. The debate on the challenges of publishing in so-called 'minority' languages, based on examples from the UNESCO report on the creative industry in Nigeria, Kenya, Haiti, and Serbia, was memorable. The Quebec Declaration on the importance of literary translation was presented and discussed in depth. The session ended with a round-table discussion on literature and war.

The conclusions of the South African meeting were integrated in the report. PEN International was awarded a grant from the UNESCO International Fund for Cultural Diversity for this research project. Coordinated by Simona Škrabec, the chair of the committee, the report included the participation of three members from PEN International Publishers Circle — Hachette, Penguin, and CH Beck — as the research was specifically dedicated to collaboration with publishers. The title of this two-year project was 'Developing the minority language creative writing industry in Kenya, Haiti, Serbia and Nigeria'. First, a mapping exercise was undertaken by the research team in each country to review and analyse the major challenges. Then, national advocacy campaigns were carried out with key stakeholders in the sector to promote the support of local publishing industries. Good practices highlighted in the report show that the publishing market can change and that readers will, with time, show their preference for editions based on linguistic diversity.

Ngũgĩ wa Thiong'o's voice has been shaping PEN during half a century.
He was elected as PEN vice-president in 2019

← Nigerian PEN participated in the research for *Culture's Oxygen*. The picture is from a PEN event, during the Port Harcourt Book Festival, UNESCO World Book Capital 2014, titled, 'What Language Means to Literature: Identity and the Importance of Literary Translation'. From left to right: Tade Ipadeola, president of Nigerian PEN, Stanley Gazemba, Bibi Bakare-Yusuf, Ken Saro-Wiwa Jnr, and Ellah Wakatama Allfrey. Bibi Bakare-Yusuf explained that Cassava Republic Press had published *Birds of Our Land*, a natural history work that included classification in the Hausa, Yoruba, and Igbo languages.

Ngũgĩ wa Thiong'o wrote the preface of the PEN/UNESCO report *Culture's Oxygen* in his native language, Gikuyu and its title came from his own words. The 2016 preface recalls that 50 years earlier he had participated in the 1966 PEN International Congress in New York:

'I welcome this wonderful PEN report in a very personal way. It was the International PEN Congress held in New York in 1966 which made me finally confront my own relationship to my language, and by extension, African languages, and others similarly situated. Arthur Miller was then president of PEN International. Held at the height of the Cold War, the conference was unique in attracting a large attendance of writers from the then Eastern Bloc, and also others previously not allowed on American soil, like Pablo Neruda, of Chile, on account of their past political affiliations.

'Among the 500 writers present, including three of us from Africa, was Ignazio Silone, author of *Bread and Wine*, first published in 1937. In making a case for more translations from Italian into English, he happened to say, in passing, that Italian was not one of those Bantu languages with one or two words in their vocabulary. Despite being mindful of the theme of the Congress, the "Writer as Independent Spirit", and Miller's opening address which had emphasised that none of us were there to represent their country, and certainly none was obliged to speak as an apologist for their culture or political beliefs, I felt obliged to speak out immediately, in defence of African languages.

'My response, and its implications for my own literary practice since 1961, would later follow me back to Leeds [in the UK] where I resumed writing my third novel, *A Grain of Wheat*, in

English, yes in English, and not in one of those Bantu languages that I had defended with fiery eloquence.

'It took me ten years, during which I published yet another novel, *Petals of Blood*, in English, and a year at a Maximum-Security Prison for my work in theatre, to come around to writing my first ever [Gikuyu-language] novel, *Caitaani Mūtharabainī*, self-translated into English as *Devil on the Cross*. And it took eight years more for me to declare in *Decolonising the Mind* that I had done away with English, that from 1984 onwards it was going to be Gikuyu and Kiswahili all the way.'

← Starting in 2010, African PEN Centres have developed projects for the promotion of creative writing in African languages in secondary and high schools. With the support of the Swedish International Development Cooperation Agency, a large network of PEN School Clubs has been established across the continent. Zambian PEN has been running workshops in schools promoting creative writing in Indigenous languages. Marita Banda, a poet in the Tumbuka language, is the coordinator of Zambian PEN's Civil Society Project. She appears in the picture at an inter-schools essay competition, with members of the Munali Girls' PEN School Club.

Perumal Murugan and an 'author's suicide'

← Perumal Murugan committed his 'author's suicide' and was a PEN main case in 2015. In 2018, at the 84th PEN International Congress in Pune, Maharashtra, he was elected vice-president of PEN International together with Nayantara Sahgal and Ngũgĩ wa Thiong'o.

Tamil-language writer Perumal Murugan's book *Madhorubagan*, published in 2010, features a controversial scene at a local Hindu shrine that depicts a fictitious, extramarital sex ritual with members of the Gounder community. Four years after it was published, with four print runs in Tamil and two in the English translation, 18 days of protests ensued, including book burnings and calls for a ban on the novel and the arrest of both its author and publisher. The book burnings were organised by Rashtriya Swayamsevak Sangh (RSS), an Indian right-wing, Hindu-nationalist, paramilitary volunteer organisation — Narendra Modi, prime minister of India since 2014, is a former member of RSS.

A 'peace meeting' took place in Namakkal, Tamil Nadu, attended by several regional religious and caste groups demanding that Murugan issue an unconditional apology, expurgate the book, recall any unsold copies, and refrain from writing on controversial or sensitive subjects. After the meeting, Murugan published a shocking declaration on his Facebook page, which read: 'Writer Perumal Murugan is Dead. He is not a God to resurrect. He doesn't believe in re-birth. The person who lives hereafter will just be an ordinary teacher by name P Murugan.' Murugan's Facebook post also asked his publishers to cease sale of any works, urged those owning copies to burn them, told literary festivals to not contact him, and requested that caste and religious outfits desist from their protests. It was an 'author's suicide'.

On 5 July 2016, the Madras High Court dismissed all the petitions, which demanded that Murugan be prosecuted. The court defended Murugan's freedom to express

himself, stating that there was no need for changes to his book *Madhorubagan* and that the police-mediated settlement imposed upon Murugan to apologise for his novel and withdraw all unsold copies was not legally binding. In its judgment, the court stated that the public should tolerate his work and emphasised that it is the state's responsibility 'to ensure proper police protection where such authors and artists come under attack from a section of the society'. The verdict added that the government should create an 'expert body to deal with situations arising from such conflicts of views' because in 'matters of art and culture, the issue cannot

→ Original Tamil version and English translation of *Madhorubagan*.

be left to the police authorities or the local administration alone, especially when there is a spurt in such conflicts'.

In response to the ruling, Murugan announced: 'I will get up.'

The following year, Murugan attended the PEN International Translation and Linguistic Rights Committee meeting in Bangalore, Karnathaka. Murugan, as a writer and professor of Tamil literature, welcomed the founding of South India PEN, which is a Centre that unites authors from six South Indian literatures.

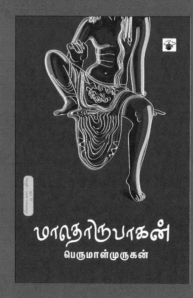

மாதொருபாகன்
பெருமாள்முருகன்

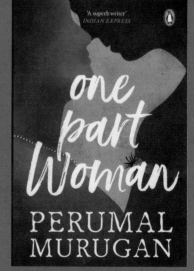

'A superb writer'
INDIAN EXPRESS

one part Woman

PERUMAL MURUGAN

↑   On 26 December 2014, an
assembly of people burned copies of
Madhorubagan in Tiruchengode,
Tamil Nadu, and demanded a ban on
the book and the arrest of Perumal
Murugan and his publisher.

Pune Congress: **a celebration of 6,000 languages**

↑→   Language Wari (pilgrimage) during the
83rd PEN International Congress in Pune, 2018.
More than 5,000 students from the university
colleges of Pune participated in a pilgrimage
across the city streets asking for the preservation
of India's languages and the world's linguistic
diversity. The students and participants carried
banners with the names of the 6,000 world
languages and the 780 languages of India.

In 2018, PEN participated in the celebration to mark the 150th anniversary of Mahatma Gandhi's birth. The 84th PEN International Congress took place in the city of Pune, in the Indian state of Maharashtra. The title of the Congress was borrowed from Gandhi's autobiography, *Experiments with Truth*, and the slogan 'Truth, Freedom, Diversity' was translated into the languages of all those who participated in the Congress. Debates were held on the critical situation for freedom of expression in India, the representation and voices of women in literature, and the life and legacy of Mohandas Gandhi and his wife, Kasturba. A unique celebration also took place, which was the Language Wari. *Wari* is the name given to massive traditional religious pilgrimages in Maharashtra, and, in recent years, literary Wari celebrations have taken place, which combine the singing, reciting, and reading of traditional and contemporary literature.

In 2017, the Lviv Congress welcomed a new South India PEN uniting writers in Tamil, Malayalam, Telugu, Konkani, Kannada, and Marathi literatures. For the Pune Congress, South India PEN prepared a Language Wari. At this historic celebration more than 5,000 students from the university colleges of Pune participated in a pilgrimage across the city streets asking for the preservation of India's languages and the world's linguistic diversity. The students and participants carried posters with the names of the 6,000 world languages, of which

780 belong to India, according to the Linguistic Survey of India. Ganesh Devy, director of the Congress, had been the chair of the voluntary network of some 3,500 scholars, teachers, activists, and nomads, who participated in the People's Linguistic Survey of India that listed all the languages of the subcontinent.

This vision of India based on its linguistic, cultural, and religious diversity contrasted with the growing intolerant climate in the country. The PEN International freedom of expression and linguistic rights report presented at the Congress was titled *Pursuing Truth in the Face of Intolerance*. Delegates paid tribute to the assassinated intellectuals Gauri Lankesh, Govind Pansare, and MM Kalburgi. The Literary Wari stopped on Maharshi Vitthal Ramji Shinde Bridge, and at the exact place where, on 20 August 2013, Narendra Dabholkar was assassinated.

The opening ceremony of the Congress took place at the Aga Khan Palace in Pune, Maharashtra, where Gandhi was kept prisoner for several years and where his most trusted life companion, Kasturba, died. Delegates paid tribute to their memorial with a minute's silence.

Writing the Future in Indigenous Languages

↑   San Cristóbal de las Casas, Chiapas, 1 May 2019 —
the inaugural event of the meeting 'Writing the Future in
Indigenous Languages', organised by PEN International's
Translation and Linguistic Rights Committee together
with UNESCO, Mexico's National Indigenous Languages
Institute, and the University of Arts and Sciences in
Chiapas. Enriqueta Lunez, the director of the Culture
House of San Juan Chamula, opens the event in tears and
speaking in Tsotsil. Lunez explains: 'Good morning to all.
Please excuse these tears. What I just said in my
language (which is not my first language, it's my second,
because I learned Spanish first) I say full of emotion
because last night I read with sadness that one of the
four people who speak Kiliwa has died. It is the story of
many languages, what it's their turn to go through:
disappearance. I know my language is also in this
process. […] Not that I don't speak it now, not at all,
I even dare to write in Tsotsil.'

In the twenty-first century, PEN's support of writers in Indigenous
languages has greatly increased. The starting point occurred at the
2003 Congress in Mexico City, which held a parallel session attended
by 30 writers in Indigenous languages. There were 15 writers from
Canada, and the rest came from Mexico. Together they debated the
integration of their literatures into the PEN community. Canadian
PEN and Quebec PEN welcomed Indigenous writers to their membership, and the literary programme of the 2015 81st PEN International
Congress in Quebec City highlighted, among others, the poetry of
Joséphine Bacon and Natasha Kanapé Fontaine.

In 2017, Argentinian PEN founded the Committee of Writers in
Indigenous Languages, and the same year Iván Prado, a Quechua
sci-fi writer, was elected president of Bolivian PEN. Guatemalan PEN

and PEN International organised workshops for Indigenous women journalists in Tegucigalpa, while in Chile the intellectual Pedro Cayuqueo began to explore the possibility of creating a Mapuche PEN Centre. In this new context, a group of Mayan writers commenced the process towards founding a Chiapas PEN Centre that would also welcome writers in the Zoque language. In May 2019, the Translation and Linguistic Rights Committee met in Chiapas, Mexico, in a meeting co-organised with UNESCO and Mexico's Instituto Nacional de Lenguas Indígenas (INALI), to celebrate the United Nation's International Year of Indigenous Languages. Under the banner of 'Writing the Future in Indigenous Languages', PEN members came from 30 PEN Centres, which included the presence of PEN Tibetan Writers Abroad as well as, among others, Norwegian PEN, Basque PEN, Croatian PEN, and Philippine PEN.

With its meeting in Chiapas, PEN's Translation and Linguistic Rights Committee reaffirmed the conviction that many worlds fit in the world and acknowledged PEN's mandate to uphold all languages, recover shared memory, and include Indigenous literatures in writing the future.

→   The poster of the conference 'Writing the Future in Indigenous Languages' was produced in eight languages: five Mayan languages, Zoque, English, and Spanish. The event was co-organised by UNESCO, INALI, the University of Science and Arts of Chiapas, and PEN International.

↙   Enrique Pérez López, poet, researcher, and teacher of three generations of Mayan writers, with Urtzi Urrutikoetxea, president of Basque PEN.

↓   Nina Jaramillo, Quechua lawyer and chair of the Committee of Writers in Indigenous Languages 'Carlos Martínez Sarasola' of Argentinian PEN, showing a condor's feather as a symbol of the group.

↘   Participants to the meeting 'Writing the Future in Indigenous Languages', including three generations of Mayan writers and Jennifer Clement, president of PEN International; Frédéric Vacheron, UNESCO's director general representative in Mexico; Juan Gregorio Regino, director of INALI; José Rodolfo Calvo Fonseca, rector of UNICACH; Cicerón Aguilar, coordinator of the meeting for UNICAH; and Simona Škrabec, chair of PEN's Translation and Linguistic Rights Committee.

PEN Philippines: literary freedom and linguistic diversity

↑   Philippine PEN has created a nationwide network of writers and schoolteachers devoted to the promotion of literature from the diverse languages in the archipelago.

Founded in 1957 by Frankie Sionil José, a novelist of Ilocano descent, Philippine PEN has developed its network for over 60 years. The Centre has created ambitious spaces for literature in the diversity of the languages of the archipelago. The Philippines, in its diversity of islands and stories, has 87 living languages. The PEN programme named 'For Love of the Word: Workshops on Teaching Philippine Literature' has been supported for more than a decade by the Swedish International Development Cooperation Agency. Philippine PEN is a decentralised Centre with a presence in Mindanao, the Visayas (both in Cebu and Samar), in different areas of Luzon, and all over the Philippines.

These workshops of Philippine literature build a strong relationship between writers and teachers and are changing the school curricula. The context is essential: because of American colonial and neocolonial influences in the shaping of the Philippine curricula for over a hundred years, emphasis has been given to the use of American English as the medium of instruction, Anglo-American literary texts as the sole canon for world literature, and Philippine literature written in English as the main texts in the literature classrooms. Philippine PEN has worked to promote a reversal: the literature that is taught through its programme is the literature of each school's cultural community. Teachers report feeling better equipped to teach literature as a result of the training they have received from the PEN Centre and resources that have been developed.

← The 85th PEN international Congress in Manila had the title 'Speaking in Tongues. Literary Freedom and Indigenous Languages', as 2019 was the International Year of Indigenous Languages. The keynote speaker was the Special Rapporteur for Minority Issues of the United Nations, Fernand de Varennes (centre). His speech was followed by a panel discussion with (from left to right): Simona Škrabec, chair of PEN's Translation and Linguistic Rights Committee; Nina Jaramillo (chair of the Committee of Writers in Indigenous Languages of PEN Argentina); Ruperta Bautista (from aspiring Chiapas PEN Centre); TS Sungkit Jr. (writer in Higaonon, Cebuano, Filipino and English), Félix Villeneuve (PEN Québec) and Genevieve L Asenjo (novelist in Kiniray, Philippines).

The development of movies rooted in the linguistic diversity of the Filipino culture has a prominent place in Philippine PEN's activities. Movies in Bikol or Visayan are connected to the literature of their communities. There is a multitude of minority literature in local theatre, speculative fiction, LGBTQI voices and the Muslim community is represented in the island of Mindanao.

→ Novelist and essayist Frankie Sionil José was elected vice-president of PEN International at the 85th PEN International Congress in Manila in 2019. He appears in the picture with vice-presidents Eric Lax and Joanne Leedom-Ackerman (American PEN), Lucina Kathmann (San Miguel de Allende PEN) and Vida Ognjenović (Serbian PEN).

↓ Frankie Sionil José, with his wife, Teresa José, at the time of founding Philippine PEN in 1957. To this day PEN meetings are held in their bookstore 'Solidaridad' in Manila.

From the magazine *PEN International* to the blog *PEN/Opp*

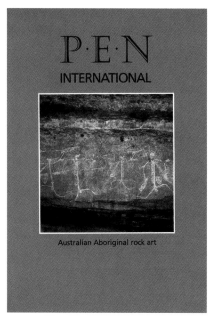

Australian Aboriginal rock art

Context: Asia Pacific
Contexte: Asie Pacifique
Contexto: Asia Pacífico

↗ In 2007, *PEN International* magazine was relaunched and renamed *Context*, showcasing writing from different regions of the world.

↓ Ola Larsmo, president of Swedish PEN and director of *The Dissident Blog* in 2015, and Elnaz Baghlanian, editor-in-chief, presenting the new version of *The Dissident Blog* at the 81st PEN International Congress in Quebec. Behind them is Tamsin Mitchell, Latin America coordinator at PEN. Larsmo was elected member of the board of PEN International in 2018.

Founded in 1950, *PEN International* magazine was originally a compendium of reviews on world literature entitled *Bulletin of Selected Books* and published with the support of UNESCO. The writer and philosopher Kathleen Nott edited it for 30 years. In 1988, at the Seoul 52nd PEN International Congress, Peter Day became editor of *PEN International* until 1999, when Jane Spender succeeded him. Over the years, the magazine was expanded to include articles, stories, and poems either from writers who contributed directly or taken from other publications. The magazine was read by more than 140 PEN Centres in 102 countries, as well as by readers all over the world, and the focus was always on translation.

In 2007, *PEN International* magazine was relaunched and renamed *Context*, which featured a new design, an assigned editor and special guest writers. *Context* showcases writing from different regions of the world with the express goal of introducing the work of new and established writers to readers everywhere. Contributors from PEN International included Adonis, Margaret Atwood, Karel Čapek, Nawal El-Saadawi, Moris Farhi, Antonia Fraser, Nadine Gordimer, Günter Grass, Han Suyin, Hongbin Liu, Chenjerai Hove, Alberto Manguel, Selim Matar, Ngũgĩ wa Thiong'o, Ben Okri, Moniro Ravanipour, Salman Rushdie, Wole Soyinka, Hilary Spurling, and many others.

In 2011, Swedish PEN launched *The Dissident Blog* to reshape the communication of PEN International, with the support of the London Secretariat and the Postcode Lottery Culture Foundation, SIDA, and Statens Kulturråd (Swedish Arts Council). A blog for 'dissidents', the site has regularly published texts that can neither be written nor published in the writers' own countries.

From the beginning, the blog had a strong approach to translation: articles are published in their original language as well as in Swedish and English, aiming to reach both a Swedish and an international audience. There are articles in Tigrinya about Eritrea, in Tsotsil about the Indigenous literature in Chiapas, in Arabic about the Arab Revolution, in Chinese about the struggle for freedom of the people of Hong Kong… Thus it has a double impact: in the societies dealt with in each monographic issue, and in the internationalising of its debates. The blog is read all over the world, and indicators show that in 2020 the countries where *The Dissident Blog* had most readers were China, the USA and Sweden.

The Dissident Blog is part of PEN International's campaigns. The 2017 mission to Caracas was followed by the corresponding issue analysing human rights and repression of freedoms in Venezuela. The Chiapas meeting entitled 'Writing the Future in Indigenous Languages' was followed by an issue on the conclusions of the conference and placed literature in Mayan languages directly on the international stage, online and in English translation. The collaboration with Hong Kong PEN had a strong impact with articles published at the very beginning of the 2019 protests. Eritrean PEN in Exile participated actively in the articles on its own country — one of the most repressive regimes on earth.

In 2019, the blog changed its name to *PEN/Opp* — opp as in opposition. It was a relaunch, with a new and modernised site broadly adapted for the computer, the mobile phone, or any e-book reader — and one that can also be accessed in places with a slow internet connection.

→
Articles from
PEN/Opp – The Dissident Blog.

Ilham Tohti, Rahile Dawut and
the persecution of the Uyghur culture in China

← In 2014, at the 80th PEN International Congress in Bishkek, Kyrgyzstan, the honorary empty chair was for Ilham Tohti, and delegates signed his portraits in several languages. The closing ceremony of the Congress was devoted to Uyghur literature and music. Over the years, Uyghur PEN has been very actively involved in the Translation and Linguistic Rights Committee of PEN International.

'Tohti has dedicated his life to advocating for the rights of the Uyghur minority in China. Despite being a voice of moderation and reconciliation, he was sentenced to life in prison following a show trial in 2014. By awarding this prize, we strongly urge the Chinese government to release Tohti and we call for the respect of minority rights in China', said David Sassoli, president of the European Parliament, at the ceremony awarding Ilham Tohti with the 2019 Sakharov Prize for Freedom of Thought in Strasbourg.

Tohti is a public Uyghur intellectual and one the world's foremost scholars on Uyghur issues. Arrested in January 2014, charged with 'Splittism' (advocating separatism) in July 2014, and convicted following an unfair trial on 23 September 2014, he was sentenced to life imprisonment as well as the confiscation of all his property. Tohti's appeal against his conviction and sentence was rejected in November 2014.

Tohti has never advocated violence or campaigned for independence. In 2006, he co-founded the website Uyghur Online, aimed at promoting understanding between Uyghurs and Han Chinese. But his criticism of the Chinese authorities for their heavy-handed treatment of the Uyghur minority made him the target of frequent harassment. PEN International first began working on Tohti's case in 2009, following his detention for speaking out about ethnic unrest that broke out in Ürümqi, capital of the Xinjiang Uyghur Autonomous Region, on 5 July 2009.

Tohti is a member of Uyghur PEN and received the PEN/Barbara Goldsmith Freedom to Write Award in 2014. He was an honorary empty chair at the 80th PEN International Congress in Bishkek, Kyrgyzstan, in 2014.

← Rahima Mahmut (left) and Aziz Isa Elkun (right), Writers in Prison Committee chair and general secretary of Uyghur PEN, at a 2018 demonstration in London with the participation of both Uyghur and English PEN in front of the Chinese Embassy. They gathered to protest against the imprisonment of two million citizens in the Uyghur gulag by Chinese authorities, the so-called 're-education camps' in Xinjiang, and to ask for the release of Ilham Tohti and all imprisoned Uyghur scholars and intellectuals.

2 YEARS GONE

#FreeRahile
freemymom.org

↑   A 2019 image from the international campaign to liberate Rahile Dawut, who vanished in 2017 and has not been heard from since. At the time of the 2014 trial, Ilham Tohti's case was a warning shot directed at Uyghur intellectuals and activists in China more broadly. On the fifth anniversary of his imprisonment, PEN International with Amnesty International, Front Line Defenders, Scholars at Risk, and several other freedom of expression organisations affirmed: 'The Chinese government [...] now operates one of the most obtrusive surveillance states in the world while arbitrarily locking up Uyghurs, Kazakhs and Kyrgyz in political indoctrination facilities. Estimates of the number detained range from several hundred thousand to well over a million. Coinciding with the construction of the camps has been the detention of hundreds more Uyghur scholars and writers in the region. Notable scholars detained include Professor Rahile Dawut, a respected specialist on Uyghur culture; Professor Halmurat Ghophur, a prominent medical scientist; Gheyret Abdurahman, the deputy head of the Linguistics Department at the Academy of Social Sciences of Xinjiang; Qurban Mamut, a writer and magazine editor; Abdulqadir Jalaleddin, a literature professor at Xinjiang Pedagogical University; and Askar Yunus, a prominent historian of the Kyrgyz ethnic community, among many others.'

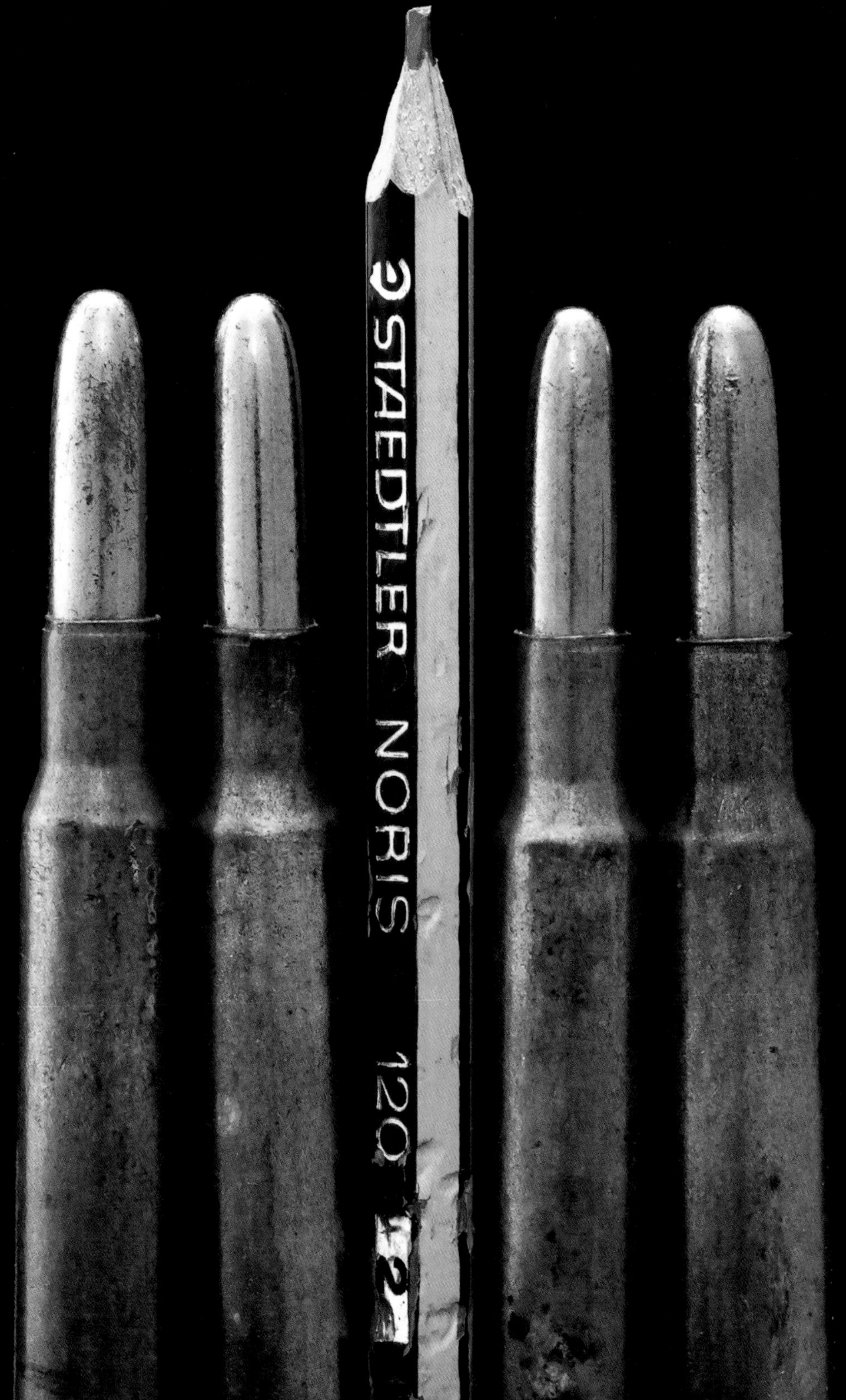
STAEDTLER NORIS 120

Writers for peace

In the same way that the founders of PEN were driven by a moral duty in response to the evil they had witnessed during the First World War, the PEN membership sought to create a bridge for writers from countries in conflict during the Cold War. PEN International looked to establish a place where writers from the Eastern and Western blocs could meet and, as communist Yugoslavia was part of the Non-Aligned Movement and could welcome writers from both sides of the Iron Curtain, the lakeside village of Bled in Slovenia was chosen. Here, in 1965, the PEN International president, Dutch writer Victor E van Vriesland, presided over the 33rd International Congress where Arthur Miller was elected the new International president.

That first Congress was the initiation of a long tradition of meetings in Bled hosted by Slovenian PEN. In fact, it was Slovenian PEN president, Miloš Mikeln, who, at the 47th PEN International Congress meeting in Tokyo in 1984, suggested the creation of a Writers for Peace Committee. Along with this proposal he invited the committee members to meet every year in Bled. This remained a tradition until 2019 when the committee decided to host meetings in other places as well.

The hopes that came with the fall of the Berlin Wall were short-lived for the Writers for Peace Committee. The aggression by Milošević's armies in Slovenia, Croatia, Bosnia, and Kosovo gave the committee a new mandate. Boris A Novak, who chaired the committee from 1991 to 2000, organised a heroic network of support. He began by helping writers in the refugee camps and soon thereafter set up a system where assistance from PEN's global community could help writers and journalists besieged in Sarajevo. In 1993, the 59th PEN International Congress was held under fire in Dubrovnik and many PEN Centres took the risk of going there to express their solidarity with the victims.

Soon after the Peace Committee faced another challenge. The 2000 Congress in Moscow, which had been prepared as a moment to celebrate Russia's step back into democracy, was transformed with the sudden and violent attack of the Russian army on Chechnya and the killing of journalists. At the Congress, Günter Grass gave a memorable speech where he led the cry against the terrible crimes by the Russian army: 'Silent no more!' Russian PEN supported the position of PEN's international community and was fearless in its defence of peace and freedom of expression.

As well as reviewing PEN's work for reconciliation and peace, the following pages will also explore the way PEN Centres have responded to their own conflicts. For example, Sierra Leonean PEN, Afghan PEN, and Malian PEN were able to create a space of inclusive dialogue even as their countries were subjected to violence and division.

The Writers for Peace Committee also stood together with Kurdish PEN and Turkish PEN in Diyarbakır/Amed in the spring of 2016 to ask the Turkish government to relaunch the peace process and abandon the aggression against the Kurds. This act of unity occurred only one month after the massacres and only days after the curfew had been lifted.

In 2014, during the Russian aggression against Ukraine and the occupation of Crimea and the Donbass, Russian and Ukrainian writers united in public events in Stockholm, Warsaw, Bled, and at the 80th PEN International Congress in Bishkek, Kyrgyzstan. This solidarity was nonstop and was an integral part of the celebration of PEN's International Congress in Lviv, Ukraine, in 2017. Here, in the very act of war and occupation, an important Russian delegation attended and set in motion the founding of Saint Petersburg PEN and Moscow PEN. The Lviv Congress explored in detail the complex mechanisms of modern propaganda. The title of the Lviv Congress was an updated formulation of PEN's mission: 'Reclaiming Truth in Times of Propaganda'.

← 'The pen is mightier than the sword' is an old adage, and a pen crossing a sword has been a motif for PEN since its early years. Artist Francesc Torres produced this image for the Day of the Imprisoned Writer 2018 (see full poster on page 150).

The creation of the Writers for Peace Committee in 1984

↑   Arthur Miller at the PEN
International Congress in Bled in
1965, debating with Yugoslav writers
Erih Kos and Miodrag Bulatović.

The Cold War meant that exiled writers from Central and Eastern
Europe had a prominent role in shaping PEN's mission with, for
example, the Hungarian Paul Tabori standing strongly behind the
creation of the Writers in Prison Committee (WiPC) at the Rio de
Janeiro PEN International Congress in 1960. But PEN's mission had
been, since its foundation, to bridge the gap between literary
communities in countries experiencing conflict and at war. As the
PEN Charter states, 'Literature knows no frontiers and must remain
common currency among people in spite of political or international upheavals.'

During the Cold War an important question arose: where might PEN find a place for writers to meet from both sides of the Iron Curtain? The place became Slovenia, an important PEN place of encounter over many decades. The Committee of Three, who were managing the WiPC, looked for a way to have greater contact with writers from the communist bloc. The Dutch writer Victor E van Vriesland had been elected president of PEN International in 1962, and in that same year the Slovenian PEN had been re-established — unable to meet since 1941 when it was banned by the Italian occupation authorities. Tito's Yugoslavia was a communist country but it was part of the Non-Aligned Movement and sufficiently open to the world to organise the event. The 33rd World Congress was held at Bled in 1965 and writers from the Soviet Union in the role of observers attended for the first time. In the divided world of the Cold War, literary links between the Eastern and Western blocs were so infrequent that the attendance of the Soviets was seen as improving inter-bloc relations. The Congress was attended by Ivo Andrić, the Yugoslav writer from Bosnia who had won the Nobel Prize in Literature four years earlier. Among the 400 participants were the prominent Latin American writers Pablo Neruda and Miguel Ángel Asturias.

The Bled Congress elected Arthur Miller as president of PEN International. In Miller's acceptance speech he said: 'All of us when we meet, meet in disguise. Alone and unobserved, we stand mystified before the questions of life and death, of meaning and meaninglessness. But facing one another we assume certain answers, pride and suspicion, the various masks of certainty. But if doubt did not exist, there could be no literature and the writer is only that member of mankind who dares to tremble in public, express with what courage he can muster his challenge to meaninglessness and the void.'

The Bled Congress was such a success that, year after year, Slovenian PEN continued to welcome writers and intellectuals from both sides and Bled became a place of literary encounter and dialogue. At the 47th PEN International Congress in Tokyo in 1984, the president of Slovenian PEN, Miloš Mikeln, proposed the creation of a Writers for Peace Committee of PEN International, reporting at Congresses and meeting every year in Bled. Mikeln himself became the first chair of the committee, and for 35 years the position was held by prominent Slovenian writers and intellectuals: Boris A Novak, Veno Taufer, Edvard Kovač, Tone Peršak, and Marjan Strojan. In 2019, at the 85th PEN International Congress in Manila, the president of French PEN Emmanuel Pierrat was elected to the chair of the committee.

↑ ↑ ↑   The Slovenian poet Veno Taufer was elected president of Slovenian PEN and chair of the Writers for Peace Committee of PEN International in 2000. Next to him is Sibila Petlevski, president of PEN Croatia and board member of PEN International in the same year.

↑ ↑   Lake Bled, Slovenia.

↑   Emmanuel Pierrat, president of French PEN and chair of the Writers for Peace Committee, and Veera Tyhtilä, president of Finnish PEN and deputy chair of the committee, reporting at the 85th PEN International Congress in Manila in 2019.

Besieged in Sarajevo...

↑   Boris A Novak was elected president of Slovenian PEN and chair of the Writers for Peace Committee in 1991 and has been a vice-president of PEN International since 2002.

Boris A Novak was chair of the Writers for Peace Committee of PEN International from 1991 to 2000. The following text is his testimony of his experience as chair, titled 'I don't want soldiers, I want civilians':

'In early October 1991, when in Slovenia we awaited with relief the final withdrawal of the Yugoslav "People's" Army and when the aggression on Croatia had just been tragically unleashed, as the president of the Slovenian PEN Centre I set in motion a humanitarian campaign for the refugees who were beginning to arrive in Slovenia from different parts of our former common state because of the dangers brought by the war and political persecution. Among the first were the Dubrovnik poet Luko Paljetak and his wife Anuška, a translator; the Montenegrin poet Jevrem Brković; and the journalist from Belgrade and founder of the Roma PEN Centre Rajko Đurić. Our humanitarian activities were very diverse: they encompassed financial help, the search for temporary work and shelter, facilitating health care for refugees and their family members, organising numerous joint literary and peace events, translating and publishing their works, resolving legal problems (mostly in connection with visas, transit visas and their legal status in Slovenia and other countries), enabling children of refugee families to attend school, and so on. Collecting financial help was actually the simplest part of these activities. During the war, we financially assisted 40 refugee writers and this number should then be multiplied by the number of their family members; the total amount was about 40,000 German marks. It soon became clear that the Slovenian PEN would be unable to bear such a heavy financial burden, and we asked for the help of PEN International, which responded with some cheques from the PEN Emergency Fund based in the Netherlands; the fund was headed by the now deceased poet Henk Bernlef.

'From November 1992, our humanitarian help focused on the besieged Sarajevo, the city where the tragedy of the twentieth century began and ended. The Bosnian poet Josip Osti, who at the start of the siege happened to be in Slovenia, suggested that we should send help to ten writers who he was certain were in Sarajevo. This was followed by another 12 consignments of money. Osti continued to offer significant help with information and connections. In the following years, the list of the recipients grew to 155; the total amount sent was 165,000 German marks. We stuck to the principle that help should be given to all writers, irrespective of their ethnicity, including Serbs — under the proviso, of course, that they did not take part in attacks on Sarajevo.

'The money was smuggled across the borders and into the areas of armed conflicts by our brave and reliable couriers, and on one occasion in November 1994, even myself. Five times, it was carried by Sašo Novak, a Slovene who had lived in Sarajevo for quite a few years. I was very touched when he told me that as a child during the Second World War he had been a courier for my father Ante, a partisan commander. All the consignments arrived at their destination. The only loss we

↖↑   The poets Ferida Duraković and Goran Simić distributed help to besieged writers around Sarajevo collected through the PEN International network.

↓   Tvrtko Kulenović, president of the Bosnian and Herzegovinian PEN Centre. Boris A Novak: 'At the PEN International World Congress in Rio de Janeiro in December 1992, I was appointed as the organiser of the help to refugee writers and our colleagues trapped in the besieged Sarajevo. At the PEN Congress in Santiago de Compostela in September 1993, the delegate assembly founded an ad hoc committee, called the Sarajevo Committee, joined by 35 Centres. I was entrusted with the position of its chair. After long-lasting efforts and painful discussions, the Bosnian and Herzegovinian PEN Centre was established, which meant a great deal to Bosnian writers: they elected Prof. Dr Tvrtko Kulenović as the first chairman.'

suffered was 500 German marks, which one of our couriers was forced to pay at the border crossing between Croatia and Bosnia and Herzegovina, as otherwise they would have taken the whole amount he was carrying. The money was delivered around Sarajevo, in very dangerous circumstances and exceptionally fairly, by the poetess Ferida Duraković and poet Goran Simić, the latter an informal leader of the community of Serbs who stayed in the besieged Sarajevo, faithful to their commitment to co-existence with their fellow townsmen and countrymen of other ethnicities. […]

'We organised a network of PEN Centres and other organisations, which donated help. The most generous amounts were contributed by the Viennese organisation Literar-Mechana at the initiative of the Austrian PEN; exceptional solidarity was also shown by the German, Swedish, French, Danish and Galician PEN Centres. Help was also sent by a group of American poets and creative writing students, led by the poet Richard Jackson. Many individuals also contributed important amounts: among them, let me mention the generous Chinese poetess Han Suyin. We also used our channels to convey to Sarajevo the help collected by other organisations, such as American and Slovene theatre workers. Taking into account all these different sources, the help we sent involved 445 intellectuals, writers and other artists.'

... and the history of ethics

From Boris A Novak's testimony:

'In addition to the joint activities, some PEN Centres that were members of the Committee also developed their own, for which they deserve special praise and gratitude. I must emphasise the huge material and moral support offered by the American PEN and brought to Sarajevo by Susan Sontag. Allow me to boast a little — during the preparations for her journey to Sarajevo, this fascinating lady studied in detail the extensive documentation I sent her via the then executive director of American PEN, Karen Kennerly. Later, Susan Sontag and I worked together on the settlement of some refugees in Western countries. As is generally known, Susan Sontag's visit did a great deal for the besieged city, both in terms of concrete help and in terms of a striking symbolic gesture: her direction of Beckett's *Waiting for Godot* in the Kamerni Teatar 55, lit only by candles, will remain written in the history of ethics. The same applies to Juan Goytisolo, Monika van Paemel, Bernard-Henry Lévy and others. I never met Susan face to face, for during those difficult years we communicated via intensive correspondence. She honoured me greatly with a nickname she gave me — *Novak Dobri* (Novak the Good).

'Let me evoke the memory of the visit of Slovene writers to the besieged city. The group included Niko Grafenauer, Drago Jančar, Josip Osti and myself. […] We had the status of a UNESCO delegation, since this UN scientific and cultural agency was organising visits by artists to the besieged city; the procuration was provided with a special letter signed by Federico Mayor Zaragoza, the then UNESCO director-general. As it later transpired, this document probably saved us many problems, maybe even our lives. I was also travelling to Sarajevo as an organiser of the PEN humanitarian help, which is why the four of us also had the status of PEN International deputies. […]

'We were received by the member of the Bosnian presidency, Mirko Pejanović, and the president of Bosnia and Herzegovina, Alija Izetbegović. We expected a short, official audience, but the increasingly lively and warm discussion stretched to over an hour. I told president Izetbegović about the humanitarian activities of the Slovene and International PEN, while Drago Jančar drew attention to the difficult position of those Serbs who had faithfully remained in the city, exposed to both Serbian cannon fire, as well as the mistrust of their neighbours of different national backgrounds. Our high-ranking host received Jančar's criticism well: he said that the Serbs were the only segment of the Sarajevo population who had the possibility of a moral choice — to either stay or leave the city, and that those who stayed had to be respected all the more. […]

'The truth of our visit was nicely summed up by Goran Simić: "Many people offering help have visited Sarajevo until now, but did nothing. But the Slovene writers first did something for us and only then visited us."'

↑↑   Susan Sontag and Juan Goytisolo in besieged Sarajevo.

↑   Josip Osti, Boris A Novak, Niko Grafenauer, and Drago Jančar in an armoured vehicle with UNPF registration number 6278.

←   The American writer Susan Sontag with the theatre company, Sarajevo, 1993.

Zoran Mutić and Svetlana Slapšak

← Zoran Mutić and
Svetlana Slapšak.

Zoran Mutić is a Bosnian Muslim translator of mixed background whose works have been banned in Serbia and have frequently protested against the rise of Serbian nationalism. When he received the PEN/Barbara Goldsmith Freedom to Write Award from American PEN in 1993 he had translated several English-language books into Bosnian/Croatian/Serbian, including Salman Rushdie's *Midnight's Children*. He was also a prominent defender of Rushdie after the issuing of the death fatwa against Rushdie in 1989. Mutić fled Sarajevo in 1992, just before the city came under siege, for Ljubljana, Slovenia, where he stayed with fellow future PEN/Barbara Goldsmith Freedom to Write Award winner Svetlana Slapšak, who had fled from Serbia one year earlier. Upon arriving in Slovenia, Mutić began work on an exhibition about the war in Bosnia and a book of testimonies by Bosnian refugees.

Writer, translator, editor, professor, and activist Svetlana Slapšak faced physical danger as well as legal troubles for her work advocating for human rights and peace in her native Serbia. She has written more than 70 books, including the popular mock-adventure novel *Leon and Leonine*. At multiple points between 1968 and 1988 her passport renewal was

denied because of her activism. In the 1980s, she defended many opposition activists who were harassed or imprisoned by the authorities as well as initiating a petition to abolish the death penalty along with her husband, Bozidar Slapšak. Slapšak served as president of the Writers' Association of Serbia's Committee for the Freedom of Expression. In the late 1980s, Slapšak was brought to court over articles critical of Slobodan Milošević and, athough she was acquitted, her staunch belief in the peace movement led to accusations of her being a traitor. Due to these

events, she lost her job at the Institute for Arts and Literature in Belgrade as well as the support of her friends and colleagues, who feared reprisal from Milošević's powerful nationalist movement.

Svetlana Slapšak fled to Slovenia in 1991 and continued her activist work there, including organising the women's anti-war group Silence Kills: Let Us Speak Up for Peace. After she received the PEN/Barbara Goldsmith Freedom to Write Award, her application for Slovenian citizenship was accepted.

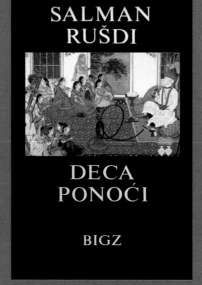

→ Zoran Mutić is the Bosnian
translator of Salman Rushdie's
Midnight's Children.

↑   The framed picture of a refugee child is by Srđan Veljović.
The picture is being eaten by fungus and held by someone in
the ruins of a burned factory in Srebrenica. The inscription is the
first verse of a popular communist song: 'Comrade Tito, we
promise to follow your path'. In July 1995, armed forces of
Republika Srpska invaded the town of Srebrenica, in eastern
Bosnia and Herzegovina. More than 8,000 Bosnian Muslim boys
and men were taken to places of detention, abused, tortured
and then executed. The International Criminal Tribunal for the
former Yugoslavia defined the crime as genocide. The artwork is
by Mireia Sallarès as part of her project *Kao malo vode na dlanu*
(*Like a Little Water in the Palm of the Hand*).

PEN International Congress in Dubrovnik during the war

PEN had faced a crisis and redefined its mission at the Dubrovnik Congress in 1933. Exactly 60 years later, at another moment of grave crisis, Croatian PEN and the Writers for Peace Committee once again invited PEN Centres from around the world to the old town of Ragusa. In the autumn of 1991, Milošević's armies had started the aggression on Croatia and Dubrovnik, with its old city a UNESCO World Heritage Site, had been under siege for a long time and was being systematically destroyed and suffering casualties. The 59th PEN International Congress took place on 19–25 April 1993 and 200 delegates from around world attended. For security reasons given the context of war, delegates gathered in Venice and sailed down the Adriatic coast. The Congress sessions took place on the island of Hvar and in Dubrovnik.

However, PEN was divided in two camps: several PEN Centres refused to participate as they wanted to remain neutral towards the conflict, and, due to these tensions, the Writers in Prison Committee announced that it would not meet during the Congress. The Writers for Peace Committee and other Centres held the opposite position: in the same way that PEN had defined its mission towards German PEN, which had been infiltrated by the Nazis in 1933, they wanted to challenge Serbian PEN, whose president, Dobrica Ćosić, was an intellectual at the service of President Milošević. The president of PEN International György Konrád and PEN International secretary Alexandre Blokh (known as Jean Blot) made a paradoxical decision: the effort by Croatian PEN was welcomed, all Centres were invited to attend the Congress and express their solidarity with the victims of war but, given the controversy, it would be a literary Congress, without resolutions or political statements.

Croatian PEN organised an extraordinary Congress. Delegates boarded the ship, travelled the coast, had passionate debates in theatres both in Hvar and Dubrovnik, and planted olive trees for peace in the nearby island of Lokrum. PEN delegates also visited the ruins of historic buildings bombed during the siege of Dubrovnik and, at times, they could even hear faint bombing in the distance.

At the following Congresses, PEN decided to enhance its governance so it could face similar situations with a united voice, which led to a change of regulations and the creation of the PEN International Board. At the Dubrovnik Congress, delegates were finally able to express their support of Croatian PEN and the victims of war. Many Centres joined the Writers for Peace Committee to stand with writers who were victims of the war and held captive in the besieged city of Sarajevo. When the sessions finished, a mission of five writers went to Zagreb to meet the Mothers of Vukovar, a group of women who were mothers, wives, sisters, or daugthers of men who had been slaughtered in the very first days of the war in the city of Vukovar and who now rested in mass graves.

↑   PEN Congress delegates arriving in the port of Hvar by ship in April 1993. The Hungarian novelist György Konrád, president of PEN International, was the first one to disembark. Behind him is Vlado Gotovac, a Croatian poet and distinguished Croatian PEN member who had been prosecuted as a dissident and jailed twice with long prison sentences in the 1970s and 1980s during the communist era in Yugoslavia.

→   Participants to the PEN International Dubrovnik Congresses in 1933 and 1993 in Gundulić Square, at the heart of the historic centre of Dubrovnik.

PEN Moscow Congress in 2000

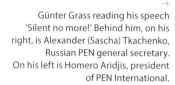
Günter Grass reading his speech 'Silent no more!' Behind him, on his right, is Alexander (Sascha) Tkachenko, Russian PEN general secretary. On his left is Homero Aridjis, president of PEN International.

For PEN, the twentieth century ended in Warsaw at its 66th International Congress. Wisława Szymborska and Czesław Miłosz, both Polish Nobel Prize winners, read together at the opening event while Adam Michnik, the renowned Polish dissident, held a talk on the clandestine movements that helped end communism in Poland 10 years earlier.

The new board was elected at this Congress and had to face a difficult decision as the following 2000 Congress had been scheduled to take place in Moscow, hosted by Russian PEN. However, six months before the Congress, Vladimir Putin had initiated the Second Chechen War with crimes, human rights abuses, curtailments to free speech and the killing of journalists. While the Russian PEN Centre had bravely denounced these abuses, the PEN International Board had to decide if holding the Congress was worth the risk of government intervention.

The PEN International Board decided to go ahead with the Moscow Congress while agreeing not to invite any government official or accept any funding from the Russian cultural ministry or Moscow city government. The board also agreed that all resolutions and statements denouncing the crimes of Putin's regime would be presented by Russian PEN, thus avoiding the accusation of 'foreign interference'.

Terry Carlbom, PEN International secretary (1998–2004), was brilliant in managing all sensiblities during the very difficult Moscow Congress. The picture is from December 2019, when Terry Carlbom donated more than 14,000 pictures and hundreds of documents to the PEN International Archive. He shows an interview in Mexico with both him and the president of USA West PEN, Eric Lax.

In addition, the board asked Günter Grass, who had won the Nobel Prize in Literature the year before, to give the opening speech titled 'Nie wieder Schweigen!' 'Silent no more!' This was a call to end the silence on the Russian army's crimes in Chechnya. Grass's opening words stated: 'Whenever and wherever writers band together, whenever and wherever the members of PEN gather, regionally or nationally, there seems to be an emergency on our agenda…' The international media covered the speech and this helped to create worldwide awareness of Vladimir Putin's crimes.

PEN delegates condemned the 'needless war', military censorship, demanded access so that NGOs could investigate 'the concentration camps set up both in Chechnya and in neighbouring territories', and mourned the irreparable damage done to the Chechen culture. Many journalists, academics and new dissidents of Putin's harsh regime joined PEN in demanding that the Russian authorities both stop all aggression and begin immediate negotiations with the legitimate Chechen government. The following year, at the 68th PEN International Congress in London, Anna Politkovskaya addressed the delegates after the first attempt against her life by the Russian army.

A delegate of the Moscow Congress asked Günter Grass to write the title of his speech 'Nie wieder Schweigen!' as a banner: 'Silent no more!' Other Congress delegates agreed to pose in the same attitude, among them Fawzia Assaad (PEN Egypt and Swiss Romand PEN), Kadija George (PEN African Writers Abroad Centre), Elisabet Middelthon (chair of Norwegian PEN's WiPC), Monica Nagler (president of Swedish PEN) and the Russian journalist Viktor Popkov, who was assassinated a few months later, shot in the back while reporting in Chechnya. The text in Popkov's banner says: 'Our hope in a better future can only be rooted in the suffering of the people, past and present. May God help us to feel their pain!'

PEN Sierra Leone: social cohesion through literature after a civil war

← Romana Cacchioli (first from right), director of International Programmes at PEN International, with delegates from Zimbabwean, Malawian, Gambian, Nigerian, and Togoan PENs, photographed during a visit to study how Sierra Leonean PEN has developed successful civil society projects such as PEN school clubs, and partnerships with the National Library, the Teachers Association, and the Ministry of Culture, Science and Technology as well as creative workshops for writers and artists to promote children's literature in Krio, Mende, Temne, and the other national languages of Sierra Leone.

↓ Mohamed Sheriff, president of PEN Sierra Leone, gives his acceptance speech after being re-elected to the PEN International Board at the 81st PEN International Congress in Quebec, 2015.

After the civil war in Sierra Leone, a national reconstruction, rehabilitation, and reintegration process started in 2000. However, Sierra Leonean writers, who have contributed immensely in documenting the history, literature, and culture of the country, were absent from any cultural policies. In order to stop the rapid decline of literary interest, and reduce the exodus of writers, Sierra Leonean PEN was formally readmitted as a fully fledged member of PEN International at the 69th PEN International Congress in Ohrid, Macedonia, in September 2002.

In 2005, Sierra Leonean PEN launched the school clubs programme with five schools in the capital, Freetown. The overall goal of the programme was to promote literature among young people in various regions across the country by generating more interest in reading and writing for both pleasure and enlightenment. In 2007, Sierra Leonean PEN became a beneficiary of both the UNESCO Innovation Fund and the SIDA Programme Fund established through PEN International. It meant the expansion of the school clubs programme beyond Freetown. Sierra Leonean PEN developed PEN school clubs all over the country, 34 of which are very active and each of which has an average of 45 members in any given academic year. The clubs have the potential to indirectly benefit thousands of children both at school and at home as well as the wider community. Experience shows that these clubs are actually schools of leadership and social awareness. The fund also supports exchange programmes between PEN Centres and, since 2007, Sierra Leonean PEN has often played host to other African PEN Centres interested in developing similar networks.

The rule of Sierra Leonean PEN is inclusivity. By giving voice to young writers from all cultural backgrounds, in a country that suffered years of war based on the confrontation of ethnic communities, the programme promotes the necessary dialogue based on the sharing of experience and the multiplication of points of view. Space is given to all mother tongues. A parallel programme by Sierra Leonean PEN organises workshops where, around a shared story, artists produce illustrations and writers produce manuscripts. More than 30 children's books have been published and the programme includes distribution to a selection of schools.

→↓
Members of the PEN school clubs participating in Sierra Leonean PEN's after-school writing workshops in 2015.

Samar Yazbek

The Syrian writer and journalist Samar Yazbek was born in Jableh in 1970. An outspoken critic of the Assad regime, Yazbek was deeply involved in the Syrian uprising, which broke out on 15 March 2011. Fearing for the life of her daughter she was forced to flee her country and lived in hiding. Determined to bear witness to the suffering of her people, she revisited her homeland repeatedly, once by even squeezing through a hole in the fence on the Turkish border. Yazbek's portraits of life in Syria are important historical documents as well as being works of art and literature. Her book *A Woman in the Crossfire: Diaries of the Syrian Revolution* won an English PEN Writers in Translation award in 2012. In France, her literary narrative *The Crossing* was awarded the prestigious Prix du Meilleur Livre Étranger (Best Foreign Book Prize).

After being forced to leave Syria, Yazbek received three PEN awards in 2012, the Oxfam Novib/PEN Award from PEN International, the Tucholsky Award from Swedish PEN, and the PEN Pinter award from English PEN. In 2019, seven years after receiving the award herself, Samar Yazbek was the keynote speaker for the Oxfam Novib/PEN Award to a Writer of

Courage given to the Ugandan poet and professor Stella Nyanzi, imprisoned in Kampala for a poem she wrote. In her keynote speech, Yazbek shared with the audience the challenge of writing about the horrors of war in Syria:

'I have been asking the same question every day: what can we do except write about the truth and demand justice for the victims? We counter terrorism through freedom of expression, educating children and providing them with opportunities to become an enlightened generation of equal citizens and not soldiers or suicidal extremists. We fight terrorism by eradicating dictatorship and the terrorism of a state that justifies its existence and fascism by the presence of extremism. Extremism is the result of ignorance and repression; ignorance breeds violence against people, as stated by the philosopher Ibn Rushd. Yes, violence transforms the victims of violence into tools of evil. I wondered how can we do something despite the war, how can we build community hotspots with the children and women? We cannot put an end to the war. We are witnessing the destruction of our country and the exclusion of women from public spaces by

the Jihadi brigades. We knew and spoke to women abused in the prisons of the Assad regime. What should we do? We should resist. We set up this action network on the ground.

'I met Maria Al Abdeh, the Syrian woman who managed, brought together and followed through every stage of our work since the foundation of "Women Now" until now. Since 2012 we have stayed with the women under bombings, during the exodus and through the bloodshed. We have accompanied them step by step, under Russian and Assad bombings. In areas controlled by extremist terrorists we build schools and deliver educational and awareness-raising lectures. We have tackled political, economic and political issues and provide psychological support. We have started up a political network project. We have provided support to women's associations in remote villages in Northern Syria, and we have encountered unbelievable war, evil and madness.'

→
Samar Yazbek was the keynote speaker at the Oxfam Novib/PEN International Awards in The Hague in January 2019. She said, 'I received this award here at The Hague seven years ago in January. Later on the same year I received two other awards: the Tucholsky Award from Swedish PEN and the Pinter Award from English PEN. With the funds of the three awards we founded a school in Syria that was able to shelter and educate children for six years. Until it was bombed by the Russian forces six months ago.'

↑   In London, in 2012, Samar Yazbek received the PEN Pinter
International Writer of Courage prize, which she shared with the
UK Poet Laureate Carol Ann Duffy as the British winner. Yazbek's
book *A Woman in the Crossfire: Diaries of the Syrian Revolution* had
already received the same year another award from English PEN,
the Writers in Translation Award, for the translation from the
Arabic by Emily Danby. In an event at the British Library, Carol
Ann Duffy explained why she had decided to share the PEN Pinter
award with Samar Yazbek: 'I have chosen Samar because of her
literary skill […] and her bravery in writing about her opposition
to the bloody Assad regime when she is already such a
prominent figure in Syria and so at increased risk. Harassment
from the security services and denouncements from her family
and clan have forced her to flee Syria to Europe.'

Afghan PEN blooming in spite of war

First board of
Afghan PEN in 2003.
In the centre, Eugene
Schoulgin and Elisabeth Eide
from Norwegian PEN.

For a century, starting with the first London meetings in 1921, PEN members have approached colleagues in other countries to support the creation of sister PEN Centres. This was the case with the creation of Afghan PEN in 2003 after a visit by the Norwegian PEN leader, Elisabeth Eide, and Eugene Schoulgin, chair of PEN International WiPC. The account of their mission is from Elisabeth Eide:

'Optimism came back to Afghans in the new millennium. They had suffered from Soviet occupation for almost 10 years (1979–88) as a last part of the Cold War with an array of stakeholders. They had witnessed a civil war (1992–96), which laid the capital in ruins, and they had survived more than five years of Taliban darkness (1996–2001). During those years, there was hardly any intellectual outlet to be found, just an extremely religious radio station and an equally fundamentalist newspaper looking like a leaflet.

'Persian and Pashto are poetic languages, and so are other minority languages. There had to be writers inside Afghanistan, old friends of the country thought, even if many had travelled into exile. In March 2003, we were out to find them. The *we* consisted of Eugene Schoulgin, veteran in International PEN, and myself from Norwegian PEN. We had a small contact list containing three Afghan writers. One of them was the poet Habibullah Rafi, who later contributed to Afghanistan's new national anthem; another was Khaleda Froagh, a young poet with an academic background, on her way to becoming one of the most renowned writers in the country; and not least Razaq Mamoon, who had spent eight years in prison during the Soviets and then published a novel based on these experiences. Our purpose seemed to go down well with these new friends. "Why did you not come earlier?" one of them asked. Yes, of course we should have come before. […] After three days, we found ourselves surrounded by 50 writers at a restaurant in central Kabul. The gathering was presided over by Dr Samay Hamed, later to become one of the most famous cultural personalities in the country. We did not know him much by then, but had vague memories of an encounter at a human rights NGO office in Peshawar some years before.

'We distributed the PEN Charter and read it aloud. All seemed eager to join the global family. Among them were writers who had been supportive of the Soviet occupation forces, as well as those who had spent years in exile or in prison during those same years; in 2003, they were miraculously united by the passion for literature and the recently gained freedom to spread their words.

'Mostly, they were poets, although some wrote short stories. There was the occasional novelist, plus a couple of editors and journalists. In a country ravaged not only by invasions and by civil war, but also divided by language, ethnicity and religion, the founding fathers and mothers decided to create a chapter of PEN recognising these divisions by an elaborate rotation system and power sharing. Thus, no single language group would dominate the organisation. Two delegates, poets Partaw Naderi (Dari) and Safia Siddiqi (Pashto), were elected to represent the new-born chapter at the PEN congress in Mexico City later that year, and arrived in triumph, after the expected visa drama. […]

'On the last evening of our visit, a request for a house, a place to gather, was raised. The year after, a writer's house in Kabul materialised and exists until this day. Fifteen years and many visits later, hopes for a safe future for Afghanistan are dwindling. We have to force the hope, said Waheed Warasta, who has run the writers' house for many years, some years ago. Hundreds of journalists have left the country. Against many odds, Afghan PEN lives on. They publish books in all Afghan languages; they organise PEN chapters in schools, vaccinating students against extremism; they host literary events every week and donate their literature to libraries and schools. The writers' house includes visual art, equipment for film editing, and a café.'

↑   Poetry reading by Afghan PEN in 2003.

↓   Eugene Schoulgin, at that time chair of PEN International's WiPC, with the governor of the district of Herat, who held a dinner for the Herat members of Afghan PEN.

↓↓   The office of Afghan PEN. From left to right: the poet Khaleda Froagh and writer Waheed Warasta, delegates of Afghan PEN at the Writers in Prison Conference in Barcelona in 2004, and Safia Siddiqi, delegate at the PEN International Congress in Mexico City in 2003.

PEN Mali, **actor of the peace process**

↑↑   The writer and publisher ismaïla Samba Traoré, founder of Malian PEN in 2015 and first president of the Centre.

↑   Cecilia Balcázar (first from the right), past president of Colombian PEN, with participants from Mali and eight West African countries, shares the lessons learned in Colombia after the signing of the peace agreement between FARC and the Colombian government.

A new Malian PEN was welcomed at the 81st PEN International Congress in Quebec in 2015. The Mali Centre gathers together writers in Bambara, Soninke, Songhay, and other languages of the area as well as Tamasheq and French. Given the conflict in the Azawad region in the north of Mali between 2012 and 2015, the respect for cultural diversity and the promotion of dialogue between all the peoples of Mali is PEN's priority in the country. Every year, Malian PEN organises regional conferences of journalists, writers, and traditional communicators, where Malian participants debate with colleagues from Morocco, Mauritania, Senegal, Ivory Coast, Guinea, Burkina Faso, Benin, Togo, and Niger. The themes of the conferences address issues relevant to the peace process. For example, in 2016, the theme was 'With the rise of violent extremism, a threat to the State, social cohesion, rights and freedoms'; in 2017, the call was 'All against ethnicisation' with the purpose of 'Deconstructing sectarian, identitarian and extremist discourses and behaviours'.

The Bamako debates organised by Malian PEN are an acknowledgement of the diversity of actors in the peace process and the need to open the national dialogue to all voices without exclusion.

Sociologists, novelists, poets, and journalists take part in the conversation, and even religious leaders and representatives of the UN peace forces of the MINUSMA (the United Nations Multidimensional Integrated Stabilisation Mission in Mali), which often help to facilitate transportation of Tuareg poets and intellectuals to Bamako.

The PEN International network actively participates in these meetings and supports Malian PEN members and their commitment to peace. In 2015 the opening speech of the *colloque* was given by John Ralston Saul, president of PEN International. In 2016, the main speaker was Colombian PEN's Cecilia Balcázar who shared the lessons from the peace process in her country, and the responsibility of writers in finding a new language for a national narrative of peace that also rejects violence. The president of Mauritanian PEN, Khadi Mint Cheickna, Abdoulaye Fodé Ndione from Senegalese PEN, Alix Parodi from Swiss Romand PEN, and Tsutomu Ide from Japanese PEN also participated in the debates.

By creating and maintaining an open and inclusive space for literature, translation, and debate, Malian PEN contributes to the peace process and is a prominent member of the Writers for Peace Committee of PEN International. The membership also promotes publishing in the national literatures of the country and campaigns for freedom of expression. Malian PEN is also the initiator of the youth movement Malivaleurs, promoting the inclusion of student voices from all cultural backgrounds in Mali's national narrative.

↑   Poster of the 2018 gathering of journalists, writers, and traditional communicators under the banner 'All against ethnicisation' with the aim of 'Deconstructing sectarian, identitarian and extremist discourses and behaviours'.

↓   Malian PEN organised in 2018 a workshop on literary freedom and copyright in Timbuktu.

Dareen Tatour

← The 2019 Oxfam Novib/PEN International Awards for Freedom of Expression were received by the Nicaraguan author and journalist Gioconda Belli, the Palestinian poet Dareen Tatour, and the Italian writer and journalist Roberto Saviano who couldn't attend the meeting because he is in hiding. The photograph shows Belli and Tatour after receiving the award from PEN International president, Jennifer Clement.

PEN International rejoiced on receiving the news that the Palestinian poet Dareen Tatour had been released from prison in Israel on 19 September 2018. Tatour had been convicted of incitement to violence and support for terror organisations in May 2018, and then handed a five-month prison sentence. However, having already served three months in prison, she was only required to serve a further two months. Tatour, a Palestinian poet and citizen of Israel, had mostly lived under house arrest from October 2015 to August 2018. Tatour's conviction was mainly related to a video in which she recites one of her poems entitled 'Qawim ya sha'abi, qawimhum' (Resist, my people, resist them).

On 8 August 2018, Tatour entered the special wing of Damoun Prison, as she was classified as a 'security' prisoner. Upon her release, Tatour commented: 'I have gained my freedom and I will continue to write. All my suffering was due to a poem I wrote and it saddens me that the Israeli authorities imprisoned me for writing the poem.'

In The Hague, in January 2019, Dareen Tatour received the Oxfam Novib/PEN Award for Freedom of Expression. In an interview after receiving the award, when asked about the relevance of PEN's work, she said: 'I will answer this question from the perspective of my case, especially given the interest and support I have received from PEN. I had never experienced any similar interest and support from any other party or organisation working to support writers, poets and artists. I believe that PEN is one of the most important organisations out there, not only among those I have heard of, but also those whose representatives I have met, such as Carles Torner and Jennifer Clement. Moreover, the messages I have received from the members have been very strengthening; they encourage me to carry on the path I have started, which is to fulfil the mission of a poet and a writer. It is one of the world's most important organisations in my opinion.'

↓ Portrait of Dareen Tatour created for a PEN campaign poster for International Women's Day in 2019.

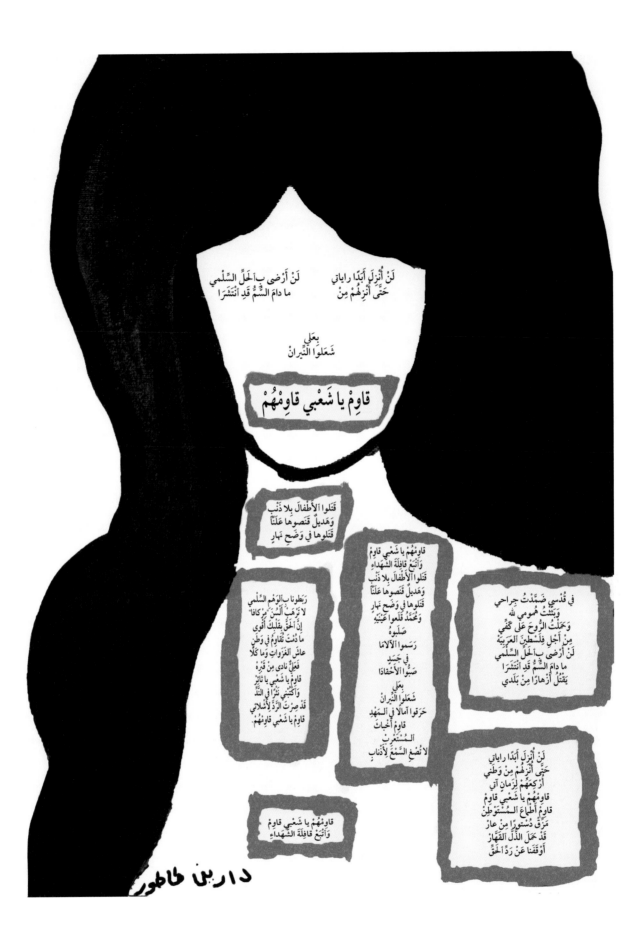

↗   Dareen Tatour's drawing *A Poet Behind Bars*
with transcriptions of her poems.

Facing the Russian aggression to Ukraine

In June 2014, Swedish PEN welcomed PEN International and both Russian PEN, represented by its vice-president, Lyudmila Ulitskaya, and Ukrainian PEN, represented by Aleksandra Hnatiuk, in Stockholm. PEN delegates stated that for three months there had been incessant acts of aggression against Ukraine from the side of the Russian Federation. The illegal annexation of Crimea had taken place, and following it armed groups had created violent disorder in the eastern parts of Ukraine with the goal of destabilising the country. All participants united in a statement:

> *Ukrainian PEN has talked about journalists and citizens being shot, murdered, kidnapped and tortured. Russian PEN points out that such violence is dependent upon the co-opting of language: 'Words are the only means we have to construct meaning and express reality. The Russian authorities are currently using words to destroy meaning. It goes without saying that this is a crime against culture.'*

↓↘   The first version of the report produced by PEN International and Moscow PEN, *Russia's Strident Stifling of Free Speech,* was presented in a panel at the Lviv PEN International Congress in 2017. As is the norm for all PEN Congresses since 2014, a report about freedom of expression and linguistic rights in the host country was presented and debated. The Ukraine report was titled *Freedom of Expression in Post-Euromaidan Ukraine: External Aggression, Internal Challenges.*

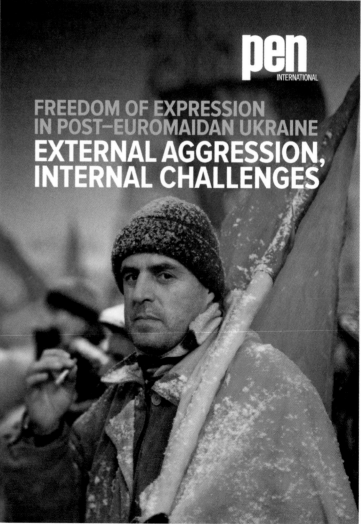

PEN is particularly concerned about the large number of anti free expression laws emerging in Russia, which include treating international NGOs as foreign agents; anti-gay laws; a law permitting the blocking of websites without a court order; laws against discussing Russian history and religious defamation law. In the name of national security, human rights are being dangerously undermined.

People wonder if we are faced by a war of interests or a war of values, or both. In either case, the only real security lies in opening channels of free expression. Those on the front lines of this situation are often the journalists, in whatever country. We admire their courage and appeal to those under pressure to remember, in Lev Rubinstein's words, that 'propaganda is the collapse of language'.

The statement was signed by John Ralston Saul, president of PEN International, Takeaki Hori, PEN International secretary, and Tone Peršak, chair of the Writers for Peace Committee, as well as Ronald Harwood, Homero Aridjis, György Konrád, Mario Vargas Llosa, and Per Wästberg, all of whom are emeritus presidents of PEN. As members of the Swedish Academy, Peter Englund and Kjell Espmark joined Wästberg in signing the statement, together with Tomas Tranströmer, Swedish Literature Nobel laureate. In the true spirit of the PEN Charter, which calls PEN to bridge the gap between literary communities in countries in conflict, Lyudmila Ulitskaya, Alexei Simonov, and Lev Rubinstein, leaders of Russian PEN, signed the statement along with the leaders of Ukrainian PEN Aleksandra Hnatiuk, Andrey Kurkov, Myroslav Marynovych, Mykola Riabchuk, and Leonid Finberg.

In the same year, PEN organised public meetings in Kiev, Warsaw, and Bled where Russian and Ukrainian PEN members together denounced the Russian aggression to Ukraine. In September 2014, at the opening of the 80th PEN International Congress in Bishkek, Kyrgyzstan, a public dialogue was held between Russian PEN member Masha Gessen and Andrei Kurkov, who at the time was vice-president of Ukrainian PEN.

Three years later, delegates from more than 80 PEN Centres met at the 83rd PEN International Congress in Lviv, Ukraine, to debate 'Reclaiming Truth in Times of Propaganda', the name of the Congress. Ukrainian PEN welcomed delegates from around the world, and their Russian colleagues presented the first version of the report *Russia's Strident Stifling of Free Speech*. Very strong political pressure from the Kremlin created a split in Russian PEN. In Lviv, delegates welcomed the creation of a new St Petersburg PEN and the following year, at the 84th PEN International Congress meeting in Pune, India, they welcomed the new Moscow PEN.

↑   Mykola Riabchuk, president of PEN Ukraine, receiving an ovation from delegates thanking him for the very successful organisation of the Lviv PEN International Congress.

↓   The opening of the 2014 80th PEN International Congress in Bishkek, Kyrgyzstan, was a panel about freedom of expression in the context of the Russian occupation of Crimea and the Donbass between Masha Gessen (Russian PEN, left) and Andrei Kurkov (Ukrainian PEN, right), moderated by Finnish reporter Anna-Lena Laurén.

↓↓   Sergey Parkhomenko and Nadezhda Azhgikhina, delegates of the Free Word Association (later Moscow PEN), presenting the report *Russia's Strident Stifling of Free Speech* at the Lviv Congress.

Oleg Sentsov

↑ Oleg Sentsov at the German PEN stand at the Frankfurt Book
Fair 2019. Left to right: Kätlin Kaldmaa, PEN International secretary;
Regula Venske, president of German PEN; Oleg Sentsov; Andrei
Kurkov, president of Ukrainian PEN; Jennifer Clement, president of
PEN International.

↑ Members of Moscow PEN with banners for the liberation of
Oleg Sentsov. At the 84th PEN International Congress in Pune in
2018 the PEN community welcomed a new PEN Moscow, created
with the mission to counter the vast number of laws against
freedom of expression after the Russian occupation of Crimea.

PEN International and Ukrainian PEN welcomed the release of the prominent Ukrainian writer and filmmaker Oleg Sentsov on 7 September 2019 as part of a prisoner exchange between Russia and Ukraine. The president of PEN International, Jennifer Clement, said: 'Oleg Sentsov's release comes as a great and long overdue relief after five gruelling years away from his loved ones in Crimea spent behind bars on trumped-up terrorism charges. His strength, selflessness and determination in the face of adversity have been an inspiration to us all. The PEN community has been actively campaigning for this wonderful moment for over five years.'

A vocal opponent of Russia's occupation and 'annexation' of Crimea, Oleg Sentsov was arrested in May 2014 and transferred to Russia in flagrant violation of international law, where he spent more than a year in pre-trial detention. He was sentenced to 20 years in prison in August 2015 on spurious terrorism charges after a grossly unfair trial by a Russian military court, further marred by allegations of torture.

The president of Ukrainian PEN Andrey Kurkov also rejoiced on the day of his release: 'Oleg Sentsov is free! Many did not believe that this was possible under the current Russian government, but finally Oleg and 34 other Ukrainians have been released from Russian prisons and are home. For five years we have been talking continuously about Oleg Sentsov, we have been calling for his freedom. And today he is finally home, though his Crimea is still annexed by Russia. But he is at home, in Ukraine, and has already stated that he is ready to fight on. For Ukraine, for its sovereignty, for other Ukrainian political prisoners kept in Russian prisons, in the territories of the Donbass controlled by separatists, and in annexed Crimea. But we all know that in the struggle for human rights, for the release of the innocently convicted, for the restoration of justice, no break can be taken. The fight must go on. The freeing of Oleg Sentsov should give us more hope, strength, and perseverance.'

Oleg Sentsov quickly became the face of the conflict in eastern Ukraine. Despite being subjected to brutal treatment, he kept using his notoriety and resolve in the service of others. In 2018, he spent 145 days on hunger strike, calling for the release of all Ukrainian nationals held in Russia on politically motivated grounds. He was subsequently awarded the European Parliament's Sakharov Prize for Freedom of Thought.

Oleg Sentsov's plight attracted considerable international attention and mobilisation. Hundreds of PEN members across the world actively campaigned for his release by sending appeals to the Russian authorities, taking part in solidarity campaigns and protests, organising film screenings, coordinating petitions, translating, publishing, and promoting his short stories, and taking part in social media actions, among other things. Before his release, Oleg Sentsov was being held in the 'Polar Bear' prison colony of Labytnangi, in Siberia, thousands of kilometres away from his home and family in Crimea.

↑   Oleg Sentsov is reunited with his daughter
in Kiev after a prisoner swap on 7 September
2019. Two months later, they both travelled to
London for Sentsov's participation in the
celebration of the Day of the Imprisoned Writer
organised by English PEN and PEN International.

PEN against the extraditions of
Edward Snowden and Julian Assange

↑   The PEN Norway Ossietzky Prize is named after Carl von Ossietzky who revealed how German authorities ran secret re-armament programmes violating the Treaty of Versailles. For these revelations he was convicted of treason and imprisoned. The PEN Paris Congress in 1937 carried unanimously a resolution protesting against his arrest and the German authorities' refusal to allow him to travel to Oslo to receive the award (see page 91). During the award ceremony of the Nobel Peace Prize in 1936, Carl von Ossietzky's chair was empty.

↘   Edward Snowden receiving the Ossietzky Prize from William Nygaard, president of PEN Norway, and its secretary general, Hege Newth Nouri, in 2017. The lithograph is by the Norwegian artist Nico Widerberg.

PEN Norway's Ossietzky Prize to Edward Snowden

In April 2017, Edward Snowden received the 2016 Ossietzky Prize. Norwegian PEN's president, William Nygaard, and its general secretary, Hege Newth Nouri, gave him the award in Moscow. In the wake of counter-terrorism strategies after the attack on the Twin Towers in September 2001, the National Security Agency (NSA) of the USA, in alliance with other states, launched a clandestine massive surveillance programme that was uncovered by Snowden in 2013. In its announcement, Norwegian PEN linked Snowden's case with the history of the prize:

'This year it is 80 years since the Nobel Peace Prize was awarded to Carl von Ossietzky, an event that we commemorate by holding the award ceremony in the University Aula of Oslo, where Ossietzky in 1936 should have come to receive his prize. […] The Ossietzky Prize is Norwegian PEN's annual award for outstanding efforts to uphold freedom of expression and can be given to a person or institution. Edward Snowden uncovered the questionable, extensive global surveillance and espionage conducted by the USA on both citizens and other countries. Snowden's disclosure of NSA's surveillance of millions of phone calls resulted in a ruling in a US court of appeals, which concluded that NSA's storage of telephone metadata is indeed illegal, because it was not approved by Congress. Nonetheless, the USA

upholds the indictment for espionage and theft of government property, and demands that Snowden be extradited to the USA, where he
faces the risk of a lifetime in prison. With this year's Ossietzky Prize,
Norwegian PEN wants to highlight that surveillance may only be
carried out within the framework of internationally accepted legal
standards for the protection of individual civil liberties. By awarding
the prize to Edward Snowden, Norwegian PEN wish to pay respect to
the unique role he has undertaken as a whistleblower.'

PEN Congress 2019 asks for Julian Assange not to be extradited to the USA

Julian Assange founded WikiLeaks in 2006, which came to international attention in 2009–10 when it published classified US government
documents that revealed that the US army, the CIA, and Iraqi and
Afghan forces had committed human rights violations. Having
exhausted every legal avenue in his attempts to avoid extradition to
Sweden, where two women had made allegations of rape and sexual
assault during a previous visit by Assange, the WikiLeaks founder
asked for asylum at the London Ecuadorian Embassy in June 2012. He
stayed there for seven years. He was arrested by British police in April
2019 for breaching his bail conditions in 2012. He was further arrested
on behalf of the US authorities under an extradition warrant. Six
months later, while he was behind bars, the Assembly of Delegates at
the 85th PEN International Congress in Manila approved a resolution
that read in its first lines:

'PEN International expresses concern over the US government's
indictment against WikiLeaks founder and publisher Julian Assange
and the threat his prosecution poses to press freedom. In May 2019,
Julian Assange was indicted by the US Justice Department on 17
counts of violating the US Espionage Act for his role in obtaining
and publishing classified military and diplomatic documents in 2010.
UN experts, free expression groups, and scores of human rights
lawyers have made it clear that this prosecution raises profound
concerns about freedom of the press under the First Amendment to
the US Constitution, and sends a dangerous signal to journalists and
publishers worldwide.' At the end of the resolution, 'The Assembly of
Delegates of PEN International calls on the United States to drop
charges against WikiLeaks founder and publisher Julian Assange,
who faces a lengthy prison sentence in the United States for obtaining
and publishing newsworthy information. Espionage laws should not
be used against journalists and publishers for disclosing information
of public interest. The Assembly of Delegates of PEN International
further calls on the United Kingdom to reject extraditing Julian Assange
to the United States.'

↑↑   Salil Tripathi, chair of the WiPC,
guiding the delegates' debate about
resolutions presented at the 85th PEN
International Congress in Manila in
October 2019.

↑   Moussa Gansore, general secretary
of PEN Mali, taking the floor at the
debate on resolutions at the 85th PEN
International Congress in Manila, where
the resolution against the extradition of
Julian Assange was approved.
Resolutions at Congresses are debated
and voted by the assembly of delegates.

In memory
of European Jews

↑   Philippe Sands gave the keynote speech at
the Lviv Congress: 'The Nuremberg Trials open on
20 November 1945. Lauterpacht is present in the
courtroom, with the British team, pushing for the
protection of individuals. Lemkin remains in
Washington, with the American team, pushing for
the protection of groups. One of the 22 men in the
dock is Hans Frank, the fourth man in my book.
An early supporter of the Nazis, from 1928 he
worked as Adolf Hitler's personal lawyer. In
October 1939, he becomes governor general of
Nazi-occupied Poland. In August 1942, he comes
here, to Lemberg and Galicia, newly incorporated
into his territory. He hosts a concert which
concludes with Beethoven's 9th symphony, and
gives a few speeches. One is in this very room.
Here, on 1 August 1942, 75 years ago, he announced
the plan to eliminate the city's entire Jewish
population.'

In October 2018, at the 83rd PEN International Congress in Lviv,
Ukraine, the keynote speech was given by Philippe Sands, president
of English PEN, in the main hall of Ivan Franko University. From the
start, delegates were told they were seated in the very chairs where, in
August 1942, Nazi leader Hans Frank announced the plan to eliminate
the Jewish population in that region. Delegates knew that the memory
of this crime against humanity, the genocide known as the Holocaust,
would mark the PEN Congress. Some delegates had their family
origins in the Yiddishland destroyed by the pogroms, the Nazis, and
the Soviet Union repression. This was the case of Jennifer Clement, as
well as Richard Stursberg, president of Canadian PEN, and Paul
Auster, who attended from American PEN, and who later wrote:

'My business was in Lviv, but I took advantage of an off-day to travel
two hours to the south and spend the afternoon in Ivano-Frankivsk,
where my paternal grandfather had been born sometime in the early
1880s. There was no reason to go there except curiosity, or else what
I would call the lure of a counterfeit nostalgia, for the fact was that
I had never known my grandfather and still know next to nothing
about him. He died 28 years before I was born, a shadow-man from the
unwritten, unremembered past, and even as I travelled to the city he
had left in the late nineteenth or early twentieth century, I understood
that the place where he had spent his boyhood and adolescence was no
longer the place where I would be spending the afternoon. Still,
I wanted to go there, and as I look back and ponder the reasons why

←   Paul Auster, next to Kätlin Kaldmaa and Jennifer Clement, president of PEN International, who said in her opening speech:

'For PEN, one of the world's oldest human rights organisations, it is important to stand on Ukrainian soil at this time in history and defend the truth, free speech, and literature. We are grateful to Ukrainian PEN, and especially to Mykola Riabchuk and Andrey Kurkov, for hosting this important Congress because it's essential to be here and speak out against propaganda and the manipulation of facts. Russian government propaganda and the dissemination of falsehoods not only manipulates world opinion, but also has divided the Ukrainian peoples.

'The problem with a lie is that even if one eventually finds out the truth, the misinformation has already contaminated minds and poisoned hearts. […] On the topic of lies and truth, and since we are a literary organisation, we know how literature constantly exposes the folly, tragedy and, sometimes even, the rewards a lie can generate. I think of Shakespeare's *Othello* and the character Iago. If Iago had confessed to Othello and admitted that what he'd said about Desdemona had all been lies, would Othello have let her live? Would she have forgiven him for mistrusting her? Would he ever be courageous again? Othello may not have killed Desdemona once he knew the truth, but those lies would have dishonoured their love forever. Untruth destroys — or tarnishes and hurts — even the purest intentions and we are witnessing this all over our world.

'On a personal note, I'm moved to be here. Ukraine was the home of my ancestors and, after over one hundred years, a daughter has returned.'

I wanted to go, perhaps it comes down to a single verifiable fact: the journey would be taking me through the bloodlands of Eastern Europe, the central horror-zone of twentieth century slaughter, and if the shadow-man responsible for giving me my name had not left that part of the world when he did, I never would have been born.'

At the Congress, Judith Rodriguez was elected vice-president of PEN International. She participated in a poetry reading with Adam Zagajewski, Halyna Kruk, Yurii Andrukhovych, and Reinaldo Montero. When she took the stage, she said, 'I will start with a poem I have written three hours ago, at the bedside table of my hotel room.'

↑   Judith Rodriguez, from Sydney PEN and at that time vice-president of PEN International, reads her poetry at the Lviv Congress.

At Lviv

Here or downriver
they lived, family of my mother.
Here or downriver
they took early warning.
Of this my mother said nothing.

What scattered cousins
underwent the darkness?
What roads and houses
miss their tread, their voices?
Did my mother ask?

Her Paris aunt and uncle
ended on the Nazi scrapheap.
Her father chose Palestine.
Her mother died in Perth.

That my mother mourned.
War came. Rumors grew.
A pond in these woods hides
the bones of thousands,
veils a regime's shame.

Here and downriver,
this painful knowledge—
but all earth's places,
all have lain in moral darkness.

My mother said nothing.
All we can do in the darkness
is shine.

Behrouz Boochani: writing a literary work on a cellphone

In 2019, Kurdish Iranian writer Behrouz Boochani won Australia's Victorian Premier's Literary Award for his book *No Friend But the Mountains: Writing from Manus Prison*. For almost five of his six years in detention and even though his phone was confiscated twice, Behrouz wrote on his phone via WhatsApp in Farsi daily notes to his translator Omid Tofighian.

In Boochani's acceptance speech, sent by WhatsApp from Manus Island, a detention centre in Papua New Guinea, the detained author wrote:

'When I arrived in Manus, I created another image for myself. I imagined a novelist in a remote prison. Sometimes I would work half naked beside the prison fences and imagine a novelist locked up right there, in that place. This image was awe inspiring. For years I maintained this image in my mind. Even while I was forced to wait in long queues to get food, or while enduring other humiliating moments.'

No Friend But the Mountains is an autobiographical account of Behrouz's attempt to make the journey from Indonesia to Australia, and of his subsequent incarceration under Australia's deterrence policy, which was developed to stop people seeking asylum by boat.

The words of his acceptance speech were a plea: 'With humility, I would like to say that this award is a victory. It is a victory not only for us, but for literature and art and above all, it is a victory for humanity. A victory for human beings, for human dignity. A victory against a system that has never recognised us as human beings. It is a victory against a system that has reduced us to numbers. This is a beautiful moment. Let us all rejoice tonight in the power of literature.'

Sydney PEN and Melbourne PEN, along with the global PEN community, celebrated the news. PEN had campaigned tirelessly for Boochani, urging the Australian government to abide by its obligations to the principle of non-refoulement, as defined by Article 33 of the United Nations Convention Relating to the Status of Refugees.

Boochani describes himself as 'a child of war', referring to the 1980s war between the Iraqi Ba'athists and 'Iranian zealots' fought largely in his Kurdish homeland in western Iran. Boochani co-founded the magazine *Werya*, promoting Kurdish culture and politics. He was lucky enough to be absent when the Islamic Revolutionary Guard Corps raided the offices of *Werya* and arrested 11 of his colleagues. He fled Iran in May 2013 and started the trip that would end in Manus prison.

Speaking at an event with Boochani (who had to attend via Skype from Manus Island) at the 2019 Byron Writers Festival in Australia, Jennifer Clement, president of PEN International, said: 'Behrouz Boochani writes of the terrible days lost at sea in a crowded boat and the loss of frontiers between people. His forlorn and crippled boat carrying refugees is the universal boat or the universal train. The no land between countries could be a boat in the Mediterranean going towards Italy or a train moving from Central America towards the US border. The frontiers and borders between people are lost and the stranger's shoulder to sleep on belongs to one's mother.'

→
The front cover
of the book
*No Friend But the
Mountains*
by Behrouz Boochani.

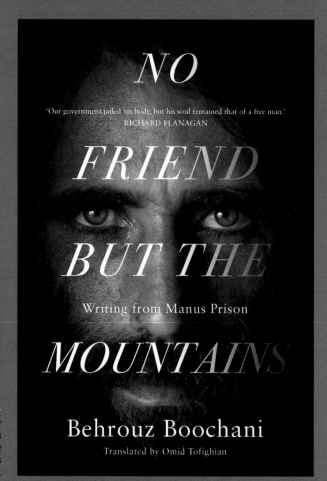

'Our government jailed his body, but his soul remained that of a free man.'
RICHARD FLANAGAN

NO FRIEND BUT THE MOUNTAINS

Writing from Manus Prison

Behrouz Boochani

Translated by Omid Tofighian

↑   The Iranian Kurdish author Behrouz Boochani wrote the award-winning book *No Friend But the Mountains* in Farsi and, word by word, on a mobile phone. He writes: 'Hopelessness arises when the prisoner realises that his discovery about the order of things is wrong. He continues trying to unlock the logic of the system, looking for solutions in his surroundings. This induces perpetual questioning. He searches for the answers to the questions that plague his mind, searches for them in the eyes of the cooks, searches for them in the eyes of the officers. Maybe there are differences in the personalities of the head chefs. Maybe some officers are less brutal.'

Women writers

PEN International was founded by Catharine Amy Dawson Scott in 1921, and yet it was not until 2015, almost 100 years later at its 81st Congress, that PEN elected Jennifer Clement, the organisation's first woman president. It seems that several women had previously been approached to run for president but most declined, including Virginia Woolf in the mid-1930s, who wrote amusingly to her sister that she had 'never been so insulted' in all her life.

Of the many exceptional women who devoted their lives to PEN's work was Margaret Storm Jameson, who was president of English PEN in the most difficult years of the Second World War. Under her leadership, English PEN sheltered a number of refugee writers as well as PEN Centres in exile. In 1960 Jameson was later part of the Committee of Three that launched a Writers in Prison Committee (WiPC) that would completely change the face of PEN. Prior to this, other prominent women left their mark on PEN, including Sophia Wadia from Bombay PEN, established in 1933, and the Turkish writer Halide Edib Adıvar. Victoria Ocampo, editor of the surrealist magazine *Sur*, from Buenos Aires PEN, was a leading figure at the 1936 Buenos Aires Congress. In more recent times important global writers such as Nadine Gordimer, Toni Morrison, and Margaret Atwood have been strong voices in PEN along with the PEN Women's Committee, founded in 1991.

Jennifer Clement as PEN International president has placed women writers at the centre of the organisation by leading the changes to the PEN Charter, which had left out gender in its list of hatreds to combat, and creating the PEN International *Women's Manifesto*. This work acknowledged that women today continue to face censorship through lack of education, inequality, and violence — violence that, in these times, often means the silencing and vilifying of women through attacks on social media. The unanimous approval of the PEN International *Women's Manifesto* at the 83rd PEN International Congress in Lviv changed PEN into an organisation in which a central part of its mission is gender equality and the struggle for the recognition of women writers, as well as the protection of women writers at risk. The *Manifesto* also opened avenues of collaboration with the United Nations and established new important partnerships with organisations such as VIDA: Women in Literary Arts and UNESCO.

The growing leadership of women in PEN was evident in Quebec, in the very room where Jennifer Clement was elected president. Among those who voted were the PEN women presidents of Argentina, Bolivia, Nicaragua, Honduras, Mexico, San Miguel de Allende, Puerto Rico, Kurdistan, Turkey, Melbourne, Sydney, Central Asia, Myanmar, Palestine, Guinea, England, Wales, Czech Republic, Germany, Finland, Romania, Croatia, Catalonia, Portugal, and the Basque Country.

At the 6th PEN Congress in Oslo in 1928, a resolution presented by Catharine Amy Dawson Scott, and carried unanimously, stated 'That women shall be considered eligible for membership of P.E.N. if writers.' In 2015, it was high time for one of them to preside over the organisation and, six years later, welcome all Centres to the celebration of PEN International's centenary.

← Tribute to the PEN Charter by Californian artist Sally Howell. The artwork illustrated a poster published by PEN USA West in 1990 containing the text of the PEN Charter (see page 72).

Women Writers protest at the New York 48th PEN International Congress, 1986

The debate at the New York Congress is represented here by three speakers.

Grace Paley

'This PEN Congress opened on Sunday. By Wednesday, many women had begun to talk to each other, in absolute amazement and perplexity, about the fact that in almost every panel, in many panels, there were only men speaking. […] About one hundred and fifty women created a statement:

'We protest the state of the imagination of the PEN International Congress, 1986. We protest the underrepresentation of women on the panels and in the readings. Although nearly half the PEN members attending the conference are women, out of 117 panellists, only 16 are women. We are outraged at PEN's failure to invite more

women writers from all parts of the world to be panellists and readers and moderators at this conference discussing the imagination of the state. There are many women writers of inter-national stature both in the US and abroad who could have spoken to the issues addressed by the panels. PEN must be an organisation which works to eradicate inequities, and should not perpetuate them within its own structure. We demand, from Norman Mailer, president of the American Centre of PEN, and from the officers of PEN, a public explanation to the members of this congress for this failure. We expect that PEN will take immediate steps to remedy this situation in the ongoing structure of American and International PEN. We are forming a committee of inquiry to investigate the structure

of PEN itself and its failure to include enough women writers. We demand that this committee be recognised, and that its work be facilitated by PEN.'

↓   At the 1986 PEN International Congress in New York, attended by 600 writers, there was a revolt and a debate that marked the history of the presence of women in PEN International. The picture shows Karen Kennerly, director of PEN America, speaking. On her left, Betty Friedan. Background, left to right: Starry Krueger, Joanne Leedom-Ackerman, and Meredith Tax, finalising the draft.

Norman Mailer: 'I will stand by this list.'

↑ Norman Mailer, president of PEN America in 1986.

'Let me clarify a few things before I come to the degree of mea culpa. […] The notion, from the beginning, was to get the very best writers we could. For this, I will take complete responsibility.

'Several times in conversation, it was brought up that in a certain country we did not have a guest of honour who was a woman. Because, frankly, there were a great many writers I knew nothing about, I said, "Who does the committee think are really good writers who are women in that country?" And the answer would be, "Well, there really aren't any." Now, that may be terribly unpleasant to a lot of you, but there are countries in the world where there are no good women writers. […] In many high places of learning there are more women intellectuals than men. That's not the point. The point is that someone who is an intellectual and an artist is rare. It's a rare phenomenon. It doesn't happen often. I can't think of too many truly talented women in America who would fit into the category of Susan Sontag, who is an intellectual and a literary artist. There are not too many.

'Now, you can name a few. I will read for you a list of the women we invited who did not come. In America, those women were Mary McCarthy, who certainly would have qualified, Ann Beattie, Diana Trilling, who would have qualified, Amy Clampitt, Eudora Welty, Francine du Plessix Gray. […] Among foreign writers, we were turned down by Iris Murdoch, Marguerite Duras, Doris Lessing, Simone de Beauvoir, Marguerite Yourcenar, Elsa Morante, Mavis Gallant, Wisława Szymborska, Christa Wolf, Elena Poniatowska. It comes to a total of twenty-four women who chose not to come. We wanted the best writers we could get. We did not want a congress that would establish a political point at the cost of considerable mediocrity. [PROTESTS FROM THE FLOOR.] I will take full responsibility for the list we ended up with. [SHOUTS FROM THE FLOOR.]'

Margaret Atwood: 'I represent an absence.'

'I am president of the Anglophone section of Canadian PEN. In concert with the Francophone section we will be holding the conference in 1989, and I will promise you right now that our conference will not only be bilingual, but also bisexual.

'I've been asked to represent a category entitled "Foreign Women at this Event." I first declined, my reason being that I was not foreign enough. […] In other words, I feel absurd doing this, but the fact that it ended up being me, all attempts at finding a substitute having failed — and Isabel Allende, who would have been much more suitable, having gone home — emphasises the nature and extent of the problem here. There just wasn't a great deal to choose from. […]

'Let me make it clear that I have no personal or national axe to grind. I experienced the delight of actually sitting on a panel. *Quelle joie!* And it was a panel that was almost 50 per cent female. I also gave a reading. […]

'But the fact is that my country and my panel were glaring exceptions in this respect. On the subject of equality — I was asked to do this, as I've said, because there wasn't much choice, and it's this lack of choice that I'm speaking to — I represent an absence. "We need someone to do it who will be equal to the men," I was also told. *Which men?* I wondered. *And how many at once?* I don't mind having to be equal to four or five men, but one hundred and seventeen is a pretty tall order. And I wouldn't have minded having a little help. I hope that at future PEN Congresses things will be so arranged that I will not be asked to make a speech of this kind, whether I'm suitable or not.'

→ Margaret Atwood, president of Canadian PEN from 1984 to 1986.

Creation of PEN International
Women Writers Committee

↑↑   From left to right: Monika van Paemel,
(Belgium Dutch-speaking PEN), Meredith Tax
(American PEN), and another delegate at the
Women's Committee Planning meeting at the
54th PEN International Congress in Toronto, 1989.

↑   From left to right: Lucina Kathmann,
president of San Miguel de Allende PEN and
chair of the Women Writers Committee (1996–
2003); the poet and children's book author Fatou
Ndiaye Sow, vice-president of Senegalese PEN;
Koumanthio Zeinab Diallo, president of Guinean
PEN. As active members of the PEN Women
Writers Committee, they attended a literary
festival organised by Senegalese PEN.

↗   Invitation by Meredith Tax
(American PEN), Buchi Emecheta (Nigerian
PEN) and Monika van Paemel (Belgium
Dutch-speaking PEN) to all PEN Centres and
to all women writers to create a PEN
International Women's Committee in 1989.

→   Reply from Antonia Fraser and
Josephine Pullein-Thompson, president
and general secretary of English PEN
respectively, to the invitation to create an
International Women's Committee in PEN.

At the time, in 1989, PEN International's leadership was all male. In its 68-year history PEN International had never had a woman president. And only one woman International secretary and few women as committee chairs, though in many centres of PEN there was a growing balance of men and women members and leaders. The consequences of the women's revolt at the 48th PEN International Congress in New York in 1986 was, first, the creation of a Women's Committee in American PEN, chaired by Meredith Tax. In a letter sent to all PEN Centres three years later, Tax described the creation of the committee in response to the underrepresentation of women at the Congress and how it had changed attitudes dramatically. Tax, together with Buchi Emecheta from Nigerian PEN and Monika van Paemel from Belgium Dutch-speaking PEN, proposed the creation of a PEN International Women's Committee at the following Congress, to take place in Canada.

There was a debate. Lady Antonia Fraser, president of English PEN, together with English PEN's general secretary, Josephine Pullein-Thompson, replied to the invitation:

'We do not favour forming an International Women's Committee, although we would not object if individual Centres felt the need to form their own in order to encourage women writers or to give them greater status in the centre.

'We are deeply committed to the PEN Charter, which states that "Membership of PEN is open to all qualified writers, editors, and translators […] without regard to nationality, race, colour or religion." We discussed adding "sex" to this list but came to the conclusion that this was unnecessary as women were covered by the phrase "all qualified writers".

'We feel that if an International Women's section is formed it may well lead to demands from other pressure groups — Black sections, Muslim sections, Jewish sections, Socialist Writers, Christian Democrat Writers — and the whole object of PEN, which is to bring writers together despite their differences, will be lost.'

A Women's Network was formed at the 54th Congress in Canada in 1989. Two years later, in Vienna, at the 56th PEN International Congress, it was approved as a permanent standing committee and named the Women Writers Committee of PEN International. Meredith Tax, one of its founders, was elected its first chair. In her acceptance speech she told the assembly of delegates that the committee would involve more women in the work of PEN at all levels. Twenty-eight PEN Centres signed up for the committee with 70 delegates and members, including men, attending the initial meeting.

July 4, 1989

To Executive Boards of all PEN Centers
and Women Writers in those Centers:

Dear Friends and Colleagues:

We are writing to urge you to help us form an International
Women's Committee in PEN. A group of Women delegates met at the
last International Congress, in Maastricht, in MAy, 1989, to
exchange information and ideas. We represented the following
centers: American, Austrian, Belgium (Dutch-speaking), English,
German Speaking Writers Abroad, Netherlands, Nigerian, Norwegian,
Thai, and USA-West. Delegates from Brazil, Israel, Kurdish Writers
Abroad, Puerto Rico, West Germany, and Writers in Exhile (N.Y.)
were unable to attend this meeting for logistical reasons but
expressed support, and since the Congress, we have spoken to
interested writers from centers in Japan Slovenia, and Switzerland
(German).

Discussion at the Maastricht meeting was lively. Some
delegates expressed dissatisfaction at the small number of women
writers in their centers and the lack of women on their boards;
others said that, while active in their centers personally, they
could not get other women to participate because of the attitudes
of the men. The delegate from PEN American Center described the
work of its Women's Committee, which formed in response to the
under-representation of women at the 1986 Congress, and said it has
changed attitudes dramatically in the last three years.

We feel that a Women's Committee on the International level
would help women writers be more effective within their own
centers; it could also initiate studies and programs that would
link us together and enable us to know each other's work. We agreed
to try to form one at the upcoming PEN Congress in Toronto and
Montreal, and appointed a continuations committee of three
delegates: Buchi Emecheta of Nigeria, Monica Van Paemel of Belgium,
and Meredith Tax of the United States. We have requested space on
the agenda, and asked the Canadian Center to allot us meeting space
in both Toronto and Montreal. A first meeting has therefore been
scheduled for Sunday, Sept. 24, from 2:00 to 5:00 P.M., to discuss
plans and perfect the following draft resolution.

> We wish to form a Women's Committee in International PEN
> to investigate the status of Women's literature and women
> writers throughout the world; to acquaint the world with
> literature by women writers; to create programs that
> focus on women's achievement in literature and on issues
> of particular interest to women writers; and to encourage
> the full participation of women writers in International
> PEN and the various PEN centers.

We are confident that the Toronto PEN Congress will be an historic
one, both for its excellent representation and program, and for the
steps taken to found an International Women's Committee. Since we
are hoping for the widest possible participation in this event by
women writers from all over the world, we are asking every PEN
center to circulate this letter among its women members and to
consider sending a woman delegate to the Toronto Congress, so their
center can play an active role in this historic event.

We are also eager to know your views about such a committee and its
tasks, to hear about women writers and their situation in each PEN
center and every country. Please give us the benefit of your
experience, so we can prepare as well as possible for the Congress.
The PEN American Center has agreed to handle communications, so you
can write to us at the following address:

Organizing Group for an International Women's Committee
PEN AMerican Center
568 Broadway
New York, New York, 10012

We hope to hear from you, and to see you in Canada.

Sincerely,

Buchi Emecheta
Monica Van Paemel
Meredith Tax

The English Centre of
INTERNATIONAL P·E·N

A WORLD ASSOCIATION OF WRITERS

7 Dilke Street, Chelsea
London SW3 4JE
Telephone: 01 - 352 6303
(Tuesday, Wednesday and Thursday)
Founded in 1921 by C. A. Dawson Scott
First Presidents: John Galsworthy OM. H. G. Wells

7th September 1989

Meredith Tax
American PEN Centre.

Dear Meredith,

At English PEN's last committee meeting we discussed your
letter proposing an International Women's Committee. Our
committee, which, by our constitution, is composed of equal
numbers of women and men, came to the following conclusions:

We do not favour forming an International Women's Committee,
although we would not object if individual centres felt a need
to form their own in order to encourage women writers or to
give them greater status in that centre.

We are all deeply committed to the PEN Charter, which states
that "Membership of P.E.N. is open to all qualified writers,
editors and translators... without regard to nationality, race,
colour or religion." We discussed adding "sex" to this list
but came to the conclusion that this was unnecessary as women
were covered by the phrase "all qualified writers."

We feel that if an International Women's section is formed it
may well lead to demands from other pressure groups - Black
Sections, Muslim Sections, Jewish Sections, Socialist Writers,
Christian Democrat Writers - and the whole object of PEN, which
is to bring writers together despite their differences, will be
lost.

We feel that ~~you~~ you have a legitimate grievance when it
comes to the election of International Vice Presidents. Of the
present 15 only three are women, and two of those, Rosamund
Lehmann and Madam Moh are too old and ill to attend PEN
meetings. We ought perhaps to encourage our centres to propose
their more distinguished women writers, or those who have given
long service to PEN, as Vice Presidents. We would like to
propose Nancy Ing.

English women writers like Rebecca West, Storm Jamieson,
Rosamund Lehmann, Veronica Wedgwood and PEN's founder, Mrs
Dawson-Scott, have from the first given English PEN a proud
record of female service. In the last twelve years the General
Secretary has been a woman and during that period we have
elected two female and two male presidents. (We normally choose
a Vice Chair of the opposite sex to the President.) If we go back to
1939 the ratio is eight men to six women. Many of
our subcommittees have been chaired by women and in fact the
only office which has remained resolutely male has been that

x AF

President: Lady Antonia Fraser *General Secretary:* Josephine Pullein-Thompson MBE *Honorary Treasurer:* Antony Horner

Vice-Presidents: Sybille Bedford OBE, Sir Isaiah Berlin OM, CBE, FBA, Lettice Cooper OBE, Peter Elstob,
William Golding CBE, Michael Holroyd, Francis King CBE, Rosamond Lehmann CBE, Malcolm Muggeridge,
Dame Iris Murdoch CBE, Kathleen Nott, Harold Pinter CBE, Sir Victor Pritchett CBE, Jasper Ridley, Sir Stephen Spender CBE,
Tom Stoppard CBE, Marjorie Watts, Dame Veronica Wedgwood DBE, OM, Sir Angus Wilson CBE.

- 2 -

of treasurer. There have been no female volunteers for this
unpopular job, but our auditor is female.

You ask about representation at congresses. We've counted up
the last 26 occasions on which we sent two delegates and find
that on 16 there was one delegate of each sex, on 5 we were
represented by two men and on 5 by two women.

We look forward to seeing you in Canada.

Yours sincerely,

Antonia Fraser

Lady Antonia Fraser
President, English PEN

Josephine Pullein-Thompson
General Secretary

Guinean PEN and the rights of women and children

→
Koumanthio Zeinab Diallo, president of Guinean PEN (right) with another PEN member in 2016. Guinean PEN has created the Petit Musée du Fouta in Labé, a cultural centre for the promotion of Fula culture and literature, as well as freedom of expression and human rights.

↓   Participants at the meeting of the Women Writers Committee at the 73rd PEN International Congress in Dakar in 2007. On the front row, in a patterned sleeveless shirt, is Judith Buckrich, chair of the committee from 2003 to 2009.

Guinean PEN was founded twice. First, in 1988, after participating in meetings with Senegalese PEN in Dakar, a group of writers founded a PEN Centre based on literature and freedom of expression in Conakry. However, the fear of repression was strong and soon thereafter the initial group broke apart. Following this, in 1990, a group of women writers united with the sociologist, poet, and novelist Koumanthio Zeinab Diallo and, based in the Fouta Djalon region, decided to create a PEN Centre devoted to the promotion of literature written by women with a strong focus on educating young women to read, write, and have a role in society. Two elements of PEN International were attractive to this group: PEN was an international platform based on the values of peace, tolerance, and freedom, where they could develop contacts with writers from abroad, and the fact that a woman, Catharine Amy Dawson Scott, had founded PEN. The new Guinean PEN was welcomed in 1992 at the 57th PEN International Congress in Barcelona and Koumanthio Zeinab Diallo, who writes in both French and Fulani, was elected president. Of the 13 members of the first board of Guinean PEN, 8 were women.

Guinean PEN has created an outstanding programme by articulating a network of school reading clubs, which educate young women as writers and social leaders. Every school year, these clubs reach over 5,000 students and develop year-long training on issues to do with human rights and women rights, based on the participation of the students and their life experiences. The network of school clubs has campaigned actively in the local communities against child marriage and female genital mutilation (FGM). Zeinab herself has written extensively on FGM both academically and through novels that help girls become aware of their rights. Unexpectedly, the PEN school network became decisive when the Ebola epidemic hit Guinea in 2014. The PEN network served as both as a space for training students and combating the disease as well as a space where, through storytelling workshops, students could express the hardships of the health crisis. Guinean PEN also took charge in the training of community-based animators who educated students in schools and society at large on how to combat Ebola. This moment underscored the unique capacity and response a network of young women readers and writers could bring to their peoples during an acute social crisis.

Guinean PEN has become one of the most active PEN Centres in West Africa and has participated in meetings of the network of francophone African PEN Centres based around Senegalese PEN. Through the work of PEN, there is now a strong exchange between Guinean women poets and their colleagues from Senegal, Mauritania, Mali, Togo, and other neighbouring countries.

↑   Koumanthio Zeinab Diallo giving an award supported by UNESCO in one of PEN Guinea's school reading and writing clubs.

↙   Koumanthio Zeinab Diallo together with the president of Malian PEN, Ismaïla Samba Traoré. They are presenting the new PEN Mauritania Centre at the 81st PEN International Congress in Quebec City in 2015. It was a moment of sadness as Djibril Ly, president of PEN Mauritania, who had travelled to Quebec to present the Centre, had fallen ill and was spending his last hours in hospital.

↓   Senegalese, Guinean, and Mauritanian women poets taking part in a reading in Dakar in 2016.

Razan Zaitouneh

↑   Razan Zaitouneh before being abducted in 2013.

→   Kamila Shamsie, a British-Pakistani writer and award-winning novelist, speaking to Salil Tripathi, chair of the Writers in Prison Committee, and Salman Rushdie at a British Library ceremony where Rushdie received the 2014 PEN Pinter award presented by English PEN.

↘   Letter written for PEN's Day of the Imprisoned Writer in November 2017.

Dear Razan,

I have to confess I'm sometimes suspicious of optimists. I think, 'These people don't want to see the reality of the world, how bad it truly is.' But then I come across people who do see the reality of the world, those who look the worst of humanity right in the eye, and still hold on to optimism — and I know those people, the ones whose optimism is forged in fire, are the ones that we need in dark times as much as we need air to breathe or water to drink. I started to know that you're such a person when I read what your sister, Reem, said about you, and your attitude to life: 'To think that you are a part of the world around you; to feel that you are not a lonely tiny creature compared to the universe; is a great start to be a human being.' And then I found an interview with you, from a time when you were in hiding from those seemingly all-powerful forces who were threatened by the work you were doing, in which you said, 'There is no doubt that the protesters and our revolution will eventually win. If we don't believe that we will win, we couldn't continue under all this violence by the regime. We couldn't bear all these crimes against our people.' How many cases of torture and abduction and killings in Syria had you documented by this point? Enough to destroy most people's optimism. But you were still able to imagine victory for your people, your country, and that gave you the strength to do your vital work. Your words made me think of the great Urdu poet, Faiz Ahmed Faiz (I know from another article that quotes your sister, Rana, that you love poetry) — in some of the darkest moments of Pakistan's history, he wrote the

lines: 'We Shall See / It is certain we shall see / That day which has been promised to us.' Those lines have been a cry of hope and resistance and — yes — victory, in the nearly 40 years since he wrote it.

People like Faiz — and like you, Razan — are not just important in the world, you are essential. You remind us to dream and to believe and to never give up. Those who've abducted you might have thought they could shut you up, but your lessons echo so powerfully and will continue to do so. We are not giving up — on you, and on everything you stand for. I hope one day after you're returned to your family, I'll have a chance to meet you. I'll bring along a book of poems by Faiz, one that contains some lines that he wrote when he was in prison (for opposing autocracy): 'though tyrants may command that lamps be smashed / in rooms where lovers are destined to meet / they cannot snuff out the moon, so today / nor tomorrow, no tyranny will succeed.'

I hope the moon is shining strong on your face. And I know that one day, in part because of the work and example of you and your colleagues, the darkness will lift entirely. You see, you've made me an optimist. Look how powerful you are, changing people's minds about the world after reading just a few words by and about you.

In solidarity and admiration,

Kamila

↑   Razan Zaitouneh is a lawyer, human rights defender, blogger, and co-founder of the Violations Documentation Centre in Syria (VDC). She is the winner of the 2011 Sakharov Prize for Freedom of Thought, the 2011 RAW in WAR Anna Politkovskaya Award and the 2012 Ibn Rushd Award for Freedom of Thought. On 9 December 2013, Zaitouneh, along with her colleagues Samira Khalil, Nazem Hamadi, and Wa'el Hamada (her husband), were abducted during a raid by a group of armed men on the offices of the VDC in Douma, near Damascus. They had been documenting human rights violations after fleeing a Syrian government-controlled area. There has been no news of their whereabouts ever since, but they are presumed to be held by an Islamic armed group in control of Douma. PEN International has been calling on the armed groups in control of the area and the governments which support them to do everything in their power to facilitate the immediate release of Zaitouneh, Hamada, Khalil, and Hamadi.

2015: the first woman president of PEN International

↑   Jorge Miralda, delegate from PEN Honduras, congratulates Jennifer Clement after her election as the 31st PEN International president at the Quebec Congress in 2015. Behind them are Takeaki Hori, PEN International secretary, and Jarkko Tontti, PEN International treasurer.

In 2015, at the Congress in Quebec, Canada, the Mexican-American writer Jennifer Clement was elected PEN International's first woman president. Clement had been president of Mexican PEN from 2009 to 2012 where she had focused on the killing of journalists. She had organised, together with president of PEN International, John Ralston Saul, the successful 2012 international mission to Mexico that was instrumental in changing the laws of the country for the protection of journalists. This is her speech as a candidate:

'It's an extraordinary experience to stand in a room where everyone wants to make the world a better place. It's extraordinary to stand in a room where everyone believes that freedom of expression and respect for the opinion of others is crucial in a world where people are jailed and killed over differences in opinion, political and religious beliefs, or for telling the truth. It's an extraordinary experience to stand in a room where everyone has worked to defend PEN's principles. Most of you have worked without a salary and spent your own money and devoted years, even decades of your lives, to PEN. It's extraordinary to stand in a room where everyone knows that the differences among us are what unite us.

'It would be an honour to hold the office of president of PEN International. I am grateful to the countries — Sweden, South Africa, and Mexico — for their nomination. It has also been a privilege to run along with two exceptional women: Vida Ognjenović and Zeynep Oral.

'It is also an extraordinary experience to stand here and know PEN will finally have its first woman president, after almost 100 years and 30 men presidents. This is a noteworthy hour for PEN and for equal rights for women. We, in this room, believe in words and know their power so, I can say here tonight what everyone in this room — a room of writers — can understand. There are languages where nouns are divided up by gender. This is true of Spanish and French — two of PEN's three working languages. What would happen if, in languages that divide things by gender, everything with female gender disappeared? Think for a minute of a world with half of everything missing — the moon, clouds and stars to begin with. Symbolically this is what is happening in the world every time a girl is not allowed to learn to read or write or own her body and mind — half the world, half the human experience is missing. There would be no magic, there would be no rain, there would be no word: *La magia, la lluvia, la palabra. La chance, la lune, la parole.* There would be no chair, no empty chair. *La silla. La chaise.*

'Gender censorship is a huge part of loss of freedom expression. How many great novels and poems are missing? How many ground breaking ideas and discoveries? I know there are whole libraries that don't exist because of gender censorship and PEN must lead. How many people in the world are not educated, silenced by laws and cultural taboos, and killed simply for being born a girl.

'Here I note: our Charter does not include gender in its call for a just and peaceful way of living. The Charter states: PEN members must do their utmost to dispel race, class and national hatreds. This should change. With millions of girls silenced all over the world, PEN must stand and say no more. No more.

'One thing I learned as president of Mexican PEN is that any country can suddenly be in the need of this esteemed league of writers. For twenty years I had been a member of Mexican PEN and my time was spent supporting other centres whose countries were in crisis. I attended the inauguration of Cuban PEN in Exile Centre in Miami and met writers who had been imprisoned for their beliefs. Never did I imagine that Mexico would become a place that needed PEN's support. Never did I imagine that we could become so fragile and broken. Never did I imagine I would speak these words: eight journalists have been killed already this year. [...]

'Like everyone here, when I look at our symbol, the empty chair, I know it is not vacant. It is so populated, so full, so inhabited by its emptiness. I see Russian poets, Bangladesh bloggers, Turkish and Ethiopian journalists, girls shot at while trying to go to school, Mexican journalists, Chinese poets, writers hiding from fatwas, assassinated cartoonists, and on and on.

'When I read the list of all the writers PEN has helped in these almost one hundred years, it is truly remarkable.

'It would be an honour to lead this organisation. PEN changes and saves lives and, life by life, one life at a time, dignifies our world.'

OSLO CONGRESS: June 1928

RESOLUTION BY MRS.DAWSON SCOTT
====================================

That women shall be considered eligible for membership of the P.E.N., if writers.

Mrs.Dawson Scott   (England)

Seconded by Mr.Theodor Daubler (Germany)

CARRIED UNANIMOUSLY.

↑   Due to rumours that one of the PEN Centres did not allow women to become members, Catharine Amy Dawson Scott presented the following resolution to the Congress in Oslo in 1928 where it was approved unanimously: 'That women shall be considered eligible for membership of P.E.N. if writers'.

↓   Delegates at the 81st PEN International Congress in Quebec, 2015. In the centre are, standing, Jennifer Clement, just elected the 31st PEN International president, and John Ralston Saul, president of PEN International (2009–15). Immediately on Jennifer's right are Gioconda Belli, president of Nicaraguan PEN, Aline Davidoff Misrachi, president of Mexican PEN, Berivan Dosky, president of Kurdish PEN, and Zeynep Oral, president of Turkish PEN.

Berta Cáceres and the voices of Indigenous women

↑   From left to right: Otilia Lux, member of
Guatemala's Historical Clarification Commission,
charged with investigating the human rights
violations committed during the nation's
30-year-long civil war; Natasha Kanapé Fontaine,
Innu poet and writer; the Quechua lawyer Nina
Jaramillo, chair of the Committee of Writers in
Indigenous Languages of Argentinian PEN;
Enriqueta Lunez, a Tsotsil-language Mayan poet
and director of Casa de la Cultura in San Juan
Chamula, Chiapas.

In May 2019, at the meeting 'Writing the Future in Indigenous
Languages' held in Chiapas, Mexico, the last panel focused on issues
related to Indigenous women writers. Innu poet and member of PEN
Quebec Natasha Kanapé Fontaine narrated the conflicts between
Indigenous communities and the huge contemporary hydroelectric
power companies exploiting their territories. Due to this permanent
aggression against the Indigenous way of life, communities organised
themselves in Quebec to draw attention to the issue. 'Poetry, therefore,
has turned more political. I want to highlight that a democratic society
like Canada does not acknowledge nevertheless the rights and public
consideration Indigenous citizens deserve. Racism is alive. But on the
other hand Indigenous peoples have gained capacity of expression, we
speak for ourselves with a critical voice. Literature, arts, cinema, theatre
are for us ways of asking pressing questions about, for example, violence
against Indigenous women and so many stolen lives among them.'

Enriqueta Lunez, a Totsil-language writer from Chiapas, thanked all
the women who had preceded her in giving voice to Indigenous women:
'We did not find a readymade meal, but at least the table to eat was set.'

Those first Indigenous women writers allowed her to build on their narratives and poetry. 'Each voice is unique, but I do not want to close myself in a given space, and want to walk as a community.' Violence against women, and especially women writers, is rampant in Mexico. However, her priority is the transmission of their work, and Enriqueta Lunez shared her enthusiasm for the programmes of the Casa de la Cultura in the village of San Juan Chamula, which she directs.

Nina Jaramillo, Argentinian PEN's chair of the Committee of Writers in Indigenous Languages, underlined, as a Quechua lawyer herself, Indigenous rights as collective rights. 'Creativity must be understood as right for Indigenous communities, and equal to all citizens. And it is the way for us to leave behind social invisibility. We must protest against laws that discriminate against us, but we need to be able to articulate our claims at the regional level and in neighbouring countries: the Indigenous movement has a social model it can offer to the urgent environmental and social problems of our societies.'

↑   In 2018, Guatemalan PEN, Canadian PEN, and PEN International organised security training workshops for women journalists in rural areas of Guatemala. These Indigenous journalists, working mainly for the network of community radios, suffer violence and discrimination both as women and as members of the Mayan people.

The assassination of the Indigenous leader Berta Cáceres

On 2 March 2016, Berta Cáceres, the coordinator of the Civic Council of Popular and Indigenous Organisations of Honduras (COPINH) was murdered. Throughout the whole of Central America, Indigenous leaders and the defenders of human rights in local communities felt this to be a warning. From the very first day, PEN called for justice as it had in 1995 with Jeanette Kawas.

Berta Cáceres, who was awarded the 2015 Goldman Environmental Prize for her resistance against the 'Agua Zarca' hydroelectric dam project, was a land rights activist and a protector of the Gualcarque River, as well as a spokesperson who amplified the Indigenous community's struggle. As a broadcaster on COPINH's two radio stations, La Voz Lenca (Lenca Voice) and Radio Guarajambala, Cáceres denounced the climate of hostility and all forms of violence towards the Lenca people and their lands.

PEN called for an independent, impartial and prompt investigation to punish those responsible for the murder, and supported the family in their demand that this investigation be led by the Inter-American Commission on Human Rights (IACHR),

↑   Berta Cáceres with members of the Lenca people in 2014.

and other international human rights organisations and national institutions born of the popular struggle. The crime has remained unpunished until the present day.

A dinner party for the
Women's Manifesto

↗   At Bute House, during the Edinburgh International Book Festival in August 2018, Nicola Sturgeon, first minister of Scotland, was given the *Women's Manifesto* from three members of the drafting committee. Left to right: Jennifer Clement, PEN International president; Ellah Wakatama Allfrey, publishing director at Indigo Press and member of English PEN; and Margie Orford, PEN International Board member and president emeritus of South African PEN.

↓   Presentation of the *Women's Manifesto* at the Buenos Aires Congress of Latin American PEN Centres in July 2018. Left to right: Emi Kasamatsu, president Paraguay PEN; Emma Wadsworth, PEN Americas coordinator (2015–19); Rosalía Gutiérrez from Pueblos Indígenas; Romana Cacchioli, director of international programmes at PEN; Luisa Valenzuela, president Argentinian PEN; Jennifer Clement, president PEN International; Kettly Mars, president Haitian PEN; Alicia Quiñones, PEN Americas coordinator since 2019; Ana Mateo Palmer, Cuban PEN in Havana; Marie Ramos Rosado, vice-president Puerto Rico PEN.

'At Aline's…' After being the president of Mexican PEN from 2013 to 2016, Aline Davidoff Misrachi moved to London and, in a tradition dating back to PEN's early days, it was at Aline's home that, in January 2017, the first PEN International *Woman's Manifesto* dinner was held. Aline welcomed Caroline Criado Perez, Lisa Appignanesi, Kamila Shamsie, Rebecca Servadio, Ellah Wakatama Allfrey, Gaby Wood, Laure Thorel, Kätlin Kaldmaa, Sarah Lawson, Deanna Rodger, Romana Cacchioli, Margie Orford, and Jennifer Clement. Clement remembers: 'It was an exceptionally cold winter night and I remember Aline saying we needed to light many candles in the room and so create small fires everywhere, which she did. Over the discussion Kamila Shamsie explained that she'd tabulated women's prizes and how, with few exceptions, every time a woman won a prize her novel's protagonist was a man. Caroline Criado Perez spoke about how she'd been vilified for creating the campaign to have a woman, who was not the queen, on a British banknote. Kätlin Kaldmaa said she was comfortable with a manifesto that did not mention men as to speak to their responsibility might create the danger of *asking for* instead of *stating* these rights. It was Lisa Appignanesi who gave us the door into the document: it needed to walk hand in hand with the PEN Charter. Over the next months Margie Orford, a member of the PEN International Board and president emeritus of South African PEN, and I drafted the document, which acknowledged that both inequality and violence against women were a censorship issue. In the fall of 2017 the *Manifesto* was presented as a resolution at the 83rd World Congress in Lviv, Ukraine, and passed with unanimity. At this Congress, the PEN Charter was modified and the resolution mentions the hope for this change.'

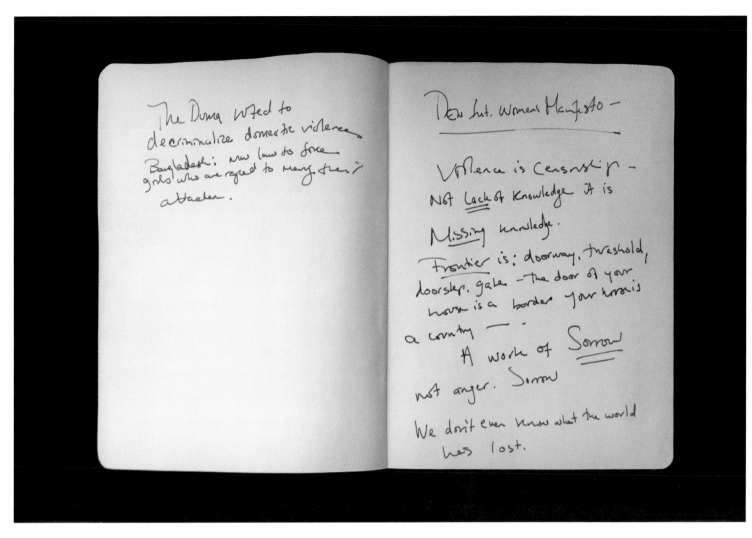

↑ 'A work of Sorrow': Jennifer Clement's
personal notes from the process of drafting
PEN International's *Women's Manifesto.*

Resolution #10: the *Women's Manifesto*

Presented by Jennifer Clement, PEN
International president and Margie Orford,
president emeritus of South African PEN and
PEN International Board member.

The Assembly of Delegates of PEN
International, meeting at their 83rd annual
Congress in Lviv, Ukraine, 18–21 September
2017.

The *Women's Manifesto* has been written in
accordance with the ideals of the PEN Charter
that calls for one humanity living in peace
and equality. We also acknowledge the
important work undertaken for 25 years by
the PEN International Women Writers
Committee.

In the manifold varieties of violence — from
murder and sex-selective abortion to stolen
girls who are sold and trafficked to female
students at universities who are rated and
slut shamed on social media — one common
result is to silence the voices of women and
hamper the transmission of their words and
stories across the boundaries of culture,
class and nation, leaving unfilled pages and
impoverished literatures.

The historical lack of freedoms for women
and girls has almost always been defended
by reference to culture, religion and tradition.
These arguments underscore that few
groups have suffered greater violations of
human rights in the name of culture than
women. Women are killed every day because
they write or speak out.

The denial of fundamental human freedoms
to millions of women, such as the right to
literacy and education, equality, participation
in political discourse as well as vilification
of their ideas and scorn of their bodies is
extreme. Victim-blaming also has a
silencing effect on women, as it can lead to
self-censorship as a way to cope and survive.

In a truly equal world, pledging to uphold
the PEN Charter (especially if it is changed to
include all hatreds and not only those of
class, nationality and race) would protect the
right to freedom of expression for women
and acknowledge that women and girls
need to be witnesses of their own lives.
However, the use of culture, religion and
tradition as the defence for keeping women
silent as well as the way in which violence
against women is a form of censorship needs
to be both acknowledged and addressed
within the organisation. This manifesto is a
public statement of our position on this
issue and our commitment to work towards
a world where women and girls can express
themselves safely, fully and freely.

The growing impact
of the *Women's Manifesto*

↓   Noma Dumezweni, Olivier Award-winning
British actor and activist, reading PEN
International's *Women's Manifesto* for the
campaign to promote it worldwide.

↓↓   'For many women in the world […] the last and perhaps the
most powerful frontier was the door of the house she lived in…'
The Palestinian poet Dareen Tatour had been on trial for a poem
she wrote. Here, under house arrest and just one week after it was
approved at the assembly of delegates at the Lviv Congress in
October 2017, she joined the international campaign by reading
PEN International's *Women's Manifesto*.

Noma Dumezweni
PEN International Women's Manifesto

Within months of the *Women's Manifesto* passing by unanimity at the
PEN Congress in Lviv, many organisations asked if they could give
their support by signing on to the document. These included United
Nations Women, the International Publishers Association (IPA), the
Ann Ida Gannon Center for Women and Leadership at Loyola
University, Chicago, VIDA: Women in Literary Arts, Moomin
Characters Ltd, as well as several literary festivals. In addition, promi-
nent women endorsed the document such as first minister of
Scotland, Nicola Sturgeon, Her Royal Highness Princess Nandi of the
Zulu Royal House, Sofi Oksanen, and Noma Dumezweni. And
Dareen Tatour, who was then under house arrest for a poem and
embodied the first lines of the manifesto:

Preface to the PEN Women's Manifesto

*The first and founding principle of the PEN Charter asserts
that 'literature knows no frontiers'. These frontiers were
traditionally thought of as borders between countries and
peoples. For many women in the world — and for almost
all women until relatively recently — the first, and the last
and perhaps the most powerful frontier was the door of the
house she lived in: her parents' or her husband's home.*

*For women to have free speech, the right to read, the right
to write, they need to have the right to roam physically,
socially and intellectually. There are few social systems that
do not regard with hostility a woman who walks by herself.*

↓   From the video of Her Royal Highness
Princess Nandi of the Zulu Royal House,
reading the translation into Zulu of
PEN International's *Women's Manifesto*.

FOR WOMEN TO HAVE FREE SPEECH, THE RIGHT TO READ, THEY NEED TO HAVE THE
RIGHT TO ROAM PHYSICALLY, SOCIALLY AND INTELLECTUALLY.

Marjorie-Ann Watts

May 28 2019

Dear Carles,

Since our recent meeting I have had a chance to look through the papers and other material you kindly gave me – including the Charter, a significant and inspiring statement. However, I found remarks included in the section entitled 'Galsworthy's inspiration', deeply disturbing.   Not only verging on the patriarchal, but untrue.

As you know, John Galsworthy and Amy Dawson Scott – my Grandmother, had very different personalities. He, a retiring, modest reserved man living a quiet well ordered life with his wife, working on his books and protected from the irritations of social life and the clamour of London; she, really the exact opposite. To begin with, she had very little money, and always rented out rooms in both Alexandra Rd and Clifton Hill to supplement her earnings as a writer. So she did not have a 'drawing room' as described, for Galsworthy to 'install himself' in. Her drawing room was a large carpeted studio with a couch where she slept, and a number of armchairs and chairs in order to entertain friends and have her famous 'At Homes'. She also – at that time, had one or two teenagers at home. She was outward going, optimistic, unconventional and undisciplined, bubbling over with good ideas and determined that other people should know about them. The idea of the staid disciplined Galsworthy sitting in her somewhat haphazard menage trying to work out the magnificent principles of the PEN charter, is completely misguided. And the heading for the paragraph concerned, certainly should not read 'Galsworthy's inspiration'. Writers and members of PEN at the time, were inspired by a remarkable woman – and her ideas marshalled and presented by her friend John Galsworthy.

I feel very strongly that the use of Galsworthy's name as publicity like this, in a statement which actually contradicts fact so blatantly, is not something that PEN should be seen to be doing – particularly currently, when gender parity is supposed to have arrived.

With best wishes,
Yours sincerely,

Marjorie-Ann Watts

Carles Torner
PEN International
Unit A, Koops Mill Mews
162-164 Abbey Street
London SE1 2AN

RECEIVED

0 4 JUN 2019

Cc Antonia Byatt President English PEN, Ginevra Avalle Archivist.

↑   Marjorie-Ann Watts is the granddaughter of the founder of PEN, Catharine Amy Dawson Scott. She actively supported the creation of the PEN Centenary Archive and, during one of her visits, she was given a copy of the PEN Charter in an edition that introduced it as 'Galsworthy's inspiration'. This letter was her reaction.

Solidarity with persecuted Mexican women writers

MEXICO: MIROSLAVA BREACH VELDUCEA

Miroslava Breach Velducea was shot dead outside her home by armed assailants on 23 March 2017. Breach Velducea, aged 54, was a well-known journalist whose twenty-year career focused on reporting on political and social issues, often covering corruption. Her most recent work exposed connections between local politicians and drug cartels. While the authorities are reported to have identified the supposed culprits, however the investigation is at a standstill, according to family members.

↑   Miroslava Breach Velducea had won prestige for her investigative journalism about the links between politicians and drug cartels in Mexico. She was killed on 23 March 2017.

↓   Hundreds of red shoes are laid out in Mexico City's main square to protest the femicides throughout the whole country.

In 2012, a PEN International mission brought to Mexico more than 50 writers around the world. They all participated in the PEN Protesta! event, claiming that the assassinations of journalists had been met with a lack of response from Mexican authorities. Surrounded by the members of the mission, the president of Mexican PEN, Jennifer Clement, gave the following speech:

'PEN International asks that at any PEN event, in any corner of the world, an empty chair, without tenant, be present that represents writers, who have been killed, assassinated, incarcerated or who have disappeared. Today we remember and honor the 67 journalists who have been killed in our country and the 10 who have disappeared.

'During the course of these months, while organising this event, I have asked myself, "How can one talk about Mexico's violence?" I feel as if the very words themselves — censure, impunity, prosecute, demand, clarify — have also been assassinated. From so much overuse these words, without weight and worn out, no longer are stones one can use to strike, but frayed cloths for wrapping bodies.

'Another consequence of this violence is self-censorship. If we cannot tell the truth and report the news because of fear, we lose not only democracy and freedom, but we also lose our history. If we don't know the story we do not know who is the saint or the killer, the outcast or the heroine. And if we do not know what happened we do not know who to pursue and punish or who to forgive and love.'

Svetlana Alexievich writes to Lydia Cacho

Minsk, 15 November 2019,
Day of the Imprisoned Writer

When you have been fighting those who are seemingly all-powerful it is easy to believe that the battle will never be won. I know this feeling, my dear Lydia, because I have felt it too. When your culture has been forged in war and barricades, as mine has been, words like freedom and love can feel like they belong in fairy tales only. You will know this feeling better than most. Over the last 40 years I have travelled collecting other people's stories — sometimes I have been shocked and frightened, wishing I could forget what I had heard. My friends and I, we are trying to resist the all-consuming darkness that is enveloping us, and so are you. You too are a collector of people's stories: not only have you exposed the worst of humanity, but you have also shown us a way forward. You don't simply share them, you also tell us what actions we must take to bring about real change.

I have been reading about the dizzying array of threats and harassment you have faced for telling the truth. And even more astounding, that the more you tell stories, the more you expose yourself, the more you make yourself vulnerable. But where most would be afraid, you endured and fought back.

When your home was attacked and your dogs killed, instead of being cowed into silence you said: *'Like many journalists, I focus on human rights, gender equality, feminism, a perspective that embraces the rights of men, women, girls, and boys. And I won't stop. We have to move from indignation to action.'*

In my own long journey, having seen all that we are capable of perpetrating against one another, it is women like you who fill me with hope. You are not alone, dear Lydia, and neither am I. We are many, and when we stand together, we cannot be silenced. It is a great comfort to me to know that, in these callous times, when writers are criminalised and murdered, when you see darkness, instead of turning away, you illuminate it.

Svetlana

↖ Svetlana Alexievich, winner of the Nobel Prize in Literature 2015 and president of PEN Belarus.

← Lydia Cacho has been a long-standing concern to PEN. A courageous Mexican writer and campaigner against sexual violence and child abuse, she has lived under threat of death since the 2005 publication of her book *Los Demonios del Edén* (*The Demons of Eden*), which implicated leading business figures in a child pornography ring. The threats have not let up, and, in July 2019, became acute after her home was broken into and her two dogs killed, forcing her to leave Mexico for her safety.

PEN women writers and the United Nations

↑   Vera Iversen-Tokombaeva (left), president of Bishkek PEN, and Kristin T Schnider, the delegate from Swiss German PEN, at the press conference of the PEN Women Writers Network meeting in Bishkek, 2005.

↓   Books published by the PEN Women Writers Committee. In the early 2000s, and at both the international level and in local PEN Centres, the PEN Women Writers Committee published anthologies of women writers. The group of writers around Salta PEN in Argentina, Finnish PEN, and Catalan PEN were successful in promoting 'Our Voice' through their publishing campaigns.

In 2018, within months of the *Women's Manifesto* being unanimously passed by the PEN Congress in Lviv, many organisations asked to sign on as supporters. These included United Nations Women, the International Publisher's Association (IPA), the Ann Ida Gannon Center for Women and Leadership at Loyola University, Chicago, and Moomin Characters Ltd, as well as several literary festivals.

Thanks to this worldwide interest, PEN International partnered with VIDA: Women in Literary Arts to establish the PEN VIDA Count in all PEN Centres. The VIDA Count, carried out annually in the USA since 2010, is based on volunteers from across the country who tally the gender breakdown in major literary publications and book reviews. VIDA has already affected change in the publishing industry by using concrete data to demonstrate the huge gap in representation between men and women in the publishing world. The PEN/VIDA Count builds on PEN's own advocacy work through its Women Writers Committee, which aims to protect free expression for women by combating and eliminating the silencing of women worldwide. Through the spirit of the PEN International *Women's Manifesto*, a regional project in Latin America has been created and, in the autumn of 2019, UNESCO became a part of this alliance and the PEN VIDA UNESCO Project was established, which will include the gender breakdown counts in the publishing industry as well as creating spaces for debate on gender equality and censorship.

The increased collaboration with the United Nations came 25 years after the Women Writers Committee began to represent PEN at its assemblies. Greta Rana from Nepalese PEN was elected chair of PEN International's Women Writers Committee (PIWWC) in 1994, and proceeded to lead PEN's delegation at the United Nations' major

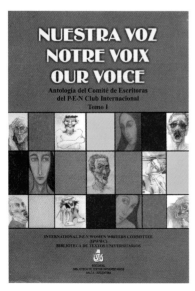

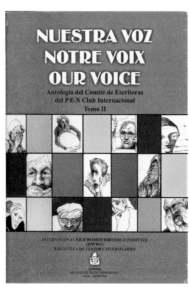

gathering in China: 'The PIWWC was in its youth when we took a team to the Fourth World Conference of Women in Beijing. I was the second chair; the first, the dynamic Meredith Tax, was busy establishing a new NGO for women. Our team included a woman poet from Nepal and the head of a famous street theatre group in Bangladesh. Nothing experienced in PEN Congresses could have prepared us for the mind-blowing experience we were about to receive. Thousands of women had gathered in Huairou, a suburb of Beijing. Official delegates, that included us, were welcomed to a grand inaugural at the Great Hall of the Peoples. I made good use of my Olympus Trip camera […]. The United Nations' Committee for the Elimination of Discrimination against Women co-opted in 2019 the Nepali journalist and social worker Bandana Rana for their committee. Bandana was with us in Beijing, and our group was instrumental in encouraging her to join the International Federation of Women Journalists. Our PIWWC group empowered her, and I think we can be proud. It rained a lot, and one day I went back to the hotel to get my umbrella. As I sped to my room I saw, through an open bedroom door, male room staff graph, quickly retrieved my umbrella from my room and rushed to re-join the last shuttle to Huairou. I forgot my camera. When I returned it had gone.' Thereafter, the PIWWC attended every year the sessions of the United Nations Commission on the Status of Women in New York.

← The United Nations under-secretary-general and executive director of UN Women, Phumzile Mlambo-Ngcuka, receives the PEN International *Women's Manifesto* from the PEN president, Jennifer Clement.

Daphne Caruana Galizia

In the autumn of 2019, for over two years, day after day, the Maltese authorities had destroyed the memorial to Daphne Caruana Galizia. And everyday citizens, friends, and resistance groups rebuilt it with pictures, candles and banners. On 16 October 2019, the second anniversary of her assassination, the government once again destroyed the memorial. On that very day, at the Frankfurt Book Fair, PEN International president Jennifer Clement presented the online poetry memorial for Daphne Caruana Galizia.
The first poem read at the event was written by PEN International Vice-president Boris A Novak:

Billiards in Malta: A mirroring memory of Daphne Caruana Galizia

1   Monday, October 16th, 2017, was a usual working day for Malta.
2   The weather was warm, 24°C, the Sun unloaded its light shipload.
3   The northeaster played billiards chasing little clouds over the blue altar.

4   At 3 PM an invisible billiard cue stick flicked a car from the road.
5   After the blast Peugeot 108 simply vanished from the asphalt.
6   A car crash? A slip down? Broken brakes? Who knows? That's Malta.

7   People froze in shining shelters, seagulls panicked squeaking their alt.
8   Nobody knew what happened. Everybody knew. The world came to a halt.
9   In Malta billiard players always disappear into the blue.

10   A young man came running from the neighbouring house. That's Matthew.
11   Tin projectiles dug shallow, smouldering craters like in a sci-fi.
12   80 metres from the road Matthew found scattered remains of his mother

13   Daphne Caruana Galizia. She was a journalist. And that is why

12   80 meters from the road Matthew found scattered remains of his mother.
11   Tin projectiles dug shallow, smouldering craters like in a sci-fi.
10   Three young men will always search for their mother: Andrew, Paul & Matthew.

9   In Malta billiard players with their billiooons always disappear into the blue.
8   Nobody ever knows. Everybody knows. The world comes to a halt.
7   People freeze in shining shelters, seagulls panic squeaking their alt.

6   A car crash? A slip down? Broken brakes? Who knows? That's Malta.
5   After the blast Peugeot 108 simply vanished from the asphalt.
4   At 3 PM an invisible billiooon cue stick flicked a car from the road.

3   The northeaster gained billiooons chasing little zeroooes over the blue altar.
2   The weather was warm, 24°C, the Sun unloaded its light shipload.
1   Monday, October 16th, 2017, was a usual working day for Malta.

Boris A Novak

↑↑   Andrew Caruana presented the empty chair devoted to his mother in an event at the Human Rights Council on repealing criminal defamation laws in May 2018. PEN has stood with the family in denouncing the dozens of ongoing civil defamation lawsuits that have continued against Caruana Galizia posthumously.

↑   On the first anniversary of Daphne Caruana Galizia's assassination, PEN participated in a mission to Malta together with Reporters Without Borders, the European Centre for Press and Media Freedom, the European Federation of Journalists, the International Press Institute, and the Committee to Protect Journalists. In the centre is Sarah Clarke, PEN International advocacy manager.

↑   Daphne Caruana Galizia, one of Malta's most influential and
widely read journalists, was assassinated on 16 October 2017 by a
powerful remote-controlled bomb placed under her car seat. Long a
household name in Malta and with a growing international reputation
through her work on the Panama Papers, Caruana Galizia's killing
raised concerns globally about press freedom, corruption, and the
rule of law in Malta. Before her death, she was subjected to systematic
and escalating intimidation and threats by government officials and
their aides and associates. She was unprotected by Malta's
institutions, the police, the attorney general, and the courts. The
mission by PEN International and five other freedom of expression
organisations paid tribute to her on the first anniversary of the killing
in the field where her car landed after the explosion.

PEN Centres
in 2021

In the year of its centenary, PEN International is a network of 145 Centres present in the five continents. Centres in exile refer to their offices abroad in 2021.

NORTH AMERICA
- America – New York
- Canada – Toronto
- Quebec – Montreal

CARIBBEAN & CENTRAL AMERICA
- Cuba – Havana
- Cuba in Exile – Miami
- Haiti – Port au Prince
- Puerto Rico – San Juan
- Mexico – Mexico City
- PEN Guadalajara – Guadalajara
- PEN San Miguel de Allende – San Miguel de Allende
- PEN Multiculturel Chiapas – San Cristóbal de las Casas
- Guatemala – Guatemala
- Honduras – Tegucigalpa
- Nicaragua – Managua

SOUTH AMERICA
- Colombia – Bogotá
- Venezuela – Caracas
- Ecuador – Quito
- Bolivia – La Paz
- PEN Quechua – La Paz
- Brazil – Rio de Janeiro
- Paraguay – Asunción
- Uruguay – Montevideo
- Argentina – Buenos Aires
- Chile – Santiago

WEST EUROPE
- Portugal – Lisbon
- Galicia – Santiago de Compostela
- Basque – Bilbao
- Catalan – Barcelona
- French – Paris
- Occitan – Montpellier
- Monaco – Monaco
- Swiss Romand – Geneva
- Swiss Italian & Reto Romansch – Lugano
- Swiss German – Bern
- Esperanto – Geneva
- Trieste – Trieste
- Italian – Rome
- Sardinia – Cagliari
- German – Darmstadt
- Belgian French Speaking – Brussels
- Belgian Dutch Speaking – Antwerp
- Liechtenstein – Vaduz
- Irish – Dublin
- English – London
- Welsh – Aberystwyth
- Scottish – Edinburgh
- The Netherlands – Amsterdam

AFRICA
- Morocco – Rabat
- Egypt – Cairo
- Mali – Bamako
- Mauritania – Nouakchott
- Senegal – Dakar
- Gambia – Banjul
- Guinea-Bissau – Bissau

NORTH & EAST EUROPE

- Denmark – Copenhagen
- Norway – Oslo
- Sweden – Stockholm
- Finland – Helsinki
- Estonia – Tallinn
- Latvia – Riga
- Lithuania – Vilnius
- Belarus – Minsk
- Ukraine – Kiev
- Poland – Warsaw
- Czech Republic – Prague
- Slovakia – Bratislava
- Hungary – Budapest
- Austria – Vienna
- Slovenia – Ljubljana
- Croatia – Zagreb
- Bosnia & Herzegovina – Sarajevo

- Macedonia – Skopje
- Serbia – Belgrade
- Kosovo – Pristina
- Montenegro – Podgorica
- Albania – Tirana
- Greece – Athens
- Cyprus – Nicosia
- Turkey – Istanbul
- Kurdish – Diyarbakır
- Armenia – Yerevan
- Georgia – Tbilisi
- Bulgaria – Sofia
- Romania – Bucharest
- Moldova – Chişinău

- Saint Petersburg – Saint Petersburg
- Moscow – Moscow
- Russian – Moscow
- Tatar – Kazan
- Chechen in Exile – Trondheim, Norway
- Central Asia – Bishkek
- Kazakhstan – Nur-Sultan

ASIA

- Afghanistan – Kabul
- Tibetan Writers Abroad – Dharamsala
- All-India – Mumbai
- Delhi – Delhi
- South India – Bangalore
- Bangladesh – Dhaka
- Nepal – Kathmandu
- Myanmar – Yangon
- Thailand – Bangkok
- Vietnamese Writers Abroad – Oviedo, USA
- Cambodia – Phnom Penh
- China – Shanghai
- Independent Chinese – Beijing

- Taiwan – Taipei
- Hong Kong Chinese Speaking – Hong Kong
- Hong Kong English Speaking – Hong Kong
- Uyghur in Exile – London, UK
- Mongolia – Ulaanbaatar
- South Korea – Seoul
- North Korea in Exile – Seoul, South Korea
- Japan – Tokyo
- Philippines – Manila
- Malaysia – Kuala Lumpur

MIDDLE EAST

- Iraq – Baghdad
- Iran in Exile – Frankfurt, Germany
- Jordan – Amman
- Palestine – Ramallah
- Lebanon – Beirut

- Guinea – Conakry
- Sierra Leone – Freetown
- Liberia – Monrovia
- Ghana – Accra
- Togo – Lomé
- Nigeria – Abuja

- Cape Verde – Praia
- Afar – Djibouti
- Somali speaking – London, UK
- Eritrea in Exile – Oslo, Norway
- Ethiopia – Addis Ababa
- Kenya – Nairobi

- Uganda – Kampala
- Malawi – Lilongwe
- Zambia – Lusaka
- Zimbabwe – Harare
- South Africa – Cape Town
- Afrikaans – Pretoria

AUSTRALIA & OCEANIA

- Australia – Perth
- Australia – Sydney
- Australia – Melbourne
- New Zealand – Wellington

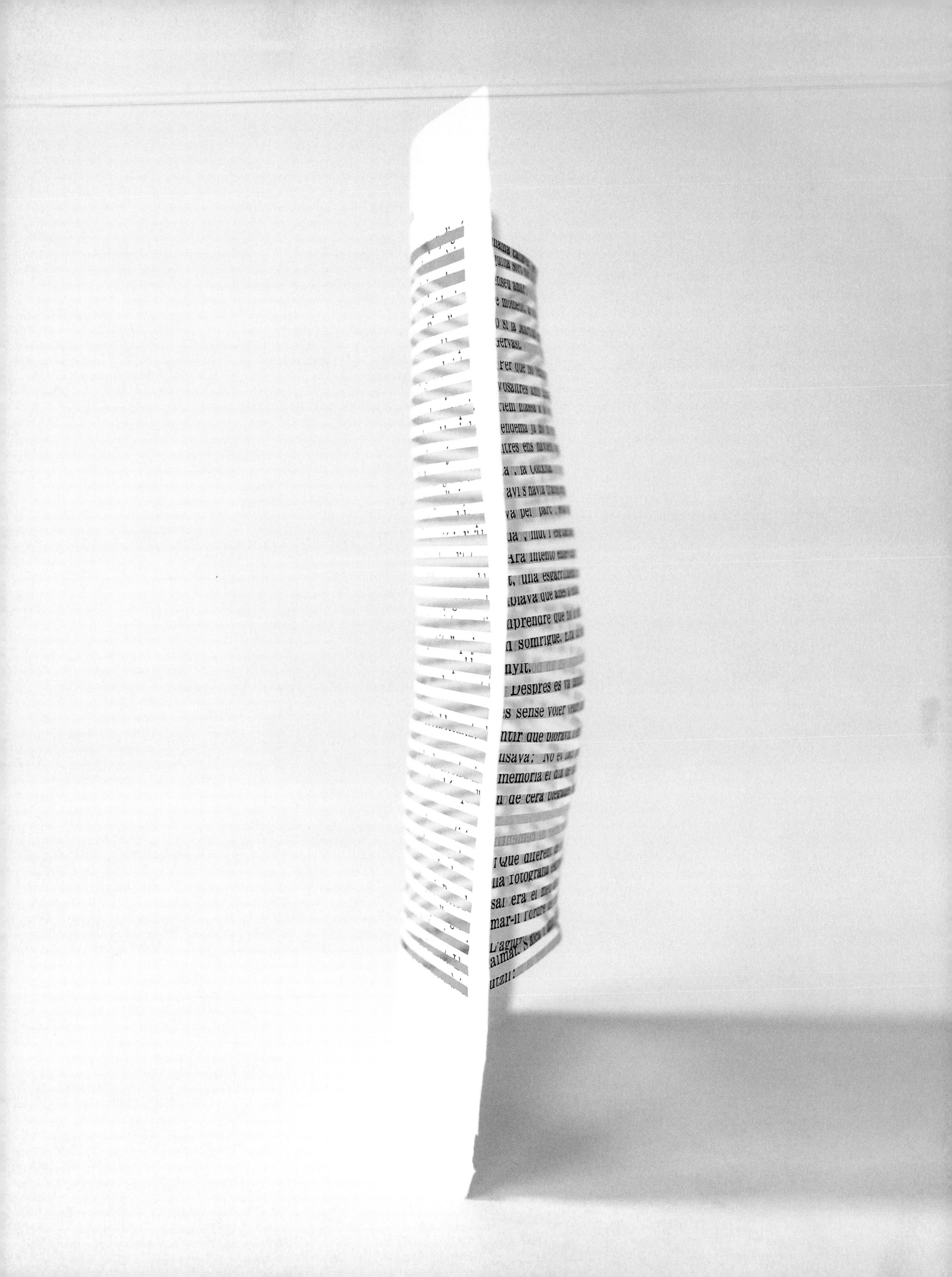

PEN *Key Documents*

The history of the PEN Charter's drafts and amendments, narrated in the second chapter, throws light on the intense debates that shaped PEN International's identity and sense of mission during a century. Since the creation of the Writers in Prison Committee in 1960, centres developed four working committees. Each of them defined PEN's mission by approving several declarations and manifestos. Committees increased the public presence of PEN in the civil societies of each given country and turned PEN International into a major actor in the development of the international civil society, in dialogue with the United Nations and other inter-governmental bodies.

At the last PEN International congress before the pandemic, meeting in Manila in 2019, PEN approved The Democracy of the Imagination Manifesto, highlighting PEN's literary vocation in front of the complexities of freedom of expression debates. PEN had also developed in previous years The PEN Declaration on Digital Freedom and The PEN Copyright manifesto.

The Committee of Translation and Linguistic Rights promoted an international platform with sixty other organizations to launch, in dialogue with UNESCO, the Universal Declaration of Linguistic Rights in 1996. The core of the declaration was later synthesized in the ten principles of the Girona Manifesto on Linguistic Rights. The Quebec Declaration on Literary Translation and Translators defined the responsibility of PEN in defence of translation and translators' rights.

The corresponding committee wrote The Bled Manifesto of Writers for Peace. It is an update of PEN's commitment, since its first meeting in 1921, to the free flow of ideas and freedom of expression in times of conflict, as well as PEN's promotion of discussion and dialogue among writers of countries in conflict and across regions of the world where wounds are open.

As for the Women Writers Committee, The PEN Women's Manifesto gave visibility to decades of commitment of PEN in defence of women writers worldwide and defined equality as a crucial value for the PEN community.

The PEN Charter

1

Literature knows no frontiers and must remain common currency among people in spite of political or international upheavals.

2

In all circumstances, and particularly in time of war, works of art, the patrimony of humanity at large, should be left untouched by national or political passion.

3

Members of PEN should at all times use what influence they have in favour of good understanding and mutual respect between nations and people; they pledge themselves to do their utmost to dispel all hatreds and to champion the ideal of one humanity living in peace and equality in one world.

4

PEN stands for the principle of unhampered transmission of thought within each nation and between all nations, and members pledge themselves to oppose any form of suppression of freedom of expression in the country and community to which they belong, as well as throughout the world wherever this is possible. PEN declares for a free press and opposes arbitrary censorship in time of peace. It believes that the necessary advance of the world towards a more highly organised political and economic order renders a free criticism of governments, administrations and institutions imperative. And since freedom implies voluntary restraint, members pledge themselves to oppose such evils of a free press as mendacious publication, deliberate falsehood and distortion of facts for political and personal ends.

The Democracy of the Imagination Manifesto

Presented by Jennifer Clement, PEN International president;
Per Wästberg, PEN International president emeritus and chair of the Nobel Prize in Literature;
Eric Lax, Nayantara Sahgal and Ngũgĩ wa Thiong'o, vice-presidents of PEN International;
and Paul Muldoon, board member of PEN America, the Democracy of the Imagination Manifesto
was adopted at the passed 85th PEN International Congress in Manila, 2019.

The opening of the PEN International Charter states that literature knows no frontiers. This speaks to both real and, no less importantly, those imagined.

PEN stands against notions of national and cultural purity that seek to stop people from listening, reading and learning from each other. One of the most treacherous forms of censorship is self-censorship — where walls are built around the imagination and often raised from fear of attack.

PEN believes the imagination allows writers and readers to transcend their own place in the world to include the ideas of others. This place for some writers has been prison where the imagination has meant interior freedom and, often, survival.

The imagination is the territory of all discovery as ideas come into being as one creates them. It is often in the confluence of contradiction, found in metaphor and simile, where the most profound human experiences reside.

For almost 100 years PEN has stood for freedom of expression. PEN also stands for, and believes in, the freedom of the empathetic imagination while recognising that many have not been the ones to tell their own stories.

PEN International upholds the following principles:

• We defend the imagination and believe it to be as free as dreams.

• We recognise and seek to counter the limits faced by so many in telling their own stories.

• We believe the imagination accesses all human experience, and reject restrictions of time, place, or origin.

• We know attempts to control the imagination may lead to xenophobia, hatred and division.

• Literature crosses all real and imagined frontiers and is always in the realm of the universal.

Women's Manifesto

*Presented by Jennifer Clement, president of PEN International, and
Margie Orford, PEN International Board member, the Women's Manifesto
was adopted at the 83rd PEN International Congress in Lviv, 2017.*

The first and founding principle of the PEN Charter asserts that 'literature knows no frontiers'. These frontiers were traditionally thought of as borders between countries and peoples. For many women in the world — and for almost all women until relatively recently — the first, and the last and perhaps the most powerful frontier was the door of the house she lived in: her parents' or her husband's home.

For women to have free speech, the right to read, the right to write, they need to have the right to roam physically, socially and intellectually. There are few social systems that do not regard with hostility a woman who walks by herself.

PEN believes that violence against women, in all its many forms, both within the walls of a home or in the public sphere, creates dangerous forms of censorship. Across the globe, culture, religion and tradition are repeatedly valued above human rights and are used as arguments to encourage or defend harm against women and girls.

PEN believes that the act of silencing a person is to deny their existence. It is a kind of death. Humanity is both wanting and bereft without the full and free expression of women's creativity and knowledge.

PEN endorses the following internationally recognised principles:

Non-violence: End violence against women and girls in all of its forms, including legal, physical, sexual, psychological, verbal and digital; promote an environment in which women and girls can express themselves freely, and ensure that all gender-based violence is comprehensively investigated and punished, and compensation provided for victims.

Safety: Protect women writers and journalists and combat impunity for violent acts and harassment committed against women writers and journalists in the world and online.

Education: Eliminate gender disparity at all levels of education by promoting full access to quality education for all women and girls, and ensuring that women can fully exercise their education rights to read and write.

Equality: Ensure that women are accorded equality with men before the law; condemn discrimination against women in all its forms and take all necessary steps to eliminate discrimination and ensure the full equality of all people through the development and advancement of women writers.

Access: Ensure that women are given the same access to the full range of civil, political, economic, social and cultural rights to enable the full and free participation and public recognition of women in all media and across the spectrum of literary forms. Additionally, ensure equal access for women and girls to all forms of media as a means of freedom of expression.

Parity: Promote the equal economic participation of women writers, and ensure that women writers and journalists are employed and paid on equal terms to men without any discrimination.

Quebec Declaration on Literary Translation and Translators

Presented by John Ralston Saul, president of PEN International,
Simona Škrabec, chair of the Translation and Linguistic Rights Committee, and
Émile Martel, president of PEN Québec, the Quebec Declaration on Literary Translation and
Translators was adopted at 81st PEN International Congress in Quebec City, 2015.

PEN's aim is to ensure that the Declaration can be read in the highest possible number of languages and we hope that other institutions and organisations will adopt its principles and help us to defend and disseminate them. The Quebec Declaration forms part of PEN International's broad strategy to promote literary creativity and collaboration between cultures.

1. Literary translation is an art of passion. Promoting values of openness, acting for peace and freedom and against injustice, intolerance and censorship, translation invites a dialogue with the world.

2. All cultures are not equal when it comes to translation. Some cultures translate by choice, others by obligation. Translation is a key to the protection of languages and cultures.

3. Respectful of authors and original texts, translators are nevertheless creators in their own right. They seek not only to reproduce a literary work but to move the work forward, to expand its presence in the world. Translators are not simply messengers: though they speak for others, their voices are also their own. In particular, they act in favour of cultural diversity by remaining loyal to marginalised authors, literary styles and social groups.

4. The rights of translators must be protected. Governments, publishers, the media, employers — all must respect the status and needs of translators, give prominence to their names, and ensure equitable remuneration and respectful working conditions — in all forms of print and digital media.

5. The physical safety and freedom of expression of translators must be guaranteed at all times.

6. As creative writers with specific skills and knowledge, translators must be shown respect and consulted for all questions related to their work. Translations belong to those who create them.

Copyright Manifesto

*Presented by Jennifer Clement, president of PEN International, and
Zoë Rodriguez, chair of the Search Committee, the Ourense Copyright Manifesto
was adopted at the 82nd PEN International Congress in Ourense, 2016.*

Going back to Britain's Statute of Anne (the first copyright act) of 1710, humankind has recognised the need to enact laws to safeguard intellectual property. In 1886 the Berne Convention for the Protection of Literary and Artistic Works was accepted, having been championed by Victor Hugo. It was then, and is now, an enlightened idea to acknowledge how individual creation and discovery elevates our collective humanity.

An author's economic independence and autonomy is central to freedom of expression and encourages a diversity of voices, which in turn fosters democracy.

To deny authors the ability to earn monetary reward from their creative works is to deny the works value and their authors a livelihood. Using the intellectual property of an author without fair recompense, and in the absence of a legitimate legal exception to the author's copyright, is theft.

PEN International believes that today, more than ever before, the rights of the individual creator are in peril from new technologies, policies and laws. PEN upholds copyright protection for all writers in every part of the world and declares the following:

1. The author is the owner of moral and copyright interests in any works they create until such time as that copyright expires.

2. Copyright includes the following uses of works: reproduction (whether analogue or digital), adaptation (including translation), publication, performance, and digital use which includes transmission of works across all digital paths and on all digital platforms.

3. Moral rights include: the right of the author to be attributed as the author of the work, and not to be falsely attributed as the author of a work they have not authored, and the right to ensure that their work are not subjected to derogatory treatment prejudicial to their reputations as authors.

4. Authors should have the right to trade freely in the copyright in their works.

5. It is a matter of choice for authors of works whether and what fee they charge for use of their works.

6. PEN International acknowledges that there are instances where governments may find it to be in the public interest to legislate exceptions to the exclusive rights of authors in the works they create. Any such exceptions must not unfairly prejudice the legitimate moral and economic interests of the author. For instance:

   • Where works are not commercially available in formats accessible to the print disabled, exceptions in domestic laws should allow for a reproduction to be made for or by a person with a print disability into an accessible format without a copyright infringement occurring. Any such copies made for the print disabled should only be made after a search for a commercial copy has been undertaken.

   • Court determinations, legislation, regulations, and other statutory instruments must be available to citizens. Faithful, unamended reproduction of these works should not be an infringement of copyright.

7. Authors' legitimate economic interests in the works they create include all existing and potential markets for their works.

8. Digital Rights Management systems applied to works should be supported by copyright legislation where necessary in order for copyright owners to exercise their copyright in works.

9. Digital reproductions of a work made on a significant scale, where no exception is in place and without the permission of the author of a work, constitute piracy. National legislation should contain appropriate punitive measures to deter piracy, while ensuring that legitimate access to works is not impeded.

Girona Manifesto on Linguistic Rights

Presented by John Ralston Saul, president of PEN International, and
Josep Maria Terricabras, chair of the Translation and Linguistic Rights Committee,
the Girona Manifesto was adopted at the 77th PEN international Congress in Belgrade, 2011.

PEN members have translated the Manifesto into various languages; we encourage you to translate it into your own and continue raising awareness about the need to protect and promote linguistic diversity.

1. Linguistic diversity is a world heritage that must be valued and protected.

2. Respect for all languages and cultures is fundamental to the process of constructing and maintaining dialogue and peace in the world.

3. All individuals learn to speak in the heart of a community that gives them life, language, culture and identity.

4. Different languages and different ways of speaking are not only means of communication; they are also the milieu in which humans grow and cultures are built.

5. Every linguistic community has the right for its language to be used as an official language in its territory.

6. School instruction must contribute to the prestige of the language spoken by the linguistic community of the territory.

7. It is desirable for citizens to have a general knowledge of various languages, because it favours empathy and intellectual openness, and contributes to a deeper knowledge of one's own tongue.

8. The translation of texts, especially the great works of various cultures,represents a very important element in the necessary process of greater understanding and respect among human beings.

9. The media is a privileged loudspeaker for making linguistic diversity work and for competently and rigorously increasing its prestige.

10. The right to use and protect one's own language must be recognised by the United Nations as one of the fundamental human rights.

Declaration on Digital Freedom

*Presented by John Ralston Saul, president of PEN International,
and Marian Botsford Fraser, chair of the Writers in Prison Committee, the PEN Declaration on Digital Freedom
was adopted by the 78th PEN International Congress in Gyeongju, South Korea, 2012.*

1. **All persons have the right to express themselves freely through digital media without fear of reprisal or persecution.**

   a. Individuals who use digital media enjoy full freedom of expression protections under international laws and standards.
   b. Governments must not prosecute individuals or exact reprisals upon individuals who convey information, opinions, or ideas through digital media.
   c. Governments must actively protect freedom of expression on digital media by enacting and enforcing effective laws and standards.

2. **All persons have the right to seek and receive information through digital media.**

   a. Governments should not censor, restrict, or control the content of digital media, including content from domestic and international sources.
   b. In exceptional circumstances, any limitations on the content of digital media must adhere to international laws and standards that govern the limits of freedom of expression, such as incitement to violence.
   c. Governments should not block access to or restrict the use of digital media, even during periods of unrest or crisis. Controlling access to digital media, especially on a broad scale, inherently violates the right to freedom of expression.
   d. Governments should foster and promote full access to digital media for all persons.

3. **All persons have the right to be free from government surveillance of digital media.**

   a. Surveillance, whether or not known by the specific intended target, chills speech by establishing the potential for persecution and the fear of reprisals. When known, surveillance fosters a climate of self-censorship that further harms free expression.
   b. As a general rule, governments should not seek to access digital communications between or among private individuals, nor should they monitor individual use of digital media, track the movements of individuals through digital media, alter the expression of individuals, or generally surveil individuals.
   c. When governments do conduct surveillance — in exceptional circumstances and in connection with legitimate law enforcement or national security investigations — any surveillance of individuals and monitoring of communications via digital media must meet international due process laws and standards that apply to lawful searches, such as obtaining a warrant by a court order.
   d. Full freedom of expression entails a right to privacy; all existing international laws and standards of privacy apply to digital media, and new laws and standards and protections may be required.
   e. Government gathering and retention of data and other information generated by digital media, including data mining, should meet international laws and standards of privacy, such as requirements that the data retention be time-limited, proportionate, and provide effective notice to persons affected.

4. **The private sector, and technology companies in particular, are bound by the right to freedom of expression and human rights.**

   a. The principles stated in this declaration equally apply to the private sector.
   b. Companies must respect human rights, including the right to freedom of expression, and must uphold these rights even when national laws and regulations do not protect them.
   c. Technology companies have a duty to determine how their products, services, and policies impact human rights in the countries in which they intend to operate. If violations are likely, or violations may be inextricably linked to the use of products or services, the companies should modify or withdraw their proposed plans in order to respect human rights.
   d. Technology companies should incorporate freedom of expression principles into core operations, such as product designs with built-in privacy protections.
   e. If their operations are found to have violated the right to freedom of expression, technology companies should provide restitution to those whose rights were violated, even when governments do not provide remedies.

Bled Manifesto of Writers for Peace

Presented by John Ralston Saul, president of PEN International, and Tone Persak, chair of the Writers for Peace Committee, the Bled Manifesto of Writers for Peace adopted by the Assembly of Delegates at the 79th PEN International Congress in Reykjavik, 2013.

1. All individuals and peoples have a right to peace and this right should be recognised by the United Nations as a universal human right.

2. PEN promotes discussion and dialogue between writers from countries in conflict and across regions of the world where wounds are open and political will is unable to address tensions.

3. PEN seeks to bring together people from around the world through literature and discussion amongst writers and with the broad public.

4. PEN considers one of the world's greatest challenges to be the transition from violence to debate, discussion and dialogue. We aim to be active participants in this process promoting where necessary the principles of international law.

5. In order to achieve the conditions for peace, freedom of expression and creativity in all its forms must be respected and protected as a fundamental right so long as it respects all other basic human rights in accordance with the principles of the Universal Declaration of Human Rights.

6. PEN acknowledges that it is of primary importance to be permanently committed to creating conditions that can lead to ending conflicts of all kinds. There is neither freedom without peace, nor peace without freedom; social and political justice is inaccessible without peace and freedom.

7. In order to achieve sustainable conditions for peace, PEN calls for the respect of the environment in conformity with the Rio Declaration on Environment and Development (1992). We condemn the excesses of technology and financial speculation that contribute to the impoverishment of a large part of the world's population.

8. PEN respects and defends the dignity of all human beings. PEN opposes injustice and violence wherever they are found, including oppression, colonisation, illegal occupation and terrorism.

9. In accordance with the principles of freedom of expression and justice, every individual or group involved in conflict has the right to demand non-violent solutions to conflict and should be free to petition and appeal to international institutions and government authorities.

10. All children have the right to receive a comprehensive peace and human rights education. PEN promotes the implementation of this right.

Universal Declaration on Linguistic Rights

*Proclaimed by PEN International, forty PEN Centres, sixty-one Non-Governmental Organizations,
forty international experts on linguistic rights and UNESCO's Linguapax Program at the First World Conference
of Linguistic Rights in Barcelona, 1996. Presented by Ronald Harwood, president of PEN International,
and Carles Torner, chair of the Follow-up Committee of the declaration, the Universal Declaration on Linguistic
Rights was adopted by the 63rd PEN International Congress in Guadalajara, Mexico, 1996.*

PRELIMINAIRES

The institutions and non-governmental organizations, signatories to the present Universal Declaration of Linguistic Rights, meeting in Barcelona from 6 to 9 June 1996.

Having regard to the 1948 Universal Declaration of Human Rights which, in its preamble, expresses its faith in fundamental human rights, in the dignity and worth of the human person and in the equal rights of men and women; and which, in its second article, establishes that everyone is entitled to all the rights and freedoms regardless of race, colour, sex, language, religion, political or other opinion, national or social origin, property, birth or other status;

Having regard to the International Covenant on Civil and Political Rights of 16 December 1966 (Article 27), and the International Covenant on Economic, Social and Cultural Rights of the same date which, in their preambles, state that human beings cannot be free unless conditions are created which enable them to enjoy both their civil and political rights and their economic, social and cultural rights;

Having regard to Resolution 47/135 of 18 December 1992 of the General Assembly of the United Nations Organization which adopted the Declaration on the Rights of Persons belonging to National, Ethnic, Religious and Linguistic Minorities;

Having regard to the declarations and conventions of the Council of Europe, such as the European Convention for the Protection of Human Rights and Fundamental Freedoms, of 4 November 1950 (Article 14); the Convention of the Council of Ministers of the Council of Europe, of 29 June 1992, approving the European Charter for Regional or Minority Languages; the Declaration on National Minorities made by the Summit Meeting of the Council of Europe on 9 October 1993; and the Framework Convention for the Protection of National Minorities of November 1994;

Having regard to the Santiago de Compostela Declaration of the International PEN Club and the Declaration of 15 December 1993 of the Translations and Linguistic Rights Committee of the International PEN Club concerning the proposal to hold a World Conference on Linguistic Rights;

Considering that, in the Recife, Brazil, Declaration of 9 October 1987, the 12th Seminar of the International Association for the Development of Intercultural Communication recommended the United Nations Organization to take the necessary steps to approve and implement a Universal Declaration of Linguistic Rights;

Having regard to Convention 169 of the International Labour Organization of 26 June 1989 concerning Indigenous and Tribal Peoples in Independent Countries;

Having regard to the Universal Declaration of the Collective Rights of Peoples, Barcelona, May 1990, which declared that all peoples have the right to express and develop their culture, language and rules of organization and, to this end, to adopt political, educational, communications and governmental structures of their own, within different political frameworks;

Having regard to the Final Declaration adopted by the General Assembly of the International Federation of Modern Language Teachers in Pécs (Hungary) on 16 August 1991, which recommended that linguistic rights be considered as fundamental rights of the individual;

Having regard to the report of the Human Rights Commission of the United Nations Economic and Social Council, of 20 April 1994, concerning the draft Declaration on the Rights of Indigenous Peoples, which viewed individual rights in the light of collective rights;

Having Regard to the draft Declaration of the Inter-American Human Rights Commission on the Rights of Indigenous Peoples, approved at session 1278 on 18 September 1995;

Considering that the majority of the world's endangered languages belong to non-sovereign peoples and that the main factors which prevent the development of these languages and accelerate the process of language substitution include the lack of self-government and the policy of states which impose their political and administrative structures and their language;

Considering that invasion, colonisation, occupation and other instances of political, economic or social subordination often involve the direct imposition of a foreign language or, at the very least, distort perceptions of the value of languages and give rise to hierarchical linguistic attitudes which undermine the language loyalty of speakers; and considering that the languages of some peoples which have attained sovereignty are consequently immersed in a process of language substitution as a result of a policy which favours the language of former colonial or imperial powers;

Considering that universalism must be based on a conception of linguistic and cultural diversity which prevails over trends towards homogenization and towards exclusionary isolation;

Considering that, in order to ensure peaceful coexistence between language communities, overall principles must be found so as to guarantee the promotion and respect of all languages and their social use in public and in private;

Considering that various factors of an extralinguistic nature (historical, political, territorial, demographic, economic, sociocultural and sociolinguistic factors and those related to collective attitudes) give rise to problems which lead to the extinction, marginalization and degeneration of numerous languages, and that linguistic rights must therefore be examined in an overall perspective, so as to apply appropriate solutions in each case;

In the belief that a Universal Declaration of Linguistic Rights is required in order to correct linguistic imbalances with a view to ensuring the respect and full development of all languages and establishing the principles for a just and equitable linguistic peace throughout the world as a key factor in the maintenance of harmonious social relations;

HEREBY DECLARE THAT

PREAMBLE

The situation of each language, in view of the foregoing considerations, is the result of the convergence and interaction of a wide range of factors of a political and legal, ideological and historical, demographic and territorial, economic and social, cultural, linguistic and sociolinguistic, interlinguistic and subjective nature.

At the present time, these factors are defined by:

- The age-old unifying tendency of the majority of states to reduce diversity and foster attitudes opposed to cultural plurality and linguistic pluralism.

- The trend towards a worldwide economy and consequently towards a worldwide market of information, communications and culture, which disrupts the spheres of interrelation and the forms of interaction that guarantee the internal cohesion of language communities.

- The economicist growth model put forward by transnational economic groups which seeks to identify deregulation with progress and competitive individualism with freedom and generates serious and growing economic, social, cultural and linguistic inequality.

Language communities are currently threatened by a lack of self-government, a limited population or one that is partially or wholly dispersed, a fragile economy, an unmodified language, or a cultural model opposed to the dominant one, which make it impossible for many languages to survive and develop unless the following basic goals are taken into account:

- In a political perspective, the goal of conceiving a way of organizing linguistic diversity so as to permit the effective participation of language communities in this new growth model.

- In a cultural perspective. the goal of rendering the worldwide communications space compatible with the equitable participation of all peoples, language communities and individuals in the development process.

- In an economic perspective, the goal of fostering sustainable development based on the participation of all and on respect for the ecological balance of societies and for equitable relationships between all languages and cultures.

For all these reasons, this Declaration takes language communities and not states as its point of departure and is to be viewed in the context of the reinforcement of international institutions capable of guaranteeing sustainable and equitable development for the whole of humanity. For these reasons also it aims to encourage the creation of a political framework for linguistic diversity based upon respect, harmonious coexistence and mutual benefit.

PRELIMINARY TITLE
Concepts

Article 1

1. This Declaration considers as a *language community* any human society established historically in a particular territorial space, whether this space be recognized or not, which identifies itself as a people and has developed a common language as a natural means of communication and cultural cohesion among its members. The term *language specific to a territory* refers to the language of the community historically established in such a space.

2. This Declaration takes as its point of departure the principle that linguistic rights are individual and collective at one and the same time. In defining the full range of linguistic rights, it adopts as its referent the case of a historical language community within its own territorial space, this space being understood, not only as the geographical area where the community lives, but also as the social and functional space vital to the full development of the language. Only on this basis is it possible to define the rights of the language groups mentioned in point 5 of the present article, and those of individuals living outside the territory of their community, in terms of a gradation or continuum.

3. For the purpose of this Declaration, groups are also deemed to be in their own territory and to belong to a language community in the following circumstances:

i. when they are separated from the main body of their community by political or administrative boundaries;

ii. when they have been historically established in a small geographical area surrounded by members of other language communities; or

iii. when they are established in a geographical area which they share with the members of other language communities with similar historical antecedents.

4. This Declaration also considers nomad peoples within their areas of migration and peoples established in geographically dispersed locations as language communities in their own historical territory.

5. This Declaration considers as a *language group* any group of persons sharing the same language which is established in the territorial space of another language community but which does not possess historical antecedents equivalent to those of that community. Examples of such groups are immigrants, refugees, deported persons and members of diasporas.

Article 2

1. This Declaration considers that, whenever various language communities and groups share the same territory, the rights formulated in this Declaration must be exercised on a basis of mutual respect and in such a way that democracy may be guaranteed to the greatest possible extent.

2. In the quest for a satisfactory sociolinguistic balance, that is, in order to establish the appropriate articulation between the respective rights of such language communities and groups and the persons belonging to them, various factors, besides their respective historical antecedents in the territory and their democratically expressed will, must be taken into account. Such factors, which may call for compensatory treatment aimed at restoring a balance, include the coercive nature of the migrations which have led to the coexistence of the different communities and groups, and their degree of political, socioeconomic and cultural vulnerability.

Article 3

1. This Declaration considers the following to be inalienable personal rights which may be exercised in any situation:

- the right to be recognized as a member of a language community;

- the right to the use of one's own language both in private and in public;

- the right to the use of one's own name;

- the right to interrelate and associate with other members of one's language community of origin;

- the right to maintain and develop one's own culture;

- and all the other rights related to language which are recognized in the International Covenant on Civil and Political Rights of 16 December 1966 and the International Covenant on Economic, Social and Cultural Rights of the same date.

2. This Declaration considers that the collective rights of language groups may include the following, in addition to the rights attributed to the members of language groups in the foregoing paragraph, and in accordance with the conditions laid down in article 2.2:

- the right for their own language and culture to be taught;

- the right of access to cultural services;

- the right to an equitable presence of their language and culture in the communications media;

- the right to receive attention in their own language from government bodies and in socioeconomic relations.

3. The aforementioned rights of persons and language groups must in no way hinder the interrelation of such persons or groups with the host language community or their integration into that community. Nor must they restrict the rights of the host community or its members to the full public use of the community's own language throughout its territorial space.

Article 4

1. This Declaration considers that persons who move to and settle in the territory of another language community have the right and the duty to maintain an attitude of *integration* towards this community. This term is understood to mean an additional socialization of such persons in such a way that they may preserve their original cultural characteristics while sharing with the society in which they have settled sufficient references, values and forms of behaviour to enable them to function socially without greater difficulties than those experienced by members of the host community.

2. This Declaration considers, on the other hand, that assimilation, a term which is understood to mean acculturation in the host society, in such a

way that the original cultural characteristics are replaced by the references, values and forms of behaviour of the host society, must on no account be forced or induced and can only be the result of an entirely free choice.

Article 5

This Declaration is based on the principle that the rights of all language communities are equal and independent of the legal or political status of their languages as official, regional or minority languages. Terms such as regional or minority languages are not used in this Declaration because, though in certain cases the recognition of regional or minority languages can facilitate the exercise of certain rights, these and other modifiers are frequently used to restrict the rights of language communities.

Article 6

This Declaration considers that a language cannot be considered specific to a territory merely on the grounds that it is the official language of the state or has been traditionally used within the territory for administrative purposes or for certain cultural activities.

TITLE ONE
General Principles

Article 7

1. All languages are the expression of a collective identity and of a distinct way of perceiving and describing reality and must therefore be able to enjoy the conditions required for their development in all functions.

2. All languages are collectively constituted and are made available within a community for individual use as tools of cohesion, identification, communication and creative expression.

Article 8

1. All language communities have the right to organize and manage their own resources so as to ensure the use of their language in all functions within society.

2. All language communities are entitled to have at their disposal whatever means are necessary to ensure the transmission and continuity of their language.

Article 9

All language communities have the right to codify, standardize, preserve, develop and promote their linguistic system, without induced or forced interference.

Article 10

1. All language communities have equal rights.

2. This Declaration considers discrimination against language communities to be inadmissible, whether it be based on their degree of political sovereignty, their situation defined in social, economic or other terms, the extent to which their languages have been codified, updated or modernized, or on any other criterion.

3. All necessary steps must be taken in order to implement this principle of equality and to render it effective.

Article 11

All language communities are entitled to have at their disposal whatever means of translation into and from other languages are needed to guarantee the exercise of the rights contained in this Declaration.

Article 12

1. Everyone has the right to carry out all activities in the public sphere in his/her language, provided it is the language specific to the territory where s/he resides.

2. Everyone has the right to use his/her language in the personal and family sphere.

Article 13

1. Everyone has the right to acquire knowledge of the language specific to the territory in which s/he lives.

2. Everyone has the right to be polyglot and to know and use the language most conducive to his/her personal development or social mobility, without prejudice to the guarantees established in this Declaration for the public use of the language specific to the territory.

Article 14

The provisions of this Declaration cannot be interpreted or used to the detriment of any norm or practice deriving from the internal or international status of a language which is more favourable to its use within the territory to which it is specific.

SECOND TITLE
Overall linguistic régime

Section I
Public administration and official bodies

Article 15

1. All language communities are entitled to the official use of their language within their territory.

2. All language communities have the right for legal and administrative acts, public and private documents and records in public registers which are drawn up in the language of the territory to be valid and effective and no one can allege ignorance of this language.

Article 16

All members of a language community have the right to interrelate with and receive attention from the public authorities in their own language. This right also applies to central, territorial, local and supraterritorial divisions which include the territory to which the language is specific.

Article 17

1. All language communities are entitled to have at their disposal and to obtain in their own language all official documents pertaining to relations which affect the territory to which the language is specific, whether such documents be in printed, machine-readable or any other form.

2. Forms and standard administrative documents, whether in printed, machine- readable or any other form, must be made available and placed at the disposal of the public in all territorial languages by the public authorities through the services which cover the territories to which each language is specific.

Article 18

1. All language communities have the right for laws and other legal provisions which concern them to be published in the language specific to the territory.

2. Public authorities who have more than one territorially historic language within their jurisdiction must publish all laws and other legal provisions of a general nature in each of these languages, whether or not their speakers understand other languages.

Article 19

1. Representative Assemblies must have as their official language(s) the language(s) historically spoken in the territory they represent.

2. This right also applies to the languages of the communities established in geographically dispersed locations referred to in Article 1, Paragraph 4.

Article 20

1. Everyone has the right to use the language historically spoken in a territory, both orally and in writing, in the Courts of Justice located within that territory. The Courts of Justice must use the language specific to the territory in their internal actions and, if on account of the legal system in force within the state, the proceedings continue elsewhere, the use of the original language must be maintained.

2. Everyone has the right, in all cases, to be tried in a language which s/he understands and can speak and to obtain the services of an interpreter free of charge.

Article 21

All language communities have the right for records in public registers to be drawn up in the language specific to the territory.

Article 22

All language communities have the right for documents authenticated by notaries public or certified by other authorized public servants to be drawn up in the language specific to the territory where the notary or other authorized public servant performs his/her functions.

Section II
Education

Article 23

1. Education must help to foster the capacity for linguistic and cultural self- expression of the language community of the territory where it is provided.

2. Education must help to maintain and develop the language spoken by the language community of the territory where it is provided.

3. Education must always be at the service of linguistic and cultural diversity and of harmonious relations between different language communities throughout the world.

4. Within the context of the foregoing principles, everyone has the right to learn any language.

Article 24

All language communities have the right to decide to what extent their language is to be present, as a vehicular language and as an object of study, at all levels of education within their territory: preschool, primary, secondary, technical and vocational, university, and adult education.

Article 25

All language communities are entitled to have at their disposal all the human and material resources necessary to ensure that their language is present to the extent they desire at all levels of education within their territory: properly trained teachers, appropriate teaching methods, text books, finance, buildings and equipment, traditional and innovative technology.

Article 26

All language communities are entitled to an education which will enable their members to acquire a full command of their own language, including the different abilities relating to all the usual spheres of use, as well as the most extensive possible command of any other language they may wish to know.

Article 27

All language communities are entitled to an education which will enable their members to acquire knowledge of any languages related to their own cultural tradition, such as literary or sacred languages which were formerly habitual languages of the community.

Article 28

All language communities are entitled to an education which will enable their members to acquire a thorough knowledge of their cultural heritage (history, geography, literature, and other manifestations of their own culture), as well as the most extensive possible knowledge of any other culture they may wish to know.

Article 29

1. Everyone is entitled to receive an education in the language specific to the territory where s/he resides.

2. This right does not exclude the right to acquire oral and written knowledge of any language which may be of use to him/her as an instrument of communication with other language communities.

Article 30

The language and culture of all language communities must be the subject of study and research at university level.

Section III
Proper names

Article 31

All language communities have the right to preserve and use their own system of proper names in all spheres and on all occasions.

Article 32

1. All language communities have the right to use place names in the language proper to the territory, both orally and in writing, in the private, public and official spheres.

2. All language communities have the right to establish, preserve and revise autochthonous place names. Such place names cannot be arbitrarily abolished, distorted or adapted, nor can they be replaced if changes in the political situation, or changes of any other type, occur.

Article 33

All language communities have the right to refer to themselves by the name used in their own language. Any translation into other languages must avoid ambiguous or pejorative denominations.

Article 34

Everyone has the right to the use of his/her own name in his/her own language in all spheres, as well as the right, only when necessary, to the most accurate possible phonetic transcription of his/her name in another writing system.

Section IV
Communications media and new technologies

Article 35

All language communities have the right to decide the extent to which their language is be present in the communications media in their territory, whether local and traditional media, those with a wider scope, or those using more advanced technology, regardless of the method of dissemination or transmission employed.

Article 36

All language communities are entitled to have at their disposal all the human and material resources required in order to ensure the desired degree of presence of their language and the desired degree of cultural self-expression in the communications media in their territory: properly trained personnel, finance, buildings and equipment, traditional and innovative technology.

Article 37

All language communities have the right to receive, through the communications media, a thorough knowledge of their cultural heritage (history, geography, literature and other manifestations of their own culture), as well as the greatest possible amount of information about any other culture their members may wish to know.

Article 38

The languages and cultures of all language communities must receive equitable and non-discriminatory treatment in the communications media throughout the world.

Article 39

The communities described in Article 1, paragraphs 3 and 4, of this Declaration, and the groups mentioned in paragraph 5 of the same article, are entitled to an equitable representation of their language in the communications media of the territory where they are established or where they migrate. This right is to be exercised in harmony with the rights of the other language groups or communities in the territory.

Article 40

In the field of information technology, all language communities are entitled to have at their disposal equipment adapted to their linguistic system and tools and products in their language, so as to derive full advantage from the potential offered by such technologies for self-expression, education, communication, publication, translation and information processing and the dissemination of culture in general.

Section V
Culture

Article 41

1. All language communities have the right to use, maintain and foster their language in all forms of cultural expression.

2. All language communities must be able to exercise this right to the full without any community's space being subjected to hegemonic occupation by a foreign culture.

Article 42

All language communities have the right to full development within their own cultural sphere.

Article 43

All language communities are entitled to access to the works produced in their language.

Article 44

All language communities are entitled to access to intercultural programmes, through the dissemination of adequate information, and to support for activities such as teaching the language to foreigners, translation, dubbing, post-synchronization and subtitling.

Article 45

All language communities have the right for the language proper to the territory to occupy a preeminent position in cultural events and services (libraries, videothèques, cinemas, theatres, museums, archives, folklore, cultural industries, and all other manifestations of cultural life).

Article 46

All language communities have the right to preserve their linguistic and cultural heritage, including its material manifestations, such as collections of documents, works of art and architecture, historic buildings and inscriptions in their own language.

Section VI
The socioeconomic sphere

Article 47

1. All language communities have the right to establish the use of their language in all socioeconomic activities within their territory.

2. All members of a language community are entitled to have at their disposal, in their own language, all the means necessary for the performance of their professional activities, such as documents and works of reference, instructions, forms, and computer equipment, tools and products.

3. The use of other languages in this sphere can only be required in so far as it is justified by the nature of the professional activity involved. In no case can a more recently arrived language relegate or supersede the use of the language proper to the territory.

Article 48

1. Within the territory of his/her language community, everyone has the right to use his/her own language with full legal validity in economic transactions of all types, such as the sale and purchase of goods and services, banking, insurance, job contracts and others.

2. No clause in such private acts can exclude or restrict the use of the language proper to the territory.

3. Within the territory of his/her language community, everyone is entitled to have the documents required for the above-mentioned operations at his/her disposal in his/her own language. Such documents include forms, cheques, contracts, invoices, receipts, delivery notes, order forms, and others.

Article 49

Within the territory of his/her language community, everyone has the right to use his/her own language in all types of socioeconomic organizations such as labour and union organizations, and employers', professional, trade and craft associations.

Article 50

1. All language communities have the right for their language to occupy a pre-eminent place in advertising, signs, external signposting, and in the image of the country as a whole.

2. Within the territory of his/her language community, everyone has the right to receive full oral and written information in his/her own language on the products and services proposed by commercial establishments, such as instructions for use, labels, lists of ingredients, advertising, guarantees and others

3. All public indications affecting the safety of persons must be expressed at least in the language proper to the territory, in conditions which are not inferior to those of any other language.

Article 51

1. Everyone has the right to use the language proper to the territory in his/her relations with firms, commercial establishments and private bodies and to be served or receive a reply in the same language.

2. Everyone has the right, as a client, customer, consumer or user, to receive oral and written information in the language proper to the territory from establishments open to the public.

Article 52

Everyone has the right to carry out his/her professional activities in the language proper to the territory unless the functions inherent to the job require the use of other languages, as in the case of language teachers, translators or tourist guides.

ADDITIONAL DISPOSITIONS

First

The public authorities must take all appropriate steps to implement the rights proclaimed in this Declaration within their respective areas of jurisdiction.

More specifically, international funds must be set up to foster the exercise of Linguistic Rights in communities which are demonstrably lacking in resources. Thus the public authorities must provide the necessary support so that the languages of the various communities may be codified, transcribed, taught, and used in the administration.

Second

The public authorities must ensure that the offial bodies, organizations and persons concerned are informed of the rights and correlative duties arising from this Declaration.

Third

The public authorities must establish, in the light of existing legislation, the sanctions to be applied in cases of violation of the linguistic rights laid down in this Declaration.

FINAL DISPOSITIONS

First

This Declaration proposes the creation of a Council of Languages within the United Nations Organization. The General Assembly of the United Nations Organization is to be responsible for setting up this Council, defining its functions and appointing its members, and for creating a body in international law to protect language communities in the exercise of the rights recognized in this Declaration.

Second

This Declaration recommends and promotes the creation of a World Commission on Linguistic Rights, a non-official, consultative body made up of representatives of non-governmental organizations and other organizations working in the field of linguistic law.

List of PEN International presidents, international secretaries, treasurers and executive directors

Founder

Catharine Amy Dawson Scott	1921

International Presidents

John Galsworthy	1921–33
HG Wells	1933–36
Jules Romains	1936–41

Wartime International Presidential Committee 1941–47

Hu Shih	1941–47
Denis Saurat	1941–47
HG Wells	1941–46
Hermon Ould	1941–47
Thornton Wilder	1941–47
EM Forster	1946–47
François Mauriac	1946–47
Ignazio Silone	1946–47

Maurice Maeterlinck	1947–49
Benedetto Croce	1949–52
Charles Morgan	1953–56
André Chamson	1956–59
Alberto Moravia	1959–62
Victor E van Vriesland	1962–65
Arthur Miller	1965–69
Pierre Emmanuel	1969–71
Heinrich Böll	1971–74
VS Pritchett	1974–76
Mario Vargas Llosa	1976–79
Per Wästberg	1979–86
Francis King	1986–89
René Tavernier	May–Nov 1989
Per Wästberg (Interim)	Nov 89–May 90
György Konrád	1990–93
Ronald Harwood	1993–97
Homero Aridjis	1997–2003
Jiří Gruša	2003–2009
John Ralston Saul	2009–2015
Jennifer Clement	2015–present

Vice-presidents*

Svetlana Alexievich
Margaret Atwood
Niels E Barfoed
Andrei Bitov
Alexandre Blokh
Sook-Hee Chun
JM Coetzee
Georges-Emmanuel Clancier
Moris Farhi
Nadine Gordimer
Gloria Guardia de Alfaro
Nancy Ing
Kata Kulavkova
Lucina Kathmann
Eric Lax
Joanne Leedom-Ackerman
Jens Lohman
Predrag Matvejević
Toni Morrison
Perumal Murugan
Boris A Novak
Vida Ognjenović
Orhan Pamuk
Elena Poniatowska
Judith Rodriguez
Michael Scammell
Eugene Schoulgin
Frankie Sionil José
Hori Takeaki
Franca Tiberto
Ngũgĩ wa Thiong'o
Nayantara Sahgal
Luisa Valenzuela

* Elected vice-presidents after the change of PEN International regulations in 1998.

International Secretaries

Marjorie Watts	1921–26
Hermon Ould	1926–51
David Carver	1951–74
Peter Elstob	1974–81
Alexandre Blokh	1981–98
Terry Carlbom	1998–2004
Joanne Leedom-Ackerman	2004–2007
Eugene Schoulgin	2007–2010
Hori Takeaki	2010–2016
Kätlin Kaldmaa	2016–present

International Treasurers

Thilo Koch	1974–91
Bill Barazetti	1991–96
Martyn Goff	1996–98
Jan Honout	1998–2001
Britta Junge Pederson	2001–07
Eric Lax	2007–13
Jarkko Tonti	2013–19
Eric Lax	2019–present

Executive Directors

Caroline McCormick	2005–10
Laura McVeigh	2011–14
Carles Torner	2014–20
Romana Cacchioli	2020–present

Ginevra Avalle is a qualified archivist and researcher working in the promotion of private collections. She has worked on different projects in a variety of environments ranging from private foundations and educational institutions (Ezio Franceschini Foundation, Florence; The Inner Temple, London), international organisations (The Institute of Ismaili Studies, London), to academia (Accademia della Crusca, Florence). Amongst her publications, *L'Archivio di Flaminio Pellegrini* (1868–1928). Lucca - Firenze: Istituto Storico Lucchese - Accademia della Crusca, 2014; *Ritratto di una generazione*. Manduria-Bari-Roma: Lacaita Editore, 2014. At present she collaborates with PEN International managing, curating, and promoting the Centenary exhibition of the PEN archive collection.

Jennifer Clement is the President of PEN International and the first woman to be elected since the organization was founded in 1921. Under her leadership the groundbreaking PEN International Women's Manifesto and The Democracy of the Imagination Manifesto were created. Clement is the author the novels *A True Story Based on Lies*, *The Poison That Fascinates*, *Prayers for the Stolen* and *Gun Love* as well as several poetry books. Clement also wrote the acclaimed memoir *Widow Basquiat* on New York City in the early 1980's and the painter Jean-Michel Basquiat. Clement is recipient of many awards including the Canongate Prize, Sara Curry Humanitarian Award, the Gran Prix des Lectrices Lyceenes de ELLE, a Guggenheim Fellowship, an NEA Fellowship and her books have twice been a *New York Times* Editor's Choice Book. *Prayers for the Stolen* was both a PEN/Faulkner Prize and Femina Prize finalist and a *New Statesman* Book of the Year, picked by Kazuo Ishiguro. Her recent novel *Gun Love* is an Oprah Book Club Selection as well as being a National Book Award, Aspen Words Literary Prize finalist, and a *New York Times* Editor's Choice Book. *Time* magazine, among other publications, named it one of the top 10 books of 2018. Clement's books have been translated into more than 35 languages.

Peter D. McDonald is Professor of English and Related Literature at the University of Oxford and a Fellow of St Hugh's College. He writes on literature, the modern state and the freedom of expression; the history of writing systems, cultural institutions and publishing; multilingualism, translation and interculturality; and on the promise of creative criticism. His main publications include *British Literary Culture and Publishing Practice*, 1888-1914 (CUP, 1997), *The Literature Police: Apartheid Censorship and its Cultural Consequences* (OUP, 2009, theliteraturepolice.com), and *Artefacts of Writing: Ideas of the State and Communities of Letters from Matthew Arnold to Xu Bing* (OUP, 2017, artefactsofwriting.com).

Jan Martens is a Belgian publisher of illustrated books on art and history and co-founder with Bato Tomasevic of the Motovun Group of International Publishers (MGIP, founded 1976) which is PEN's editorial partner of the book celebrating the centennial. He has been commissioned by PEN and MGIP to create the editorial concept and to coordinate the many language versions of the book and its distribution worldwide as a co-editor of the project together with Carles Torner. He has also been teaching comparative Indo-European linguistics and literature at several universities and cooperates with institutions in defence of secular education and freedom of expression.

Rachel Potter is Professor of Modern Literature at the University of East Anglia. She writes on literature and censorship, free expression and writers organisations, modernist literature and early twentieth century culture. She has been exploring the early history of International PEN for a number of years, research which is central to her forthcoming book, *The World Literary Republic: Literature and Free Expression 1921-1948*. Her published books include *Obscene Modernism: Literary Censorship and Experiment 1900-1940* (OUP, 2013), *The Edinburgh Guide to Modernist Literature* (EUP, 2012), and *Modernism and Democracy: Literary Culture 1900-1930* (OUP, 2006).

Carles Torner is a Catalan poet and writer. He has published seven volumes of poetry, among them *Life Afterwards* (1998, National Critic's Award), *Europe's Bride* (2008), and *Twenty-Seven Christmas and a King* (2019). English translations of his poetry have appeared in *Six Catalan Poets* (2013). He has also written essays in French, among them *Shoah, a Pedagogy of Memory* (2002) and *The Indigenous Converted Me* (2003), which was co-written with the late Bishop of Chiapas, Samuel Ruiz. Torner has participated in missions for imprisoned writers in Peru, Venezuela, Kazakhstan, and Turkey —trips that gave shape to a collection of 35 letters to foreign women writers and civil society leaders titled *Babel's Arch* (2005). As chair of PEN's Translation and Linguistic Rights Committee, he conceived and promoted the Universal Declaration of Linguistic Rights and the report *To be translated or not to be* (2007). He was PEN International Executive Director from 2014 to 2020 and is at present the director of the PEN Centenary.

Laetitia Zecchini is a research fellow at the CNRS (Paris). Her research focuses on contemporary Indian poetry and the politics of literature. She is the author of a monograph on the poet Arun Kolatkar (*Arun Kolatkar and Modernism in India, Moving Lines*, Bloomsbury, 2014), whom she has also translated into French, and has more recently co-edited several special issues and volumes including "The Worlds of Bombay Poetry" (2017), "The Locations of (World) Literature: Perspectives from Africa and South Asia" (2019). She is at work on a monograph around issues of literary activism and struggles for cultural/literary freedoms in postcolonial India.

⬎ Next pages:
January 2017, PEN International mission of writers and publishers from 13 countries after reading a statement in front of Silivri prison in Istanbul, where 150 journalists were detained. See page 152.

Picture Credits

Pictures, documents and works of art appearing in this book may be protected by copyright and may not be reproduced without the permission of the rights holders. In reproducing the images contained in this publication, PEN International obtained the permission of the rights holders whenever possible. Should PEN have been unable to locate a rights holder, notwithstanding good-faith efforts, it requests that any contact information concerning such rights holders be forwarded, so that they may be contacted for future editions. The copyright credit lines listed below are in some instances provided at the request of the rights holders.

PEN has researched for this book in partnership with the Harry Ransom Centre / University of Texas at Austin. Documents of t148he centre are reproduced by courtesy on pp. 6, 17, 20, 25, 28 (PEN News), 29, 31, 34–35, 40, 42, 47, 49, 54, 55, 56, 70, 71, 82, 90 (J Chance letter), 91, 92 (S Zweig letter), 98 (P Tabori letter), 126 (Rio Congress minutes), 139, 194 (PEN News), 197 (IB Singer card), 201 and 277.

Documents and pictures are courtesy of Marjorie-Ann Watts on pp. 18, 24, 198 and 289.

Artworks are reproduced by courtesy of the artists: Heirs Antoni Tàpies/VEGAP p. 146; Frederic Amat/ VEGAP pp. 14, 148; Sally Howell pp. 72, 272; Narcís Comadira p. 147; Eulàlia Valldosera/ VEGAP p. 148; Joan Fontcuberta/VEGAP pp. 122, 148; Jaume Plensa/VEGAP pp. 84, 149; Francesc Torres/VEGAP pp. 150, 238; Francesc Abad p. 151; Mar Arza pp. 151, 298; Mireia Sallarès pp. 151, 247; Christopher Downes p. 110 (*I am a cartoonist*); Eaten Fish p. 110 (*I am only a refugee*), 111; Caroline Glover pp. 117, 260 (D Tatour); Maxine Young pp. 170–171, 281, 290 (M Breach Velducea); Zehra Doğan p. 220 (*Nusaybin*); Sergi Rucabado Rebés p. 192; Dareen Tatour p. 261.

Pictures on the following pages are reproduced by courtesy of photographers: Núria Cases, heir of Gabriel Cases p. 94; Simone Ahrend, sah-photo, p. 104 (F Sarkohi); Mike Halmshaw for PEN Int. p. 110 (A Dorani, C McCann & L Hovda Løkeland); Alex Teame for PEN Eritrea p. 115 (Action PEN Eritrea); Ingrid Scammell p. 135; Caspar von Vegesack p. 136 (T von Vegesack); Domènec Umbert p. 142 (J Sarsanedas); Calla Fleischer p. 206 (A Fleischer); John Leffmann p. 207 (O Paz); Wojciech Plewinski p. 207 (W Szymborska); Nathaniel Wice p. 212 (E Allen); Kemal Hadžić p. 243 (G Simić); Paul Lowe p. 244 (S Sontag & troupe); Gervasio Sánchez p. 245 (J Goytisolo & S Sontag); Iztok Dimc p. 246 (S Slapšak); Tymchenko Mykola (Day newspaper, Kyiv) p. 265; Mattias Axelsson p. 288 (Princess Nandi).

The following copyrights are claimed for pictures: Getty Images for pp. 30, 31, 38, 41 (League of Nations), 50 (F Marinetti), 53, 60, 77 (M Vargas Llosa & P Elstob), 112, 121, 124 (L Renn), 125, 126, 127 (P Tabori, S Jameson), 156 (burning *Satanic Verses*), 177, 206 (AP Esquivel), 220 (Banksy), 240, 275

(N Mailer, M Atwood); AFP for pp. 113 (Liu Xia), 214 (S Rushdie & M Otamendi); Alamy for pp. 124 (J Roumain), 127 (VE van Vriesland), 206-207 (N Mandela, J Ramos-Horta, W Szymborska, S Heany); Robert Carrithers for p. 162.

The following photographs and documents are by and courtesy: Penguin Random House p. 48; Vor Der Morgenröte, X Filme Creative Pool pp. 51, 92 (movie poster) ; Atelier Rambow/ Lienemeyer/van de Sand p. 86; Deutsche Nationalbibliothek, Deutsches Exilarchiv 1933–45, Frankfurt am Main, pp. 88, 89, 90 (list); ICORN pp. 108, 109; Royal Shakespeare Company p. 120; Fundación Federico García Lorca p. 124; Linda Kokalari/Musine Kokalari Institute p. 128; Albanian Telegraphic Agency p. 129; The Willye Agency p. 153 (A Miller, H Pinter & O Pamuk); Ari and Sturla Gunnarsson for PEN Canada pp. 158–159; Maynooth University Library p. 167; Swedish Academy p. 168 (L Xiaobo Nobel ceremony); *Charlie Hebdo* p. 174; *Dagens Nyheter* p. 191; National Library of Scotland p. 194 (H Cruickshank); *Enciclopèdia Catalana* p. 198 (P Fabra & HG Wells); Associació Memòria i Història de Manresa p. 199 (P Casals); Creative Commons pp. 206 (D Tutu), 266 (C Ossietzky); Tibetan Centre for Human Rights & Democracy p. 209 (report cover); *Chomei (The Lamp)* p. 211; UCLA p. 212 (MH Heim); Institut Ramon Llull p. 213 (J Lange, report cover); *Egunkaria* p. 214 (demonstration), 215; UNESCO México p. 231 (E Pérez López & U Urutikoetexea, group photo); Freemymom.org p. 237; *Delo* p. 245 (Sarajevo group); *New York Times* p. 274; Grupo Milenio p. 290 (red shoes).

The following pictures and documents are courtesy of PEN Centres: All-India PEN pp. 27, 59; American PEN pp. 134, 181 (poster), 212 (P Nadas); Brazilian PEN p. 93; Belgium Francophone PEN p. 194 (press card L Piérard); Canadian PEN pp. 158–159, 182 (B de Caires), 270, 285 (radio) ; Catalan PEN pp. 95–97, 173, 204, 205, 207 (group), 292 (*Memòria de l'aigua*); Central Asia PEN p. 292 (V Iversen-Tokombaeva & KT Schnider); Croatian PEN pp. 144, 241 (V Taufer & S Petlevski), 242 (BA Novak); Cuban Writers in Exile PEN pp. 248–249; Cuban Writers in Exile PEN pp. 100 (Havana restaurant), 101; Czech PEN p. 19 (caricature by Adolf Hoffmeister); Danish PEN p. 182 (J Lohman), 183; English PEN pp. 137 (AR Chowdury & M Atwood), 168 (AR Chowdury), 202 (Ngũgĩ & A Hopkinson), 203, 255, 280 (S Rushdie, S Tripathi & C Shamsie); Eritrean PEN pp. 114, 115 (book cover), 116 (DA Berekhet); Finnish PEN p. 32 (letter CA Dawson Scott), 292 (*Kyltymätön uunni*); Galician PEN p. 157 (G Kónrad, S Rushdie & R Harwood), 219 (panel); German PEN pp. 118 (group), 119, 264 (O Sentsov with group); Guinea PEN pp. 276 (L Kathmann, F Ndiaye Sow & KZ Diallo), 278 (Musée du Fouta), 279 (UNESCO award, women poets); Iranian PEN in Exile p. 104 (assembly, demonstration); Japanese PEN p. 74 (Tokyo Congress), 77 (D Carver); Kurdish PEN pp. 218 (Slemani, Diyarbakır, Dresden, Rojava), 219 (Kurdish PEN office assault); Malian PEN pp. 258 (I Samba Traoré), 259; Moscow PEN p. 264 (group

with banners); Norwegian PEN p. 266 (E Snowden, H Newth Nouri & W Nygaard); PEN Quebec p. 283 (group); Philippine PEN p. 232; Polish PEN pp. 12–13, 33, 99 (C Miłosz), 194 (S Asch, S Zahorska & M Weinzieher); Serbian PEN p. 100 (Belgrade Congress); Sierra Leone PEN p. 253; Slovene PEN p. 241 (Lake Bled); South African PEN p. 143; Swedish PEN & *PEN/Opp* pp. 200, 235; Tibetan PEN Abroad pp. 106 (board meeting), 107, 142 (N Tso on Day Imprisoned Writer), 210; Ugandan PEN p. 178; Ukrainian PEN pp. 145, 263 (M Riabchuk, Lviv panel), 269; Uyghur PEN pp. 105, 236 (demonstration); Vietnamese PEN in Exile pp. 102–103; Zambian PEN p. 225 (students group).

The following pictures are courtesy of PEN members: Jennifer Clement p. 283 (notebook); Zehra Doğan p. 220 ; Ferida Duraković p. 234; Alma Dzubur Kulenović p. 234 (T Kulenović); Hilde Keteleer p. 176 (H Dink & H Keteleer); Joanne Leedom-Ackerman p. 136 (group), 152 (group with megaphone), 154, 155, 217 (panel); Basim Mardan p. 222; Zoran Mutić p. 246; Eugene Schoulgin pp. 256–257; Larry Siems p. 222; Dr Ma Thida pp. 160 (group), 161; Frankie Sionil José p. 233 (couple); Kannan Surdaram pp. 226–227; Carles Torner pp. 113 (M Botsford Fraser, Tienchi Martin & Liu Xia), 120 (C Dündar & T Bonet), 138 (writing letters), 165, 169, 172, 174–175, 178 (M Socorro), 179, 190, 209 (panel), 216, 218 (Z Mohammadi), 221, 228–229, 230, 231 (N Jaramillo), 233 (F Sionil & VPs), 234, 236 (I Tohti), 250–251, 254 (S Yazbek), 258 (C Balcázar & panel), 260 (group), 268, 284, 286 (group Edinburgh, group Buenos Aires), 288 (D Tatour), 294 (group, A Caruana Galizia).

The following pictures and documents are owned by PEN International: pp. 2, 16, 19 (PEN founders), 21, 22, 23, 28 (minutes), 43, 61, 62, 65 (London map), 66–67, 69, 73, 74 (Manila Congress), 74 (manuscript), 75, 78–81, 98 (book cover), 99 (minutes), 106 (Dalai Lama), 110 (A Dorani, C McCann & L Løkeland Hovda), 116 (Y Fisseha award), 118 (J Haslinger), 130, 131, 138 (S Demirtaş, card), 140 (book cover), 152, 157 (W Nygaard & Ethiopian PEN), 160 (WiPC newsletter), 163, 164, 166, 168 (A Askarov empty chair), 175 (report covers), 178 (report covers), 180, 181 (JG Morfin & JR Saul), 182 (*Vivan los Periodistas*, E Poniatowska), 184, 185, 186, 187, 188, 195, 196, 197 (Yiddish resolution), 208, 213 (report cover), 223, 224, 225 (Port Harcourt), 233 (panel), 234, 241 (E Pierrat & V Tyhtilä), 252, 262, 263 (M Gessen, AL Laurén & A Kurkov), 267, 276 (M van Paemel & M Tax), 278 (group), 279 (I Samba Traoré & KZ Diallo), 282, 283 (resolution), 288 (N Dumezweni), 289, 292 (*Nuestra voz*), 293, 295.

·

On the cover:
Antoni Tàpies, *Llibertat*, Day of the Imprisoned
Writer 2003 (detail). See page 146.

First published in the USA in 2021 by

INTERLINK BOOKS
An imprint of Interlink Publishing Group, Inc.
46 Crosby Street
Northampton, Massachusetts 01060
www.interlinkbooks.com

Published in association with PEN International and
the Motovun Group of International Publishers.
Copyright © 2021 PEN International, London and MGIP, Brussels
American edition copyright © 2021 Interlink Publishing

Library of Congress Cataloging-in-Publication Data available
ISBN 978-1-62371-902-9

Printed and bound in Belgium

10 9 8 7 6 5 4 3 2 1

Editorial directors
Jan Martens (MGIP – Marot, Brussels)
Carles Torner (PEN International)

Archives Collection Manager
Ginevra Avalle (PEN International)

Picture research
Ginevra Avalle, Isabel Jacobs et Carles Torner
(PEN International)

**Graphic design, typesetting and
colour separation**
Thierry Julliand (MGIP – T'ink Studio, Brussels)

Art direction
Thierry Julliand (MGIP – T'ink Studio, Brussels)
Marc Sapir (MGIP – MoMA, New York)

Production
Jan Martens (MGIP – Marot, Brussels)
Ronny Gobyn (MGIP – Tijdsbeeld, Ghent)

Production coordination
Barbara Costermans (Tijdsbeeld, Ghent)
Ann Mestdag (MGIP – Tijdsbeeld, Ghent)

Printing and binding
Graphius, Belgium

This book was produced by the Motovun Group of International Publishers on the initiative of PEN International to mark PEN's centennial. The English edition, published by Thames & Hudson in London and Interlink Publishing in Northampton (MA), was issued with six foreign-language co-editions, all translated from the original English. An edition in French, with a supplement on Belgian PEN, was published by Marot, Brussels, and by Actes Sud, Arles. Marot was also responsible for a Spanish edition, that was distributed by Galaxia Gutenberg, Barcelona. Elisabeth Sandmann Verlag, Munich, published a German edition with a supplement on German PEN. Galaxia Gutenberg, Barcelona, translated the book into Catalan, and Editorial Txalaparta, based in Tafalla (Navarre), produced an edition in Basque, both with a supplement on the local PEN. Kaunitz-Olsson in Stockholm was responsible for a Swedish edition. In addition to these translations of the complete book, Tibetan PEN in Exile published part of the English edition in Tibetan. In addition, Slovenian PEN adopted the English-language edition with a supplement in the local language. All other PEN representations worldwide adopted the book in one of the existing languages of their choice.